CONTENTS

CHAPTER 1 BREAKFASTS 7
Maple Granola 7
Bacon Knots with Maple Sugar 7
Cheddar Ham Toast 7
Cinnamon Monkey Bread 7
Vanilla French Toast withBourbon 7
Hash Brown Cups with Cheddar Cheese 8
Buttermilk Biscuits 8
Grits with Cheddar Cheese 8
Tater Tot and Chicken Sausage Casserole 8
Egg and Bacon Bread Cups 9
Baked Cornmeal Pancake 9
Bell Pepper Rings with Eggs 9
English Muffins with Spinach and Pear 9
Corn Frittata with Avocado Dressing 10
Cheese and Bacon Muffin Sandwiches 10
Breakfast Sausage Quiche 10
Bell Pepper and Carrot Frittata 10
Broccoli and Red Pepper Quiche 11
Vanilla Banana Bread Pudding 11
Shrimp and Spinach Frittata 11
Cheddar Bacon Casserole 12
Cheddar Hash Brown Casserole 12
Bell Pepper and Ham Omelet 12
Mushroom and Spinach Frittata 12
Vanilla Pancake with Walnuts 13
Vanilla Pancake with Mixed Berries 13
Brown Rice Porridge with Dates 13
Vanilla Blueberry Cobbler 13
Asparagus Strata with Havarti Cheese 14
Garlic Potatoes with Peppers and Onions 14
Brown Rice Quiches with Pimiento 14
Avocado and Egg Burrito 14
Banana Chocolate Bread with Walnuts 15
Baked Eggs with Kale Pesto 15
Chicken Breakfast Sausages 15
Blueberries Quesadillas 15
Maple Banana Bread Pudding 16
Baked Avocado with Eggs and Tomato 16
Spinach and Egg Florentine 16
Cinnamon Rolls with Brown Sugar 16
Banana Carrot Muffin 17
Artichoke and Mushroom Frittata 17
Whole-Wheat Blueberries Muffins 17
Orange Scones with Blueberries 18
French Toast Sticks with Strawberries 18
Blueberry Cake with Lemon 18
Cinnamon Apple Turnovers 18
Beef Hash with Eggs 19
Maple French Toast Casserole 19
Honey Cashew Granola with Cranberries 19
CHAPTER 2 APPETIZERS AND SNACKS 21
Cheddar Baked Potatoes with Chives 21
Sausage and Onion Rolls with Mustard 21
Honey Roasted Grapes with Basil 21
Parmesan Cauliflower with Turmeric 21
Cheddar Mushrooms with Pimientos 22

Roasted Mushrooms with Garlic 22
Jalapeño Poppers with Cheddar 22
Lemon-Pepper Chicken Wings 22
Green Chiles and Cheese Nachos 23
Pepperoni Pizza Bites with Marinara 23
Cheddar Sausage Balls 23
Tuna Melts with Mayo 23
Sugar Roasted Walnuts 24
Balsamic Prosciutto-Wrapped Pears 24
Breaded Zucchini Tots 24
Ginger Shrimp with Sesame Seeds 24
Paprika Polenta Fries with Chili-Lime Mayo .. 25
Lemon Ricotta with Capers 25
Deviled Eggs with Mayo 25
Honey Snack Mix 26
Parmesan Snack Mix 26
Paprika Potato Chips 26
Hush Puppies with Jalapeño 26
Fried Pickle Spears with Chili 27
Cinnamon Apple Chips 27
Avocado Chips with Lime 27
Ginger Apple Wedges 27
Cumin Tortilla Chips 27
Old Bay Fried Chicken Wings 28
Carrot Chips 28
Mushroom and Sausage Empanadas 28
Cumin Fried Chickpeas 28
Paprika Nut Mix 29
Garlic Fried Edamame 29
Nutmeg Apple Chips 29
Parmesan Bruschetta with Tomato 29
Sesame Kale Chips 30
Cheddar Black Bean and Corn Salsa 30
Cinnamon Peach Wedges 30
BBQ Cheese Chicken Pizza 30
Brie Pear Sandwiches 30
Breaded Artichoke Bites 31
Parmesan Crab Toasts 31
Buttermilk-Marinated Chicken Wings 31
Pork and Turkey Sandwiches 31
Horseradish Green Tomatoes 32
Spinach Calzones with Mushrooms 32
Turkey-Wrapped Dates and Almonds 32
Italian Rice Balls with Olives 33
Muffuletta Sliders with Olive Mix 33
CHAPTER 3 WRAPS AND SANDWICHES 34
Gochujang Beef and Onion Tacos 34
Curried Shrimp and Zucchini Potstickers 34
Cod Fish Tacos with Mango Salsa 34
Bacon and Egg Wraps with Salsa 35
Chicken Wraps with Ricotta Cheese 35
Sweet Potato and Spinach Burritos 35
Cabbage and Prawn Wraps 35
Ricotta Spinach and Basil Pockets 36
Carrot and Mushroom Spring Rolls 36
Avocado and Tomato Wraps 36
Chicken and Cabbage Wraps 37

Cajun Beef and Bell Pepper Fajitas 37
Potato Taquitos with Mexican Cheese............ 37
Parmesan Eggplant Hoagies 38
Chickpea and Mushroom Wraps 38
Mozzarella Chicken Taquitos........................... 38
Curried Pork Sliders... 38
Pork Momos with Carrot.................................. 39
Crispy Cream Cheese Wontons........................ 39
Beef Steak and Bell Pepper Rolls 39
Cream Cheese and Crab Wontons 40
Pork and Cabbage Gyoza................................. 40
Jalapeño Turkey Sliders with Chive Mayo 40
Beef Burgers with Korean Mayo 40
Lamb Hamburgers with Feta Cheese 41
Smoked Paprika Chicken Burgers 41
Beef Burgers with Seeds 42
Potato Samosas with Mint Chutney 42
Cheddar Chicken Empanadas........................... 43
Turkey and Pepper Hamburger 43
CHAPTER 4 STAPLES..44
Ginger-Garlic Dipping Sauce 44
Lemon Anchovy Dressing................................. 44
Buttery Mushrooms.. 44
Garlic Tomato Sauce... 44
Teriyaki Sauce.. 44
Creamy Grits.. 44
Poblano Garlic Sauce.. 45
Shawarma Seasoning.. 45
Baked White Rice... 45
Paprika-Oregano Seasoning............................. 45
CHAPTER 5 VEGAN AND VEGETARIAN................46
Roasted Veggie and Tofu.................................. 46
Black Bean and Salsa Tacos............................. 46
Thai Curried Veggies.. 46
Eggplant and Bell Peppers with Basil 46
Vinegary Asparagus.. 47
Baked Eggs with Spinach and Basil................. 47
Cheesy Broccoli with Rosemary....................... 47
Kale with Tahini-Lemon Dressing.................... 47
Vegetable Mélange with Garlic 47
Garlic Carrots with Sesame Seeds 48
Thai-Flavored Brussels Sprouts 48
Honey Eggplant with Yogurt Sauce.................. 48
Parmesan Cabbage Wedges 48
Sesame Mushrooms with Thyme...................... 49
Ratatouille with Bread Crumb Topping........... 49
Butternut Squash and Parsnip with Thyme ... 49
Butternut Squash with Goat Cheese 49
Ginger-Pepper Broccoli.................................... 50
Parmesan Brussels Sprouts.............................. 50
Roasted Veggie Rice with Eggs 50
Air Fried Tofu Sticks.. 50
Garlic Eggplant Slices with Parsley.................. 51
Cayenne Green Beans 51
Honey Baby Carrots with Dill.......................... 51
Garlic Tofu with Basil....................................... 51
Zucchini Quesadilla with Gouda Cheese 51
Curried Cauliflower with Cashews................... 52
Fried Root Veggies with Thyme 52
Red Chili Okra 52

Veggie and Oat Meatballs 53
Garlic Bell Peppers with Marjoram.................. 53
Carrot, Tofu and Cauliflower Rice 53
Halloumi Zucchinis and Eggplant 54
Breaded Zucchini Chips with Parmesan 54
Roasted Veggies with Honey-Garlic Glaze....... 54
Garlic Ratatouille 54
Cauliflower with Teriyaki Sauce 55
Onion-Stuffed Mushrooms............................... 55
Garlic Turnip and Zucchini 55
Balsamic-Glazed Beets..................................... 55
Mozzarella Walnut Stuffed Mushrooms........... 56
Tomato-Stuffed Portobello Mushrooms 56
Roasted Veggie Salad with Lemon.................... 56
Spinach-Stuffed Beefsteak Tomatoes............... 56
Potato and Asparagus Platter........................... 57
Pepper-Stuffed Portobellos.............................. 57
Chickpea-Stuffed Bell Peppers........................ 57
Stuffed Bell Peppers with Cream Cheese.......... 58
Mozzarella Tomato-Stuffed Squash 58
Rice and Olives Stuffed Peppers...................... 58
CHAPTER 6 VEGETABLE SIDES 60
Garlic-Lime Shishito Peppers 60
Garlic Zucchini Sticks...................................... 60
Garlic Potatoes with Heavy Cream................... 60
Garlic Zucchini Crisps 60
Garlicky Cabbage with Red Pepper 60
Maple Garlic Brussels Sprouts 61
Garlic Butternut Squash Croquettes................ 61
Lime Sweet Potatoes with Allspice 61
Citrus Carrots with Balsamic Glaze................. 61
Sesame Green Beans with Sriracha................... 62
Corn Casserole with Swiss Cheese 62
Parmesan Corn on the Cob 62
Brown Sugar Acorn Squash.............................. 62
Greek Potatoes with Chives............................. 63
Garlic Broccoli with Parmesan......................... 63
Breaded Asparagus Fries 63
Cheddar Broccoli Gratin 63
Roasted Potatoes with Rosemary..................... 63
Balsamic Asparagus.. 64
Breaded Brussels Sprouts with Paprika 64
CHAPTER 7 MEATS 65
Beef-Stuffed Bell Peppers................................ 65
Prosciutto-Wrapped Beef Rolls 65
Teriyaki-Marinated Rump Steak...................... 65
Beef Meatballs with Salsa................................. 66
Rosemary Ground Beef with Zucchini 66
Fried Calf's Liver Sticks................................... 66
Sirloin Steaks with Cucumber Salad................ 66
Beef and Pork Sausage Meatloaf 67
Beef Pizza with Bell Pepper............................. 67
Curried Beef Meatballs..................................... 67
Rosemary Veal Loin with Fennel Seeds 68
Fried Venison Backstrap................................... 68
Dijon Lamb Rack with Pistachio...................... 68
Beef Tenderloin with Feta Cheese.................... 68
Garlic Lamb Chops with Asparagus 69
Lamb Kofta with Mint...................................... 69
Horseradish Lamb Loin Chops......................... 69

Bacon-Wrapped Sausage with Tomato Relish70
Wasabi Spam 70
Rosemary Pork with Apple Glaze 70
Curried Lamb Chops with Potatoes 70
Dijon Pork Tenderloin... 71
Prosciutto Tart with Asparagus 71
Paprika Lamb Chops with Sage 72
Ginger Pork Shoulder in Shaoxing Wine.......... 72
Citrus Pork Ribs with Oregano 72
Vinegary Pork Schnitzel...................................... 72
Nut-Crusted Pork Rack.. 73
Teriyaki-Glazed Pork Ribs 73
Bacon-Wrapped Pork Hot Dogs......................... 73
Garlic Pork Belly with Bay Leaves 74
Lemon Pork Loin Chop with Marjoram............. 74
Pork and Veggie Kebabs 74
Pork and Pineapple Kebabs 74
Pork, Squash and Pepper Kebabs 75
BBQ Kielbasa Sausage.. 75
Pork Butt withCoriander-Parsley Sauce 75
Colby Pork Sausage with Cauliflower 76
Pork Chops with Sour Cream and Dill Sauce . 76
Pork Sausage Ratatouille..................................... 76
Pork Meatballs with Scallions 77
Chuck and Sausage Meatballs............................ 77
Garlic Pork Leg Roast with Candy Onions........ 77
Breaded Pork Loin Chops 78
Thyme Pork Chops with Carrots........................ 78
Balsamic Italian Sausages and Red Grapes..... 78
Beef Meatloaves with Spinach 78
Breaded Calf's Liver Strips 79
Pork Chops and Apple Bake 79
Pork Tenderloin with Rice................................... 79
Pork and Lettuce Wraps with Almonds 80
Pork Chop Roast with Worcestershire 80
Worcestershire Ribeye Steaks with Garlic...... 80
Orange Beef and Broccoli with Sriracha.......... 80
Mexican Sirloin Steak and Pepper Fajitas....... 81
Beef Ravioli with Parmesan 81
Pork Cutlets with Aloha Salsa............................ 81
Dijon-Honey Pork Tenderloin............................. 82
Pork Loin Chops with Butternut Squash 82
Mozzarella Sausage Calzones 82
CHAPTER 8 FISH AND SEAFOOD **84**
Tuna Casserole with Basil................................... 84
Salmon Spring Rolls with Parsley...................... 84
Cajun Tilapia Tacos.. 84
Hoisin Tuna with Lemongrass 84
Tilapia Meunière with Parsley............................ 85
Tuna and Fruit Kebabs with Honey Glaze....... 85
Breaded Fish Fillets with Mustard 85
Cayenne Cod Fillets... 86
Breaded Fish Sticks.. 86
Tuna and Veggie Salad 86
Salmon with Roasted Asparagus....................... 86
Salmon with Cherry Tomatoes 87
Teriyaki Salmon and Bok Choy 87
Honey-Lemon Snapper with Grapes 87
Ginger Swordfish Steaks with Jalapeño 87
Baked Salmon in Wine.. 88

Fried Cod Fillets in Beer 88
Cayenne Cod Fillets with Garlic 88
Lemon Red Snapper with Thyme....................... 88
Snapper Fillets with Capers 89
Salmon and Pepper Bowl 89
Curried Halibut Fillets with Parmesan............. 89
Cajun Cod Fillets with Lemon Pepper.............. 89
Honey Halibut Steaks with Parsley 90
Catfish Fillets with Pecan Crust 90
Breaded Catfish Nuggets 90
Paprika Tilapia with Garlic Aioli 90
Shrimp Salad with Caesar Dressing.................. 91
Lemon Tilapia Fillets with Garlic 91
Old Bay Shrimp with Potatoes 91
Breaded Fish Sticks.. 92
Dijon Hake Fillets with Garlic Sauce 92
Cayenne Prawns with Cumin............................. 92
Parmesan Fish Fillets with Tarragon 92
Cajun Catfish Cakes with Parmesan................. 93
Coconut Curried Fish with Chilies 93
Shrimp and Veggie Spring Rolls 93
Orange Shrimp with Cayenne............................ 94
Flounder Fillets with Lemon Pepper................. 94
Paprika Tiger Shrimp...94
Curried Prawns with Coconut............................ 94
Parsley Shrimp with Lemon............................... 95
Shrimp Kebabs with Cherry Tomatoes 95
Shrimp Scampi with Garlic Butter..................... 95
Lemon Shrimp with Cumin................................. 95
Hoisin Scallops with Sesame Seeds.................. 96
Curried King Prawns with Cumin 96
Old Bay Crab Sticks with Mayo Sauce 96
Balsamic Shrimp with Goat Cheese.................. 96
Jumbo Shrimp with Dijon-Mayo Sauce 97
Crab and Fish Cakes.. 97
Shrimp and Artichoke Paella 97
Shrimp and Veggie Patties 97
Lemon Crab Cakes with Mayo 98
Balsamic Ginger Scallops.................................... 98
Fried Bacon-Wrapped Scallops.......................... 98
Fried Breaded Scallops.. 99
Fried Scallops with Thyme 99
Garlic Calamari Rings.. 99
Basil Scallops with Broccoli................................ 99
Crab Ratatouille with Thyme 99
CHAPTER 9 POULTRY **101**
Chicken Drumsticks with BBQ-Honey Sauce101
Chicken and Ham Rochambeau 101
Breaded Chicken Fingers.................................... 101
Breaded Chicken Tenders with Thyme 102
Barbecue Chicken with Coleslaw 102
Mustard Chicken Thighs in Waffles 102
Gochujang Chicken Wings.................................. 103
Chili Chicken Skin with Dill 103
Chicken Drumsticks with Cajun Seasoning.. 103
Breaded Chicken Livers 103
Ginger Chicken Bites in Sherry 104
Honey-Ginger Chicken Breasts 104
Parmesan Chicken Cutlets 104
Rosemary Chicken Breasts with Tomatoes. 105

Chicken Tacos with Lettuce 105
Buttermilk Chicken Drumsticks 105
Lime Chicken Breasts with Cilantro 105
Ground Chicken with Tomatoes.........................106
Chicken with Veggie Couscous Salad 106
Breaded Chicken Nuggets...................................106
Chicken Thighs with Mirin 107
Garlicky Whole Chicken Bake...........................107
Garlic Chicken Wings 107
Chicken and Pepper Baguette with Mayo 107
Satay Chicken Skewers..108
Sweet-and-Sour Chicken Breasts......................108
Teriyaki Chicken Thighs 108
Five-Spice Turkey Thighs...................................109
Dijon Turkey Breast with Sage 109
Turkey and Mushroom Meatballs.....................109
Maple Turkey Breast with Rosemary 110
Whole Duck with Cherry Sauce 110
Chicken Thighs with Peppers............................110
Turkey Breast with Strawberries......................111
Turkey and Cauliflower Meatloaf.....................111
Garlic Duck Leg Quarters 111
Balsamic Duck Breasts with Orange
Marmalade 112
Game Hens with Cucumber Salad.....................112
Turkey Scotch Eggs with Rosemary 112
Dijon Turkey with Carrots.................................112
Chicken and Cheese Sandwiches 113
Balsamic Chicken Breast with Oregano 113
Chicken Kebabs with Corn Salad......................114
Cheddar Turkey Burgers with Mayo 114
Curried Chicken and Brussels Sprouts 114
Chicken Thighs with Cherry Tomatoes..........115
Mozzarella Chicken Breasts with Basil...........115
Chicken Thighs with Cabbage Slaw 116
Buttery Chicken with Corn 116
Vinegary Chicken with Pineapple....................116
Chicken Gnocchi with Spinach 117
Peach Chicken with Dark Cherry......................117
Turkey Meatloaves with Onion.........................117
Paprika Hens with Creole Seasoning................117
Paprika Hens in Wine 118
Chili Chicken Fries...118
Paprika Whole Chicken Roast 118
Lemon Chicken with Oregano 119
Chicken Drumsticks with Green Beans 119
Turkey-Stuffed Peppers with Cheddar............119
CHAPTER 10 DESSERTS 121
Lemon Caramelized Pear Tart 121
Honey Walnut and Pistachios Baklava...........121
Monk Fruit and Hazelnut Cake 121
Blueberry and Peach Tart...................................122
Butter Shortbread with Lemon 122
Chocolate Coconut Cake 122
Coffee Chocolate Cake with Cinnamon...........122
Vanilla Cookies with Chocolate Chips.............123
Chocolate Vanilla Cheesecake 123
Strawberry Crumble with Rhubarb..................123
Raspberry Muffins..124
Peach and Apple Crisp with Oatmeal...............124
Vanilla Walnuts Tart with Cloves.................... 124
Mixed Berry Bake with Almond Topping..... 124
Vanilla Coconut Cookies with Pecans............. 125
Cinnamon Apple Fritters.................................... 125
Chocolate Blueberry Cupcakes 125
Vanilla Chocolate Chip Cookies....................... 126
Vanilla Chocolate Cake 126
Coconut Orange Cake.. 126
Peach and Blueberry Galette 127
Honey Apple-Peach Crumble............................ 127
Cinnamon Apple with Apricots 127
Honey-Glazed Peach and Plum Kebabs 127
Vanilla Pound Cake 128
Pumpkin Pudding with Vanilla Wafers 128
Vanilla Ricotta Cake with Lemon 128
Apple Bake with Cinnamon 128
Vanilla Fudge Pie 129
Chocolate Cake with Blackberries.................... 129
Blackberry Cobbler.. 129
Chocolate Chip Brownies 129
White Chocolate Cookies with Nutmeg......... 130
Peanut Butter Bread Pudding............................ 130
Cinnamon Pineapple Rings................................ 130
Mixed Berry Crisp with Cloves......................... 130
Pineapple Sticks with Coconut.......................... 131
Chocolate S'mores 131
Pecan Pie with Chocolate Chips 131
Vanilla Baked Peaches and Blueberries........ 131
**CHAPTER 11 CASSEROLES, FRITTATA, AND
QUICHE 132**
Mushroom and Beef Casserole........................... 132
Cauliflower Casserole with Pecan Butter..... 132
Cheddar Chicken Sausage Casserole 132
Corn Casserole with Bell Pepper...................... 132
Asparagus Casserole with Grits 133
Cheddar Broccoli Casserole................................ 133
Tilapia and Rockfish Casserole 133
Parmesan Green Bean Casserole....................... 133
Cheddar Pastrami Casserole 133
Swiss Chicken and Ham Casserole 134
Spinach and Mushroom Frittata....................... 134
Cauliflower and Okra Casserole 134
Turkey Casserole with Almond Mayo 134
Peppery Sausage Casserole with Cheddar ... 135
Chickpea and Spinach Casserole 135
Beef and Bean Casserole..................................... 135
Cheddar Chicken and Broccoli Divan 135
Smoked Trout Frittata with Dill 136
Cheddar and Egg Frittata with Parsley.......... 136
Cheddar Broccoli and Carrot Quiche.............. 136
Mexican Beef and Chile Casserole.................... 137
Chicken and Broccoli Casserole........................ 137
Ricotta Pork Gratin with Mustard 137
Potato and Chorizo Frittata............................... 137
Asparagus Frittata with Goat Cheese 138
Kale and Egg Frittata with Feta 138
Spinach and Shrimp Frittata.............................. 138
Zucchini and Spinach Frittata........................... 138
Cheese and Egg Quiche....................................... 139
Tomato and Olive Quiche 139

CHAPTER 12 HOLIDAY SPECIALS....................**140**
    Mozzarella Rice Arancini..............................140
    Pork Egg Rolls with Vinegar Dipping............140
    Cinnamon Churros..140
    Vanilla Banana Cake 141
    Chocolate Macaroons with Coconut...............141
    Chocolate-Glazed Donut Holes......................141
    Balsamic Cherry Tomatoes...........................142
    Vanilla Butter Cake 142
    Dill Pickles with Buttermilk Dressing............142
    Olive and Basil Stromboli with Garlic 143
    Pigs in a Blanket with Sesame Seeds.............143
    Cream-Glazed Cinnamon Rolls 143
    Buttermilk Chocolate Cake 144
    Teriyaki-Marinated Shrimp Skewers..............144
    Garlic Nuggets..144
    Vanilla Cheese Blintzes 144
    Maple Pecan Tart..145
    Asiago Balls 145
    Sriracha Shrimp with Mayo...........................145
    Risotto Croquettes with Tomato Sauce..........146
CHAPTER 13 ROTISSERIE RECIPES **147**

    Whiskey-Basted Prime Rib Roast....................147
    Paprika Pulled Pork Butt..............................147
    Porchetta with Lemony Sage Rub....................147
    Orange Honey Glazed Ham 148
    Ham with Dijon Bourbon Baste 148
    Spareribs with Paprika Rub 149
    Smoked Paprika Lamb Leg 149
    BBQ Chicken with Mustard Rub 150
    Sirloin Roast with Porcini-Wine Baste 150
    Balsamic Chuck Roast..................................151
    Baby Back Ribs with Paprika Rub 151
    Teriyaki Chicken 152
    Chicken Roast with Mustard Paste..................152
    Chicken with Brown Sugar Brine.....................152
    Turkey with Thyme-Sage Brine.......................153
    Pork Loin Roast with Brown Sugar Brine 153
    Dried Fruit Stuffed Pork Loin 153
    Feta Stuffed Lamb Leg 154
    Mustard Lamb Shoulder 154
    Bacon-Wrapped Sirloin Roast........................154
APPENDIX : RECIPES INDEX...............................**156**

CHAPTER 1 BREAKFASTS

Maple Granola

Prep time: 5 minutes | Cook time: 40 minutes | Serves 4

1 cup rolled oats
3 tablespoons maple syrup
1 tablespoon sunflower oil
1 tablespoon coconut sugar
¼ teaspoon vanilla
¼ teaspoon cinnamon
¼ teaspoon sea salt

1. Mix together the oats, maple syrup, sunflower oil, coconut sugar, vanilla, cinnamon, and sea salt in a medium bowl and stir to combine. Transfer the mixture to a baking pan.
2. Select Bake. Set temperature to 248ºF (120ºC) and set time to 40 minutes. Press Start to begin preheating.
3. Once preheated, place the pan into the oven. Stir the granola four times during cooking.
4. When cooking is complete, the granola will be mostly dry and lightly browned.
5. Let the granola stand for 5 to 10 minutes before serving.

Bacon Knots with Maple Sugar

Prep time: 5 minutes | Cook time: 7 to 8 minutes | Serves 6

1 pound (454 g) maple smoked center-cut bacon
¼ cup maple syrup
¼ cup brown sugar
Coarsely cracked black peppercorns, to taste

1. On a clean work surface, tie each bacon strip in a loose knot.
2. Stir together the maple syrup and brown sugar in a bowl. Generously brush this mixture over the bacon knots.
3. Place the bacon knots in the perforated pan and sprinkle with the coarsely cracked black peppercorns.
4. Select Air Fry. Set temperature to 390ºF (199ºC) and set time to 8 minutes. Press Start to begin preheating.
5. Once preheated, place the pan into the oven.
6. After 5 minutes, remove the pan from the oven and flip the bacon knots. Return the pan to the oven and continue cooking for 2 to 3 minutes more.
7. When cooking is complete, the bacon should be crisp. Remove from the oven to a paper towel-lined plate. Let the bacon knots cool for a few minutes and serve warm.

Cheddar Ham Toast

Prep time: 5 minutes | Cook time: 6 minutes | Serves: 1

1 slice bread
1 teaspoon butter, at room temperature
1 egg
Salt and freshly ground black pepper, to taste
2 teaspoons diced ham
1 tablespoon grated Cheddar cheese

1. On a clean work surface, use a 2½-inch biscuit cutter to make a hole in the center of the bread slice with about ½-inch of bread remaining.
2. Spread the butter on both sides of the bread slice. Crack the egg into the hole and season with salt and pepper to taste. Transfer the bread to the perforated pan.
3. Select Air Fry. Set temperature to 325ºF (163ºC) and set time to 6 minutes. Press Start to begin preheating.
4. Once preheated, place the pan into the oven.
5. After 5 minutes, remove the pan from the oven. Scatter the cheese and diced ham on top and continue cooking for an additional 1 minute.
6. When cooking is complete, the egg should be set and the cheese should be melted. Remove the toast from the oven to a plate and let cool for 5 minutes before serving.

Cinnamon Monkey Bread

Prep time: 5 minutes | Cook time: 8 minutes | Serves 4

1 (8-ounce / 227-g) can refrigerated biscuits
3 tablespoons melted unsalted butter
¼ cup white sugar
3 tablespoons brown sugar
½ teaspoon cinnamon
⅛ teaspoon nutmeg

1. On a clean work surface, cut each biscuit into 4 pieces.
2. In a shallow bowl, place the melted butter. In another shallow bowl, stir together the white sugar, brown sugar, cinnamon, and nutmeg until combined.
3. Dredge the biscuits, one at a time, in the melted butter, then roll them in the sugar mixture to coat well. Spread the biscuits evenly in a baking pan.
4. Select Bake. Set temperature to 350ºF (180ºC) and set time to 8 minutes. Press Start to begin preheating.
5. Once the oven has preheated, place the pan into the oven.
6. When cooked, the biscuits should be golden brown.
7. Cool for 5 minutes before serving.

Vanilla French Toast withBourbon

Prep time: 15 minutes | Cook time: 6 minutes | Serves 4

2 large eggs
2 tablespoons water
²/₃ cup whole or 2% milk
1 tablespoon butter, melted

2 tablespoons bourbon
1 teaspoon vanilla extract
8 (1-inch-thick) French bread slices
Cooking spray
1.	Line the perforated pan with parchment paper and spray it with cooking spray.
2.	Beat the eggs with the water in a shallow bowl until combined. Add the milk, melted butter, bourbon, and vanilla and stir to mix well.
3.	Dredge 4 slices of bread in the batter, turning to coat both sides evenly. Transfer the bread slices onto the parchment paper.
4.	Select Bake. Set temperature to 320ºF (160ºC) and set time to 6 minutes. Press Start to begin preheating.
5.	Once the oven has preheated, place the pan into the oven. Flip the slices halfway through the cooking time.
6.	When cooking is complete, the bread slices should be nicely browned.
7.	Remove from the oven to a plate and serve warm.

Hash Brown Cups with Cheddar Cheese

Prep time: 10 minutes | Cook time: 9 minutes | Serves 6
4 eggs, beaten
2¼ cups frozen hash browns, thawed
1 cup diced ham
½ cup shredded Cheddar cheese
½ teaspoon Cajun seasoning
Cooking spray
1.	Lightly spritz a 12-cup muffin tin with cooking spray.
2.	Combine the beaten eggs, hash browns, diced ham, cheese, and Cajun seasoning in a medium bowl and stir until well blended.
3.	Spoon a heaping 1½ tablespoons of egg mixture into each muffin cup.
4.	Select Bake. Set temperature to 350ºF (180ºC) and set time to 9 minutes. Press Start to begin preheating.
5.	Once preheated, place the muffin tin into the oven.
6.	When cooked, the muffins will be golden brown.
7.	Allow to cool for 5 to 10 minutes on a wire rack and serve warm.

Buttermilk Biscuits

Prep time: 5 minutes | Cook time: 18 minutes | Makes 16 biscuits
2½ cups all-purpose flour
1 tablespoon baking powder
1 teaspoon kosher salt
1 teaspoon sugar
½ teaspoon baking soda
8 tablespoons (1 stick) unsalted butter, at room temperature

1 cup buttermilk, chilled
1.	Stir together the flour, baking powder, salt, sugar, and baking powder in a large bowl.
2.	Add the butter and stir to mix well. Pour in the buttermilk and stir with a rubber spatula just until incorporated.
3.	Place the dough onto a lightly floured surface and roll the dough out to a disk, ½ inch thick. Cut out the biscuits with a 2-inch round cutter and re-roll any scraps until you have 16 biscuits.
4.	Arrange the biscuits in the perforated pan in a single layer.
5.	Select Bake. Set temperature to 325ºF (163ºC) and set time to 18 minutes. Press Start to begin preheating.
6.	Once preheated, place the pan into the oven.
7.	When cooked, the biscuits will be golden brown.
8.	Remove from the oven to a plate and serve hot.

Grits with Cheddar Cheese

Prep time: 10 minutes | Cook time: 11 minutes | Serves 4
$^2/_3$ cup instant grits
1 teaspoon salt
1 teaspoon freshly ground black pepper
¾ cup whole or 2% milk
3 ounces (85 g) cream cheese, at room temperature
1 large egg, beaten
1 tablespoon butter, melted
1 cup shredded mild Cheddar cheese
Cooking spray
1.	Mix the grits, salt, and black pepper in a large bowl. Add the milk, cream cheese, beaten egg, and melted butter and whisk to combine. Fold in the Cheddar cheese and stir well.
2.	Spray a baking pan with cooking spray. Spread the grits mixture into the baking pan.
3.	Select Air Fry. Set temperature to 400ºF (205ºC) and set time to 11 minutes. Press Start to begin preheating.
4.	Once preheated, place the pan into the oven. Stir the mixture halfway through the cooking time.
5.	When done, a knife inserted in the center should come out clean.
6.	Rest for 5 minutes and serve warm.

Tater Tot and Chicken Sausage Casserole

Prep time: 5 minutes | Cook time: 17 to 18 minutes | Serves 4
4 eggs
1 cup milk
Salt and pepper, to taste
12 ounces (340 g) ground chicken sausage
1 pound (454 g) frozen tater tots, thawed
¾ cup grated Cheddar cheese
Cooking spray

1. Whisk together the eggs and milk in a medium bowl. Season with salt and pepper to taste and stir until mixed. Set aside.
2. Place a skillet over medium-high heat and spritz with cooking spray. Place the ground sausage in the skillet and break it into smaller pieces with a spatula or spoon. Cook for 3 to 4 minutes until the sausage Starts to brown, stirring occasionally. Remove from heat and set aside.
3. Coat a baking pan with cooking spray. Arrange the tater tots in the baking pan.
4. Select Bake. Set temperature to 400ºF (205ºC) and set time to 14 minutes. Press Start to begin preheating.
5. Once preheated, place the pan into the oven.
6. After 6 minutes, remove the pan from the oven. Stir the tater tots and add the egg mixture and cooked sausage. Return the pan to the oven and continue cooking.
7. After another 6 minutes, remove the pan from the oven. Scatter the cheese on top of the tater tots. Return the pan to the oven and continue to cook for 2 minutes more.
8. When done, the cheese should be bubbly and melted.
9. Let the mixture cool for 5 minutes and serve warm.

Egg and Bacon Bread Cups

Prep time: 10 minutes | Cook time: 10 minutes | Serves 4

4 (3-by-4-inch) crusty rolls
4 thin slices Gouda or Swiss cheese mini wedges
5 eggs
2 tablespoons heavy cream
3 strips precooked bacon, chopped
½ teaspoon dried thyme
Pinch salt
Freshly ground black pepper, to taste
1. On a clean work surface, cut the tops off the rolls. Using your fingers, remove the insides of the rolls to make bread cups, leaving a ½-inch shell. Place a slice of cheese onto each roll bottom.
2. Whisk together the eggs and heavy cream in a medium bowl until well combined. Fold in the bacon, thyme, salt, and pepper and stir well.
3. Scrape the egg mixture into the prepared bread cups. Arrange the bread cups in the perforated pan.
4. Select Bake. Set temperature to 330ºF (166ºC) and set time to 10 minutes. Press Start to begin preheating.
5. Once preheated, place the pan into the oven.
6. When cooked, the eggs should be cooked to your preference.
7. Serve warm.

Baked Cornmeal Pancake

Prep time: 10 minutes | Cook time: 6 minutes | Serves 4

1½ cups yellow cornmeal
½ cup all-purpose flour
2 tablespoons sugar
1 teaspoon salt
1 teaspoon baking powder
1 cup whole or 2% milk
1 large egg, lightly beaten
1 tablespoon butter, melted
Cooking spray
1. Line the perforated pan with parchment paper.
2. Stir together the cornmeal, flour, sugar, salt, and baking powder in a large bowl. Mix in the milk, egg, and melted butter and whisk to combine.
3. Drop tablespoonfuls of the batter onto the parchment paper for each pancake. Spray the pancakes with cooking spray.
4. Select Bake. Set temperature to 350ºF (180ºC) and set time to 6 minutes. Press Start to begin preheating.
5. Once the oven has preheated, place the pan into the oven. Flip the pancakes and spray with cooking spray again halfway through the cooking time.
6. When cooking is complete, remove the pancakes from the oven to a plate.
7. *Cool for 5 minutes and serve immediately.*

Bell Pepper Rings with Eggs

Prep time: 5 minutes | Cook time: 7 minutes | Serves 4

1 large red, yellow, or orange bell pepper, cut into four ¾-inch rings
4 eggs
Salt and freshly ground black pepper, to taste
2 teaspoons salsa
Cooking spray
1. Coat a baking pan lightly with cooking spray.
2. Put 4 bell pepper rings in the prepared baking pan. Crack one egg into each bell pepper ring and sprinkle with salt and pepper. Top each egg with ½ teaspoon of salsa.
3. Select Air Fry. Set temperature to 350ºF (180ºC) and set time to 7 minutes. Press Start to begin preheating.
4. Once preheated, place the pan into the oven.
5. When done, the eggs should be cooked to your desired doneness.
6. Remove the rings from the pan to a plate and serve warm.

English Muffins with Spinach and Pear

Prep time: 5 minutes | Cook time: 10 minutes | Serves 4

2 strips turkey bacon, cut in half crosswise
2 whole-grain English muffins, split

1 cup fresh baby spinach, long stems removed
¼ ripe pear, peeled and thinly sliced
4 slices Provolone cheese
1.	Put the turkey bacon strips in the perforated pan.
2.	Select Air Fry. Set temperature to 390ºF (199ºC) and set time to 6 minutes. Press Start to begin preheating.
3.	Once preheated, place the pan into the oven. Flip the strips halfway through the cooking time.
4.	When cooking is complete, the bacon should be crisp.
5.	Remove from the oven and drain on paper towels. Set aside.
6.	Put the muffin halves in the perforated pan.
7.	Select Air Fry and set time to 2 minutes. Return the pan to the oven. When done, the muffin halves will be lightly browned.
8.	Remove the pan from the oven. Top each muffin half with ¼ of the baby spinach, several pear slices, a strip of turkey bacon, followed by a slice of cheese.
9.	Select Bake. Set temperature to 360ºF (182ºC) and set time to 2 minutes. Place the pan back to the oven. When done, the cheese will be melted.
10.	Serve warm.

Corn Frittata with Avocado Dressing

Prep time: 10 minutes | Cook time: 20 minutes | Serves 2 or 3
½ cup cherry tomatoes, halved
Kosher salt and freshly ground black pepper, to taste
6 large eggs, lightly beaten
½ cup fresh corn kernels
¼ cup milk
1 tablespoon finely chopped fresh dill
½ cup shredded Monterey Jack cheese
Avocado Dressing:
1 ripe avocado, pitted and peeled
2 tablespoons fresh lime juice
¼ cup olive oil
1 scallion, finely chopped
8 fresh basil leaves, finely chopped
1.	Put the tomato halves in a colander and lightly season with salt. Set aside for 10 minutes to drain well. Pour the tomatoes into a large bowl and fold in the eggs, corn, milk, and dill. Sprinkle with salt and pepper and stir until mixed.
2.	Pour the egg mixture into a baking pan.
3.	Select Bake. Set temperature to 300ºF (150ºC) and set time to 15 minutes. Press Start to begin preheating.
4.	Once the oven has preheated, place the pan into the oven.
5.	When done, remove the pan from the oven. Scatter the cheese on top.
6.	Select Bake. Set temperature to 315ºF (157ºC) and set time to 5 minutes. Return the pan to the oven.

7.	Meanwhile, make the avocado dressing: Mash the avocado with the lime juice in a medium bowl until smooth. Mix in the olive oil, scallion, and basil and stir until well incorporated.
8.	When cooking is complete, the frittata will be puffy and set. Let the frittata cool for 5 minutes and serve alongside the avocado dressing.

Cheese and Bacon Muffin Sandwiches

Prep time: 5 minutes | Cook time: 8 minutes | Serves 4
4 English muffins, split
8 slices Canadian bacon
4 slices cheese
Cooking spray
1.	Make the sandwiches: Top each of 4 muffin halves with 2 slices of Canadian bacon, 1 slice of cheese, and finish with the remaining muffin half.
2.	Put the sandwiches in the perforated pan and spritz the tops with cooking spray.
3.	Select Bake. Set temperature to 370ºF (188ºC) and set time to 8 minutes. Press Start to begin preheating.
4.	Once preheated, place the pan into the oven. Flip the sandwiches halfway through the cooking time.
5.	When cooking is complete, remove the pan from the oven. Divide the sandwiches among four plates and serve warm.

Breakfast Sausage Quiche

Prep time: 5 minutes | Cook time: 25 minutes | Serves 4
12 large eggs
1 cup heavy cream
Salt and black pepper, to taste
12 ounces (340 g) sugar-free breakfast sausage
2 cups shredded Cheddar cheese
Cooking spray
1.	Coat a casserole dish with cooking spray.
2.	Beat together the eggs, heavy cream, salt and pepper in a large bowl until creamy. Stir in the breakfast sausage and Cheddar cheese.
3.	Pour the sausage mixture into the prepared casserole dish.
4.	Select Bake. Set temperature to 375ºF (190ºC) and set time to 25 minutes. Press Start to begin preheating.
5.	Once the oven has preheated, place the dish into the oven.
6.	When done, the top of the quiche should be golden brown and the eggs will be set.
7.	Remove from the oven and let sit for 5 to 10 minutes before serving.

Bell Pepper and Carrot Frittata

Prep time: 10 minutes | Cook time: 12 minutes | Serves 4
½ cup chopped red bell pepper

$^1/_3$ cup grated carrot
$^1/_3$ cup minced onion
1 teaspoon olive oil
1 egg
6 egg whites
$^1/_3$ cup 2% milk
1 tablespoon shredded Parmesan cheese
1.	Mix together the red bell pepper, carrot, onion, and olive oil in a baking pan and stir to combine.
2.	Select Bake. Set temperature to 350ºF (180ºC) and set time to 12 minutes. Press Start to begin preheating.
3.	Once preheated, place the pan into the oven.
4.	After 3 minutes, remove the pan from the oven. Stir the vegetables. Return the pan to the oven and continue cooking.
5.	Meantime, whisk together the egg, egg whites, and milk in a medium bowl until creamy.
6.	After 3 minutes, remove the pan from the oven. Pour the egg mixture over the top and scatter with the Parmesan cheese. Return the pan to the oven and continue cooking for additional 6 minutes.
7.	When cooking is complete, the eggs will be set and the top will be golden around the edges.
8.	Allow the frittata to cool for 5 minutes before slicing and serving.

Broccoli and Red Pepper Quiche

Prep time: 5 minutes | Cook time: 10 minutes | Serves 4

1 cup broccoli florets
¾ cup chopped roasted red peppers
1¼ cups grated Fontina cheese
6 eggs
¾ cup heavy cream
½ teaspoon salt
Freshly ground black pepper, to taste
Cooking spray
1.	Spritz a baking pan with cooking spray
2.	Add the broccoli florets and roasted red peppers to the pan and scatter the grated Fontina cheese on top.
3.	In a bowl, beat together the eggs and heavy cream. Sprinkle with salt and pepper. Pour the egg mixture over the top of the cheese. Wrap the pan in foil.
4.	Select Air Fry. Set temperature to 325ºF (163ºC) and set time to 10 minutes. Press Start to begin preheating.
5.	Once preheated, place the pan into the oven.
6.	After 8 minutes, remove the pan from the oven. Remove the foil. Return the pan to the oven and continue to cook another 2 minutes.
7.	When cooked, the quiche should be golden brown.
8.	Rest for 5 minutes before cutting into wedges and serve warm.

Vanilla Banana Bread Pudding

Prep time: 10 minutes | Cook time: 16 minutes | Serves 4

2 medium ripe bananas, mashed
½ cup low-fat milk
2 tablespoons maple syrup
2 tablespoons peanut butter
1 teaspoon vanilla extract
1 teaspoon ground cinnamon
2 slices whole-grain bread, cut into bite-sized cubes
¼ cup quick oats
Cooking spray
1.	Spritz a baking dish lightly with cooking spray.
2.	Mix the bananas, milk, maple syrup, peanut butter, vanilla, and cinnamon in a large mixing bowl and stir until well incorporated.
3.	Add the bread cubes to the banana mixture and stir until thoroughly coated. Fold in the oats and stir to combine.
4.	Transfer the mixture to the baking dish. Wrap the baking dish in aluminum foil.
5.	Select Air Fry. Set temperature to 350ºF (180ºC) and set time to 16 minutes. Press Start to begin preheating.
6.	Once the oven has preheated, place the pan into the oven.
7.	After 10 minutes, remove the baking dish from the oven. Remove the foil. Return the baking dish to the oven and continue to cook another 6 minutes.
8.	When done, the pudding should be set.
9.	Let the pudding cool for 5 minutes before serving.

Shrimp and Spinach Frittata

Prep time: 15 minutes | Cook time: 16 minutes | Serves 4

4 eggs
Pinch salt
½ cup cooked rice
½ cup chopped cooked shrimp
½ cup baby spinach
½ cup grated Monterey Jack cheese
Nonstick cooking spray
1.	Spritz a baking pan with nonstick cooking spray.
2.	Whisk the eggs and salt in a small bowl until frothy.
3.	Place the cooked rice, shrimp, and baby spinach in the baking pan. Pour in the whisked eggs and scatter the cheese on top.
4.	Select Bake. Set temperature to 320ºF (160ºC) and set time to 16 minutes. Press Start to begin preheating.
5.	Once the oven has preheated, place the pan into the oven.
6.	When cooking is complete, the frittata should be golden and puffy.
7.	Let the frittata cool for 5 minutes before slicing to serve.

Cheddar Bacon Casserole

Prep time: 10 minutes | Cook time: 16 minutes | Serves 4

6 slices bacon
6 eggs
Salt and pepper, to taste
Cooking spray
½ cup chopped green bell pepper
½ cup chopped onion
¾ cup shredded Cheddar cheese

1. Place the bacon in a skillet over medium-high heat and cook each side for about 4 minutes until evenly crisp. Remove from the heat to a paper towel-lined plate to drain. Crumble it into small pieces and set aside.
2. Whisk the eggs with the salt and pepper in a medium bowl.
3. Spritz a baking pan with cooking spray.
4. Place the whisked eggs, crumbled bacon, green bell pepper, and onion in the prepared pan.
5. Select Bake. Set temperature to 400ºF (205ºC) and set time to 8 minutes. Press Start to begin preheating.
6. Once preheated, place the pan into the oven.
7. After 6 minutes, remove the pan from the oven. Scatter the Cheddar cheese all over. Return the pan to the oven and continue to cook another 2 minutes.
8. When cooking is complete, let sit for 5 minutes and serve on plates.

Cheddar Hash Brown Casserole

Prep time: 15 minutes | Cook time: 30 minutes | Serves 4

3½ cups frozen hash browns, thawed
1 teaspoon salt
1 teaspoon freshly ground black pepper
3 tablespoons butter, melted
1 (10.5-ounce / 298-g) can cream of chicken soup
½ cup sour cream
1 cup minced onion
½ cup shredded sharp Cheddar cheese
Cooking spray

1. Put the hash browns in a large bowl and season with salt and black pepper. Add the melted butter, cream of chicken soup, and sour cream and stir until well incorporated. Mix in the minced onion and cheese and stir well.
2. Spray a baking pan with cooking spray.
3. Spread the hash brown mixture evenly into the baking pan.
4. Select Bake. Set temperature to 325ºF (163ºC) and set time to 30 minutes. Press Start to begin preheating.
5. Once the oven has preheated, place the pan into the oven.
6. When cooked, the hash brown mixture will be browned.
7. Cool for 5 minutes before serving.

Bell Pepper and Ham Omelet

Prep time: 5 minutes | Cook time: 20 minutes | Serves 2

¼ cup chopped bell pepper, green or red
¼ cup chopped onion
¼ cup diced ham
1 teaspoon butter
4 large eggs
2 tablespoons milk
⅛ teaspoon salt
¾ cup shredded sharp Cheddar cheese

1. Put the bell pepper, onion, ham, and butter in a baking pan and mix well.
2. Select Air Fry. Set temperature to 390ºF (199ºC) and set time to 5 minutes. Press Start to begin preheating.
3. Once the oven has preheated, place the pan into the oven.
4. After 1 minute, remove the pan from the oven. Stir the mixture. Return the pan to the oven and continue to cook for another 4 minutes.
5. When done, the veggies should be softened.
6. Whisk together the eggs, milk, and salt in a bowl. Pour the egg mixture over the veggie mixture.
7. Select Bake. Set temperature to 360ºF (182ºC) and set time to 15 minutes. place the pan into the oven.
8. After 14 minutes, remove the pan from the oven. Scatter the omelet with the shredded cheese. Return the pan to the oven and continue to cook for another 1 minute.
9. When cooking is complete, the top will be lightly golden browned, the eggs will be set and the cheese will be melted.
10. Let the omelet cool for 5 minutes before serving.

Mushroom and Spinach Frittata

Prep time: 10 minutes | Cook time: 22 minutes | Serves 2

4 large eggs
4 ounces (113 g) baby bella mushrooms, chopped
1 cup baby spinach, chopped
½ cup shredded Cheddar cheese
$1/3$ cup chopped leek, white part only
¼ cup halved grape tomatoes
1 tablespoon 2% milk
¼ teaspoon dried oregano
¼ teaspoon garlic powder
½ teaspoon kosher salt
Freshly ground black pepper, to taste
Cooking spray

1. Lightly spritz a baking dish with cooking spray.
2. Whisk the eggs in a large bowl until frothy. Add the mushrooms, baby spinach, cheese, leek, tomatoes, milk, oregano, garlic powder, salt, and pepper and stir until well blended. Pour the mixture into the prepared baking dish.

3.   Select Bake. Set temperature to 300ºF (150ºC) and set time to 22 minutes. Press Start to begin preheating.
4.   Once the oven has preheated, place the dish into the oven.
5.   When cooked, the center will be puffed up and the top will be golden brown.
6.   Let the frittata cool for 5 minutes before slicing to serve.

Vanilla Pancake with Walnuts

Prep time: 10 minutes | Cook time: 20 minutes | Serves 4

3 tablespoons melted butter, divided
1 cup flour
2 tablespoons sugar
1½ teaspoons baking powder
¼ teaspoon salt
1 egg, beaten
¾ cup milk
1 teaspoon pure vanilla extract
½ cup roughly chopped walnuts
Maple syrup or fresh sliced fruit, for serving

1.   Grease a baking pan with 1 tablespoon of melted butter.
2.   Mix together the flour, sugar, baking powder, and salt in a medium bowl. Add the beaten egg, milk, the remaining 2 tablespoons of melted butter, and vanilla and stir until the batter is sticky but slightly lumpy.
3.   Slowly pour the batter into the greased baking pan and scatter with the walnuts.
4.   Select Bake. Set temperature to 330ºF (166ºC) and set time to 20 minutes. Press Start to begin preheating.
5.   Once preheated, place the pan into the oven.
6.   When cooked, the pancake should be golden brown and cooked through.
7.   Let the pancake rest for 5 minutes and serve topped with the maple syrup or fresh fruit, if desired.

Vanilla Pancake with Mixed Berries

Prep time: 10 minutes | Cook time: 14 minutes | Serves 4

1 tablespoon unsalted butter, at room temperature
1 egg
2 egg whites
½ cup 2% milk
½ cup whole-wheat pastry flour
1 teaspoon pure vanilla extract
1 cup sliced fresh strawberries
½ cup fresh raspberries
½ cup fresh blueberries

1.   Grease a baking pan with the butter.
2.   Using a hand mixer, beat together the egg, egg whites, milk, pastry flour, and vanilla in a medium mixing bowl until well incorporated.
3.   Pour the batter into the pan.

4.   Select Bake. Set temperature to 330ºF (166ºC) and set time to 14 minutes. Press Start to begin preheating.
5.   Once the oven has preheated, place the pan into the oven.
6.   When cooked, the pancake should puff up in the center and the edges should be golden brown
7.   Allow the pancake to cool for 5 minutes and serve topped with the berries.

Brown Rice Porridge with Dates

Prep time: 5 minutes | Cook time: 23 minutes | Serves 1 or 2

½ cup cooked brown rice
1 cup canned coconut milk
¼ cup unsweetened shredded coconut
¼ cup packed dark brown sugar
4 large Medjool dates, pitted and roughly chopped
½ teaspoon kosher salt
¼ teaspoon ground cardamom
Heavy cream, for serving (optional)

1.   Place all the ingredients except the heavy cream in a baking pan and stir until blended.
2.   Select Bake. Set temperature to 375ºF (190ºC) and set time to 23 minutes. Press Start to begin preheating.
3.   Once the oven has preheated, place the pan into the oven. Stir the porridge halfway through the cooking time.
4.   When cooked, the porridge will be thick and creamy.
5.   Remove from the oven and ladle the porridge into bowls.
6.   Serve hot with a drizzle of the cream, if desired.

Vanilla Blueberry Cobbler

Prep time: 5 minutes | Cook time: 15 minutes | Serves 4

¾ teaspoon baking powder
$^1/_3$ cup whole-wheat pastry flour
Dash sea salt
$^1/_3$ cup unsweetened nondairy milk
2 tablespoons maple syrup
½ teaspoon vanilla
Cooking spray
½ cup blueberries
¼ cup granola
Nondairy yogurt, for topping (optional)

1.   Spritz a baking pan with cooking spray.
2.   Mix together the baking powder, flour, and salt in a medium bowl. Add the milk, maple syrup, and vanilla and whisk to combine.
3.   Scrape the mixture into the prepared pan. Scatter the blueberries and granola on top.
4.   Select Bake. Set temperature to 347ºF (175ºC) and set time to 15 minutes. Press Start to begin preheating.
5.   Once preheated, place the pan into the oven.

6.   When done, the top should begin to brown and a knife inserted in the center should come out clean.
7.   Let the cobbler cool for 5 minutes and serve with a drizzle of nondairy yogurt.

Asparagus Strata with Havarti Cheese

Prep time: 10 minutes | Cook time: 17 minutes | Serves 4
6 asparagus spears, cut into 2-inch pieces
1 tablespoon water
2 slices whole-wheat bread, cut into ½-inch cubes
4 eggs
3 tablespoons whole milk
2 tablespoons chopped flat-leaf parsley
½ cup grated Havarti or Swiss cheese
Pinch salt
Freshly ground black pepper, to taste
Cooking spray
1.   Add the asparagus spears and 1 tablespoon of water in a baking pan.
2.   Select Bake. Set temperature to 330ºF (166ºC) and set time to 4 minutes. Press Start to begin preheating.
3.   Once preheated, place the pan into the oven.
4.   When cooking is complete, the asparagus spears will be crisp-tender.
5.   Remove the asparagus from the pan and drain on paper towels.
6.   Spritz the pan with cooking spray. Place the bread and asparagus in the pan.
7.   Whisk together the eggs and milk in a medium mixing bowl until creamy. Fold in the parsley, cheese, salt, and pepper and stir to combine. Pour this mixture into the baking pan.
8.   Select Bake and set time to 13 minutes. Place the pan back to the oven. When done, the eggs will be set and the top will be lightly browned.
9.   Let cool for 5 minutes before slicing and serving.

Garlic Potatoes with Peppers and Onions

Prep time: 10 minutes | Cook time: 35 minutes | Serves 4
1 pound (454 g) red potatoes, cut into ½-inch dices
1 large red bell pepper, cut into ½-inch dices
1 large green bell pepper, cut into ½-inch dices
1 medium onion, cut into ½-inch dices
1½ tablespoons extra-virgin olive oil
1¼ teaspoons kosher salt
¾ teaspoon sweet paprika
¾ teaspoon garlic powder
Freshly ground black pepper, to taste
1.   Mix together the potatoes, bell peppers, onion, oil, salt, paprika, garlic powder, and black pepper in a large mixing and toss to coat.
2.   Transfer the potato mixture to the perforated pan.

3.   Select Air Fry. Set temperature to 350ºF (180ºC) and set time to 35 minutes. Press Start to begin preheating.
4.   Once preheated, place the pan into the oven. Stir the potato mixture three times during cooking.
5.   When done, the potatoes should be nicely browned.
6.   Remove from the oven to a plate and serve warm.

Brown Rice Quiches with Pimiento

Prep time: 10 minutes | Cook time: 14 minutes | Serves 6
4 ounces (113 g) diced green chilies
3 cups cooked brown rice
1 cup shredded reduced-fat Cheddar cheese, divided
½ cup egg whites
$^1/_3$ cup fat-free milk
¼ cup diced pimiento
½ teaspoon cumin
1 small eggplant, cubed
1 bunch fresh cilantro, finely chopped
Cooking spray
1.   Spritz a 12-cup muffin pan with cooking spray.
2.   In a large bowl, stir together all the ingredients, except for ½ cup of the cheese.
3.   Scoop the mixture evenly into the muffin cups and sprinkle the remaining ½ cup of the cheese on top.
4.   Select Bake. Set temperature to 400ºF (205ºC) and set time to 14 minutes. Press Start to begin preheating.
5.   Once the unit has preheated, place the pan into the oven.
6.   When cooking is complete, remove the pan and check the quiches. They should be set.
7.   Carefully transfer the quiches to a platter and serve immediately.

Avocado and Egg Burrito

Prep time: 10 minutes | Cook time: 4 minutes | Serves 4
4 low-sodium whole-wheat flour tortillas
Filling:
1 hard-boiled egg, chopped
2 hard-boiled egg whites, chopped
1 ripe avocado, peeled, pitted, and chopped
1 red bell pepper, chopped
1 (1.2-ounce / 34-g) slice low-sodium, low-fat American cheese, torn into pieces
3 tablespoons low-sodium salsa, plus additional for serving (optional)
Special Equipment:
4 toothpicks (optional) soaked in water for at least 30 minutes
1.   Make the filling: Combine the egg, egg whites, avocado, red bell pepper, cheese, and salsa in a medium bowl and stir until blended.

2.   Assemble the burritos: Arrange the tortillas on a clean work surface and place ¼ of the prepared filling in the middle of each tortilla, leaving about 1½-inch on each end unfilled. Fold in the opposite sides of each tortilla and roll up. Secure with toothpicks through the center, if needed.
3.   Transfer the burritos to the perforated pan.
4.   Select Air Fry. Set temperature to 390ºF (199ºC) and set time to 4 minutes. Press Start to begin preheating.
5.   Once the oven has preheated, place the pan into the oven.
6.   When cooking is complete, the burritos should be crisp and golden brown.
7.   Allow to cool for 5 minutes and serve with salsa, if desired.

Banana Chocolate Bread with Walnuts

Prep time: 10 minutes | Cook time: 30 minutes | Serves 4
¼ cup cocoa powder
6 tablespoons plus 2 teaspoons all-purpose flour, divided
½ teaspoon kosher salt
¼ teaspoon baking soda
1½ ripe bananas
1 large egg, whisked
¼ cup vegetable oil
½ cup sugar
3 tablespoons buttermilk or plain yogurt (not Greek)
½ teaspoon vanilla extract
6 tablespoons chopped white chocolate
6 tablespoons chopped walnuts
1.   Mix together the cocoa powder, 6 tablespoons of the flour, salt, and baking soda in a medium bowl.
2.   Mash the bananas with a fork in another medium bowl until smooth. Fold in the egg, oil, sugar, buttermilk, and vanilla, and whisk until thoroughly combined. Add the wet mixture to the dry mixture and stir until well incorporated.
3.   Combine the white chocolate, walnuts, and the remaining 2 tablespoons of flour in a third bowl and toss to coat. Add this mixture to the batter and stir until well incorporated. Pour the batter into a baking pan and smooth the top with a spatula.
4.   Select Bake. Set temperature to 310ºF (154ºC) and set time to 30 minutes. Press Start to begin preheating.
5.   Once the oven has preheated, place the pan into the oven.
6.   When done, a toothpick inserted into the center of the bread should come out clean.
7.   Remove from the oven and allow to cool on a wire rack for 10 minutes before serving.

Baked Eggs with Kale Pesto

Prep time: 5 minutes | Cook time: 11 minutes | Serves 2

1 cup roughly chopped kale leaves, stems and center ribs removed
¼ cup grated pecorino cheese
¼ cup olive oil
1 garlic clove, peeled
3 tablespoons whole almonds
Kosher salt and freshly ground black pepper, to taste
4 large eggs
2 tablespoons heavy cream
3 tablespoons chopped pitted mixed olives
1.   Place the kale, pecorino, olive oil, garlic, almonds, salt, and pepper in a small blender and blitz until well incorporated.
2.   One at a time, crack the eggs in a baking pan. Drizzle the kale pesto on top of the egg whites. Top the yolks with the cream and swirl together the yolks and the pesto.
3.   Select Bake. Set temperature to 300ºF (150ºC) and set time to 11 minutes. Press Start to begin preheating.
4.   Once preheated, place the pan into the oven.
5.   When cooked, the top should begin to brown and the eggs should be set.
6.   Allow the eggs to cool for 5 minutes. Scatter the olives on top and serve warm.

Chicken Breakfast Sausages

Prep time: 15 minutes | Cook time: 10 minutes | Makes 8 patties
1 Granny Smith apple, peeled and finely chopped
2 tablespoons apple juice
2 garlic cloves, minced
1 egg white
$^1/_3$ cup minced onion
3 tablespoons ground almonds
⅛ teaspoon freshly ground black pepper
1 pound (454 g) ground chicken breast
1.   Combine all the ingredients except the chicken in a medium mixing bowl and stir well.
2.   Add the chicken breast to the apple mixture and mix with your hands until well incorporated.
3.   Divide the mixture into 8 equal portions and shape into patties. Arrange the patties in the perforated pan.
4.   Select Air Fry. Set temperature to 330ºF (166ºC) and set time to 10 minutes. Press Start to begin preheating.
5.   Once the oven has preheated, place the pan into the oven.
6.   When done, a meat thermometer inserted in the center of the chicken should reach at least 165ºF (74ºC).
7.   Remove from the oven to a plate. Let the chicken cool for 5 minutes and serve warm.

Blueberries Quesadillas

Prep time: 5 minutes | Cook time: 4 minutes | Serves 2
¼ cup nonfat Ricotta cheese

¼ cup plain nonfat Greek yogurt
2 tablespoons finely ground flaxseeds
1 tablespoon granulated stevia
½ teaspoon cinnamon
¼ teaspoon vanilla extract
2 (8-inch) low-carb whole-wheat tortillas
½ cup fresh blueberries, divided
1.	Line the sheet pan with the aluminum foil.
2.	In a small bowl, whisk together the Ricotta cheese, yogurt, flaxseeds, stevia, cinnamon and vanilla.
3.	Place the tortillas on the sheet pan. Spread half of the yogurt mixture on each tortilla, almost to the edges. Top each tortilla with ¼ cup of blueberries. Fold the tortillas in half.
4.	Select Bake. Set temperature to 400ºF (205ºC) and set time to 4 minutes. Press Start to begin preheating.
5.	Once the unit has preheated, place the pan into the oven.
6.	When cooking is complete, remove the pan from the oven. Serve immediately.

Maple Banana Bread Pudding

Prep time: 10 minutes | Cook time: 18 minutes | Serves 4
2 medium ripe bananas, mashed
½ cup low-fat milk
2 tablespoons maple syrup
2 tablespoons peanut butter
1 teaspoon vanilla extract
1 teaspoon ground cinnamon
2 slices whole-grain bread, torn into bite-sized pieces
¼ cup quick oats
Cooking spray
1.	Spritz the sheet pan with cooking spray.
2.	In a large bowl, combine the bananas, milk, maple syrup, peanut butter, vanilla extract and cinnamon. Use an immersion blender to mix until well combined.
3.	Stir in the bread pieces to coat well. Add the oats and stir until everything is combined.
4.	Transfer the mixture to the sheet pan. Cover with the aluminum foil.
5.	Select Air Fry. Set temperature to 375ºF (190ºC) and set time to 18 minutes. Press Start to begin preheating.
6.	Once the unit has preheated, place the pan into the oven.
7.	After 10 minutes, remove the foil and continue to cook for 8 minutes.
8.	Serve immediately.

Baked Avocado with Eggs and Tomato

Prep time: 5 minutes | Cook time: 9 minutes | Serves 2
1 large avocado, halved and pitted
2 large eggs
2 tomato slices, divided
½ cup nonfat Cottage cheese, divided
½ teaspoon fresh cilantro, for garnish
1.	Line the sheet pan with the aluminium foil.
2.	Slice a thin piece from the bottom of each avocado half so they sit flat. Remove a small amount from each avocado half to make a bigger hole to hold the egg.
3.	Arrange the avocado halves on the pan, hollow-side up. Break 1 egg into each half. Top each half with 1 tomato slice and ¼ cup of the Cottage cheese.
4.	Select Bake. Set temperature to 425ºF (220ºC) and set time to 9 minutes. Press Start to begin preheating.
5.	Once the unit has preheated, place the pan into the oven.
6.	When cooking is complete, remove the pan from the oven. Garnish with the fresh cilantro and serve.

Spinach and Egg Florentine

Prep time: 10 minutes | Cook time: 15 minutes | Serves 4
3 cups frozen spinach, thawed and drained
2 tablespoons heavy cream
¼ teaspoon kosher salt
⅛ teaspoon freshly ground black pepper
4 ounces (113 g) Ricotta cheese
2 garlic cloves, minced
½ cup panko bread crumbs
3 tablespoons grated Parmesan cheese
2 teaspoons unsalted butter, melted
4 large eggs
1.	In a medium bowl, whisk together the spinach, heavy cream, salt, pepper, Ricotta cheese and garlic.
2.	In a small bowl, whisk together the bread crumbs, Parmesan cheese and butter. Set aside.
3.	Spoon the spinach mixture on the sheet pan and form four even circles.
4.	Select Roast. Set temperature to 375ºF (190ºC) and set time to 15 minutes. Press Start to begin preheating.
5.	Once the unit has preheated, place the pan into the oven.
6.	After 8 minutes, remove the pan from the oven. The spinach should be bubbling. With the back of a large spoon, make indentations in the spinach for the eggs. Crack the eggs into the indentations and sprinkle the panko mixture over the surface of the eggs. Return the pan to the oven to continue cooking.
7.	When cooking is complete, remove the pan from the oven. Serve hot.

Cinnamon Rolls with Brown Sugar

Prep time: 5 minutes | Cook time: 25 minutes | Makes 18 rolls
$^1/_3$ cup light brown sugar
2 teaspoons cinnamon

1 (9-by-9-inch) frozen puff pastry sheet, thawed
All-purpose flour, for dusting
6 teaspoons unsalted butter, melted, divided
1.	In a small bowl, stir together the brown sugar and cinnamon.
2.	On a clean work surface, lightly dust with the flour and lay the puff pastry sheet. Using a rolling pin, press the folds together and roll the dough out in one direction so that it measures about 9 by 11 inches. Cut it in half to form two squat rectangles of about 5½ by 9 inches.
3.	Brush 2 teaspoons of the butter over each pastry half. Sprinkle with 2 tablespoons of the cinnamon sugar. Pat it down lightly with the palm of your hand to help it adhere to the butter.
4.	Starting with the 9-inch side of one rectangle. Using your hands, carefully roll the dough into a cylinder. Repeat with the other rectangle. To make slicing easier, refrigerate the rolls for 10 to 20 minutes.
5.	Using a sharp knife, slice each roll into nine 1-inch pieces. Transfer the rolls to the center of the sheet pan. They should be very close to each other, but not quite touching. Drizzle the remaining 2 teaspoons of the butter over the rolls and sprinkle with the remaining cinnamon sugar.
6.	Select Bake. Set temperature to 350ºF (180ºC) and set time to 25 minutes. Press Start to begin preheating.
7.	Once the unit has preheated, place the pan into the oven.
8.	When cooking is complete, remove the pan and check the rolls. They should be puffed up and golden brown.
9.	Let the rolls rest for 5 minutes and transfer them to a wire rack to cool completely. Serve.

Banana Carrot Muffin

Prep time: 10 minutes | Cook time: 20 minutes | Serves 12
1½ cups whole-wheat flour
1 cup grated carrot
1 cup mashed banana
½ cup bran
½ cup low-fat buttermilk
2 tablespoons agave nectar
2 teaspoons baking powder
1 teaspoon vanilla
1 teaspoon baking soda
½ teaspoon nutmeg
Pinch cloves
2 egg whites
1.	Line a muffin pan with 12 paper liners.
2.	In a large bowl, stir together all the ingredients. Mix well, but do not over beat.
3.	Scoop the mixture into the muffin cups.
4.	Select Bake. Set temperature to 400ºF (205ºC) and set time to 20 minutes. Press Start to begin preheating.

5.	Once the unit has preheated, place the pan into the oven.
6.	When cooking is complete, remove the pan and let rest for 5 minutes.
7.	Serve warm or at room temperature.

Artichoke and Mushroom Frittata

Prep time: 10 minutes | Cook time: 15 minutes | Serves 6
8 eggs
½ teaspoon kosher salt
¼ cup whole milk
¾ cup shredded Mozzarella cheese, divided
2 tablespoons unsalted butter, melted
1 cup coarsely chopped artichoke hearts
¼ cup chopped onion
½ cup mushrooms
¼ cup grated Parmesan cheese
¼ teaspoon freshly ground black pepper
1.	In a medium bowl, whisk together the eggs and salt. Let rest for a minute or two, then pour in the milk and whisk again. Stir in ½ cup of the Mozzarella cheese.
2.	Grease the sheet pan with the butter. Stir in the artichoke hearts and onion and toss to coat with the butter.
3.	Select Roast. Set temperature to 375ºF (190ºC) and set time to 12 minutes. Press Start to begin preheating.
4.	Once the unit has preheated, place the pan into the oven.
5.	After 5 minutes, remove the pan. Spread the mushrooms over the vegetables. Pour the egg mixture on top. Stir gently just to distribute the vegetables evenly. Return the pan to the oven and continue cooking for 5 to 7 minutes, or until the edges are set. The center will still be quite liquid.
6.	Select Broil. Set temperature to Low and set time to 3 minutes. Place the pan into the oven.
7.	After 1 minute, remove the pan and sprinkle the remaining ¼ cup of the Mozzarella and Parmesan cheese over the frittata. Return the pan to the oven and continue cooking for 2 minutes.
8.	When cooking is complete, the cheese should be melted with the top completely set but not browned. Sprinkle the black pepper on top and serve.

Whole-Wheat Blueberries Muffins

Prep time: 5 minutes | Cook time: 25 minutes | Makes 8 muffins
½ cup unsweetened applesauce
½ cup plant-based milk
½ cup maple syrup
1 teaspoon vanilla extract
2 cups whole-wheat flour
½ teaspoon baking soda
1 cup blueberries
Cooking spray

1.	Spritz a 8-cup muffin pan with cooking spray.
2.	In a large bowl, stir together the applesauce, milk, maple syrup and vanilla extract. Whisk in the flour and baking soda until no dry flour is left and the batter is smooth. Gently mix in the blueberries until they are evenly distributed throughout the batter.
3.	Spoon the batter into the muffin cups, three-quarters full.
4.	Select Bake. Set temperature to 375ºF (190ºC) and set time to 25 minutes. Press Start to begin preheating.
5.	Once preheated, place the pan into the oven.
6.	When cooking is complete, remove the pan and check the muffins. You can stick a knife into the center of a muffin and it should come out clean.
7.	Let rest for 5 minutes before serving.

Orange Scones with Blueberries

Prep time: 5 minutes | Cook time: 20 minutes | Serves 14
½ cup low-fat buttermilk
¾ cup orange juice
Zest of 1 orange
2¼ cups whole-wheat pastry flour
$^1/_3$ cup agave nectar
¼ cup canola oil
1 teaspoon baking soda
1 teaspoon cream of tartar
1 cup fresh blueberries
1.	In a small bowl, stir together the buttermilk, orange juice and orange zest.
2.	In a large bowl, whisk together the flour, agave nectar, canola oil, baking soda and cream of tartar.
3.	Add the buttermilk mixture and blueberries to the bowl with the flour mixture. Mix gently by hand until well combined.
4.	Transfer the batter onto a lightly floured baking sheet. Pat into a circle about ¾ inch thick and 8 inches across. Use a knife to cut the circle into 14 wedges, cutting almost all the way through.
5.	Select Bake. Set temperature to 375ºF (190ºC) and set time to 20 minutes. Press Start to begin preheating.
6.	Once the unit has preheated, place the baking sheet into the oven.
7.	When cooking is complete, remove the baking sheet and check the scones. They should be lightly browned.
8.	Let rest for 5 minutes and cut completely through the wedges before serving.

French Toast Sticks with Strawberries

Prep time: 5 minutes | Cook time: 12 minutes | Serves 4
3 slices low-sodium whole-wheat bread, each cut into 4 strips
1 tablespoon unsalted butter, melted
1 tablespoon 2 percent milk
1 tablespoon sugar
1 egg, beaten
1 egg white
1 cup sliced fresh strawberries
1 tablespoon freshly squeezed lemon juice
1.	Arrange the bread strips on a plate and drizzle with the melted butter.
2.	In a bowl, whisk together the milk, sugar, egg and egg white.
3.	Dredge the bread strips into the egg mixture and place on a wire rack to let the batter drip off. Arrange half the coated bread strips on the sheet pan.
4.	Select Air Fry. Set temperature to 380ºF (193ºC) and set time to 6 minutes. Press Start to begin preheating.
5.	Once preheated, place the pan into the oven.
6.	After 3 minutes, remove the pan from the oven. Use tongs to turn the strips over. Rotate the pan and return the pan to the oven to continue cooking.
7.	When cooking is complete, the strips should be golden brown.
8.	In a small bowl, mash the strawberries with a fork and stir in the lemon juice. Serve the French toast sticks with the strawberry sauce.

Blueberry Cake with Lemon

Prep time: 5 minutes | Cook time: 10 minutes | Serves 8
1½ cups Bisquick
¼ cup granulated sugar
2 large eggs, beaten
¾ cup whole milk
1 teaspoon vanilla extract
½ teaspoon lemon zest
Cooking spray
2 cups blueberries
1.	Stir together the Bisquick and sugar in a medium bowl. Stir together the eggs, milk, vanilla and lemon zest. Add the wet ingredients to the dry ingredients and stir until well combined.
2.	Spritz the sheet pan with cooking spray and line with the parchment paper, pressing it into place. Spray the parchment paper with cooking spray. Pour the batter on the pan and spread it out evenly. Sprinkle the blueberries evenly over the top.
3.	Select Bake. Set temperature to 375ºF (190ºC) and set time to 10 minutes. Press Start to begin preheating.
4.	Once the unit has preheated, place the pan into the oven.
5.	When cooking is complete, the cake should be pulling away from the edges of the pan and the top should be just starting to turn golden brown.
6.	Let the cake rest for a minute before cutting into 16 squares. Serve immediately.

Cinnamon Apple Turnovers

Prep time: 10 minutes | Cook time: 20 minutes | Serves 4

1 cup diced apple
1 tablespoon brown sugar
1 teaspoon freshly squeezed lemon juice
1 teaspoon all-purpose flour, plus more for dusting
¼ teaspoon cinnamon
⅛ teaspoon allspice
½ package frozen puff pastry, thawed
1 large egg, beaten
2 teaspoons granulated sugar

1. Whisk together the apple, brown sugar, lemon juice, flour, cinnamon and allspice in a medium bowl.
2. On a clean work surface, lightly dust with the flour and lay the puff pastry sheet. Using a rolling pin, gently roll the dough to smooth out the folds, seal any tears and form it into a square. Cut the dough into four squares.
3. Spoon a quarter of the apple mixture into the center of each puff pastry square and spread it evenly in a triangle shape over half the pastry, leaving a border of about ½ inch around the edges of the pastry. Fold the pastry diagonally over the filling to form triangles. With a fork, crimp the edges to seal them. Place the turnovers on the sheet pan, spacing them evenly.
4. Cut two or three small slits in the top of each turnover. Brush with the egg. Sprinkle evenly with the granulated sugar.
5. Select Bake. Set temperature to 350ºF (180ºC) and set time to 20 minutes. Press Start to begin preheating.
6. Once the unit has preheated, place the pan into the oven.
7. After 10 to 12 minutes, remove the pan from the oven. Check the pastries. If they are browned unevenly, rotate the pan. Return the pan to the oven and continue cooking.
8. When cooking is complete, remove the pan from the oven. The turnovers should be golden brown and the filling bubbling. Let cool for about 10 minutes before serving.

Beef Hash with Eggs

Prep time: 10 minutes | Cook time: 25 minutes | Serves 4

2 medium Yukon Gold potatoes, peeled and cut into ¼-inch cubes
1 medium onion, chopped
$^1/_3$ cup diced red bell pepper
3 tablespoons vegetable oil
½ teaspoon dried thyme
½ teaspoon kosher salt, divided
½ teaspoon freshly ground black pepper, divided
¾ pound (340 g) corned beef, cut into ¼-inch pieces
4 large eggs

1. In a large bowl, stir together the potatoes, onion, red pepper, vegetable oil, thyme, ¼ teaspoon of the salt and ¼ teaspoon of the pepper. Spread the vegetable mixture on the sheet pan in an even layer.
2. Select Roast. Set temperature to 375ºF (190ºC) and set time to 25 minutes. Press Start to begin preheating.
3. Once the unit has preheated, place the pan into the oven.
4. After 15 minutes, remove the pan from the oven and add the corned beef. Stir the mixture to incorporate the corned beef. Return the pan to the oven and continue cooking.
5. After 5 minutes, remove the pan from the oven. Using a large spoon, create 4 circles in the hash to hold the eggs. Gently crack an egg into each circle. Season the eggs with the remaining ¼ teaspoon of the salt and ¼ teaspoon of the pepper. Return the pan to the oven. Continue cooking for 3 to 5 minutes, depending on how you like your eggs.
6. When cooking is complete, remove the pan from the oven. Serve immediately.

Maple French Toast Casserole

Prep time: 5 minutes | Cook time: 12 minutes | Serves 6

3 large eggs, beaten
1 cup whole milk
1 tablespoon pure maple syrup
1 teaspoon vanilla extract
¼ teaspoon cinnamon
¼ teaspoon kosher salt
3 cups stale bread cubes
1 tablespoon unsalted butter, at room temperature

1. In a medium bowl, whisk together the eggs, milk, maple syrup, vanilla extract, cinnamon and salt. Stir in the bread cubes to coat well.
2. Grease the bottom of the sheet pan with the butter. Spread the bread mixture into the pan in an even layer.
3. Select Roast. Set temperature to 350ºF (180ºC) and set time to 12 minutes. Press Start to begin preheating.
4. Once the unit has preheated, place the pan into the oven.
5. After about 10 minutes, remove the pan and check the casserole. The top should be browned and the middle of the casserole just set. If more time is needed, return the pan to the oven and continue cooking.
6. When cooking is complete, serve warm.

Honey Cashew Granola with Cranberries

Prep time: 5 minutes | Cook time: 12 minutes | Serves 6

3 cups old-fashioned rolled oats
2 cups raw cashews
1 cup unsweetened coconut chips
½ cup honey
¼ cup vegetable oil
$^1/_3$ cup packed light brown sugar

¼ teaspoon kosher salt
1 cup dried cranberries
1. In a large bowl, stir together all the ingredients, except for the cranberries. Spread the mixture on the sheet pan in an even layer.
2. Select Bake. Set temperature to 325ºF (163ºC) and set time to 12 minutes. Press Start to begin preheating.
3. Once the unit has preheated, place the pan into the oven.
4. After 5 to 6 minutes, remove the pan and stir the granola. Return the pan to the oven and continue cooking.
5. When cooking is complete, remove the pan. Let the granola cool to room temperature. Stir in the cranberries before serving.

CHAPTER 2 APPETIZERS AND SNACKS

Cheddar Baked Potatoes with Chives

Prep time: 5 minutes | Cook time: 20 minutes | Serves 6

12 small red potatoes
1 teaspoon kosher salt, divided
1 tablespoon extra-virgin olive oil
¼ cup grated sharp Cheddar cheese
¼ cup sour cream
2 tablespoons chopped chives
2 tablespoons grated Parmesan cheese

1. Add the potatoes to a large bowl. Sprinkle with the ½ teaspoon of the salt and drizzle with the olive oil. Toss to coat. Place the potatoes in the sheet pan.
2. Select Roast. Set temperature to 375ºF (190ºC) and set time to 15 minutes. Press Start to begin preheating.
3. When the unit has preheated, place the pan into the oven.
4. After 10 minutes, rotate the pan and continue cooking.
5. When cooking is complete, remove the pan and let the potatoes rest for 5 minutes. Halve the potatoes lengthwise. Using a spoon, scoop the flesh into a bowl, leaving a thin shell of skin. Arrange the potato halves on the sheet pan.
6. Mash the potato flesh until smooth. Stir in the remaining ½ teaspoon of the salt, Cheddar cheese, sour cream and chives. Transfer the filling into a pastry bag with one corner snipped off. Pipe the filling into the potato shells, mounding up slightly. Sprinkle with the Parmesan cheese.
7. Select Roast. Set temperature to 375ºF (190ºC) and set time to 5 minutes. Place the pan into the oven.
8. When cooking is complete, the tops should be browning slightly. Remove the pan from the oven and let the potatoes cool slightly before serving.

Sausage and Onion Rolls with Mustard

Prep time: 15 minutes | Cook time: 15 minutes | Serves 12

1 pound (454 g) bulk breakfast sausage
½ cup finely chopped onion
½ cup fresh bread crumbs
½ teaspoon dried mustard
½ teaspoon dried sage
¼ teaspoon cayenne pepper
1 large egg, beaten
1 garlic clove, minced
2 sheets (1 package) frozen puff pastry, thawed
All-purpose flour, for dusting

1. In a medium bowl, break up the sausage. Stir in the onion, bread crumbs, mustard, sage, cayenne pepper, egg and garlic. Divide the sausage mixture in half and tightly wrap each half in plastic wrap. Refrigerate for 5 to 10 minutes.
2. Lay the pastry sheets on a lightly floured work surface. Using a rolling pin, lightly roll out the pastry to smooth out the dough. Take out one of the sausage packages and form the sausage into a long roll. Remove the plastic wrap and place the sausage on top of the puff pastry about 1 inch from one of the long edges. Roll the pastry around the sausage and pinch the edges of the dough together to seal. Repeat with the other pastry sheet and sausage.
3. Slice the logs into lengths about 1½ inches long. Place the sausage rolls on the sheet pan, cut-side down.
4. Select Roast. Set temperature to 350ºF (180ºC) and set time to 15 minutes. Press Start to begin preheating.
5. Once the unit has preheated, place the pan into the oven.
6. After 7 or 8 minutes, rotate the pan and continue cooking.
7. When cooking is complete, the rolls will be golden brown and sizzling. Remove the pan from the oven and let cool for 5 minutes.

Honey Roasted Grapes with Basil

Prep time: 5 minutes | Cook time: 10 minutes | Serves 6

2 cups seedless red grapes, rinsed and patted dry
1 tablespoon apple cider vinegar
1 tablespoon honey
1 cup low-fat Greek yogurt
2 tablespoons 2 percent milk
2 tablespoons minced fresh basil

1. Spread the red grapes in the perforated pan and drizzle with the cider vinegar and honey. Lightly toss to coat.
2. Select Roast. Set temperature to 380ºF (193ºC) and set time to 10 minutes. Press Start to begin preheating.
3. Once the unit has preheated, place the pan into the oven.
4. When cooking is complete, the grapes will be wilted but still soft. Remove the pan from the oven.
5. In a medium bowl, whisk together the yogurt and milk. Gently fold in the grapes and basil.
6. Serve immediately.

Parmesan Cauliflower with Turmeric

Prep time: 15 minutes | Cook time: 15 minutes | Makes 5 cups

8 cups small cauliflower florets (about 1¼ pounds / 567 g)
3 tablespoons olive oil
1 teaspoon garlic powder
½ teaspoon salt
½ teaspoon turmeric
¼ cup shredded Parmesan cheese

1.	In a bowl, combine the cauliflower florets, olive oil, garlic powder, salt, and turmeric and toss to coat. Transfer to the perforated pan.
2.	Select Air Fry. Set temperature to 390ºF (199ºC) and set time to 15 minutes. Press Start to begin preheating.
3.	Once preheated, place the pan into the oven.
4.	After 5 minutes, remove from the oven and stir the cauliflower florets. Return the pan to the oven and continue cooking.
5.	After 6 minutes, remove from the oven and stir the cauliflower. Return the pan to the oven and continue cooking for 4 minutes. The cauliflower florets should be crisp-tender.
6.	When cooking is complete, remove from the oven to a plate. Sprinkle with the shredded Parmesan cheese and toss well. Serve warm.

Cheddar Mushrooms with Pimientos

Prep time: 10 minutes | Cook time: 18 minutes | Serves 12
24 medium raw white button mushrooms, rinsed and drained
4 ounces (113 g) shredded extra-sharp Cheddar cheese
2 ounces (57 g) cream cheese, at room temperature
1 ounce (28 g) chopped jarred pimientos
2 tablespoons grated onion
⅛ teaspoon smoked paprika
⅛ teaspoon hot sauce
2 tablespoons butter, melted, divided
$1/3$ cup panko bread crumbs
2 tablespoons grated Parmesan cheese
1.	Gently pull out the stems of the mushrooms and discard. Set aside.
2.	In a medium bowl, stir together the Cheddar cheese, cream cheese, pimientos, onion, paprika and hot sauce.
3.	Brush the sheet pan with 1 tablespoon of the melted butter. Arrange the mushrooms evenly on the pan, hollow-side up.
4.	Place the cheese mixture into a large heavy plastic bag and cut off the end. Fill the mushrooms with the cheese mixture.
5.	In a small bowl, whisk together the remaining 1 tablespoon of the melted butter, bread crumbs and Parmesan cheese. Sprinkle the panko mixture over each mushroom.
6.	Select Roast. Set temperature to 350ºF (180ºC) and set time to 18 minutes. Press Start to begin preheating.
7.	When the unit has preheated, place the pan into the oven.
8.	After about 9 minutes, rotate the pan and continue cooking.
9.	When cooking is complete, let the stuffed mushrooms rest for 2 minutes before serving.

Roasted Mushrooms with Garlic

Prep time: 5 minutes | Cook time: 27 minutes | Serves 4
16 garlic cloves, peeled
2 teaspoons olive oil, divided
16 button mushrooms
½ teaspoon dried marjoram
⅛ teaspoon freshly ground black pepper
1 tablespoon white wine
1.	Place the garlic cloves on the sheet pan and drizzle with 1 teaspoon of the olive oil. Toss to coat well.
2.	Select Roast. Set temperature to 350ºF (180ºC) and set time to 12 minutes. Press Start to begin preheating.
3.	Once the unit has preheated, place the pan into the oven.
4.	When cooking is complete, remove the pan from the oven. Stir in the mushrooms, marjoram and pepper. Drizzle with the remaining 1 teaspoon of the olive oil and the white wine. Toss to coat well. Return the pan to the oven.
5.	Select Roast. Set temperature to 350ºF (180ºC) and set time to 15 minutes. place the pan into the oven.
6.	Once done, the mushrooms and garlic cloves will be softened. Remove the pan from the oven.
7.	Serve warm.

Jalapeño Poppers with Cheddar

Prep time: 10 minutes | Cook time: 15 minutes | Serves 8
6 ounces (170 g) cream cheese, at room temperature
4 ounces (113 g) shredded Cheddar cheese
1 teaspoon chili powder
12 large jalapeño peppers, deseeded and sliced in half lengthwise
2 slices cooked bacon, chopped
¼ cup panko bread crumbs
1 tablespoon butter, melted
1.	In a medium bowl, whisk together the cream cheese, Cheddar cheese and chili powder. Spoon the cheese mixture into the jalapeño halves and arrange them on the sheet pan.
2.	In a small bowl, stir together the bacon, bread crumbs and butter. Sprinkle the mixture over the jalapeño halves.
3.	Select Roast. Set temperature to 375ºF (190ºC) and set time to 15 minutes. Press Start to begin preheating.
4.	When the unit has preheated, place the pan into the oven.
5.	After 7 or 8 minutes, rotate the pan and continue cooking until the peppers are softened, the filling is bubbling and the bread crumbs are browned.
6.	When cooking is complete, remove the pan from the oven. Let the poppers cool for 5 minutes before serving.

Lemon-Pepper Chicken Wings

Prep time: 5 minutes | Cook time: 24 minutes | Serves 10

2 pounds (907 g) chicken wings
4½ teaspoons salt-free lemon pepper seasoning
1½ teaspoons baking powder
1½ teaspoons kosher salt
1.   In a large bowl, toss together all the ingredients until well coated. Place the wings on the sheet pan, making sure they don't crowd each other too much.
2.   Select Air Fry. Set temperature to 375ºF (190ºC) and set time to 24 minutes. Press Start to begin preheating.
3.   Once preheated, slide the pan into the oven.
4.   After 12 minutes, remove the pan from the oven. Use tongs to turn the wings over. Rotate the pan and return the pan to the oven to continue cooking.
5.   When cooking is complete, the wings should be dark golden brown and a bit charred in places. Remove the pan from the oven and let rest for 5 minutes before serving.

Green Chiles and Cheese Nachos

Prep time: 10 minutes | Cook time: 10 minutes | Serves 6

8 ounces (227 g) tortilla chips
3 cups shredded Monterey Jack cheese, divided
2 (7-ounce / 198-g) cans chopped green chiles, drained
1 (8-ounce / 227-g) can tomato sauce
¼ teaspoon dried oregano
¼ teaspoon granulated garlic
¼ teaspoon freshly ground black pepper
Pinch cinnamon
Pinch cayenne pepper
1.   Arrange the tortilla chips close together in a single layer on the sheet pan. Sprinkle 1½ cups of the cheese over the chips. Arrange the green chiles over the cheese as evenly as possible. Top with the remaining 1½ cups of the cheese.
2.   Select Roast. Set temperature to 375ºF (190ºC) and set time to 10 minutes. Press Start to begin preheating.
3.   When the unit has preheated, place the pan into the oven.
4.   After 5 minutes, rotate the pan and continue cooking.
5.   Meanwhile, stir together the remaining ingredients in a bowl.
6.   When cooking is complete, the cheese will be melted and starting to crisp around the edges of the pan. Remove the pan from the oven. Drizzle the sauce over the nachos and serve warm.

Pepperoni Pizza Bites with Marinara

Prep time: 5 minutes | Cook time: 12 minutes | Serves 8

1 cup finely shredded Mozzarella cheese

½ cup chopped pepperoni
¼ cup Marinara sauce
1 (8-ounce / 227-g) can crescent roll dough
All-purpose flour, for dusting
1.   In a small bowl, stir together the cheese, pepperoni and Marinara sauce.
2.   Lay the dough on a lightly floured work surface. Separate it into 4 rectangles. Firmly pinch the perforations together and pat the dough pieces flat.
3.   Divide the cheese mixture evenly between the rectangles and spread it out over the dough, leaving a ¼-inch border. Roll a rectangle up tightly, starting with the short end. Pinch the edge down to seal the roll. Repeat with the remaining rolls.
4.   Slice the rolls into 4 or 5 even slices. Place the slices on the sheet pan, leaving a few inches between each slice.
5.   Select Roast. Set temperature to 350ºF (180ºC) and set time to 12 minutes. Press Start to begin preheating.
6.   Once the unit has preheated, place the pan into the oven.
7.   After 6 minutes, rotate the pan and continue cooking.
8.   When cooking is complete, the rolls will be golden brown with crisp edges. Remove the pan from the oven. Serve hot.

Cheddar Sausage Balls

Prep time: 10 minutes | Cook time: 10 minutes | Serves 8

12 ounces (340 g) mild ground sausage
1½ cups baking mix
1 cup shredded mild Cheddar cheese
3 ounces (85 g) cream cheese, at room temperature
1 to 2 tablespoons olive oil
1.   Line the perforated pan with parchment paper. Set aside.
2.   Mix together the ground sausage, baking mix, Cheddar cheese, and cream cheese in a large bowl and stir to incorporate.
3.   Divide the sausage mixture into 16 equal portions and roll them into 1-inch balls with your hands. Arrange the sausage balls on the parchment, leaving space between each ball. Brush the sausage balls with the olive oil.
4.   Select Air Fry. Set temperature to 325ºF (163ºC) and set time to 10 minutes. Press Start to begin preheating.
5.   Once preheated, place the pan into the oven. Flip the balls halfway through the cooking time.
6.   When cooking is complete, the balls should be firm and lightly browned on both sides. Remove from the oven to a plate and serve warm.

Tuna Melts with Mayo

Prep time: 10 minutes | Cook time: 6 minutes | Serves 6

2 (5- to 6-ounce / 142- to 170-g) cans oil-packed tuna, drained
1 large scallion, chopped
1 small stalk celery, chopped
$^1/_3$ cup mayonnaise
1 tablespoon chopped fresh dill
1 tablespoon capers, drained
¼ teaspoon celery salt
12 slices cocktail rye bread
2 tablespoons butter, melted
6 slices sharp Cheddar cheese
1.	In a medium bowl, stir together the tuna, scallion, celery, mayonnaise, dill, capers and celery salt.
2.	Brush one side of the bread slices with the butter. Arrange the bread slices on the sheet pan, buttered-side down. Scoop a heaping tablespoon of the tuna mixture on each slice of bread, spreading it out evenly to the edges.
3.	Cut the cheese slices to fit the dimensions of the bread and place a cheese slice on each piece.
4.	Select Roast. Set temperature to 375ºF (190ºC) and set time to 6 minutes. Press Start to begin preheating.
5.	Once the unit has preheated, place the pan into the oven.
6.	After 4 minutes, remove the pan from the oven and check the tuna melts. The tuna melts are done when the cheese has melted and the tuna is heated through. If needed, continue cooking.
7.	When cooking is complete, remove the pan from the oven. Use a spatula to transfer the tuna melts to a clean work surface and slice each one in half diagonally. Serve warm.

Sugar Roasted Walnuts

Prep time: 5 minutes | Cook time: 15 minutes | Makes 4 cups
1 pound (454 g) walnut halves and pieces
½ cup granulated sugar
3 tablespoons vegetable oil
1 teaspoon cayenne pepper
½ teaspoon fine salt
1.	Soak the walnuts in a large bowl with boiling water for a minute or two. Drain the walnuts. Stir in the sugar, oil and cayenne pepper to coat well. Spread the walnuts in a single layer on the sheet pan.
2.	Select Roast. Set temperature to 325ºF (163ºC) and set time to 15 minutes. Press Start to begin preheating.
3.	When the unit has preheated, place the pan into the oven.
4.	After 7 or 8 minutes, remove the pan from the oven. Stir the nuts. Return the pan to the oven and continue cooking, check frequently.
5.	When cooking is complete, the walnuts should be dark golden brown. Remove the pan from the oven. Sprinkle the nuts with the salt and let cool. Serve.

Balsamic Prosciutto-Wrapped Pears

Prep time: 12 minutes | Cook time: 6 minutes | Serves 8
2 large, ripe Anjou pears
4 thin slices Parma prosciutto
2 teaspoons aged balsamic vinegar
1.	Peel the pears. Slice into 8 wedges and cut out the core from each wedge.
2.	Cut the prosciutto into 8 long strips. Wrap each pear wedge with a strip of prosciutto. Place the wrapped pears in the sheet pan.
3.	Select Broil. Set temperature to High and set time to 6 minutes. Press Start to begin preheating.
4.	When the unit has preheated, place the pan into the oven.
5.	After 2 or 3 minutes, check the pears. The pears should be turned over if the prosciutto is beginning to crisp up and brown. Return the pan to the oven and continue cooking.
6.	When cooking is complete, remove the pan from the oven. Drizzle the pears with the balsamic vinegar and serve warm.

Breaded Zucchini Tots

Prep time: 15 minutes | Cook time: 6 minutes | Serves 8
2 medium zucchini (about 12 ounces / 340 g) shredded
1 large egg, whisked
½ cup grated pecorino romano cheese
½ cup panko bread crumbs
¼ teaspoon black pepper
1 clove garlic, minced
Cooking spray
1.	Using your hands, squeeze out as much liquid from the zucchini as possible. In a large bowl, mix the zucchini with the remaining ingredients except the oil until well incorporated.
2.	Make the zucchini tots: Use a spoon or cookie scoop to place tablespoonfuls of the zucchini mixture onto a lightly floured cutting board and form into 1-inch logs.
3.	Spritz the perforated pan with cooking spray. Place the zucchini tots in the pan.
4.	Select Air Fry. Set temperature to 375ºF (190ºC) and set time to 6 minutes. Press Start to begin preheating.
5.	Once preheated, place the pan into the oven.
6.	When cooking is complete, the tots should be golden brown. Remove from the oven to a serving plate and serve warm.

Ginger Shrimp with Sesame Seeds

Prep time: 15 minutes | Cook time: 8 minutes | Serves 4 to 6
½ pound (227 g) raw shrimp, peeled and deveined
1 egg, beaten
2 scallions, chopped, plus more for garnish

2 tablespoons chopped fresh cilantro
2 teaspoons grated fresh ginger
1 to 2 teaspoons sriracha sauce
1 teaspoon soy sauce
½ teaspoon toasted sesame oil
6 slices thinly sliced white sandwich bread
½ cup sesame seeds
Cooking spray
Thai chili sauce, for serving
1.	In a food processor, add the shrimp, egg, scallions, cilantro, ginger, sriracha sauce, soy sauce and sesame oil, and pulse until chopped finely. You'll need to stop the food processor occasionally to scrape down the sides. Transfer the shrimp mixture to a bowl.
2.	On a clean work surface, cut the crusts off the sandwich bread. Using a brush, generously brush one side of each slice of bread with shrimp mixture.
3.	Place the sesame seeds on a plate. Press bread slices, shrimp-side down, into sesame seeds to coat evenly. Cut each slice diagonally into quarters.
4.	Spritz the perforated pan with cooking spray. Spread the coated slices in a single layer in the perforated pan.
5.	Select Air Fry. Set temperature to 400ºF (205ºC) and set time to 8 minutes. Press Start to begin preheating.
6.	Once preheated, place the pan into the oven. Flip the bread slices halfway through.
7.	When cooking is complete, they should be golden and crispy. Remove from the oven to a plate and let cool for 5 minutes. Top with the chopped scallions and serve warm with Thai chili sauce.

Paprika Polenta Fries with Chili-Lime Mayo

Prep time: 10 minutes | Cook time: 28 minutes | Serves 4
Polenta Fries:
2 teaspoons vegetable or olive oil
¼ teaspoon paprika
1 pound (454 g) prepared polenta, cut into 3-inch × ½-inch strips
Salt and freshly ground black pepper, to taste
Chili-Lime Mayo:
½ cup mayonnaise
1 teaspoon chili powder
1 teaspoon chopped fresh cilantro
¼ teaspoon ground cumin
Juice of ½ lime
Salt and freshly ground black pepper, to taste
1.	Mix the oil and paprika in a bowl. Add the polenta strips and toss until evenly coated. Transfer the polenta strips to the perforated pan.
2.	Select Air Fry. Set temperature to 400ºF (205ºC) and set time to 28 minutes. Press Start to begin preheating.
3.	Once preheated, place the pan into the oven. Stir the polenta strips halfway through the cooking time.

4.	Meanwhile, whisk together all the ingredients for the chili-lime mayo in a small bowl.
5.	When cooking is complete, remove the polenta fries from the oven to a plate. Season as desired with salt and pepper. Serve alongside the chili-lime mayo as a dipping sauce.

Lemon Ricotta with Capers

Prep time: 10 minutes | Cook time: 8 minutes | Serves 4 to 6
1½ cups whole milk ricotta cheese
2 tablespoons extra-virgin olive oil
2 tablespoons capers, rinsed
Zest of 1 lemon, plus more for garnish
1 teaspoon finely chopped fresh rosemary
Pinch crushed red pepper flakes
Salt and freshly ground black pepper, to taste
1 tablespoon grated Parmesan cheese
1.	In a mixing bowl, stir together the ricotta cheese, olive oil, capers, lemon zest, rosemary, red pepper flakes, salt, and pepper until well combined.
2.	Spread the mixture evenly in a baking dish.
3.	Select Air Fry. Set temperature to 380ºF (193ºC) and set time to 8 minutes. Press Start to begin preheating.
4.	Once preheated, place the baking dish in the oven.
5.	When cooking is complete, the top should be nicely browned. Remove from the oven and top with a sprinkle of grated Parmesan cheese. Garnish with the lemon zest and serve warm.

Deviled Eggs with Mayo

Prep time: 20 minutes | Cook time: 16 minutes | Serves 12
3 cups ice
12 large eggs
½ cup mayonnaise
10 hamburger dill pickle chips, diced
¼ cup diced onion
2 teaspoons salt
2 teaspoons yellow mustard
1 teaspoon freshly ground black pepper
½ teaspoon paprika
1.	Put the ice in a large bowl and set aside. Carefully place the eggs in the perforated pan.
2.	Select Bake. Set temperature to 250ºF (121ºC) and set time to 16 minutes. Press Start to begin preheating.
3.	Once preheated, place the pan into the oven.
4.	When cooking is complete, transfer the eggs to the large bowl of ice to cool.
5.	When cool enough to handle, peel the eggs. Slice them in half lengthwise and scoop out yolks into a small bowl. Stir in the mayonnaise, pickles, onion, salt, mustard, and pepper. Mash the mixture with a fork until well combined.
6.	Fill each egg white half with 1 to 2 teaspoons of the egg yolk mixture.

7. Sprinkle the paprika on top and serve immediately.

Honey Snack Mix

Prep time: 5 minutes | Cook time: 10 minutes | Makes about 10 cups
3 tablespoons butter, melted
½ cup honey
1 teaspoon salt
2 cups granola
2 cups sesame sticks
2 cups crispy corn puff cereal
2 cups mini pretzel crisps
1 cup cashews
1 cup pepitas
1 cup dried cherries
1. In a small mixing bowl, mix together the butter, honey, and salt until well incorporated.
2. In a large bowl, combine the granola, sesame sticks, corn puff cereal and pretzel crisps, cashews, and pepitas. Drizzle with the butter mixture and toss until evenly coated. Transfer the snack mix to a sheet pan.
3. Select Air Fry. Set temperature to 370ºF (188ºC) and set time to 10 minutes. Press Start to begin preheating.
4. Once preheated, slide the pan into the oven. Stir the snack mix halfway through the cooking time.
5. When cooking is complete, they should be lightly toasted. Remove from the oven and allow to cool completely. Scatter with the dried cherries and mix well. Serve immediately.

Parmesan Snack Mix

Prep time: 5 minutes | Cook time: 6 minutes | Makes 6 cups
2 cups oyster crackers
2 cups Chex rice
1 cup sesame sticks
$^2/_3$ cup finely grated Parmesan cheese
8 tablespoons unsalted butter, melted
1½ teaspoons granulated garlic
½ teaspoon kosher salt
1. Toss together all the ingredients in a large bowl until well coated. Spread the mixture on the sheet pan in an even layer.
2. Select Roast. Set temperature to 350ºF (180ºC) and set time to 6 minutes. Press Start to begin preheating.
3. When the unit has preheated, place the pan into the oven.
4. After 3 minutes, remove the pan and stir the mixture. Return the pan to the oven and continue cooking.
5. When cooking is complete, the mixture should be lightly browned and fragrant. Let cool before serving.

Paprika Potato Chips

Prep time: 5 minutes | Cook time: 22 minutes | Serves 3
2 medium potatoes, preferably Yukon Gold, scrubbed
Cooking spray
2 teaspoons olive oil
½ teaspoon garlic granules
¼ teaspoon paprika
¼ teaspoon plus ⅛ teaspoon sea salt
¼ teaspoon freshly ground black pepper
Ketchup or hot sauce, for serving
1. Spritz the perforated pan with cooking spray.
2. On a flat work surface, cut the potatoes into ¼-inch-thick slices. Transfer the potato slices to a medium bowl, along with the olive oil, garlic granules, paprika, salt, and pepper and toss to coat well. Transfer the potato slices to the perforated pan.
3. Select Air Fry. Set temperature to 392ºF (200ºC) and set time to 22 minutes. Press Start to begin preheating.
4. Once preheated, place the pan into the oven. Stir the potato slices twice during the cooking process.
5. When cooking is complete, the potato chips should be tender and nicely browned. Remove from the oven and serve alongside the ketchup for dipping.

Hush Puppies with Jalapeño

Prep time: 45 minutes | Cook time: 10 minutes | Serves 12
1 cup self-rising yellow cornmeal
½ cup all-purpose flour
1 teaspoon sugar
1 teaspoon salt
1 teaspoon freshly ground black pepper
1 large egg
$^1/_3$ cup canned creamed corn
1 cup minced onion
2 teaspoons minced jalapeño pepper
2 tablespoons olive oil, divided
1. Thoroughly combine the cornmeal, flour, sugar, salt, and pepper in a large bowl.
2. Whisk together the egg and corn in a small bowl. Pour the egg mixture into the bowl of cornmeal mixture and stir to combine. Stir in the minced onion and jalapeño. Cover the bowl with plastic wrap and place in the refrigerator for 30 minutes.
3. Line the perforated pan with parchment paper and lightly brush it with 1 tablespoon of olive oil.
4. Scoop out the cornmeal mixture and form into 24 balls, about 1 inch.
5. Arrange the balls on the parchment, leaving space between each ball.
6. Select Air Fry. Set temperature to 375ºF (190ºC) and set time to 10 minutes. Press Start to begin preheating.
7. Once preheated, place the pan into the oven.
8. After 5 minutes, remove the pan from the oven. Flip the balls and brush them with the

remaining 1 tablespoon of olive oil. Return to the oven and continue cooking for 5 minutes until golden brown.

9. When cooking is complete, remove the balls (hush puppies) from the oven and serve on a plate.

Fried Pickle Spears with Chili

Prep time: 5 minutes | Cook time: 15 minutes | Serves 6

2 jars sweet and sour pickle spears, patted dry
2 medium-sized eggs
$^1/_3$ cup milk
1 teaspoon garlic powder
1 teaspoon sea salt
½ teaspoon shallot powder
$^1/_3$ teaspoon chili powder
$^1/_3$ cup all-purpose flour
Cooking spray

1. Spritz the perforated pan with cooking spray.
2. In a bowl, beat together the eggs with milk. In another bowl, combine garlic powder, sea salt, shallot powder, chili powder and all-purpose flour until well blended.
3. One by one, roll the pickle spears in the powder mixture, then dredge them in the egg mixture. Dip them in the powder mixture a second time for additional coating.
4. Place the coated pickles in the perforated pan.
5. Select Air Fry. Set temperature to 385ºF (196ºC) and set time to 15 minutes. Press Start to begin preheating.
6. Once preheated, place the pan into the oven. Stir the pickles halfway through the cooking time.
7. When cooking is complete, they should be golden and crispy. Transfer to a plate and let cool for 5 minutes before serving.

Cinnamon Apple Chips

Prep time: 10 minutes | Cook time: 10 minutes | Serves 4

2 apples, cored and cut into thin slices
2 heaped teaspoons ground cinnamon
Cooking spray

1. Spritz the perforated pan with cooking spray.
2. In a medium bowl, sprinkle the apple slices with the cinnamon. Toss until evenly coated. Spread the coated apple slices on the pan in a single layer.
3. Select Air Fry. Set temperature to 350ºF (180ºC) and set time to 10 minutes. Press Start to begin preheating.
4. Once preheated, place the pan into the oven.
5. After 5 minutes, remove the pan from the oven. Stir the apple slices and return the pan to the oven to continue cooking.

6. When cooking is complete, the slices should be until crispy Remove the pan from the oven and let rest for 5 minutes before serving.

Avocado Chips with Lime

Prep time: 15 minutes | Cook time: 10 minutes | Serves 4

1 egg
1 tablespoon lime juice
⅛ teaspoon hot sauce
2 tablespoons flour
¾ cup panko bread crumbs
¼ cup cornmeal
¼ teaspoon salt
1 large avocado, pitted, peeled, and cut into ½-inch slices
Cooking spray

1. Whisk together the egg, lime juice, and hot sauce in a small bowl.
2. On a sheet of wax paper, place the flour. In a separate sheet of wax paper, combine the bread crumbs, cornmeal, and salt.
3. Dredge the avocado slices one at a time in the flour, then in the egg mixture, finally roll them in the bread crumb mixture to coat well.
4. Place the breaded avocado slices in the perforated pan and mist them with cooking spray.
5. Select Air Fry. Set temperature to 390ºF (199ºC) and set time to 10 minutes. Press Start to begin preheating.
6. Once preheated, place the pan into the oven.
7. When cooking is complete, the slices should be nicely browned and crispy. Transfer the avocado slices to a plate and serve.

Ginger Apple Wedges

Prep time: 10 minutes | Cook time: 12 minutes | Serves 4

2 medium apples, cored and sliced into ¼-inch wedges
1 teaspoon canola oil
2 teaspoons peeled and grated fresh ginger
½ teaspoon ground cinnamon
½ cup low-fat Greek vanilla yogurt, for serving

1. In a large bowl, toss the apple wedges with the canola oil, ginger, and cinnamon until evenly coated. Put the apple wedges in the perforated pan.
2. Select Air Fry. Set temperature to 360ºF (182ºC) and set time to 12 minutes. Press Start to begin preheating.
3. Once preheated, place the pan into the oven.
4. When cooking is complete, the apple wedges should be crisp-tender. Remove the apple wedges from the oven and serve drizzled with the yogurt.

Cumin Tortilla Chips

Prep time: 5 minutes | Cook time: 5 minutes | Serves 4

½ teaspoon ground cumin
½ teaspoon paprika
½ teaspoon chili powder
½ teaspoon salt
Pinch cayenne pepper
8 (6-inch) corn tortillas, each cut into 6 wedges
Cooking spray
1.	Lightly spritz the perforated pan with cooking spray.
2.	Stir together the cumin, paprika, chili powder, salt, and pepper in a small bowl.
3.	Place the tortilla wedges in the perforated pan in a single layer. Lightly mist them with cooking spray. Sprinkle the seasoning mixture on top of the tortilla wedges.
4.	Select Air Fry. Set temperature to 375ºF (190ºC) and set time to 5 minutes. Press Start to begin preheating.
5.	Once preheated, place the pan into the oven. Stir the tortilla wedges halfway through the cooking time.
6.	When cooking is complete, the chips should be lightly browned and crunchy. Remove the pan from the oven. Let the tortilla chips cool for 5 minutes and serve.

Old Bay Fried Chicken Wings

Prep time: 10 minutes | Cook time: 13 minutes | Serves 4
2 tablespoons Old Bay seasoning
2 teaspoons baking powder
2 teaspoons salt
2 pounds (907 g) chicken wings, patted dry
Cooking spray
1.	Combine the Old Bay seasoning, baking powder, and salt in a large zip-top plastic bag. Add the chicken wings, seal, and shake until the wings are thoroughly coated in the seasoning mixture.
2.	Lightly spray the perforated pan with cooking spray. Lay the chicken wings in the perforated pan in a single layer and lightly mist them with cooking spray.
3.	Select Air Fry. Set temperature to 400ºF (205ºC) and set time to 13 minutes. Press Start to begin preheating.
4.	Once preheated, place the pan into the oven. Flip the wings halfway through the cooking time.
5.	When cooking is complete, the wings should reach an internal temperature of 165ºF (74ºC) on a meat thermometer. Remove from the oven to a plate and serve hot.

Carrot Chips

Prep time: 15 minutes | Cook time: 10 minutes | Serves 4
4 to 5 medium carrots, trimmed and thinly sliced
1 tablespoon olive oil, plus more for greasing
1 teaspoon seasoned salt
1.	Toss the carrot slices with 1 tablespoon of olive oil and salt in a medium bowl until thoroughly coated.
2.	Grease the perforated pan with the olive oil. Place the carrot slices in the greased pan.
3.	Select Air Fry. Set temperature to 390ºF (199ºC) and set time to 10 minutes. Press Start to begin preheating.
4.	Once preheated, place the pan into the oven. Stir the carrot slices halfway through the cooking time.
5.	When cooking is complete, the chips should be crisp-tender. Remove the pan from the oven and allow to cool for 5 minutes before serving.

Mushroom and Sausage Empanadas

Prep time: 5 minutes | Cook time: 12 minutes | Serves 4
½ pound (227 g) Kielbasa smoked sausage, chopped
4 chopped canned mushrooms
2 tablespoons chopped onion
½ teaspoon ground cumin
¼ teaspoon paprika
Salt and black pepper, to taste
½ package puff pastry dough, at room temperature
1 egg, beaten
Cooking spray
1.	Combine the sausage, mushrooms, onion, cumin, paprika, salt, and pepper in a bowl and stir to mix well.
2.	Make the empanadas: Place the puff pastry dough on a lightly floured surface. Cut circles into the dough with a glass. Place 1 tablespoon of the sausage mixture into the center of each pastry circle. Fold each in half and pinch the edges to seal. Using a fork, crimp the edges. Brush them with the beaten egg and mist with cooking spray.
3.	Spritz the perforated pan with cooking spray. Place the empanadas in the perforated pan.
4.	Select Air Fry. Set temperature to 360ºF (182ºC) and set time to 12 minutes. Press Start to begin preheating.
5.	Once preheated, place the pan into the oven. Flip the empanadas halfway through the cooking time.
6.	When cooking is complete, the empanadas should be golden brown. Remove the pan from the oven. Allow them to cool for 5 minutes and serve hot.

Cumin Fried Chickpeas

Prep time: 5 minutes | Cook time: 18 minutes | Serves 4
½ teaspoon chili powder
½ teaspoon ground cumin
¼ teaspoon cayenne pepper
¼ teaspoon salt
1 (19-ounce / 539-g) can chickpeas, drained and rinsed
Cooking spray

1. Lina the perforated pan with parchment paper and lightly spritz with cooking spray.
2. Mix the chili powder, cumin, cayenne pepper, and salt in a small bowl.
3. Place the chickpeas in a medium bowl and lightly mist with cooking spray.
4. Add the spice mixture to the chickpeas and toss until evenly coated. Transfer the chickpeas to the parchment.
5. Select Air Fry. Set temperature to 390ºF (199ºC) and set time to 18 minutes. Press Start to begin preheating.
6. Once preheated, place the pan into the oven. Stir the chickpeas twice during cooking.
7. When cooking is complete, the chickpeas should be crunchy. Remove the pan from the oven. Let the chickpeas cool for 5 minutes before serving.

Paprika Nut Mix

Prep time: 5 minutes | Cook time: 20 minutes | Serves 6
2 cups mixed nuts (walnuts, pecans, and almonds)
2 tablespoons egg white
2 tablespoons sugar
1 teaspoon paprika
1 teaspoon ground cinnamon
Cooking spray
1. Line the perforated pan with parchment paper and spray with cooking spray.
2. Stir together the mixed nuts, egg white, sugar, paprika, and cinnamon in a small bowl until the nuts are fully coated. Place the nuts in the perforated pan.
3. Select Roast. Set temperature to 300ºF (150ºC) and set time to 20 minutes. Press Start to begin preheating.
4. Once preheated, place the pan into the oven. Stir the nuts halfway through the cooking time.
5. When cooking is complete, remove the pan from the oven. Transfer the nuts to a bowl and serve warm.

Garlic Fried Edamame

Prep time: 5 minutes | Cook time: 9 minutes | Serves 4
1 (16-ounce / 454-g) bag frozen edamame in pods
2 tablespoon olive oil, divided
½ teaspoon garlic salt
½ teaspoon salt
¼ teaspoon freshly ground black pepper
½ teaspoon red pepper flakes (optional)
1. Place the edamame in a medium bowl and drizzle with 1 tablespoon of olive oil. Toss to coat well.
2. Stir together the garlic salt, salt, pepper, and red pepper flakes (if desired) in a small bowl. Pour the mixture into the bowl of edamame and toss until the edamame is fully coated.

3. Grease the perforated pan with the remaining 1 tablespoon of olive oil.
4. Place the edamame in the greased pan.
5. Select Air Fry. Set temperature to 375ºF (190ºC) and set time to 9 minutes. Press Start to begin preheating.
6. Once preheated, place the pan into the oven. Stir the edamame once halfway through the cooking time.
7. When cooking is complete, the edamame should be crisp. Remove from the oven to a plate and serve warm.

Nutmeg Apple Chips

Prep time: 10 minutes | Cook time: 10 minutes | Serves 4
4 medium apples (any type will work) cored and thinly sliced
¼ teaspoon nutmeg
¼ teaspoon cinnamon
Cooking spray
1. Place the apple slices in a large bowl and sprinkle the spices on top. Toss to coat.
2. Put the apple slices in the perforated pan in a single layer and spray them with cooking spray.
3. Select Air Fry. Set temperature to 360ºF (182ºC) and set time to 10 minutes. Press Start to begin preheating.
4. Once preheated, place the pan into the oven. Stir the apple slices halfway through.
5. When cooking is complete, the apple chips should be crispy. Transfer the apple chips to a paper towel-lined plate and rest for 5 minutes before serving.

Parmesan Bruschetta with Tomato

Prep time: 5 minutes | Cook time: 3 minutes | Serves 6
4 tomatoes, diced
$^1/_3$ cup shredded fresh basil
¼ cup shredded Parmesan cheese
1 tablespoon balsamic vinegar
1 tablespoon minced garlic
1 teaspoon olive oil
1 teaspoon salt
1 teaspoon freshly ground black pepper
1 loaf French bread, cut into 1-inch-thick slices
Cooking spray
1. Mix together the tomatoes and basil in a medium bowl. Add the cheese, vinegar, garlic, olive oil, salt, and pepper and stir until well incorporated. Set aside.
2. Spritz the perforated pan with cooking spray and lay the bread slices in the pan in a single layer. Spray the slices with cooking spray.
3. Select Bake. Set temperature to 250ºF (121ºC) and set time to 3 minutes. Press Start to begin preheating.
4. Once preheated, place the pan into the oven.

5.   When cooking is complete, remove from the oven to a plate. Top each slice with a generous spoonful of the tomato mixture and serve.

Sesame Kale Chips

Prep time: 15 minutes | Cook time: 8 minutes | Serves 5

8 cups deribbed kale leaves, torn into 2-inch pieces
1½ tablespoons olive oil
¾ teaspoon chili powder
¼ teaspoon garlic powder
½ teaspoon paprika
2 teaspoons sesame seeds

1.   In a large bowl, toss the kale with the olive oil, chili powder, garlic powder, paprika, and sesame seeds until well coated.
2.   Transfer the kale to the perforated pan.
3.   Select Air Fry. Set temperature to 350ºF (180ºC) and set time to 8 minutes. Press Start to begin preheating.
4.   Once preheated, place the pan into the oven. Flip the kale twice during cooking.
5.   When cooking is complete, the kale should be crispy. Remove from the oven and serve warm.

Cheddar Black Bean and Corn Salsa

Prep time: 10 minutes | Cook time: 10 minutes | Serves 4

½ (15-ounce / 425-g) can corn, drained and rinsed
½ (15-ounce / 425-g) can black beans, drained and rinsed
¼ cup chunky salsa
2 ounces (57 g) reduced-fat cream cheese, softened
¼ cup shredded reduced-fat Cheddar cheese
½ teaspoon paprika
½ teaspoon ground cumin
Salt and freshly ground black pepper, to taste

1.   Combine the corn, black beans, salsa, cream cheese, Cheddar cheese, paprika, and cumin in a medium bowl. Sprinkle with salt and pepper and stir until well blended.
2.   Pour the mixture into a baking dish.
3.   Select Air Fry. Set temperature to 325ºF (163ºC) and set time to 10 minutes. Press Start to begin preheating.
4.   Once preheated, place the baking dish in the oven.
5.   When cooking is complete, the mixture should be heated through. Rest for 5 minutes and serve warm.

Cinnamon Peach Wedges

Prep time: 10 minutes | Cook time: 10 to 13 minutes | Serves 4

2 tablespoons sugar
¼ teaspoon ground cinnamon
4 peaches, cut into wedges
Cooking spray

1.   Toss the peaches with the sugar and cinnamon in a medium bowl until evenly coated.
2.   Lightly spray the perforated pan with cooking spray. Place the peaches in the perforated pan in a single layer. Lightly mist the peaches with cooking spray.
3.   Select Air Fry. Set temperature to 350ºF (180ºC) and set time to 10 minutes. Press Start to begin preheating.
4.   Once preheated, place the pan into the oven.
5.   After 5 minutes, remove from the oven and flip the peaches. Return to the oven and continue cooking for 5 minutes.
6.   When cooking is complete, the peaches should be caramelized. If necessary, continue cooking for 3 minutes. Remove the pan from the oven. Let the peaches cool for 5 minutes and serve warm.

BBQ Cheese Chicken Pizza

Prep time: 5 minutes | Cook time: 8 minutes | Serves 1

1 piece naan bread
¼ cup Barbecue sauce
¼ cup shredded Monterrey Jack cheese
¼ cup shredded Mozzarella cheese
½ chicken herby sausage, sliced
2 tablespoons red onion, thinly sliced
Chopped cilantro or parsley, for garnish
Cooking spray

1.   Spritz the bottom of naan bread with cooking spray, then transfer to the perforated pan.
2.   Brush with the Barbecue sauce. Top with the cheeses, sausage, and finish with the red onion.
3.   Select Air Fry. Set temperature to 400ºF (205ºC) and set time to 8 minutes. Press Start to begin preheating.
4.   Once preheated, place the pan into the oven.
5.   When cooking is complete, the cheese should be melted. Remove the pan from the oven. Garnish with the chopped cilantro or parsley before slicing to serve.

Brie Pear Sandwiches

Prep time: 10 minutes | Cook time: 6 minutes | Serves 4 to 8

8 ounces (227 g) Brie
8 slices oat nut bread
1 large ripe pear, cored and cut into ½-inch-thick slices
2 tablespoons butter, melted

1.   Make the sandwiches: Spread each of 4 slices of bread with ¼ of the Brie. Top the Brie with the pear slices and remaining 4 bread slices.
2.   Brush the melted butter lightly on both sides of each sandwich.
3.   Arrange the sandwiches in the perforated pan.

4.	Select Bake. Set temperature to 360ºF (182ºC) and set time to 6 minutes. Press Start to begin preheating.
5.	Once preheated, place the pan into the oven.
6.	When cooking is complete, the cheese should be melted. Remove the pan from the oven and serve warm.

Breaded Artichoke Bites

Prep time: 10 minutes | Cook time: 8 minutes | Serves 4
14 whole artichoke hearts packed in water
½ cup all-purpose flour
1 egg
$^1/_3$ cup panko bread crumbs
1 teaspoon Italian seasoning
Cooking spray
1.	Drain the artichoke hearts and dry thoroughly with paper towels.
2.	Place the flour on a plate. Beat the egg in a shallow bowl until frothy. Thoroughly combine the bread crumbs and Italian seasoning in a separate shallow bowl.
3.	Dredge the artichoke hearts in the flour, then in the beaten egg, and finally roll in the bread crumb mixture until evenly coated.
4.	Place the artichoke hearts in the perforated pan and mist them with cooking spray.
5.	Select Air Fry. Set temperature to 375ºF (190ºC) and set time to 8 minutes. Press Start to begin preheating.
6.	Once preheated, place the pan into the oven. Flip the artichoke hearts halfway through the cooking time.
7.	When cooking is complete, the artichoke hearts should start to brown and the edges should be crispy. Remove the pan from the oven. Let the artichoke hearts sit for 5 minutes before serving.

Parmesan Crab Toasts

Prep time: 10 minutes | Cook time: 5 minutes | Makes 15 to 18 toasts
1 (6-ounce / 170-g) can flaked crab meat, well drained
3 tablespoons light mayonnaise
¼ cup shredded Parmesan cheese
¼ cup shredded Cheddar cheese
1 teaspoon Worcestershire sauce
½ teaspoon lemon juice
1 loaf artisan bread, French bread, or baguette, cut into ⅜-inch-thick slices
1.	In a large bowl, stir together all the ingredients except the bread slices.
2.	On a clean work surface, lay the bread slices. Spread ½ tablespoon of crab mixture onto each slice of bread.
3.	Arrange the bread slices in the perforated pan in a single layer.

4.	Select Bake. Set temperature to 360ºF (182ºC) and set time to 5 minutes. Press Start to begin preheating.
5.	Once preheated, place the pan into the oven.
6.	When cooking is complete, the tops should be lightly browned. Remove the pan from the oven. Serve warm.

Buttermilk-Marinated Chicken Wings

Prep time: 20 minutes | Cook time: 18 minutes | Serves 4
2 pounds (907 g) chicken wings
Cooking spray
Marinade:
1 cup buttermilk
½ teaspoon salt
½ teaspoon black pepper
Coating:
1 cup flour
1 cup panko bread crumbs
2 tablespoons poultry seasoning
2 teaspoons salt
1.	Whisk together all the ingredients for the marinade in a large bowl.
2.	Add the chicken wings to the marinade and toss well. Transfer to the refrigerator to marinate for at least an hour.
3.	Spritz the perforated pan with cooking spray. Set aside.
4.	Thoroughly combine all the ingredients for the coating in a shallow bowl.
5.	Remove the chicken wings from the marinade and shake off any excess. Roll them in the coating mixture.
6.	Place the chicken wings in the perforated pan in a single layer. Mist the wings with cooking spray.
7.	Select Air Fry. Set temperature to 360ºF (182ºC) and set time to 18 minutes. Press Start to begin preheating.
8.	Once preheated, place the pan into the oven. Flip the wings halfway through the cooking time.
9.	When cooking is complete, the wings should be crisp and golden brown on the outside. Remove from the oven to a plate and serve hot.

Pork and Turkey Sandwiches

Prep time: 20 minutes | Cook time: 8 minutes | Makes 4 sandwiches
8 slices ciabatta bread, about ¼-inch thick
Cooking spray
1 tablespoon brown mustard
Toppings:
6 to 8 ounces (170 to 227 g) thinly sliced leftover roast pork
4 ounces (113 g) thinly sliced deli turkey
$^1/_3$ cup bread and butter pickle slices
2 to 3 ounces (57 to 85 g) Pepper Jack cheese slices

1.   On a clean work surface, spray one side of each slice of bread with cooking spray. Spread the other side of each slice of bread evenly with brown mustard.
2.   Top 4 of the bread slices with the roast pork, turkey, pickle slices, cheese, and finish with remaining bread slices. Transfer to the perforated pan.
3.   Select Air Fry. Set temperature to 390ºF (199ºC) and set time to 8 minutes. Press Start to begin preheating.
4.   Once preheated, place the pan into the oven.
5.   When cooking is complete, remove the pan from the oven. Cool for 5 minutes and serve warm.

Horseradish Green Tomatoes

Prep time: 18 minutes | Cook time: 13 minutes | Serves 4
2 eggs
¼ cup buttermilk
½ cup bread crumbs
½ cup cornmeal
¼ teaspoon salt
1½ pounds (680 g) firm green tomatoes, cut into ¼-inch slices
Cooking spray
Horseradish Sauce:
¼ cup sour cream
¼ cup mayonnaise
2 teaspoons prepared horseradish
½ teaspoon lemon juice
½ teaspoon Worcestershire sauce
⅛ teaspoon black pepper
1.   Spritz the perforated pan with cooking spray. Set aside.
2.   In a small bowl, whisk together all the ingredients for the horseradish sauce until smooth. Set aside.
3.   In a shallow dish, beat the eggs and buttermilk.
4.   In a separate shallow dish, thoroughly combine the bread crumbs, cornmeal, and salt.
5.   Dredge the tomato slices, one at a time, in the egg mixture, then roll in the bread crumb mixture until evenly coated.
6.   Place the tomato slices in the perforated pan in a single layer. Spray them with cooking spray.
7.   Select Air Fry. Set temperature to 390ºF (199ºC) and set time to 13 minutes. Press Start to begin preheating.
8.   Once preheated, place the pan into the oven. Flip the tomato slices halfway through the cooking time.
9.   When cooking is complete, the tomato slices should be nicely browned and crisp. Remove from the oven to a platter and serve drizzled with the prepared horseradish sauce.

Spinach Calzones with Mushrooms

Prep time: 15 minutes | Cook time: 26 to 27 minutes | Serves 4
2 tablespoons olive oil
1 onion, chopped
2 garlic cloves, minced
¼ cup chopped mushrooms
1 pound (454 g) spinach, chopped
1 tablespoon Italian seasoning
½ teaspoon oregano
Salt and black pepper, to taste
1½ cups marinara sauce
1 cup ricotta cheese, crumbled
1 (13-ounce / 369-g) pizza crust
Cooking spray
Make the Filling:
1.   Heat the olive oil in a pan over medium heat until shimmering.
2.   Add the onion, garlic, and mushrooms and sauté for 4 minutes, or until softened.
3.   Stir in the spinach and sauté for 2 to 3 minutes, or until the spinach is wilted. Sprinkle with the Italian seasoning, oregano, salt, and pepper and mix well.
4.   Add the marinara sauce and cook for about 5 minutes, stirring occasionally, or until the sauce is thickened.
5.   Remove the pan from the heat and stir in the ricotta cheese. Set aside.
Make the Calzones:
6.   Spritz the perforated pan with cooking spray. Set aside.
7.   Roll the pizza crust out with a rolling pin on a lightly floured work surface, then cut it into 4 rectangles.
8.   Spoon ¼ of the filling into each rectangle and fold in half. Crimp the edges with a fork to seal. Mist them with cooking spray. Transfer the calzones to the perforated pan.
9.   Select Air Fry. Set temperature to 375ºF (190ºC) and set time to 15 minutes. Press Start to begin preheating.
10.   Once preheated, place the pan into the oven. Flip the calzones halfway through the cooking time.
11.   When cooking is complete, the calzones should be golden brown and crisp. Transfer the calzones to a paper towel-lined plate and serve.

Turkey-Wrapped Dates and Almonds

Prep time: 10 minutes | Cook time: 6 minutes | Makes 16 appetizers
16 whole dates, pitted
16 whole almonds
6 to 8 strips turkey bacon, cut in half
Special Equipment:
16 toothpicks, soaked in water for at least 30 minutes
1.   On a flat work surface, stuff each pitted date with a whole almond.
2.   Wrap half slice of bacon around each date and secure it with a toothpick.

3. Place the bacon-wrapped dates in the perforated pan.
4. Select Air Fry. Set temperature to 390ºF (199ºC) and set time to 6 minutes. Press Start to begin preheating.
5. Once preheated, place the pan into the oven.
6. When cooking is complete, transfer the dates to a paper towel-lined plate to drain. Serve hot.

Italian Rice Balls with Olives

Prep time: 20 minutes | Cook time: 10 minutes | Makes 8 rice balls
1½ cups cooked sticky rice
½ teaspoon Italian seasoning blend
¾ teaspoon salt, divided
8 black olives, pitted
1 ounce (28 g) Mozzarella cheese, cut into tiny pieces (small enough to stuff into olives)
2 eggs
$^1/_3$ cup Italian bread crumbs
¾ cup panko bread crumbs
Cooking spray
1. Stuff each black olive with a piece of Mozzarella cheese.
2. In a bowl, combine the cooked sticky rice, Italian seasoning blend, and ½ teaspoon of salt and stir to mix well. Form the rice mixture into a log with your hands and divide it into 8 equal portions. Mold each portion around a black olive and roll into a ball.
3. Transfer to the freezer to chill for 10 to 15 minutes until firm.
4. In a shallow dish, place the Italian bread crumbs. In a separate shallow dish, whisk the eggs. In a third shallow dish, combine the panko bread crumbs and remaining salt.
5. One by one, roll the rice balls in the Italian bread crumbs, then dip in the whisked eggs, finally coat them with the panko bread crumbs.
6. Arrange the rice balls in the perforated pan and spritz both sides with cooking spray.
7. Select Air Fry. Set temperature to 390ºF (199ºC) and set time to 10 minutes. Press Start to begin preheating.

8. Once preheated, place the pan into the oven. Flip the balls halfway through the cooking time.
9. When cooking is complete, the rice balls should be golden brown. Remove from the oven and serve warm.

Muffuletta Sliders with Olive Mix

Prep time: 10 minutes | Cook time: 6 minutes | Makes 8 sliders
¼ pound (113 g) thinly sliced deli ham
¼ pound (113 g) thinly sliced pastrami
4 ounces (113 g) low-fat Mozzarella cheese, grated
8 slider buns, split in half
Cooking spray
1 tablespoon sesame seeds
Olive Mix:
½ cup sliced green olives with pimentos
¼ cup sliced black olives
¼ cup chopped kalamata olives
1 teaspoon red wine vinegar
¼ teaspoon basil
⅛ teaspoon garlic powder
1. Combine all the ingredients for the olive mix in a small bowl and stir well.
2. Stir together the ham, pastrami, and cheese in a medium bowl and divide the mixture into 8 equal portions.
3. Assemble the sliders: Top each bottom bun with 1 portion of meat and cheese, 2 tablespoons of olive mix, finished by the remaining buns. Lightly spritz the tops with cooking spray. Scatter the sesame seeds on top.
4. Arrange the sliders in the perforated pan.
5. Select Bake. Set temperature to 360ºF (182ºC) and set time to 6 minutes. Press Start to begin preheating.
6. Once preheated, place the pan into the oven.
7. When cooking is complete, the cheese should be melted. Remove the pan from the oven and serve.

Gochujang Beef and Onion Tacos

Prep time: 1 hour 15 minutes | Cook time: 12 minutes | Serves 6

2 tablespoons gochujang
1 tablespoon soy sauce
2 tablespoons sesame seeds
2 teaspoons minced fresh ginger
2 cloves garlic, minced
2 tablespoons toasted sesame oil
2 teaspoons sugar
½ teaspoon kosher salt
1½ pounds (680 g) thinly sliced beef chuck
1 medium red onion, sliced
6 corn tortillas, warmed
¼ cup chopped fresh cilantro
½ cup kimchi
½ cup chopped green onions

1.	Combine the gochujang, soy sauce, sesame seeds, ginger, garlic, sesame oil, sugar, and salt in a large bowl. Stir to mix well.
2.	Dunk the beef chunk in the large bowl. Press to submerge, then wrap the bowl in plastic and refrigerate to marinate for at least 1 hour.
3.	Remove the beef chunk from the marinade and transfer to the perforated pan. Add the onion to the pan.
4.	Select Air Fry. Set temperature to 400ºF (205ºC) and set time to 12 minutes. Press Start to begin preheating.
5.	Once preheated, place the pan into the oven. Stir the mixture halfway through the cooking time.
6.	When cooked, the beef will be well browned.
7.	Unfold the tortillas on a clean work surface, then divide the fried beef and onion on the tortillas. Spread the cilantro, kimchi, and green onions on top.
8.	Serve immediately.

Curried Shrimp and Zucchini Potstickers

Prep time: 35 minutes | Cook time: 5 minutes | Serves 10

½ pound (227 g) peeled and deveined shrimp, finely chopped
1 medium zucchini, coarsely grated
1 tablespoon fish sauce
1 tablespoon green curry paste
2 scallions, thinly sliced
¼ cup basil, chopped
30 round dumpling wrappers
Cooking spray

1.	Combine the chopped shrimp, zucchini, fish sauce, curry paste, scallions, and basil in a large bowl. Stir to mix well.
2.	Unfold the dumpling wrappers on a clean work surface, dab a little water around the edges of each wrapper, then scoop up 1 teaspoon of filling in the middle of each wrapper.
3.	Make the potstickers: Fold the wrappers in half and press the edges to seal.
4.	Spritz the perforated pan with cooking spray.
5.	Transfer the potstickers to the pan and spritz with cooking spray.
6.	Select Air Fry. Set temperature to 350ºF (180ºC) and set time to 5 minutes. Press Start to begin preheating.
7.	Once preheated, place the pan into the oven. Flip the potstickers halfway through the cooking time.
8.	When cooking is complete, the potstickers should be crunchy and lightly browned.
9.	Serve immediately.

Cod Fish Tacos with Mango Salsa

Prep time: 15 minutes | Cook time: 17 minutes | Makes 6 tacos

1 egg
5 ounces (142 g) Mexican beer
¾ cup all-purpose flour
¾ cup cornstarch
¼ teaspoon chili powder
½ teaspoon ground cumin
½ pound (227 g) cod, cut into large pieces
6 corn tortillas
Cooking spray
Salsa:
1 mango, peeled and diced
¼ red bell pepper, diced
½ small jalapeño, diced
¼ red onion, minced
Juice of half a lime
Pinch chopped fresh cilantro
¼ teaspoon salt
¼ teaspoon ground black pepper

1.	Spritz the perforated pan with cooking spray.
2.	Whisk the egg with beer in a bowl. Combine the flour, cornstarch, chili powder, and cumin in a separate bowl.
3.	Dredge the cod in the egg mixture first, then in the flour mixture to coat well. Shake the excess off.
4.	Arrange the cod in the perforated pan and spritz with cooking spray.
5.	Select Air Fry. Set temperature to 380ºF (193ºC) and set time to 17 minutes. Press Start to begin preheating.
6.	Once preheated, place the pan into the oven. Flip the cod halfway through the cooking time.
7.	When cooked, the cod should be golden brown and crunchy.
8.	Meanwhile, combine the ingredients for the salsa in a small bowl. Stir to mix well.
9.	Unfold the tortillas on a clean work surface, then divide the fish on the tortillas and spread the salsa on top. Fold to serve.

Bacon and Egg Wraps with Salsa

Prep time: 15 minutes | Cook time: 10 minutes | Serves 3

3 corn tortillas
3 slices bacon, cut into strips
2 scrambled eggs
3 tablespoons salsa
1 cup grated Pepper Jack cheese
3 tablespoons cream cheese, divided
Cooking spray

1.   Spritz the perforated pan with cooking spray.
2.   Unfold the tortillas on a clean work surface, divide the bacon and eggs in the middle of the tortillas, then spread with salsa and scatter with cheeses. Fold the tortillas over.
3.   Arrange the tortillas in the pan.
4.   Select Air Fry. Set temperature to 390ºF (199ºC) and set time to 10 minutes. Press Start to begin preheating.
5.   Once the oven has preheated, place the pan into the oven. Flip the tortillas halfway through the cooking time.
6.   When cooking is complete, the cheeses will be melted and the tortillas will be lightly browned.
7.   Serve immediately.

Chicken Wraps with Ricotta Cheese

Prep time: 30 minutes | Cook time: 5 minutes | Serves 12

2 large-sized chicken breasts, cooked and shredded
2 spring onions, chopped
10 ounces (284 g) Ricotta cheese
1 tablespoon rice vinegar
1 tablespoon molasses
1 teaspoon grated fresh ginger
¼ cup soy sauce
$^{1}/_{3}$ teaspoon sea salt
¼ teaspoon ground black pepper, or more to taste
48 wonton wrappers
Cooking spray

1.   Spritz the perforated pan with cooking spray.
2.   Combine all the ingredients, except for the wrappers in a large bowl. Toss to mix well.
3.   Unfold the wrappers on a clean work surface, then divide and spoon the mixture in the middle of the wrappers.
4.   Dab a little water on the edges of the wrappers, then fold the edge close to you over the filling. Tuck the edge under the filling and roll up to seal.
5.   Arrange the wraps in the pan.
6.   Select Air Fry. Set temperature to 375ºF (190ºC) and set time to 5 minutes. Press Start to begin preheating.
7.   Once preheated, place the pan into the oven. Flip the wraps halfway through the cooking time.

8.   When cooking is complete, the wraps should be lightly browned.
9.   Serve immediately.

Sweet Potato and Spinach Burritos

Prep time: 15 minutes | Cook time: 30 minutes | Makes 6 burritos

2 sweet potatoes, peeled and cut into a small dice
1 tablespoon vegetable oil
Kosher salt and ground black pepper, to taste
6 large flour tortillas
1 (16-ounce / 454-g) can refried black beans, divided
1½ cups baby spinach, divided
6 eggs, scrambled
¾ cup grated Cheddar cheese, divided
¼ cup salsa
¼ cup sour cream
Cooking spray

1.   Put the sweet potatoes in a large bowl, then drizzle with vegetable oil and sprinkle with salt and black pepper. Toss to coat well.
2.   Place the potatoes in the perforated pan.
3.   Select Air Fry. Set temperature to 400ºF (205ºC) and set time to 10 minutes. Press Start to begin preheating.
4.   Once preheated, place the pan into the oven. Flip the potatoes halfway through the cooking time.
5.   When done, the potatoes should be lightly browned. Remove the potatoes from the oven.
6.   Unfold the tortillas on a clean work surface. Divide the black beans, spinach, air fried sweet potatoes, scrambled eggs, and cheese on top of the tortillas.
7.   Fold the long side of the tortillas over the filling, then fold in the shorter side to wrap the filling to make the burritos.
8.   Wrap the burritos in the aluminum foil and put in the pan.
9.   Select Air Fry. Set temperature to 350ºF (180ºC) and set time to 20 minutes. Place the pan into the oven. Flip the burritos halfway through the cooking time.
10.   Remove the burritos from the oven and spread with sour cream and salsa. Serve immediately.

Cabbage and Prawn Wraps

Prep time: 20 minutes | Cook time: 18 minutes | Serves 4

2 tablespoons olive oil
1 carrot, cut into strips
1-inch piece fresh ginger, grated
1 tablespoon minced garlic
2 tablespoons soy sauce
¼ cup chicken broth
1 tablespoon sugar
1 cup shredded Napa cabbage
1 tablespoon sesame oil
8 cooked prawns, minced
8 egg roll wrappers

1 egg, beaten
Cooking spray
1. Spritz the perforated pan with cooking spray. Set aside.
2. Heat the olive oil in a nonstick skillet over medium heat until shimmering.
3. Add the carrot, ginger, and garlic and sauté for 2 minutes or until fragrant.
4. Pour in the soy sauce, broth, and sugar. Bring to a boil. Keep stirring.
5. Add the cabbage and simmer for 4 minutes or until the cabbage is tender.
6. Turn off the heat and mix in the sesame oil. Let sit for 15 minutes.
7. Use a strainer to remove the vegetables from the liquid, then combine with the minced prawns.
8. Unfold the egg roll wrappers on a clean work surface, then divide the prawn mixture in the center of wrappers.
9. Dab the edges of a wrapper with the beaten egg, then fold a corner over the filling and tuck the corner under the filling. Fold the left and right corner into the center. Roll the wrapper up and press to seal. Repeat with remaining wrappers.
10. Arrange the wrappers in the pan and spritz with cooking spray.
11. Select Air Fry. Set temperature to 370ºF (188ºC) and set time to 12 minutes. Press Start to begin preheating.
12. Once the oven has preheated, place the pan into the oven. Flip the wrappers halfway through the cooking time.
13. When cooking is complete, the wrappers should be golden.
14. Serve immediately.

Ricotta Spinach and Basil Pockets

Prep time: 20 minutes | Cook time: 10 minutes | Makes 8 pockets

2 large eggs, divided
1 tablespoon water
1 cup baby spinach, roughly chopped
¼ cup sun-dried tomatoes, finely chopped
1 cup ricotta cheese
1 cup basil, chopped
¼ teaspoon red pepper flakes
¼ teaspoon kosher salt
2 refrigerated rolled pie crusts
2 tablespoons sesame seeds
1. Spritz the perforated pan with cooking spray.
2. Whisk an egg with water in a small bowl.
3. Combine the spinach, tomatoes, the other egg, ricotta cheese, basil, red pepper flakes, and salt in a large bowl. Whisk to mix well.
4. Unfold the pie crusts on a clean work surface and slice each crust into 4 wedges. Scoop up 3 tablespoons of the spinach mixture on each crust and leave ½ inch space from edges.
5. Fold the crust wedges in half to wrap the filling and press the edges with a fork to seal.
6. Arrange the wraps in the pan and spritz with cooking spray. Sprinkle with sesame seeds.
7. Select Air Fry. Set temperature to 380ºF (193ºC) and set time to 10 minutes. Press Start to begin preheating.
8. Once the oven has preheated, place the pan into the oven. Flip the wraps halfway through the cooking time.
9. When cooked, the wraps will be crispy and golden.
10. Serve immediately.

Carrot and Mushroom Spring Rolls

Prep time: 10 minutes | Cook time: 18 minutes | Serves 4

4 spring roll wrappers
½ cup cooked vermicelli noodles
1 teaspoon sesame oil
1 tablespoon freshly minced ginger
1 tablespoon soy sauce
1 clove garlic, minced
½ red bell pepper, deseeded and chopped
½ cup chopped carrot
½ cup chopped mushrooms
¼ cup chopped scallions
Cooking spray
1. Spritz the perforated pan with cooking spray and set aside.
2. Heat the sesame oil in a saucepan on medium heat. Sauté the ginger and garlic in the sesame oil for 1 minute, or until fragrant. Add soy sauce, red bell pepper, carrot, mushrooms and scallions. Sauté for 5 minutes or until the vegetables become tender. Mix in vermicelli noodles. Turn off the heat and remove them from the saucepan. Allow to cool for 10 minutes.
3. Lay out one spring roll wrapper with a corner pointed toward you. Scoop the noodle mixture on spring roll wrapper and fold corner up over the mixture. Fold left and right corners toward the center and continue to roll to make firmly sealed rolls.
4. Arrange the spring rolls in the pan and spritz with cooking spray.
5. Select Air Fry. Set temperature to 340ºF (171ºC) and set time to 12 minutes. Press Start to begin preheating.
6. Once the oven has preheated, place the pan into the oven. Flip the spring rolls halfway through the cooking time.
7. When done, the spring rolls will be golden brown and crispy.
8. Serve warm.

Avocado and Tomato Wraps

Prep time: 10 minutes | Cook time: 5 minutes | Serves 5

10 egg roll wrappers
3 avocados, peeled and pitted
1 tomato, diced
Salt and ground black pepper, to taste
Cooking spray
1.   Spritz the perforated pan with cooking spray.
2.   Put the tomato and avocados in a food processor. Sprinkle with salt and ground black pepper. Pulse to mix and coarsely mash until smooth.
3.   Unfold the wrappers on a clean work surface, then divide the mixture in the center of each wrapper. Roll the wrapper up and press to seal.
4.   Transfer the rolls to the pan and spritz with cooking spray.
5.   Select Air Fry. Set temperature to 350ºF (180ºC) and set time to 5 minutes. Press Start to begin preheating.
6.   Once the oven has preheated, place the pan into the oven. Flip the rolls halfway through the cooking time.
7.   When cooked, the rolls should be golden brown.
8.   Serve immediately.

Chicken and Cabbage Wraps

Prep time: 10 minutes | Cook time: 23 to 24 minutes | Serves 4
1 pound (454 g) ground chicken
2 teaspoons olive oil
2 garlic cloves, minced
1 teaspoon grated fresh ginger
2 cups white cabbage, shredded
1 onion, chopped
¼ cup soy sauce
8 egg roll wrappers
1 egg, beaten
Cooking spray
1.   Spritz the perforated pan with cooking spray.
2.   Heat olive oil in a saucepan over medium heat. Sauté the garlic and ginger in the olive oil for 1 minute, or until fragrant. Add the ground chicken to the saucepan. Sauté for 5 minutes, or until the chicken is cooked through. Add the cabbage, onion and soy sauce and sauté for 5 to 6 minutes, or until the vegetables become soft. Remove the saucepan from the heat.
3.   Unfold the egg roll wrappers on a clean work surface. Divide the chicken mixture among the wrappers and brush the edges of the wrappers with the beaten egg. Tightly roll up the egg rolls, enclosing the filling. Arrange the rolls in the pan.
4.   Select Air Fry. Set temperature to 370ºF (188ºC) and set time to 12 minutes. Press Start to begin preheating.
5.   Once the oven has preheated, place the pan into the oven. Flip the rolls halfway through the cooking time.
6.   When cooked, the rolls will be crispy and golden brown.
7.   Transfer to a platter and let cool for 5 minutes before serving.

Cajun Beef and Bell Pepper Fajitas

Prep time: 15 minutes | Cook time: 10 minutes | Serves 4
1 pound (454 g) beef sirloin steak, cut into strips
2 shallots, sliced
1 orange bell pepper, sliced
1 red bell pepper, sliced
2 garlic cloves, minced
2 tablespoons Cajun seasoning
1 tablespoon paprika
Salt and ground black pepper, to taste
4 corn tortillas
½ cup shredded Cheddar cheese
Cooking spray
1.   Spritz the perforated pan with cooking spray.
2.   Combine all the ingredients, except for the tortillas and cheese, in a large bowl. Toss to coat well.
3.   Pour the beef and vegetables in the pan and spritz with cooking spray.
4.   Select Air Fry. Set temperature to 360ºF (182ºC) and set time to 10 minutes. Press Start to begin preheating.
5.   Once preheated, place the pan into the oven. Stir the beef and vegetables halfway through the cooking time.
6.   When cooking is complete, the meat will be browned and the vegetables will be soft and lightly wilted.
7.   Unfold the tortillas on a clean work surface and spread the cooked beef and vegetables on top. Scatter with cheese and fold to serve.

Potato Taquitos with Mexican Cheese

Prep time: 5 minutes | Cook time: 6 minutes | Makes 12 taquitos
2 cups mashed potatoes
½ cup shredded Mexican cheese
12 corn tortillas
Cooking spray
1.   Line a baking pan with parchment paper.
2.   In a bowl, combine the potatoes and cheese until well mixed. Microwave the tortillas on high heat for 30 seconds, or until softened. Add some water to another bowl and set alongside.
3.   On a clean work surface, lay the tortillas. Scoop 3 tablespoons of the potato mixture in the center of each tortilla. Roll up tightly and secure with toothpicks if necessary.
4.   Arrange the filled tortillas, seam side down, in the prepared baking pan. Spritz the tortillas with cooking spray.

5.	Select Air Fry. Set temperature to 400ºF (205ºC) and set time to 6 minutes. Press Start to begin preheating.
6.	Once preheated, place the pan into the oven. Flip the tortillas halfway through the cooking time.
7.	When cooked, the tortillas should be crispy and golden brown.
8.	Serve hot.

Parmesan Eggplant Hoagies

Prep time: 15 minutes | Cook time: 12 minutes | Makes 3 hoagies
6 peeled eggplant slices (about ½ inch thick and 3 inches in diameter)
¼ cup jarred pizza sauce
6 tablespoons grated Parmesan cheese
3 Italian sub rolls, split open lengthwise, warmed
Cooking spray
1.	Spritz the perforated pan with cooking spray.
2.	Arrange the eggplant slices in the pan and spritz with cooking spray.
3.	Select Air Fry. Set temperature to 350ºF (180ºC) and set time to 10 minutes. Press Start to begin preheating.
4.	Once the oven has preheated, place the pan into the oven. Flip the slices halfway through the cooking time.
5.	When cooked, the eggplant slices should be lightly wilted and tender.
6.	Divide and spread the pizza sauce and cheese on top of the eggplant slice
7.	Select Air Fry. Set temperature to 375ºF (190ºC) and set time to 2 minutes. place the pan into the oven. When cooked, the cheese will be melted.
8.	Assemble each sub roll with two slices of eggplant and serve immediately.

Chickpea and Mushroom Wraps

Prep time: 15 minutes | Cook time: 9 minutes | Serves 4
8 ounces (227 g) green beans
2 portobello mushroom caps, sliced
1 large red pepper, sliced
2 tablespoons olive oil, divided
¼ teaspoon salt
1 (15-ounce / 425-g) can chickpeas, drained
3 tablespoons lemon juice
¼ teaspoon ground black pepper
4 (6-inch) whole-grain wraps
4 ounces (113 g) fresh herb or garlic goat cheese, crumbled
1 lemon, cut into wedges
1.	Add the green beans, mushrooms, red pepper to a large bowl. Drizzle with 1 tablespoon olive oil and season with salt. Toss until well coated.
2.	Transfer the vegetable mixture to a baking pan.

3.	Select Air Fry. Set temperature to 400ºF (205ºC) and set time to 9 minutes. Press Start to begin preheating.
4.	Once preheated, slide the pan into the oven. Stir the vegetable mixture three times during cooking.
5.	When cooked, the vegetables should be tender.
6.	Meanwhile, mash the chickpeas with lemon juice, pepper and the remaining 1 tablespoon oil until well blended
7.	Unfold the wraps on a clean work surface. Spoon the chickpea mash on the wraps and spread all over.
8.	Divide the cooked veggies among wraps. Sprinkle 1 ounce crumbled goat cheese on top of each wrap. Fold to wrap. Squeeze the lemon wedges on top and serve.

Mozzarella Chicken Taquitos

Prep time: 15 minutes | Cook time: 12 minutes | Serves 4
1 cup cooked chicken, shredded
¼ cup Greek yogurt
¼ cup salsa
1 cup shredded Mozzarella cheese
Salt and ground black pepper, to taste
4 flour tortillas
Cooking spray
1.	Spritz the perforated pan with cooking spray.
2.	Combine all the ingredients, except for the tortillas, in a large bowl. Stir to mix well.
3.	Make the taquitos: Unfold the tortillas on a clean work surface, then scoop up 2 tablespoons of the chicken mixture in the middle of each tortilla. Roll the tortillas up to wrap the filling.
4.	Arrange the taquitos in the pan and spritz with cooking spray.
5.	Select Air Fry. Set temperature to 380ºF (193ºC) and set time to 12 minutes. Press Start to begin preheating.
6.	Once preheated, place the pan into the oven. Flip the taquitos halfway through the cooking time.
7.	When cooked, the taquitos should be golden brown and the cheese should be melted.
8.	Serve immediately.

Curried Pork Sliders

Prep time: 10 minutes | Cook time: 14 minutes | Makes 6 sliders
1 pound (454 g) ground pork
1 tablespoon Thai curry paste
1½ tablespoons fish sauce
¼ cup thinly sliced scallions, white and green parts
2 tablespoons minced peeled fresh ginger
1 tablespoon light brown sugar
1 teaspoon ground black pepper
6 slider buns, split open lengthwise, warmed
Cooking spray

1.   Spritz the perforated pan with cooking spray.
2.   Combine all the ingredients, except for the buns in a large bowl. Stir to mix well.
3.   Divide and shape the mixture into six balls, then bash the balls into six 3-inch-diameter patties.
4.   Arrange the patties in the pan and spritz with cooking spray.
5.   Select Air Fry. Set temperature to 375ºF (190ºC) and set time to 14 minutes. Press Start to begin preheating.
6.   Once the oven has preheated, place the pan into the oven. Flip the patties halfway through the cooking time.
7.   When cooked, the patties should be well browned.
8.   Assemble the buns with patties to make the sliders and serve immediately.

Pork Momos with Carrot

Prep time: 20 minutes | Cook time: 20 minutes | Serves 4

2 tablespoons olive oil
1 pound (454 g) ground pork
1 shredded carrot
1 onion, chopped
1 teaspoon soy sauce
16 wonton wrappers
Salt and ground black pepper, to taste
Cooking spray

1.   Heat the olive oil in a nonstick skillet over medium heat until shimmering.
2.   Add the ground pork, carrot, onion, soy sauce, salt, and ground black pepper and sauté for 10 minutes or until the pork is well browned and carrots are tender.
3.   Unfold the wrappers on a clean work surface, then divide the cooked pork and vegetables on the wrappers. Fold the edges around the filling to form momos. Nip the top to seal the momos.
4.   Arrange the momos in the perforated pan and spritz with cooking spray.
5.   Select Air Fry. Set temperature to 320ºF (160ºC) and set time to 10 minutes. Press Start to begin preheating.
6.   Once the oven has preheated, place the pan into the oven.
7.   When cooking is complete, the wrappers will be lightly browned.
8.   Serve immediately.

Crispy Cream Cheese Wontons

Prep time: 5 minutes | Cook time: 6 minutes | Serves 4

2 ounces (57 g) cream cheese, softened
1 tablespoon sugar
16 square wonton wrappers
Cooking spray

1.   Spritz the perforated pan with cooking spray.
2.   In a mixing bowl, stir together the cream cheese and sugar until well mixed. Prepare a small bowl of water alongside.
3.   On a clean work surface, lay the wonton wrappers. Scoop ¼ teaspoon of cream cheese in the center of each wonton wrapper. Dab the water over the wrapper edges. Fold each wonton wrapper diagonally in half over the filling to form a triangle.
4.   Arrange the wontons in the pan. Spritz the wontons with cooking spray.
5.   Select Air Fry. Set temperature to 350ºF (180ºC) and set time to 6 minutes. Press Start to begin preheating.
6.   Once preheated, place the pan into the oven. Flip the wontons halfway through the cooking time.
7.   When cooking is complete, the wontons will be golden brown and crispy.
8.   Divide the wontons among four plates. Let rest for 5 minutes before serving.

Beef Steak and Bell Pepper Rolls

Prep time: 20 minutes | Cook time: 20 minutes | Serves 2

12 ounces (340 g) boneless rib-eye steak, sliced thinly
½ teaspoon Worcestershire sauce
½ teaspoon soy sauce
Kosher salt and ground black pepper, to taste
½ green bell pepper, stemmed, deseeded, and thinly sliced
½ small onion, halved and thinly sliced
1 tablespoon vegetable oil
2 soft hoagie rolls, split three-fourths of the way through
1 tablespoon butter, softened
2 slices provolone cheese, halved

1.   Combine the steak, Worcestershire sauce, soy sauce, salt, and ground black pepper in a large bowl. Toss to coat well. Set aside.
2.   Combine the bell pepper, onion, salt, ground black pepper, and vegetable oil in a separate bowl. Toss to coat the vegetables well.
3.   Pour the steak and vegetables in the perforated pan.
4.   Select Air Fry. Set temperature to 400ºF (205ºC) and set time to 15 minutes. Press Start to begin preheating.
5.   Once preheated, place the pan into the oven.
6.   When cooked, the steak will be browned and vegetables will be tender. Transfer them on a plate. Set aside.
7.   Brush the hoagie rolls with butter and place in the pan.
8.   Select Toast and set time to 3 minutes. Place the pan into the oven. When done, the rolls should be lightly browned.
9.   Transfer the rolls to a clean work surface and divide the steak and vegetable mix in between

the rolls. Spread with cheese. Place the stuffed rolls back in the pan.

10.   Select Air Fry and set time to 2 minutes. Place the pan into the oven. When done, the cheese should be melted.

11.   Serve immediately.

Cream Cheese and Crab Wontons

Prep time: 10 minutes | Cook time: 10 minutes | Serves 6 to 8

24 wonton wrappers, thawed if frozen
Cooking spray
Filling:
5 ounces (142 g) lump crabmeat, drained and patted dry
4 ounces (113 g) cream cheese, at room temperature
2 scallions, sliced
1½ teaspoons toasted sesame oil
1 teaspoon Worcestershire sauce
Kosher salt and ground black pepper, to taste

1.   Spritz the perforated pan with cooking spray.

2.   In a medium-size bowl, place all the ingredients for the filling and stir until well mixed. Prepare a small bowl of water alongside.

3.   On a clean work surface, lay the wonton wrappers. Scoop 1 teaspoon of the filling in the center of each wrapper. Wet the edges with a touch of water. Fold each wonton wrapper diagonally in half over the filling to form a triangle.

4.   Arrange the wontons in the pan. Spritz the wontons with cooking spray.

5.   Select Air Fry. Set temperature to 350ºF (180ºC) and set time to 10 minutes. Press Start to begin preheating.

6.   Once preheated, place the pan into the oven. Flip the wontons halfway through the cooking time.

7.   When cooking is complete, the wontons will be crispy and golden brown.

8.   Serve immediately.

Pork and Cabbage Gyoza

Prep time: 10 minutes | Cook time: 10 minutes | Makes 48 gyozas

1 pound (454 g) ground pork
1 head Napa cabbage (about 1 pound / 454 g) sliced thinly and minced
½ cup minced scallions
1 teaspoon minced fresh chives
1 teaspoon soy sauce
1 teaspoon minced fresh ginger
1 tablespoon minced garlic
1 teaspoon granulated sugar
2 teaspoons kosher salt
48 to 50 wonton or dumpling wrappers
Cooking spray

1.   Spritz the perforated pan with cooking spray. Set aside.

2.   Make the filling: Combine all the ingredients, except for the wrappers in a large bowl. Stir to mix well.

3.   Unfold a wrapper on a clean work surface, then dab the edges with a little water. Scoop up 2 teaspoons of the filling mixture in the center.

4.   Make the gyoza: Fold the wrapper over to filling and press the edges to seal. Pleat the edges if desired. Repeat with remaining wrappers and fillings.

5.   Arrange the gyozas in the pan and spritz with cooking spray.

6.   Select Air Fry. Set temperature to 360ºF (182ºC) and set time to 10 minutes. Press Start to begin preheating.

7.   Once preheated, place the pan into the oven. Flip the gyozas halfway through the cooking time.

8.   When cooked, the gyozas will be golden brown.

9.   Serve immediately.

Jalapeño Turkey Sliders with Chive Mayo

Prep time: 10 minutes | Cook time: 15 minutes | Serves 6

12 burger buns
Cooking spray
Turkey Sliders:
¾ pound (340 g) turkey, minced
1 tablespoon oyster sauce
¼ cup pickled jalapeño, chopped
2 tablespoons chopped scallions
1 tablespoon chopped fresh cilantro
1 to 2 cloves garlic, minced
Sea salt and ground black pepper, to taste
Chive Mayo:
1 tablespoon chives
1 cup mayonnaise
Zest of 1 lime
1 teaspoon salt

1.   Spritz the perforated pan with cooking spray.

2.   Combine the ingredients for the turkey sliders in a large bowl. Stir to mix well. Shape the mixture into 6 balls, then bash the balls into patties.

3.   Arrange the patties in the pan and spritz with cooking spray.

4.   Select Air Fry. Set temperature to 365ºF (185ºC) and set time to 15 minutes. Press Start to begin preheating.

5.   Once preheated, place the pan into the oven. Flip the patties halfway through the cooking time.

6.   Meanwhile, combine the ingredients for the chive mayo in a small bowl. Stir to mix well.

7.   When cooked, the patties will be well browned.

8.   Smear the patties with chive mayo, then assemble the patties between two buns to make the sliders. Serve immediately.

Beef Burgers with Korean Mayo

Prep time: 15 minutes | Cook time: 10 minutes | Serves 4
Burgers:
1 pound (454 g) 85% lean ground beef
2 tablespoons gochujang
¼ cup chopped scallions
2 teaspoons minced garlic
2 teaspoons minced fresh ginger
1 tablespoon soy sauce
1 tablespoon toasted sesame oil
2 teaspoons sugar
½ teaspoon kosher salt
4 hamburger buns
Cooking spray
Korean Mayo:
1 tablespoon gochujang
¼ cup mayonnaise
2 teaspoons sesame seeds
¼ cup chopped scallions
1 tablespoon toasted sesame oil
1. Combine the ingredients for the burgers, except for the buns, in a large bowl. Stir to mix well, then wrap the bowl in plastic and refrigerate to marinate for at least an hour.
2. Spritz the perforated pan with cooking spray.
3. Divide the meat mixture into four portions and form into four balls. Bash the balls into patties.
4. Arrange the patties in the pan and spritz with cooking spray.
5. Select Air Fry. Set temperature to 350ºF (180ºC) and set time to 10 minutes. Press Start to begin preheating.
6. Once the oven has preheated, place the pan into the oven. Flip the patties halfway through the cooking time.
7. Meanwhile, combine the ingredients for the Korean mayo in a small bowl. Stir to mix well.
8. When cooking is complete, the patties should be golden brown.
9. Remove the patties from the oven and assemble with the buns, then spread the Korean mayo over the patties to make the burgers. Serve immediately.

Lamb Hamburgers with Feta Cheese

Prep time: 15 minutes | Cook time: 16 minutes | Makes 4 burgers
1½ pounds (680 g) ground lamb
¼ cup crumbled feta
1½ teaspoons tomato paste
1½ teaspoons minced garlic
1 teaspoon ground dried ginger
1 teaspoon ground coriander
¼ teaspoon salt
¼ teaspoon cayenne pepper
4 kaiser rolls or hamburger buns, split open lengthwise, warmed
Cooking spray

1. Spritz the perforated pan with cooking spray.
2. Combine all the ingredients, except for the buns, in a large bowl. Coarsely stir to mix well.
3. Shape the mixture into four balls, then pound the balls into four 5-inch diameter patties.
4. Arrange the patties in the pan and spritz with cooking spray.
5. Select Air Fry. Set temperature to 375ºF (190ºC) and set time to 16 minutes. Press Start to begin preheating.
6. Once preheated, place the pan into the oven. Flip the patties halfway through the cooking time.
7. When cooking is complete, the patties should be well browned.
8. Assemble the buns with patties to make the burgers and serve immediately.

Smoked Paprika Chicken Burgers

Prep time: 15 minutes | Cook time: 20 minutes | Serves 6 to 8
4 skinless and boneless chicken breasts
1 small head of cauliflower, sliced into florets
1 jalapeño pepper
3 tablespoons smoked paprika
1 tablespoon thyme
1 tablespoon oregano
1 tablespoon mustard powder
1 teaspoon cayenne pepper
1 egg
Salt and ground black pepper, to taste
2 tomatoes, sliced
2 lettuce leaves, chopped
6 to 8 brioche buns, sliced lengthwise
¾ cup taco sauce
Cooking spray
1. Spritz the perforated pan with cooking spray. Set aside.
2. In a blender, add the cauliflower florets, jalapeño pepper, paprika, thyme, oregano, mustard powder and cayenne pepper and blend until the mixture has a texture similar to bread crumbs.
3. Transfer ¾ of the cauliflower mixture to a medium bowl and set aside. Beat the egg in a different bowl and set aside.
4. Add the chicken breasts to the blender with remaining cauliflower mixture. Sprinkle with salt and pepper. Blend until finely chopped and well mixed.
5. Remove the mixture from the blender and form into 6 to 8 patties. One by one, dredge each patty in the reserved cauliflower mixture, then into the egg. Dip them in the cauliflower mixture again for additional coating.
6. Place the coated patties into the pan and spritz with cooking spray.
7. Select Air Fry. Set temperature to 350ºF (180ºC) and set time to 20 minutes. Press Start to begin preheating.
8. Once preheated, place the pan into the oven. Flip the patties halfway through the cooking time.

9.	When cooking is complete, the patties should be golden and crispy.
10.	Transfer the patties to a clean work surface and assemble with the buns, tomato slices, chopped lettuce leaves and taco sauce to make burgers. Serve and enjoy.

Beef Burgers with Seeds

Prep time: 15 minutes | Cook time: 10 minutes | Serves 4
1 teaspoon cumin seeds
1 teaspoon mustard seeds
1 teaspoon coriander seeds
1 teaspoon dried minced garlic
1 teaspoon dried red pepper flakes
1 teaspoon kosher salt
2 teaspoons ground black pepper
1 pound (454 g) 85% lean ground beef
2 tablespoons Worcestershire sauce
4 hamburger buns
Mayonnaise, for serving
Cooking spray
1.	Spritz the perforated pan with cooking spray.
2.	Put the seeds, garlic, red pepper flakes, salt, and ground black pepper in a food processor. Pulse to coarsely ground the mixture.
3.	Put the ground beef in a large bowl. Pour in the seed mixture and drizzle with Worcestershire sauce. Stir to mix well.
4.	Divide the mixture into four parts and shape each part into a ball, then bash each ball into a patty. Arrange the patties in the pan.
5.	Select Air Fry. Set temperature to 350ºF (180ºC) and set time to 10 minutes. Press Start to begin preheating.
6.	Once the oven has preheated, place the pan into the oven. Flip the patties with tongs halfway through the cooking time.
7.	When cooked, the patties will be well browned.
8.	Assemble the buns with the patties, then drizzle the mayo over the patties to make the burgers. Serve immediately.

Potato Samosas with Mint Chutney

Prep time: 30 minutes | Cook time: 22 minutes | Makes 16 samosas
Dough:
4 cups all-purpose flour, plus more for flouring the work surface
¼ cup plain yogurt
½ cup cold unsalted butter, cut into cubes
2 teaspoons kosher salt
1 cup ice water
Filling:
2 tablespoons vegetable oil
1 onion, diced
1½ teaspoons coriander
1½ teaspoons cumin
1 clove garlic, minced
1 teaspoon turmeric
1 teaspoon kosher salt
½ cup peas, thawed if frozen
2 cups mashed potatoes
2 tablespoons yogurt
Cooking spray
Chutney:
1 cup mint leaves, lightly packed
2 cups cilantro leaves, lightly packed
1 green chile pepper, deseeded and minced
½ cup minced onion
Juice of 1 lime
1 teaspoon granulated sugar
1 teaspoon kosher salt
2 tablespoons vegetable oil
1.	Put the flour, yogurt, butter, and salt in a food processor. Pulse to combine until grainy. Pour in the water and pulse until a smooth and firm dough forms.
2.	Transfer the dough on a clean and lightly floured working surface. Knead the dough and shape it into a ball. Cut in half and flatten the halves into 2 discs. Wrap them in plastic and let sit in refrigerator until ready to use.
3.	Meanwhile, make the filling: Heat the vegetable oil in a saucepan over medium heat.
4.	Add the onion and sauté for 5 minutes or until lightly browned.
5.	Add the coriander, cumin, garlic, turmeric, and salt and sauté for 2 minutes or until fragrant.
6.	Add the peas, potatoes, and yogurt and stir to combine well. Turn off the heat and allow to cool.
7.	Meanwhile, combine the ingredients for the chutney in a food processor. Pulse to mix well until glossy. Pour the chutney in a bowl and refrigerate until ready to use.
8.	Make the samosas: Remove the dough discs from the refrigerator and cut each disc into 8 parts. Shape each part into a ball, then roll the ball into a 6-inch circle. Cut the circle in half and roll each half into a cone.
9.	Scoop up 2 tablespoons of the filling into the cone, press the edges of the cone to seal and form into a triangle. Repeat with remaining dough and filling.
10.	Spritz the perforated pan with cooking spray. Arrange the samosas in the pan and spritz with cooking spray.
11.	Select Air Fry. Set temperature to 360ºF (182ºC) and set time to 15 minutes. Press Start to begin preheating.
12.	Once the oven has preheated, place the pan into the oven. Flip the samosas halfway through the cooking time.
13.	When cooked, the samosas will be golden brown and crispy.
14.	Serve the samosas with the chutney.

Cheddar Chicken Empanadas

Prep time: 25 minutes | Cook time: 12 minutes | Makes 12 empanadas

1 cup boneless, skinless rotisserie chicken breast meat, chopped finely
¼ cup salsa verde
$^2/_3$ cup shredded Cheddar cheese
1 teaspoon ground cumin
1 teaspoon ground black pepper
2 purchased refrigerated pie crusts, from a minimum 14.1-ounce (400 g) box
1 large egg
2 tablespoons water
Cooking spray

1. Spritz the perforated pan with cooking spray. Set aside.
2. Combine the chicken meat, salsa verde, Cheddar, cumin, and black pepper in a large bowl. Stir to mix well. Set aside.
3. Unfold the pie crusts on a clean work surface, then use a large cookie cutter to cut out 3½-inch circles as much as possible.
4. Roll the remaining crusts to a ball and flatten into a circle which has the same thickness of the original crust. Cut out more 3½-inch circles until you have 12 circles in total.
5. Make the empanadas: Divide the chicken mixture in the middle of each circle, about 1½ tablespoons each. Dab the edges of the circle with water. Fold the circle in half over the filling to shape like a half-moon and press to seal, or you can press with a fork.
6. Whisk the egg with water in a small bowl.
7. Arrange the empanadas in the pan and spritz with cooking spray. Brush with whisked egg.
8. Select Air Fry. Set temperature to 350ºF (180ºC) and set time to 12 minutes. Press Start to begin preheating.
9. Once preheated, place the pan into the oven. Flip the empanadas halfway through the cooking time.
10. When cooking is complete, the empanadas will be golden and crispy.
11. Serve immediately.

Turkey and Pepper Hamburger

Prep time: 10 minutes | Cook time: 20 minutes | Serves 4

1 cup leftover turkey, cut into bite-sized chunks
1 leek, sliced
1 Serrano pepper, seeded and chopped
2 bell peppers, seeded and chopped
2 tablespoons Tabasco sauce
½ cup sour cream
1 heaping tablespoon fresh cilantro, chopped
1 teaspoon hot paprika
¾ teaspoon kosher salt
½ teaspoon ground black pepper
4 hamburger buns
Cooking spray

1. Spritz a baking pan with cooking spray.
2. Mix all the ingredients, except for the buns, in a large bowl. Toss to combine well.
3. Pour the mixture in the baking pan.
4. Select Bake. Set temperature to 385ºF (196ºC) and set time to 20 minutes. Press Start to begin preheating.
5. Once preheated, place the pan into the oven.
6. When done, the turkey will be well browned and the leek will be tender.
7. Assemble the hamburger buns with the turkey mixture and serve immediately.

CHAPTER 4 STAPLES

Ginger-Garlic Dipping Sauce

Prep time: 15 minutes | Cook time: 0 minutes | Makes about 1 cup

¼ cup rice vinegar
¼ cup hoisin sauce
¼ cup low-sodium chicken or vegetable stock
3 tablespoons soy sauce
1 tablespoon minced or grated ginger
1 tablespoon minced or pressed garlic
1 teaspoon chili-garlic sauce or sriracha (or more to taste)

1. Stir together all the ingredients in a small bowl, or place in a jar with a tight-fitting lid and shake until well mixed.
2. Use immediately.

Lemon Anchovy Dressing

Prep time: 5 minutes | Cook time: 0 minutes | Makes about ⅔ cup

½ cup extra-virgin olive oil
2 tablespoons freshly squeezed lemon juice
1 teaspoon anchovy paste
¼ teaspoon kosher salt or ⅛ teaspoon fine salt
¼ teaspoon minced or pressed garlic
1 egg, beaten

1. Add all the ingredients to a tall, narrow container.
2. Purée the mixture with an immersion blender until smooth.
3. Use immediately.

Buttery Mushrooms

Prep time: 8 minutes | Cook time: 30 minutes | Makes about 1½ cups

1 pound (454 g) button or cremini mushrooms, washed, stems trimmed, and cut into quarters or thick slices
¼ cup water
1 teaspoon kosher salt or ½ teaspoon fine salt
3 tablespoons unsalted butter, cut into pieces, or extra-virgin olive oil

1. Place a large piece of aluminum foil on the sheet pan. Place the mushroom pieces in the middle of the foil. Spread them out into an even layer. Pour the water over them, season with the salt, and add the butter. Wrap the mushrooms in the foil.
2. Select Roast. Set temperature to 325ºF (163ºC) and set time to 15 minutes. Press Start to begin preheating.
3. Once the unit has preheated, place the pan into the oven.
4. After 15 minutes, remove the pan from the oven. Transfer the foil packet to a cutting board and carefully unwrap it. Pour the mushrooms and cooking liquid from the foil onto the sheet pan.
5. Select Roast. Set temperature to 350ºF (180ºC) and set time to 15 minutes. place the pan into the oven. Press Start to begin preheating.
6. After about 10 minutes, remove the pan from the oven and stir the mushrooms. Return the pan to the oven and continue cooking for 5 to 15 more minutes, or until the liquid is mostly gone and the mushrooms start to brown.
7. Serve immediately.

Garlic Tomato Sauce

Prep time: 15 minutes | Cook time: 30 minutes | Makes about 3 cups

¼ cup extra-virgin olive oil
3 garlic cloves, minced
1 small onion, chopped (about ½ cup)
2 tablespoons minced or puréed sun-dried tomatoes (optional)
1 (28-ounce / 794-g) can crushed tomatoes
½ teaspoon dried basil
½ teaspoon dried oregano
¼ teaspoon red pepper flakes
1 teaspoon kosher salt or ½ teaspoon fine salt, plus more as needed

1. Heat the oil in a medium saucepan over medium heat.
2. Add the garlic and onion and sauté for 2 to 3 minutes, or until the onion is softened. Add the sun-dried tomatoes (if desired) and cook for 1 minute until fragrant. Stir in the crushed tomatoes, scraping any brown bits from the bottom of the pot. Fold in the basil, oregano, red pepper flakes, and salt. Stir well.
3. Bring to a simmer. Cook covered for about 30 minutes, stirring occasionally.
4. Turn off the heat and allow the sauce to cool for about 10 minutes.
5. Taste and adjust the seasoning, adding more salt if needed.
6. Use immediately.

Teriyaki Sauce

Prep time: 5 minutes | Cook time: 0 minutes | Makes ¾ cup

½ cup soy sauce
3 tablespoons honey
1 tablespoon rice wine or dry sherry
1 tablespoon rice vinegar
2 teaspoons minced fresh ginger
2 garlic cloves, smashed

1. Beat together all the ingredients in a small bowl.
2. Use immediately.

Creamy Grits

Prep time: 3 minutes | Cook time: 1 hour 5 minutes | Makes about 4 cups

1 cup grits or polenta (not instant or quick cook)
2 cups chicken or vegetable stock
2 cups milk
2 tablespoons unsalted butter, cut into 4 pieces
1 teaspoon kosher salt or ½ teaspoon fine salt
1.	Add the grits to the baking pan. Stir in the stock, milk, butter, and salt.
2.	Select Bake. set temperature to 325ºF (163ºC) and set time to 1 hour and 5 minutes. Press Start to begin preheating.
3.	Once the unit has preheated, place the pan into the oven.
4.	After 15 minutes, remove the pan from the oven and stir the polenta. Return the pan to the oven and continue cooking.
5.	After 30 minutes, remove the pan again and stir the polenta again. Return the pan to the oven and continue cooking for 15 to 20 minutes, or until the polenta is soft and creamy and the liquid is absorbed.
6.	When done, remove the pan from the oven.
7.	Serve immediately.

Poblano Garlic Sauce

Prep time: 15 minutes | Cook time: 0 minutes | Makes 2 cups

3 large ancho chiles, stems and seeds removed, torn into pieces
1½ cups very hot water
2 garlic cloves, peeled and lightly smashed
2 tablespoons wine vinegar
1½ teaspoons sugar
½ teaspoon dried oregano
½ teaspoon ground cumin
2 teaspoons kosher salt or 1 teaspoon fine salt
1.	Mix together the chile pieces and hot water in a bowl and let stand for 10 to 15 minutes.
2.	Pour the chiles and water into a blender jar. Fold in the garlic, vinegar, sugar, oregano, cumin, and salt and blend until smooth.
3.	Use immediately.

Shawarma Seasoning

Prep time: 5 minutes | Cook time: 0 minutes | Makes about 1 tablespoon

1 teaspoon smoked paprika
1 teaspoon cumin
¼ teaspoon turmeric
¼ teaspoon kosher salt or ⅛ teaspoon fine salt
¼ teaspoon cinnamon
¼ teaspoon allspice

¼ teaspoon red pepper flakes
¼ teaspoon freshly ground black pepper
1.	Stir together all the ingredients in a small bowl.
2.	Use immediately or place in an airtight container in the pantry.

Baked White Rice

Prep time: 3 minutes | Cook time: 35 minutes | Makes about 4 cups

1 cup long-grain white rice, rinsed and drained
1 tablespoon unsalted butter, melted, or 1 tablespoon extra-virgin olive oil
2 cups water
1 teaspoon kosher salt or ½ teaspoon fine salt
1.	Add the butter and rice to the baking pan and stir to coat. Pour in the water and sprinkle with the salt. Stir until the salt is dissolved.
2.	Select Bake. Set temperature to 325ºF (163ºC) and set time to 35 minutes. Press Start to begin preheating.
3.	Once the unit has preheated, place the pan into the oven.
4.	After 20 minutes, remove the pan from the oven. Stir the rice. Transfer the pan back to the oven and continue cooking for 10 to 15 minutes, or until the rice is mostly cooked through and the water is absorbed.
5.	When done, remove the pan from the oven and cover with aluminum foil. Let stand for 10 minutes. Using a fork, gently fluff the rice.
6.	Serve immediately.

Paprika-Oregano Seasoning

Prep time: 5 minutes | Cook time: 0 minutes | Makes about ¾ cups

3 tablespoons ancho chile powder
3 tablespoons paprika
2 tablespoons dried oregano
2 tablespoons freshly ground black pepper
2 teaspoons cayenne
2 teaspoons cumin
1 tablespoon granulated onion
1 tablespoon granulated garlic
1.	Stir together all the ingredients in a small bowl.
2.	Use immediately or place in an airtight container in the pantry.

CHAPTER 5 VEGAN AND VEGETARIAN

Roasted Veggie and Tofu

Prep time: 10 minutes | Cook time: 10 minutes | Serves 4

$^1/_3$ cup Asian-Style sauce
1 teaspoon cornstarch
½ teaspoon red pepper flakes, or more to taste
1 pound (454 g) firm or extra-firm tofu, cut into 1-inch cubes
1 small carrot, peeled and cut into ¼-inch-thick coins
1 small green bell pepper, cut into bite-size pieces
3 scallions, sliced, whites and green parts separated
3 tablespoons roasted unsalted peanuts
1.	In a large bowl, whisk together the sauce, cornstarch, and red pepper flakes. Fold in the tofu, carrot, pepper, and the white parts of the scallions and toss to coat. Spread the mixture evenly on the sheet pan.
2.	Select Roast. Set temperature to 375ºF (190ºC) and set time to 10 minutes. Press Start to begin preheating.
3.	Once preheated, place the pan into the oven. Stir the ingredients once halfway through the cooking time.
4.	When done, remove the pan from the oven. Serve sprinkled with the peanuts and scallion greens.

Black Bean and Salsa Tacos

Prep time: 12 minutes | Cook time: 7 minutes | Serves 4

1 (15-ounce / 425-g) can black beans, drained and rinsed
½ cup prepared salsa
1½ teaspoons chili powder
4 ounces (113 g) grated Monterey Jack cheese
2 tablespoons minced onion
8 (6-inch) flour tortillas
2 tablespoons vegetable or extra-virgin olive oil
Shredded lettuce, for serving
1.	In a medium bowl, add the beans, salsa and chili powder. Coarsely mash them with a potato masher. Fold in the cheese and onion and stir until combined.
2.	Arrange the flour tortillas on a cutting board and spoon 2 to 3 tablespoons of the filling into each tortilla. Fold the tortillas over, pressing lightly to even out the filling. Brush the tacos on one side with half the olive oil and put them, oiled side down, on the sheet pan. Brush the top side with the remaining olive oil.
3.	Select Air Fry. Set temperature to 400ºF (205ºC) and set time to 7 minutes. Press Start to begin preheating.
4.	Once preheated, place the pan into the oven. Flip the tacos halfway through the cooking time.
5.	Remove the pan from the oven and allow to cool for 5 minutes. Serve with the shredded lettuce on the side.

Thai Curried Veggies

Prep time: 10 minutes | Cook time: 8 minutes | Serves 4

1 small head Napa cabbage, shredded, divided
1 medium carrot, cut into thin coins
8 ounces (227 g) snow peas
1 red or green bell pepper, sliced into thin strips
1 tablespoon vegetable oil
2 tablespoons soy sauce
1 tablespoon sesame oil
2 tablespoons brown sugar
2 tablespoons freshly squeezed lime juice
2 teaspoons red or green Thai curry paste
1 serrano chile, deseeded and minced
1 cup frozen mango slices, thawed
½ cup chopped roasted peanuts or cashews
1.	Put half the Napa cabbage in a large bowl, along with the carrot, snow peas, and bell pepper. Drizzle with the vegetable oil and toss to coat. Spread them evenly on the sheet pan.
2.	Select Roast. Set temperature to 375ºF (190ºC) and set time to 8 minutes. Press Start to begin preheating.
3.	Once preheated, place the pan into the oven.
4.	Meanwhile, whisk together the soy sauce, sesame oil, brown sugar, lime juice, and curry paste in a small bowl.
5.	When done, the vegetables should be tender and crisp. Remove the pan and put the vegetables back into the bowl. Add the chile, mango slices, and the remaining cabbage. Pour over the dressing and toss to coat. Top with the roasted nuts and serve.

Eggplant and Bell Peppers with Basil

Prep time: 15 minutes | Cook time: 20 minutes | Serves 2

1 small eggplant, halved and sliced
1 yellow bell pepper, cut into thick strips
1 red bell pepper, cut into thick strips
2 garlic cloves, quartered
1 red onion, sliced
1 tablespoon extra-virgin olive oil
Salt and freshly ground black pepper, to taste
½ cup chopped fresh basil, for garnish
Cooking spray
1.	Grease a nonstick baking dish with cooking spray.
2.	Place the eggplant, bell peppers, garlic, and red onion in the greased baking dish. Drizzle with the olive oil and toss to coat well. Spritz any uncoated surfaces with cooking spray.
3.	Select Bake. Set temperature to 350ºF (180ºC) and set time to 20 minutes. Press Start to begin preheating.

4.	Once preheated, place the baking dish into the oven. Flip the vegetables halfway through the cooking time.
5.	When done, remove from the oven and sprinkle with salt and pepper.
6.	Sprinkle the basil on top for garnish and serve.

Vinegary Asparagus

Prep time: 15 minutes | Cook time: 10 minutes | Serves 4
4 tablespoons olive oil, plus more for greasing
4 tablespoons balsamic vinegar
1½ pounds (680 g) asparagus spears, trimmed
Salt and freshly ground black pepper, to taste
1.	Grease the perforated pan with olive oil.
2.	In a shallow bowl, stir together the 4 tablespoons of olive oil and balsamic vinegar to make a marinade.
3.	Put the asparagus spears in the bowl so they are thoroughly covered by the marinade and allow to marinate for 5 minutes.
4.	Put the asparagus in the greased pan in a single layer and season with salt and pepper.
5.	Select Air Fry. Set temperature to 350ºF (180ºC) and set time to 10 minutes. Press Start to begin preheating.
6.	Once preheated, place the pan into the oven. Flip the asparagus halfway through the cooking time.
7.	When done, the asparagus should be tender and lightly browned. Cool for 5 minutes before serving.

Baked Eggs with Spinach and Basil

Prep time: 10 minutes | Cook time: 10 minutes | Serves 2
2 tablespoons olive oil
4 eggs, whisked
5 ounces (142 g) fresh spinach, chopped
1 medium-sized tomato, chopped
1 teaspoon fresh lemon juice
½ teaspoon ground black pepper
½ teaspoon coarse salt
½ cup roughly chopped fresh basil leaves, for garnish
1.	Generously grease a baking pan with olive oil.
2.	Stir together the remaining ingredients except the basil leaves in the greased baking pan until well incorporated.
3.	Select Bake. Set temperature to 280ºF (137ºC) and set time to 10 minutes. Press Start to begin preheating.
4.	Once preheated, place the pan into the oven.
5.	When cooking is complete, the eggs should be completely set and the vegetables should be tender. Remove from the oven and serve garnished with the fresh basil leaves.

Cheesy Broccoli with Rosemary

Prep time: 5 minutes | Cook time: 18 minutes | Serves 4
1 large-sized head broccoli, stemmed and cut into small florets
2½ tablespoons canola oil
2 teaspoons dried basil
2 teaspoons dried rosemary
Salt and ground black pepper, to taste
$^1/_3$ cup grated yellow cheese
1.	Bring a pot of lightly salted water to a boil. Add the broccoli florets to the boiling water and let boil for about 3 minutes.
2.	Drain the broccoli florets well and transfer to a large bowl. Add the canola oil, basil, rosemary, salt, and black pepper to the bowl and toss until the broccoli is fully coated. Place the broccoli in the perforated pan.
3.	Select Air Fry. Set temperature to 390ºF (199ºC) and set time to 15 minutes. Press Start to begin preheating.
4.	Once preheated, place the pan into the oven. Stir the broccoli halfway through the cooking time.
5.	When cooking is complete, the broccoli should be crisp. Remove the pan from the oven. Serve the broccoli warm with grated cheese sprinkled on top.

Kale with Tahini-Lemon Dressing

Prep time: 5 minutes | Cook time: 15 minutes | Serves 2 to 4
Dressing:
¼ cup tahini
¼ cup fresh lemon juice
2 tablespoons olive oil
1 teaspoon sesame seeds
½ teaspoon garlic powder
¼ teaspoon cayenne pepper
Kale:
4 cups packed torn kale leaves (stems and ribs removed and leaves torn into palm-size pieces)
Kosher salt and freshly ground black pepper, to taste
1.	Make the dressing: Whisk together the tahini, lemon juice, olive oil, sesame seeds, garlic powder, and cayenne pepper in a large bowl until well mixed.
2.	Add the kale and massage the dressing thoroughly all over the leaves. Sprinkle the salt and pepper to season.
3.	Place the kale in the perforated pan in a single layer.
4.	Select Air Fry. Set temperature to 350ºF (180ºC) and set time to 15 minutes. Press Start to begin preheating.
5.	Once preheated, place the pan into the oven.
6.	When cooking is complete, the leaves should be slightly wilted and crispy. Remove from the oven and serve on a plate.

Vegetable Mélange with Garlic

Prep time: 10 minutes | Cook time: 16 minutes | Serves 4
1 (8-ounce / 227-g) package sliced mushrooms
1 yellow summer squash, sliced
1 red bell pepper, sliced
3 cloves garlic, sliced
1 tablespoon olive oil
½ teaspoon dried basil
½ teaspoon dried thyme
½ teaspoon dried tarragon
1.   Toss the mushrooms, squash, and bell pepper with the garlic and olive oil in a large bowl until well coated. Mix in the basil, thyme, and tarragon and toss again.
2.   Spread the vegetables evenly in the perforated pan.
3.   Select Roast. Set temperature to 350ºF (180ºC) and set time to 16 minutes. Press Start to begin preheating.
4.   Once preheated, place the pan into the oven.
5.   When cooking is complete, the vegetables should be fork-tender. Remove the pan from the oven. Cool for 5 minutes before serving.

Garlic Carrots with Sesame Seeds

Prep time: 5 minutes | Cook time: 16 minutes | Serves 4 to 6
1 pound (454 g) baby carrots
1 tablespoon sesame oil
½ teaspoon dried dill
Pinch salt
Freshly ground black pepper, to taste
6 cloves garlic, peeled
3 tablespoons sesame seeds
1.   In a medium bowl, drizzle the baby carrots with the sesame oil. Sprinkle with the dill, salt, and pepper and toss to coat well.
2.   Place the baby carrots in the perforated pan.
3.   Select Roast. Set temperature to 380ºF (193ºC) and set time to 16 minutes. Press Start to begin preheating.
4.   Once preheated, place the pan into the oven.
5.   After 8 minutes, remove the pan from the oven and stir in the garlic. Return the pan to the oven and continue roasting for 8 minutes more.
6.   When cooking is complete, the carrots should be lightly browned. Remove the pan from the oven and serve sprinkled with the sesame seeds.

Thai-Flavored Brussels Sprouts

Prep time: 5 minutes | Cook time: 20 minutes | Serves 2
¼ cup Thai sweet chili sauce
2 tablespoons black vinegar or balsamic vinegar
½ teaspoon hot sauce
2 small shallots, cut into ¼-inch-thick slices
8 ounces (227 g) Brussels sprouts, trimmed (large sprouts halved)
Kosher salt and freshly ground black pepper, to taste
2 teaspoons lightly packed fresh cilantro leaves, for garnish
1.   Place the chili sauce, vinegar, and hot sauce in a large bowl and whisk to combine.
2.   Add the shallots and Brussels sprouts and toss to coat. Sprinkle with the salt and pepper. Transfer the Brussels sprouts and sauce to a baking pan.
3.   Select Roast. Set temperature to 390ºF (199ºC) and set time to 20 minutes. Press Start to begin preheating.
4.   Once preheated, place the pan into the oven. Stir the Brussels sprouts twice during cooking.
5.   When cooking is complete, the Brussels sprouts should be crisp-tender. Remove from the oven. Sprinkle the cilantro on top for garnish and serve warm.

Honey Eggplant with Yogurt Sauce

Prep time: 5 minutes | Cook time: 15 minutes | Serves 2
1 medium eggplant, quartered and cut crosswise into ½-inch-thick slices
2 tablespoons vegetable oil
Kosher salt and freshly ground black pepper, to taste
½ cup plain yogurt (not Greek)
2 tablespoons harissa paste
1 garlic clove, grated
2 teaspoons honey
1.   Toss the eggplant slices with the vegetable oil, salt, and pepper in a large bowl until well coated.
2.   Lay the eggplant slices in the perforated pan.
3.   Select Air Fry. Set temperature to 400ºF (205ºC) and set time to 15 minutes. Press Start to begin preheating.
4.   Once preheated, place the pan into the oven. Stir the slices two to three times during cooking.
5.   Meanwhile, make the yogurt sauce by whisking together the yogurt, harissa paste, and garlic in a small bowl.
6.   When cooking is complete, the eggplant slices should be golden brown. Spread the yogurt sauce on a platter, and pile the eggplant slices over the top. Serve drizzled with the honey.

Parmesan Cabbage Wedges

Prep time: 5 minutes | Cook time: 20 minutes | Serves 4
4 tablespoons melted butter
1 head cabbage, cut into wedges
1 cup shredded Parmesan cheese
Salt and black pepper, to taste
½ cup shredded Mozzarella cheese
1.   Brush the melted butter over the cut sides of cabbage wedges and sprinkle both sides with the Parmesan cheese. Season with salt and pepper to taste.

2.	Place the cabbage wedges in the perforated pan.
3.	Select Air Fry. Set temperature to 380ºF (193ºC) and set time to 20 minutes. Press Start to begin preheating.
4.	Once preheated, place the pan into the oven. Flip the cabbage halfway through the cooking time.
5.	When cooking is complete, the cabbage wedges should be lightly browned. Transfer the cabbage wedges to a plate and serve with the Mozzarella cheese sprinkled on top.

Sesame Mushrooms with Thyme

Prep time: 5 minutes | Cook time: 15 minutes | Serves 2

1 tablespoon soy sauce
2 teaspoons toasted sesame oil
3 teaspoons vegetable oil, divided
1 garlic clove, minced
7 ounces (198 g) maitake (hen of the woods) mushrooms
½ teaspoon flaky sea salt
½ teaspoon sesame seeds
½ teaspoon finely chopped fresh thyme leaves
1.	Whisk together the soy sauce, sesame oil, 1 teaspoon of vegetable oil, and garlic in a small bowl.
2.	Arrange the mushrooms in the perforated pan in a single layer. Drizzle the soy sauce mixture over the mushrooms.
3.	Select Roast. Set temperature to 300ºF (150ºC) and set time to 15 minutes. Press Start to begin preheating.
4.	Once preheated, place the pan into the oven.
5.	After 10 minutes, remove the pan from the oven. Flip the mushrooms and sprinkle the sea salt, sesame seeds, and thyme leaves on top. Drizzle the remaining 2 teaspoons of vegetable oil all over. Return to the oven and continue roasting for an additional 5 minutes.
6.	When cooking is complete, remove the mushrooms from the oven to a plate and serve hot.

Ratatouille with Bread Crumb Topping

Prep time: 10 minutes | Cook time: 12 minutes | Serves 6

1 medium zucchini, sliced ½-inch thick
1 small eggplant, peeled and sliced ½-inch thick
2 teaspoons kosher salt, divided
4 tablespoons extra-virgin olive oil, divided
3 garlic cloves, minced
1 small onion, chopped
1 small red bell pepper, cut into ½-inch chunks
1 small green bell pepper, cut into ½-inch chunks
½ teaspoon dried oregano
¼ teaspoon freshly ground black pepper
1 pint cherry tomatoes
2 tablespoons minced fresh basil
1 cup panko bread crumbs
½ cup grated Parmesan cheese (optional)

1.	Season one side of the zucchini and eggplant slices with ¾ teaspoon of salt. Put the slices, salted side down, on a rack set over a baking sheet. Sprinkle the other sides with ¾ teaspoon of salt. Allow to sit for 10 minutes, or until the slices begin to exude water. When ready, rinse and dry them. Cut the zucchini slices into quarters and the eggplant slices into eighths.
2.	Pour the zucchini and eggplant into a large bowl, along with 2 tablespoons of olive oil, garlic, onion, bell peppers, oregano, and black pepper. Toss to coat well. Arrange the vegetables on the sheet pan.
3.	Select Roast. Set temperature to 375ºF (190ºC) and set time to 12 minutes. Press Start to begin preheating.
4.	Once preheated, place the pan into the oven.
5.	Meanwhile, add the tomatoes and basil to the large bowl. Sprinkle with the remaining ½ teaspoon of salt and 1 tablespoon of olive oil. Toss well and set aside.
6.	Stir together the remaining 1 tablespoon of olive oil, panko, and Parmesan cheese (if desired) in a small bowl.
7.	After 6 minutes, remove the pan and add the tomato mixture to the sheet pan and stir to mix well. Scatter the panko mixture on top. Return the pan to the oven and continue cooking for 6 minutes, or until the vegetables are softened and the topping is golden brown.
8.	Cool for 5 minutes before serving.

Butternut Squash and Parsnip with Thyme

Prep time: 5 minutes | Cook time: 16 minutes | Serves 2

1 parsnip, sliced
1 cup sliced butternut squash
1 small red onion, cut into wedges
½ chopped celery stalk
1 tablespoon chopped fresh thyme
2 teaspoons olive oil
Salt and black pepper, to taste
1.	Toss all the ingredients in a large bowl until the vegetables are well coated.
2.	Transfer the vegetables to the perforated pan.
3.	Select Air Fry. Set temperature to 380ºF (193ºC) and set time to 16 minutes. Press Start to begin preheating.
4.	Once preheated, place the pan into the oven. Stir the vegetables halfway through the cooking time.
5.	When cooking is complete, the vegetables should be golden brown and tender. Remove from the oven and serve warm.

Butternut Squash with Goat Cheese

Prep time: 5 minutes | Cook time: 20 minutes | Serves 2

1 pound (454 g) butternut squash, cut into wedges
2 tablespoons olive oil

1 tablespoon dried rosemary
Salt, to salt
1 cup crumbled goat cheese
1 tablespoon maple syrup
1.   Toss the squash wedges with the olive oil, rosemary, and salt in a large bowl until well coated.
2.   Transfer the squash wedges to the perforated pan, spreading them out in as even a layer as possible.
3.   Select Air Fry. Set temperature to 350ºF (180ºC) and set time to 20 minutes. Press Start to begin preheating.
4.   Once preheated, place the pan into the oven.
5.   After 10 minutes, remove from the oven and flip the squash. Return the pan to the oven and continue cooking for 10 minutes.
6.   When cooking is complete, the squash should be golden brown. Remove the pan from the oven. Sprinkle the goat cheese on top and serve drizzled with the maple syrup.

Ginger-Pepper Broccoli

Prep time: 5 minutes | Cook time: 10 minutes | Serves 2
12 ounces (340 g) broccoli florets
2 tablespoons Asian hot chili oil
1 teaspoon ground Sichuan peppercorns (or black pepper)
2 garlic cloves, finely chopped
1 (2-inch) piece fresh ginger, peeled and finely chopped
Kosher salt and freshly ground black pepper
1.   Toss the broccoli florets with the chili oil, Sichuan peppercorns, garlic, ginger, salt, and pepper in a mixing bowl until thoroughly coated.
2.   Transfer the broccoli florets to the perforated pan.
3.   Select Air Fry. Set temperature to 375ºF (190ºC) and set time to 10 minutes. Press Start to begin preheating.
4.   Once preheated, place the pan into the oven. Stir the broccoli florets halfway through the cooking time.
5.   When cooking is complete, the broccoli florets should be lightly browned and tender. Remove the broccoli from the oven and serve on a plate.

Parmesan Brussels Sprouts

Prep time: 10 minutes | Cook time: 20 minutes | Serves 4
1 pound (454 g) fresh Brussels sprouts, trimmed
1 tablespoon olive oil
½ teaspoon salt
⅛ teaspoon pepper
¼ cup grated Parmesan cheese
1.   In a large bowl, combine the Brussels sprouts with olive oil, salt, and pepper and toss until evenly coated.

2.   Spread the Brussels sprouts evenly in the perforated pan.
3.   Select Air Fry. Set temperature to 330ºF (166ºC) and set time to 20 minutes. Press Start to begin preheating.
4.   Once preheated, place the pan into the oven. Stir the Brussels sprouts twice during cooking.
5.   When cooking is complete, the Brussels sprouts should be golden brown and crisp. Remove the pan from the oven. Sprinkle the grated Parmesan cheese on top and serve warm.

Roasted Veggie Rice with Eggs

Prep time: 5 minutes | Cook time: 12 minutes | Serves 4
2 teaspoons melted butter
1 cup chopped mushrooms
1 cup cooked rice
1 cup peas
1 carrot, chopped
1 red onion, chopped
1 garlic clove, minced
Salt and black pepper, to taste
2 hard-boiled eggs, grated
1 tablespoon soy sauce
1.   Coat a baking dish with melted butter.
2.   Stir together the mushrooms, cooked rice, peas, carrot, onion, garlic, salt, and pepper in a large bowl until well mixed. Pour the mixture into the prepared baking dish.
3.   Select Roast. Set temperature to 380ºF (193ºC) and set time to 12 minutes. Press Start to begin preheating.
4.   Once preheated, place the baking dish into the oven.
5.   When cooking is complete, remove from the oven. Divide the mixture among four plates. Serve warm with a sprinkle of grated eggs and a drizzle of soy sauce.

Air Fried Tofu Sticks

Prep time: 5 minutes | Cook time: 14 minutes | Serves 4
2 tablespoons olive oil, divided
½ cup flour
½ cup crushed cornflakes
Salt and black pepper, to taste
14 ounces (397 g) firm tofu, cut into ½-inch-thick strips
1.   Grease the perforated pan with 1 tablespoon of olive oil.
2.   Combine the flour, cornflakes, salt, and pepper on a plate.
3.   Dredge the tofu strips in the flour mixture until they are completely coated. Transfer the tofu strips to the greased pan.
4.   Drizzle the remaining 1 tablespoon of olive oil over the top of tofu strips.

5.	Select Air Fry. Set temperature to 360ºF (182ºC) and set time to 14 minutes. Press Start to begin preheating.
6.	Once preheated, place the pan into the oven. Flip the tofu strips halfway through the cooking time.
7.	When cooking is complete, the tofu strips should be crispy. Remove from the oven and serve warm.

Garlic Eggplant Slices with Parsley

Prep time: 5 minutes | Cook time: 12 minutes | Serves 4
1 cup flour
4 eggs
Salt, to taste
2 cups bread crumbs
1 teaspoon Italian seasoning
2 eggplants, sliced
2 garlic cloves, sliced
2 tablespoons chopped parsley
Cooking spray
1.	Spritz the perforated pan with cooking spray. Set aside.
2.	On a plate, place the flour. In a shallow bowl, whisk the eggs with salt. In another shallow bowl, combine the bread crumbs and Italian seasoning.
3.	Dredge the eggplant slices, one at a time, in the flour, then in the whisked eggs, finally in the bread crumb mixture to coat well.
4.	Lay the coated eggplant slices in the perforated pan.
5.	Select Air Fry. Set temperature to 390ºF (199ºC) and set time to 12 minutes. Press Start to begin preheating.
6.	Once preheated, place the pan into the oven. Flip the eggplant slices halfway through the cooking time.
7.	When cooking is complete, the eggplant slices should be golden brown and crispy. Transfer the eggplant slices to a plate and sprinkle the garlic and parsley on top before serving.

Cayenne Green Beans

Prep time: 5 minutes | Cook time: 15 minutes | Serves 4
½ cup flour
2 eggs
1 cup panko bread crumbs
½ cup grated Parmesan cheese
1 teaspoon cayenne pepper
Salt and black pepper, to taste
1½ pounds (680 g) green beans
1.	In a bowl, place the flour. In a separate bowl, lightly beat the eggs. In a separate shallow bowl, thoroughly combine the bread crumbs, cheese, cayenne pepper, salt, and pepper.
2.	Dip the green beans in the flour, then in the beaten eggs, finally in the bread crumb mixture to coat well. Transfer the green beans to the perforated pan.
3.	Select Air Fry. Set temperature to 400ºF (205ºC) and set time to 15 minutes. Press Start to begin preheating.
4.	Once preheated, place the pan into the oven. Stir the green beans halfway through the cooking time.
5.	When cooking is complete, remove from the oven to a bowl and serve.

Honey Baby Carrots with Dill

Prep time: 5 minutes | Cook time: 12 minutes | Serves 4
1 pound (454 g) baby carrots
2 tablespoons olive oil
1 tablespoon honey
1 teaspoon dried dill
Salt and black pepper, to taste
1.	Place the carrots in a large bowl. Add the olive oil, honey, dill, salt, and pepper and toss to coat well.
2.	Transfer the carrots to the perforated pan.
3.	Select Roast. Set temperature to 350ºF (180ºC) and set time to 12 minutes. Press Start to begin preheating.
4.	Once preheated, place the pan into the oven. Stir the carrots once during cooking.
5.	When cooking is complete, the carrots should be crisp-tender. Remove from the oven and serve warm.

Garlic Tofu with Basil

Prep time: 5 minutes | Cook time: 10 minutes | Serves 2
1 tablespoon soy sauce
1 tablespoon water
$^1/_3$ teaspoon garlic powder
$^1/_3$ teaspoon onion powder
$^1/_3$ teaspoon dried oregano
$^1/_3$ teaspoon dried basil
Black pepper, to taste
6 ounces (170 g) extra firm tofu, pressed and cubed
1.	In a large mixing bowl, whisk together the soy sauce, water, garlic powder, onion powder, oregano, basil, and black pepper. Add the tofu cubes, stirring to coat, and let them marinate for 10 minutes.
2.	Arrange the tofu in the perforated pan.
3.	Select Bake. Set temperature to 390ºF (199ºC) and set time to 10 minutes. Press Start to begin preheating.
4.	Once preheated, place the pan into the oven. Flip the tofu halfway through the cooking time.
5.	When cooking is complete, the tofu should be crisp.
6.	Remove from the oven to a plate and serve.

Zucchini Quesadilla with Gouda Cheese

Prep time: 5 minutes | Cook time: 10 minutes | Serves 1

1 teaspoon olive oil
2 flour tortillas
¼ zucchini, sliced
¼ yellow bell pepper, sliced
¼ cup shredded Gouda cheese
1 tablespoon chopped cilantro
½ green onion, sliced
1. Coat the perforated pan with 1 teaspoon of olive oil.
2. Arrange a flour tortilla in the perforated pan and scatter the top with zucchini, bell pepper, Gouda cheese, cilantro, and green onion. Place the other flour tortilla on top.
3. Select Air Fry. Set temperature to 390ºF (199ºC) and set time to 10 minutes. Press Start to begin preheating.
4. Once preheated, place the pan into the oven.
5. When cooking is complete, the tortillas should be lightly browned and the vegetables should be tender. Remove from the oven and cool for 5 minutes before slicing into wedges.

Curried Cauliflower with Cashews

Prep time: 5 minutes | Cook time: 12 minutes | Serves 2

4 cups cauliflower florets (about half a large head)
1 tablespoon olive oil
1 teaspoon curry powder
Salt, to taste
½ cup toasted, chopped cashews, for garnish
Yogurt Sauce:
¼ cup plain yogurt
2 tablespoons sour cream
1 teaspoon honey
1 teaspoon lemon juice
Pinch cayenne pepper
Salt, to taste
1 tablespoon chopped fresh cilantro, plus leaves for garnish
1. In a large mixing bowl, toss the cauliflower florets with the olive oil, curry powder, and salt.
2. Place the cauliflower florets in the perforated pan.
3. Select Air Fry. Set temperature to 400ºF (205ºC) and set time to 12 minutes. Press Start to begin preheating.
4. Once preheated, place the pan into the oven. Stir the cauliflower florets twice during cooking.
5. When cooking is complete, the cauliflower should be golden brown.
6. Meanwhile, mix all the ingredients for the yogurt sauce in a small bowl and whisk to combine.
7. Remove the cauliflower from the oven and drizzle with the yogurt sauce. Scatter the toasted cashews and cilantro on top and serve immediately.

Fried Root Veggies with Thyme

Prep time: 10 minutes | Cook time: 22 minutes | Serves 4

2 carrots, sliced
2 potatoes, cut into chunks
1 rutabaga, cut into chunks
1 turnip, cut into chunks
1 beet, cut into chunks
8 shallots, halved
2 tablespoons olive oil
Salt and black pepper, to taste
2 tablespoons tomato pesto
2 tablespoons water
2 tablespoons chopped fresh thyme
1. Toss the carrots, potatoes, rutabaga, turnip, beet, shallots, olive oil, salt, and pepper in a large mixing bowl until the root vegetables are evenly coated.
2. Place the root vegetables in the perforated pan.
3. Select Air Fry. Set temperature to 400ºF (205ºC) and set time to 22 minutes. Press Start to begin preheating.
4. Once preheated, place the pan into the oven. Stir the vegetables twice during cooking.
5. When cooking is complete, the vegetables should be tender.
6. Meanwhile, in a small bowl, whisk together the tomato pesto and water until smooth.
7. When ready, remove the root vegetables from the oven to a platter. Drizzle with the tomato pesto mixture and sprinkle with the thyme. Serve immediately.

Red Chili Okra

Prep time: 5 minutes | Cook time: 10 minutes | Serves 4

3 tablespoons sour cream
2 tablespoons flour
2 tablespoons semolina
½ teaspoon red chili powder
Salt and black pepper, to taste
1 pound (454 g) okra, halved
Cooking spray
1. Spray the perforated pan with cooking spray. Set aside.
2. In a shallow bowl, place the sour cream. In another shallow bowl, thoroughly combine the flour, semolina, red chili powder, salt, and pepper.
3. Dredge the okra in the sour cream, then roll in the flour mixture until evenly coated. Transfer the okra to the perforated pan.
4. Select Air Fry. Set temperature to 400ºF (205ºC) and set time to 10 minutes. Press Start to begin preheating.
5. Once preheated, place the pan into the oven. Flip the okra halfway through the cooking time.
6. When cooking is complete, the okra should be golden brown and crispy. Remove the pan from the oven. Cool for 5 minutes before serving.

Veggie and Oat Meatballs

Prep time: 15 minutes | Cook time: 18 minutes | Serves 3

½ cup grated carrots
½ cup sweet onions
2 tablespoons olive oil
1 cup rolled oats
½ cup roasted cashews
2 cups cooked chickpeas
Juice of 1 lemon
2 tablespoons soy sauce
1 tablespoon flax meal
1 teaspoon garlic powder
1 teaspoon cumin
½ teaspoon turmeric

1. Mix the carrots, onions, and olive oil in a baking dish and stir to combine.
2. Select Roast. Set temperature to 350ºF (180ºC) and set time to 6 minutes. Press Start to begin preheating.
3. Once preheated, place the baking dish into the oven. Stir the vegetables halfway through.
4. When cooking is complete, the vegetables should be tender.
5. Meanwhile, put the oats and cashews in a food processor or blender and pulse until coarsely ground. Transfer the mixture to a large bowl. Add the chickpeas, lemon juice, and soy sauce to the food processor and pulse until smooth. Transfer the chickpea mixture to the bowl of oat and cashew mixture.
6. Remove the carrots and onions from the oven to the bowl of chickpea mixture. Add the flax meal, garlic powder, cumin, and turmeric and stir to incorporate.
7. Scoop tablespoon-sized portions of the veggie mixture and roll them into balls with your hands. Transfer the balls to the perforated pan.
8. Increase the temperature to 370ºF (188ºC) and set time to 12 minutes on Bake. Place the pan into the oven. Flip the balls halfway through the cooking time.
9. When cooking is complete, the balls should be golden brown.
10. Serve warm.

Garlic Bell Peppers with Marjoram

Prep time: 10 minutes | Cook time: 22 minutes | Serves 4

1 green bell pepper, sliced into 1-inch strips
1 red bell pepper, sliced into 1-inch strips
1 orange bell pepper, sliced into 1-inch strips
1 yellow bell pepper, sliced into 1-inch strips
2 tablespoons olive oil, divided
½ teaspoon dried marjoram
Pinch salt
Freshly ground black pepper, to taste
1 head garlic

1. Toss the bell peppers with 1 tablespoon of olive oil in a large bowl until well coated. Season with the marjoram, salt, and pepper. Toss again and set aside.
2. Cut off the top of a head of garlic. Place the garlic cloves on a large square of aluminum foil. Drizzle the top with the remaining 1 tablespoon of olive oil and wrap the garlic cloves in foil.
3. Transfer the garlic to the perforated pan.
4. Select Roast. Set temperature to 330ºF (166ºC) and set time to 15 minutes. Press Start to begin preheating.
5. Once preheated, place the pan into the oven.
6. After 15 minutes, remove the perforated pan from the oven and add the bell peppers. Return to the oven and set time to 7 minutes.
7. When cooking is complete or until the garlic is soft and the bell peppers are tender.
8. TRANSFER THE COOKED BELL PEPPERS TO A PLATE. REMOVE THE GARLIC AND UNWRAP THE FOIL. LET THE GARLIC REST FOR A FEW MINUTES. ONCE COOLED, SQUEEZE THE ROASTED GARLIC CLOVES OUT OF THEIR SKINS AND ADD THEM TO THE PLATE OF BELL PEPPERS. STIR WELL AND SERVE IMMEDIATELY.

Carrot, Tofu and Cauliflower Rice

Prep time: 10 minutes | Cook time: 22 minutes | Serves 4

½ block tofu, crumbled
1 cup diced carrot
½ cup diced onions
2 tablespoons soy sauce
1 teaspoon turmeric

Cauliflower:

3 cups cauliflower rice
½ cup chopped broccoli
½ cup frozen peas
2 tablespoons soy sauce
1 tablespoon minced ginger
2 garlic cloves, minced
1 tablespoon rice vinegar
1½ teaspoons toasted sesame oil

1. Mix the tofu, carrot, onions, soy sauce, and turmeric in a baking dish and stir until well incorporated.
2. Select Roast. Set temperature to 370ºF (188ºC) and set time to 10 minutes. Press Start to begin preheating.
3. Once preheated, place the baking dish into the oven. Flip the tofu and carrot halfway through the cooking time.
4. When cooking is complete, the tofu should be crisp.
5. Meanwhile, in a large bowl, combine all the ingredients for the cauliflower and toss well.
6. Remove the dish from the oven and add the cauliflower mixture to the tofu and stir to combine.

7.	Return the baking dish to the oven and set time to 12 minutes on Roast. Place the baking dish into the oven
8.	When cooking is complete, the vegetables should be tender.
9.	Cool for 5 minutes before serving.

Halloumi Zucchinis and Eggplant

Prep time: 5 minutes | Cook time: 14 minutes | Serves 2
2 zucchinis, cut into even chunks
1 large eggplant, peeled, cut into chunks
1 large carrot, cut into chunks
6 ounces (170 g) halloumi cheese, cubed
2 teaspoons olive oil
Salt and black pepper, to taste
1 teaspoon dried mixed herbs
1.	Combine the zucchinis, eggplant, carrot, cheese, olive oil, salt, and pepper in a large bowl and toss to coat well.
2.	Spread the mixture evenly in the perforated pan.
3.	Select Air Fry. Set temperature to 340ºF (171ºC) and set time to 14 minutes. Press Start to begin preheating.
4.	Once preheated, place the pan into the oven. Stir the mixture once during cooking.
5.	When cooking is complete, they should be crispy and golden. Remove from the oven and serve topped with mixed herbs.

Breaded Zucchini Chips with Parmesan

Prep time: 5 minutes | Cook time: 14 minutes | Serves 4
2 egg whites
Salt and black pepper, to taste
½ cup seasoned bread crumbs
2 tablespoons grated Parmesan cheese
¼ teaspoon garlic powder
2 medium zucchini, sliced
Cooking spray
1.	Spritz the perforated pan with cooking spray.
2.	In a bowl, beat the egg whites with salt and pepper. In a separate bowl, thoroughly combine the bread crumbs, Parmesan cheese, and garlic powder.
3.	Dredge the zucchini slices in the egg white, then coat in the bread crumb mixture.
4.	Arrange the zucchini slices in the perforated pan.
5.	Select Air Fry. Set temperature to 400ºF (205ºC) and set time to 14 minutes. Press Start to begin preheating.
6.	Once preheated, place the pan into the oven. Flip the zucchini halfway through.
7.	When cooking is complete, the zucchini should be tender.
8.	Remove from the oven to a plate and serve.

Roasted Veggies with Honey-Garlic Glaze

Prep time: 15 minutes | Cook time: 20 minutes | Makes 3 cups
Glaze:
2 tablespoons raw honey
2 teaspoons minced garlic
¼ teaspoon dried marjoram
¼ teaspoon dried basil
¼ teaspoon dried oregano
⅛ teaspoon dried sage
⅛ teaspoon dried rosemary
⅛ teaspoon dried thyme
½ teaspoon salt
¼ teaspoon ground black pepper
Veggies:
3 to 4 medium red potatoes, cut into 1- to 2-inch pieces
1 small zucchini, cut into 1- to 2-inch pieces
1 small carrot, sliced into ¼-inch rounds
1 (10.5-ounce / 298-g) package cherry tomatoes, halved
1 cup sliced mushrooms
3 tablespoons olive oil
1.	Combine the honey, garlic, marjoram, basil, oregano, sage, rosemary, thyme, salt, and pepper in a small bowl and stir to mix well. Set aside.
2.	Place the red potatoes, zucchini, carrot, cherry tomatoes, and mushroom in a large bowl. Drizzle with the olive oil and toss to coat.
3.	Pour the veggies into the perforated pan.
4.	Select Roast. Set temperature to 380ºF (193ºC) and set time to 15 minutes. Press Start to begin preheating.
5.	Once preheated, place the pan into the oven. Stir the veggies halfway through.
6.	When cooking is complete, the vegetables should be tender.
7.	When ready, transfer the roasted veggies to the large bowl. Pour the honey mixture over the veggies, tossing to coat.
8.	Spread out the veggies in a baking pan and place in the oven.
9.	Increase the temperature to 390ºF (199ºC) and set time to 5 minutes on Roast. Place the pan into the oven.
10.	When cooking is complete, the veggies should be tender and glazed. Serve warm.

Garlic Ratatouille

Prep time: 15 minutes | Cook time: 16 minutes | Serves 2
2 Roma tomatoes, thinly sliced
1 zucchini, thinly sliced
2 yellow bell peppers, sliced
2 garlic cloves, minced
2 tablespoons olive oil
2 tablespoons herbes de Provence
1 tablespoon vinegar
Salt and black pepper, to taste

1.	Place the tomatoes, zucchini, bell peppers, garlic, olive oil, herbes de Provence, and vinegar in a large bowl and toss until the vegetables are evenly coated. Sprinkle with salt and pepper and toss again. Pour the vegetable mixture into a baking dish.
2.	Select Roast. Set temperature to 390ºF (199ºC) and set time to 16 minutes. Press Start to begin preheating.
3.	Once preheated, place the baking dish into the oven. Stir the vegetables halfway through.
4.	When cooking is complete, the vegetables should be tender.
5.	Let the vegetable mixture stand for 5 minutes in the oven before removing and serving.

Cauliflower with Teriyaki Sauce

Prep time: 5 minutes | Cook time: 14 minutes | Serves 4
½ cup soy sauce
$^1/_3$ cup water
1 tablespoon brown sugar
1 teaspoon sesame oil
1 teaspoon cornstarch
2 cloves garlic, chopped
½ teaspoon chili powder
1 big cauliflower head, cut into florets
1.	Make the teriyaki sauce: In a small bowl, whisk together the soy sauce, water, brown sugar, sesame oil, cornstarch, garlic, and chili powder until well combined.
2.	Place the cauliflower florets in a large bowl and drizzle the top with the prepared teriyaki sauce and toss to coat well.
3.	Put the cauliflower florets in the perforated pan.
4.	Select Air Fry. Set temperature to 340ºF (171ºC) and set time to 14 minutes. Press Start to begin preheating.
5.	Once preheated, place the pan into the oven. Stir the cauliflower halfway through.
6.	When cooking is complete, the cauliflower should be crisp-tender.
7.	Let the cauliflower cool for 5 minutes before serving.

Onion-Stuffed Mushrooms

Prep time: 5 minutes | Cook time: 12 minutes | Serves 2
18 medium-sized white mushrooms
1 small onion, peeled and chopped
4 garlic cloves, peeled and minced
2 tablespoons olive oil
2 teaspoons cumin powder
A pinch ground allspice
Fine sea salt and freshly ground black pepper, to taste
1.	On a clean work surface, remove the mushroom stems. Using a spoon, scoop out the mushroom gills and discard.

2.	Thoroughly combine the onion, garlic, olive oil, cumin powder, allspice, salt, and pepper in a mixing bowl. Stuff the mushrooms evenly with the mixture.
3.	Place the stuffed mushrooms in the perforated pan.
4.	Select Roast. Set temperature to 345ºF (174ºC) and set time to 12 minutes. Press Start to begin preheating.
5.	Once preheated, place the pan into the oven.
6.	When cooking is complete, the mushroom should be browned.
7.	Cool for 5 minutes before serving.

Garlic Turnip and Zucchini

Prep time: 5 minutes | Cook time: 18 minutes | Serves 4
3 turnips, sliced
1 large zucchini, sliced
1 large red onion, cut into rings
2 cloves garlic, crushed
1 tablespoon olive oil
Salt and black pepper, to taste
1.	Put the turnips, zucchini, red onion, and garlic in a baking pan. Drizzle the olive oil over the top and sprinkle with the salt and pepper.
2.	Select Bake. Set temperature to 330ºF (166ºC) and set time to 18 minutes. Press Start to begin preheating.
3.	Once preheated, place the pan into the oven.
4.	When cooking is complete, the vegetables should be tender. Remove from the oven and serve on a plate.

Balsamic-Glazed Beets

Prep time: 5 minutes | Cook time: 10 minutes | Serves 2
Beet:
2 beets, cubed
2 tablespoons olive oil
2 springs rosemary, chopped
Salt and black pepper, to taste
Balsamic Glaze:
$^1/_3$ cup balsamic vinegar
1 tablespoon honey
1.	Combine the beets, olive oil, rosemary, salt, and pepper in a mixing bowl and toss until the beets are completely coated.
2.	Place the beets in the perforated pan.
3.	Select Air Fry. Set temperature to 400ºF (205ºC) and set time to 10 minutes. Press Start to begin preheating.
4.	Once preheated, place the pan into the oven. Stir the vegetables halfway through.
5.	When cooking is complete, the beets should be crisp and browned at the edges.
6.	Meanwhile, make the balsamic glaze: Place the balsamic vinegar and honey in a small saucepan and bring to a boil over medium heat. When the

sauce boils, reduce the heat to medium-low heat and simmer until the liquid is reduced by half.

7.   When ready, remove the beets from the oven to a platter. Pour the balsamic glaze over the top and serve immediately.

Mozzarella Walnut Stuffed Mushrooms

Prep time: 5 minutes | Cook time: 10 minutes | Serves 4

4 large portobello mushrooms
1 tablespoon canola oil
½ cup shredded Mozzarella cheese
$^1/_3$ cup minced walnuts
2 tablespoons chopped fresh parsley
Cooking spray

1.   Spritz the perforated pan with cooking spray.
2.   On a clean work surface, remove the mushroom stems. Scoop out the gills with a spoon and discard. Coat the mushrooms with canola oil. Top each mushroom evenly with the shredded Mozzarella cheese, followed by the minced walnuts.
3.   Arrange the mushrooms in the perforated pan.
4.   Select Roast. Set temperature to 350ºF (180ºC) and set time to 10 minutes. Press Start to begin preheating.
5.   Once preheated, place the pan into the oven.
6.   When cooking is complete, the mushroom should be golden brown.
7.   Transfer the mushrooms to a plate and sprinkle the parsley on top for garnish before serving.

Tomato-Stuffed Portobello Mushrooms

Prep time: 5 minutes | Cook time: 8 minutes | Serves 4

4 portobello mushrooms, stem removed
1 tablespoon olive oil
1 tomato, diced
½ green bell pepper, diced
½ small red onion, diced
½ teaspoon garlic powder
Salt and black pepper, to taste
½ cup grated Mozzarella cheese

1.   Using a spoon to scoop out the gills of the mushrooms and discard them. Brush the mushrooms with the olive oil.
2.   In a mixing bowl, stir together the remaining ingredients except the Mozzarella cheese. Using a spoon to stuff each mushroom with the filling and scatter the Mozzarella cheese on top.
3.   Arrange the mushrooms in the perforated pan.
4.   Select Roast. Set temperature to 330ºF (166ºC) and set time to 8 minutes. Press Start to begin preheating.
5.   Once preheated, place the pan into the oven.
6.   When cooking is complete, the cheese should be melted.

7.   Serve warm.

Roasted Veggie Salad with Lemon

Prep time: 5 minutes | Cook time: 20 minutes | Serves 2

1 potato, chopped
1 carrot, sliced diagonally
1 cup cherry tomatoes
½ small beetroot, sliced
¼ onion, sliced
½ teaspoon turmeric
½ teaspoon cumin
¼ teaspoon sea salt
2 tablespoons olive oil, divided
A handful of arugula
A handful of baby spinach
Juice of 1 lemon
3 tablespoons canned chickpeas, for serving
Parmesan shavings, for serving

1.   Combine the potato, carrot, cherry tomatoes, beetroot, onion, turmeric, cumin, salt, and 1 tablespoon of olive oil in a large bowl and toss until well coated.
2.   Arrange the veggies in the perforated pan.
3.   Select Roast. Set temperature to 370ºF (188ºC) and set time to 20 minutes. Press Start to begin preheating.
4.   Once preheated, place the pan into the oven. Stir the vegetables halfway through.
5.   When cooking is complete, the potatoes should be golden brown.
6.   Let the veggies cool for 5 to 10 minutes in the oven.
7.   Put the arugula, baby spinach, lemon juice, and remaining 1 tablespoon of olive oil in a salad bowl and stir to combine. Mix in the roasted veggies and toss well.
8.   Scatter the chickpeas and Parmesan shavings on top and serve immediately.

Spinach-Stuffed Beefsteak Tomatoes

Prep time: 10 minutes | Cook time: 18 minutes | Serves 4

4 medium beefsteak tomatoes, rinsed
½ cup grated carrot
1 medium onion, chopped
1 garlic clove, minced
2 teaspoons olive oil
2 cups fresh baby spinach
¼ cup crumbled low-sodium feta cheese
½ teaspoon dried basil

1.   On your cutting board, cut a thin slice off the top of each tomato. Scoop out a ¼- to ½-inch-thick tomato pulp and place the tomatoes upside down on paper towels to drain. Set aside.
2.   Stir together the carrot, onion, garlic, and olive oil in a baking pan.

3.	Select Bake. Set temperature to 350ºF (180ºC) and set time to 5 minutes. Press Start to begin preheating.
4.	Once preheated, place the pan into the oven. Stir the vegetables halfway through.
5.	When cooking is complete, the carrot should be crisp-tender.
6.	Remove the pan from the oven and stir in the spinach, feta cheese, and basil.
7.	Spoon ¼ of the vegetable mixture into each tomato and transfer the stuffed tomatoes to the oven. Set time to 13 minutes on Bake.
8.	When cooking is complete, the filling should be hot and the tomatoes should be lightly caramelized.
9.	Let the tomatoes cool for 5 minutes and serve.

Potato and Asparagus Platter

Prep time: 5 minutes | Cook time: 26 minutes | Serves 5
4 medium potatoes, cut into wedges
Cooking spray
1 bunch asparagus, trimmed
2 tablespoons olive oil
Salt and pepper, to taste
Cheese Sauce:
¼ cup crumbled cottage cheese
¼ cup buttermilk
1 tablespoon whole-grain mustard
Salt and black pepper, to taste
1.	Spritz the perforated pan with cooking spray.
2.	Put the potatoes in the perforated pan.
3.	Select Roast. Set temperature to 400ºF (205ºC) and set time to 20 minutes. Press Start to begin preheating.
4.	Once preheated, place the pan into the oven. Stir the potatoes halfway through.
5.	When cooking is complete, the potatoes should be golden brown.
6.	Remove the potatoes from the oven to a platter. Cover the potatoes with foil to keep warm. Set aside.
7.	Place the asparagus in the perforated pan and drizzle with the olive oil. Sprinkle with salt and pepper.
8.	Select Roast. Set temperature to 400ºF (205ºC) and set time to 6 minutes. Place the pan into the oven. Stir the asparagus halfway through.
9.	When cooking is complete, the asparagus should be crispy.
10.	Meanwhile, make the cheese sauce by stirring together the cottage cheese, buttermilk, and mustard in a small bowl. Season as needed with salt and pepper.
11.	Transfer the asparagus to the platter of potatoes and drizzle with the cheese sauce. Serve immediately.

Pepper-Stuffed Portobellos

Prep time: 15 minutes | Cook time: 15 minutes | Serves 4
4 tablespoons sherry vinegar or white wine vinegar
6 garlic cloves, minced, divided
1 tablespoon fresh thyme leaves
1 teaspoon Dijon mustard
1 teaspoon kosher salt, divided
¼ cup plus 3¼ teaspoons extra-virgin olive oil, divided
8 portobello mushroom caps, each about 3 inches across, patted dry
1 small red or yellow bell pepper, thinly sliced
1 small green bell pepper, thinly sliced
1 small onion, thinly sliced
¼ teaspoon red pepper flakes
Freshly ground black pepper, to taste
4 ounces (113 g) shredded Fontina cheese
1.	Stir together the vinegar, 4 minced garlic cloves, thyme, mustard, and ½ teaspoon of kosher salt in a small bowl. Slowly pour in ¼ cup of olive oil, whisking constantly, or until an emulsion is formed. Reserve 2 tablespoons of the marinade and set aside.
2.	Put the mushrooms in a resealable plastic bag and pour in the marinade. Seal and shake the bag, coating the mushrooms in the marinade. Transfer the mushrooms to the sheet pan, gill-side down.
3.	Put the remaining 2 minced garlic cloves, bell peppers, onion, red pepper flakes, remaining ½ teaspoon of salt, and black pepper in a medium bowl. Drizzle with the remaining 3¼ teaspoons of olive oil and toss well. Transfer the bell pepper mixture to the sheet pan.
4.	Select Roast. Set temperature to 375ºF (190ºC) and set time to 12 minutes. Press Start to begin preheating.
5.	Once preheated, place the pan into the oven.
6.	After 7 minutes, remove the pan and stir the peppers and flip the mushrooms. Return the pan to the oven and continue cooking for 5 minutes.
7.	Remove the pan from the oven and place the pepper mixture onto a cutting board and coarsely chop.
8.	Brush both sides of the mushrooms with the reserved 2 tablespoons marinade. Stuff the caps evenly with the pepper mixture. Scatter the cheese on top.
9.	Select Broil. Set temperature to High and set time to 3 minutes. Place the pan into the oven.
10.	When done, the mushrooms should be tender and the cheese should be melted.
11.	Serve warm.

Chickpea-Stuffed Bell Peppers

Prep time: 10 minutes | Cook time: 18 minutes | Serves 4
4 medium red, green, or yellow bell peppers, halved and deseeded
4 tablespoons extra-virgin olive oil, divided

½ teaspoon kosher salt, divided
1 (15-ounce / 425-g) can chickpeas
1½ cups cooked white rice
½ cup diced roasted red peppers
¼ cup chopped parsley
½ small onion, finely chopped
3 garlic cloves, minced
½ teaspoon cumin
¼ teaspoon freshly ground black pepper
¾ cup panko bread crumbs

1. Brush the peppers inside and out with 1 tablespoon of olive oil. Season the insides with ¼ teaspoon of kosher salt. Arrange the peppers on the sheet pan, cut side up.
2. Place the chickpeas with their liquid into a large bowl. Lightly mash the beans with a potato masher. Sprinkle with the remaining ¼ teaspoon of kosher salt and 1 tablespoon of olive oil. Add the rice, red peppers, parsley, onion, garlic, cumin, and black pepper to the bowl and stir to incorporate.
3. Divide the mixture among the bell pepper halves.
4. Stir together the remaining 2 tablespoons of olive oil and panko in a small bowl. Top the pepper halves with the panko mixture.
5. Select Roast. Set temperature to 375ºF (190ºC) and set time to 18 minutes. Press Start to begin preheating.
6. Once preheated, place the pan into the oven.
7. When done, the peppers should be slightly wrinkled, and the panko should be golden brown.
8. Remove from the oven and serve on a plate.

Stuffed Bell Peppers with Cream Cheese

Prep time: 5 minutes | Cook time: 15 minutes | Serves 2
2 bell peppers, tops and seeds removed
Salt and pepper, to taste
²/₃ cup cream cheese
2 tablespoons mayonnaise
1 tablespoon chopped fresh celery stalks
Cooking spray

1. Spritz the perforated pan with cooking spray.
2. Place the peppers in the perforated pan.
3. Select Roast. Set temperature to 400ºF (205ºC) and set time to 10 minutes. Press Start to begin preheating.
4. Once preheated, place the pan into the oven. Flip the peppers halfway through.
5. When cooking is complete, the peppers should be crisp-tender.
6. Remove from the oven to a plate and season with salt and pepper.
7. Mix the cream cheese, mayo, and celery in a small bowl and stir to incorporate. Evenly stuff the roasted peppers with the cream cheese mixture with a spoon. Serve immediately.

Mozzarella Tomato-Stuffed Squash

Prep time: 5 minutes | Cook time: 30 minutes | Serves 4
1 pound (454 g) butternut squash, ends trimmed
2 teaspoons olive oil, divided
6 grape tomatoes, halved
1 poblano pepper, cut into strips
Salt and black pepper, to taste
¼ cup grated Mozzarella cheese

1. Using a large knife, cut the squash in half lengthwise on a flat work surface. This recipe just needs half of the squash. Scoop out the flesh to make room for the stuffing. Coat the squash half with 1 teaspoon of olive oil.
2. Put the squash half in the perforated pan.
3. Select Bake. Set temperature to 350ºF (180ºC) and set time to 15 minutes. Press Start to begin preheating.
4. Once preheated, place the pan into the oven. Flip the squash halfway through.
5. When cooking is complete, the squash should be tender.
6. Meanwhile, thoroughly combine the tomatoes, poblano pepper, remaining 1 teaspoon of olive oil, salt, and pepper in a bowl.
7. Remove the pan from the oven and spoon the tomato mixture into the squash. Return to the oven.
8. Select Roast. Set time to 15 minutes. Place the pan into the oven
9. After 12 minutes, remove the pan from the oven. Scatter the Mozzarella cheese on top. Return the pan to the oven and continue cooking.
10. When cooking is complete, the tomatoes should be soft and the cheese should be melted.
11. Cool for 5 minutes before serving.

Rice and Olives Stuffed Peppers

Prep time: 5 minutes | Cook time: 16 to 17 minutes | Serves 4
4 red bell peppers, tops sliced off
2 cups cooked rice
1 cup crumbled feta cheese
1 onion, chopped
¼ cup sliced kalamata olives
¾ cup tomato sauce
1 tablespoon Greek seasoning
Salt and black pepper, to taste
2 tablespoons chopped fresh dill, for serving

1. Microwave the red bell peppers for 1 to 2 minutes until tender.
2. When ready, transfer the red bell peppers to a plate to cool.
3. Mix the cooked rice, feta cheese, onion, kalamata olives, tomato sauce, Greek seasoning, salt, and pepper in a medium bowl and stir until well combined.
4. Divide the rice mixture among the red bell peppers and transfer to a greased baking dish.

5.	Select Bake. Set temperature to 360ºF (182ºC) and set time to 15 minutes. Press Start to begin preheating.
6.	Once preheated, place the baking dish into the oven.

7.	When cooking is complete, the rice should be heated through and the vegetables should be soft.
8.	Remove from the oven and serve with the dill sprinkled on top.

CHAPTER 6 VEGETABLE SIDES

Garlic-Lime Shishito Peppers

Prep time: 5 minutes | Cook time: 9 minutes | Serves 3
½ pound (227 g) shishito peppers, rinsed
Cooking spray
Sauce:
1 tablespoon tamari or shoyu
2 teaspoons fresh lime juice
2 large garlic cloves, minced
1.	Spritz the perforated pan with cooking spray.
2.	Place the shishito peppers in the perforated pan and spritz them with cooking spray.
3.	Select Roast. Set temperature to 392ºF (200ºC) and set time to 9 minutes. Press Start to begin preheating.
4.	Once preheated, place the pan into the oven.
5.	Meanwhile, whisk together all the ingredients for the sauce in a large bowl. Set aside.
6.	After 3 minutes, remove the pan from the oven. Flip the peppers and spritz them with cooking spray. Return to the oven and continue cooking.
7.	After another 3 minutes, remove the pan from the oven. Flip the peppers and spray with cooking spray. Return to the oven and continue roasting for 3 minutes more, or until the peppers are blistered and nicely browned.
8.	When cooking is complete, remove the peppers from the oven to the bowl of sauce. Toss to coat well and serve immediately.

Garlic Zucchini Sticks

Prep time: 5 minutes | Cook time: 14 minutes | Serves 4
2 small zucchini, cut into 2-inch × ½-inch sticks
3 tablespoons chickpea flour
2 teaspoons arrowroot (or cornstarch)
½ teaspoon garlic granules
¼ teaspoon sea salt
⅛ teaspoon freshly ground black pepper
1 tablespoon water
Cooking spray
1.	Combine the zucchini sticks with the chickpea flour, arrowroot, garlic granules, salt, and pepper in a medium bowl and toss to coat. Add the water and stir to mix well.
2.	Spritz the perforated pan with cooking spray and spread out the zucchini sticks in the pan. Mist the zucchini sticks with cooking spray.
3.	Select Air Fry. Set temperature to 392ºF (200ºC) and set time to 14 minutes. Press Start to begin preheating.
4.	Once preheated, place the pan into the oven. Stir the sticks halfway through the cooking time.
5.	When cooking is complete, the zucchini sticks should be crispy and nicely browned. Remove from the oven and serve warm.

Garlic Potatoes with Heavy Cream

Prep time: 5 minutes | Cook time: 15 to 20 minutes | Serves 4
2 cup sliced frozen potatoes, thawed
3 cloves garlic, minced
Pinch salt
Freshly ground black pepper, to taste
¾ cup heavy cream
1.	Toss the potatoes with the garlic, salt, and black pepper in a baking pan until evenly coated. Pour the heavy cream over the top.
2.	Select Bake. Set temperature to 380ºF (193ºC) and set time to 15 minutes. Press Start to begin preheating.
3.	Once preheated, place the pan into the oven.
4.	When cooking is complete, the potatoes should be tender and the top golden brown. Check for doneness and bake for another 5 minutes if needed. Remove from the oven and serve hot.

Garlic Zucchini Crisps

Prep time: 5 minutes | Cook time: 14 minutes | Serves 4
2 zucchini, sliced into ¼- to ½-inch-thick rounds (about 2 cups)
¼ teaspoon garlic granules
⅛ teaspoon sea salt
Freshly ground black pepper, to taste (optional)
Cooking spray
1.	Spritz the perforated pan with cooking spray.
2.	Put the zucchini rounds in the perforated pan, spreading them out as much as possible. Top with a sprinkle of garlic granules, sea salt, and black pepper (if desired). Spritz the zucchini rounds with cooking spray.
3.	Select Roast. Set temperature to 392ºF (200ºC) and set time to 14 minutes. Press Start to begin preheating.
4.	Once preheated, place the pan into the oven. Flip the zucchini rounds halfway through.
5.	When cooking is complete, the zucchini rounds should be crisp-tender. Remove from the oven. Let them rest for 5 minutes and serve.

Garlicky Cabbage with Red Pepper

Prep time: 5 minutes | Cook time: 7 minutes | Serves 4
1 head cabbage, sliced into 1-inch-thick ribbons
1 tablespoon olive oil
1 teaspoon garlic powder
1 teaspoon red pepper flakes
1 teaspoon salt
1 teaspoon freshly ground black pepper

1. Toss the cabbage with the olive oil, garlic powder, red pepper flakes, salt, and pepper in a large mixing bowl until well coated.
2. Transfer the cabbage to the perforated pan.
3. Select Roast. Set temperature to 350ºF (180ºC) and set time to 7 minutes. Press Start to begin preheating.
4. Once preheated, place the pan into the oven. Flip the cabbage with tongs halfway through the cooking time.
5. When cooking is complete, the cabbage should be crisp. Remove from the oven to a plate and serve warm.

Maple Garlic Brussels Sprouts

Prep time: 10 minutes | Cook time: 11 minutes | Serves 4
2½ cups trimmed Brussels sprouts
Sauce:
1½ teaspoons mellow white miso
1½ tablespoons maple syrup
1 teaspoon toasted sesame oil
1 teaspoons tamari or shoyu
1 teaspoon grated fresh ginger
2 large garlic cloves, finely minced
¼ to ½ teaspoon red chili flakes
Cooking spray
1. Spritz the perforated pan with cooking spray.
2. Arrange the Brussels sprouts in the perforated pan and spray them with cooking spray.
3. Select Air Fry. Set temperature to 392ºF (200ºC) and set time to 11 minutes. Press Start to begin preheating.
4. Once preheated, place the pan into the oven.
5. After 6 minutes, remove the pan from the oven. Flip the Brussels sprouts and spritz with cooking spray again. Return to the oven and continue cooking for 5 minutes more.
6. Meanwhile, make the sauce: Stir together the miso and maple syrup in a medium bowl. Add the sesame oil, tamari, ginger, garlic, and red chili flakes and whisk to combine.
7. When cooking is complete, the Brussels sprouts should be crisp-tender. Transfer the Brussels sprouts to the bowl of sauce, tossing to coat well. If you prefer a saltier taste, you can add additional ½ teaspoon tamari to the sauce. Serve immediately.

Garlic Butternut Squash Croquettes

Prep time: 5 minutes | Cook time: 17 minutes | Serves 4
$^1/_3$ butternut squash, peeled and grated
$^1/_3$ cup all-purpose flour
2 eggs, whisked
4 cloves garlic, minced
1½ tablespoons olive oil
1 teaspoon fine sea salt

$^1/_3$ teaspoon freshly ground black pepper, or more to taste
$^1/_3$ teaspoon dried sage
A pinch of ground allspice
1. Line the perforated pan with parchment paper. Set aside.
2. In a mixing bowl, stir together all the ingredients until well combined.
3. Make the squash croquettes: Use a small cookie scoop to drop tablespoonfuls of the squash mixture onto a lightly floured surface and shape into balls with your hands. Transfer them to the perforated pan.
4. Select Air Fry. Set temperature to 345ºF (174ºC) and set time to 17 minutes. Press Start to begin preheating.
5. Once preheated, place the pan into the oven.
6. When cooking is complete, the squash croquettes should be golden brown. Remove from the oven to a plate and serve warm.

Lime Sweet Potatoes with Allspice

Prep time: 5 minutes | Cook time: 22 minutes | Serves 4
5 garnet sweet potatoes, peeled and diced
1½ tablespoons fresh lime juice
1 tablespoon butter, melted
2 teaspoons tamarind paste
1½ teaspoon ground allspice
$^1/_3$ teaspoon white pepper
½ teaspoon turmeric powder
A few drops liquid stevia
1. In a large mixing bowl, combine all the ingredients and toss until the sweet potatoes are evenly coated. Place the sweet potatoes in the perforated pan.
2. Select Air Fry. Set temperature to 400ºF (205ºC) and set time to 22 minutes. Press Start to begin preheating.
3. Once preheated, place the pan into the oven. Stir the potatoes twice during cooking.
4. When cooking is complete, the potatoes should be crispy on the outside and soft on the inside. Let the potatoes cool for 5 minutes before serving.

Citrus Carrots with Balsamic Glaze

Prep time: 5 minutes | Cook time: 18 minutes | Serves 3
3 medium-size carrots, cut into 2-inch × ½-inch sticks
1 tablespoon orange juice
2 teaspoons balsamic vinegar
1 teaspoon maple syrup
1 teaspoon avocado oil
½ teaspoon dried rosemary
¼ teaspoon sea salt
¼ teaspoon lemon zest
1. Put the carrots in a baking pan and sprinkle with the orange juice, balsamic vinegar, maple syrup,

avocado oil, rosemary, sea salt, finished by the lemon zest. Toss well.
2.   Select Roast. Set temperature to 392ºF (200ºC) and set time to 18 minutes. Press Start to begin preheating.
3.   Once preheated, place the pan into the oven. Stir the carrots several times during the cooking process.
4.   When cooking is complete, the carrots should be nicely glazed and tender. Remove from the oven and serve hot.

Sesame Green Beans with Sriracha

Prep time: 5 minutes | Cook time: 8 minutes | Serves 4
1 tablespoon reduced-sodium soy sauce or tamari
½ tablespoon Sriracha sauce
4 teaspoons toasted sesame oil, divided
12 ounces (340 g) trimmed green beans
½ tablespoon toasted sesame seeds
1.   Whisk together the soy sauce, Sriracha sauce, and 1 teaspoon of sesame oil in a small bowl until smooth. Set aside.
2.   Toss the green beans with the remaining sesame oil in a large bowl until evenly coated.
3.   Place the green beans in the perforated pan in a single layer.
4.   Select Air Fry. Set temperature to 375ºF (190ºC) and set time to 8 minutes. Press Start to begin preheating.
5.   Once preheated, place the pan into the oven. Stir the green beans halfway through the cooking time.
6.   When cooking is complete, the green beans should be lightly charred and tender. Remove from the oven to a platter. Pour the prepared sauce over the top of green beans and toss well. Serve sprinkled with the toasted sesame seeds.

Corn Casserole with Swiss Cheese

Prep time: 5 minutes | Cook time: 15 minutes | Serves 4
2 cups frozen yellow corn
1 egg, beaten
3 tablespoons flour
½ cup grated Swiss or Havarti cheese
½ cup light cream
¼ cup milk
Pinch salt
Freshly ground black pepper, to taste
2 tablespoons butter, cut into cubes
Nonstick cooking spray
1.   Spritz a baking pan with nonstick cooking spray.
2.   Stir together the remaining ingredients except the butter in a medium bowl until well incorporated. Transfer the mixture to the prepared baking pan and scatter with the butter cubes.

3.   Select Bake. Set temperature to 320ºF (160ºC) and set time to 15 minutes. Press Start to begin preheating.
4.   Once preheated, place the pan into the oven.
5.   When cooking is complete, the top should be golden brown and a toothpick inserted in the center should come out clean. Remove the pan from the oven. Let the casserole cool for 5 minutes before slicing into wedges and serving.

Parmesan Corn on the Cob

Prep time: 10 minutes | Cook time: 15 minutes | Serves 4
2 tablespoon olive oil, divided
2 tablespoons grated Parmesan cheese
1 teaspoon garlic powder
1 teaspoon chili powder
1 teaspoon ground cumin
1 teaspoon paprika
1 teaspoon salt
¼ teaspoon cayenne pepper (optional)
4 ears fresh corn, shucked
1.   Grease the perforated pan with 1 tablespoon of olive oil. Set aside.
2.   Combine the Parmesan cheese, garlic powder, chili powder, cumin, paprika, salt, and cayenne pepper (if desired) in a small bowl and stir to mix well.
3.   Lightly coat the ears of corn with the remaining 1 tablespoon of olive oil. Rub the cheese mixture all over the ears of corn until completely coated.
4.   Arrange the ears of corn in the greased pan in a single layer.
5.   Select Air Fry. Set temperature to 400ºF (205ºC) and set time to 15 minutes. Press Start to begin preheating.
6.   Once preheated, place the pan into the oven. Flip the ears of corn halfway through the cooking time.
7.   When cooking is complete, they should be lightly browned. Remove from the oven and let them cool for 5 minutes before serving.

Brown Sugar Acorn Squash

Prep time: 5 minutes | Cook time: 15 minutes | Serves 2
1 medium acorn squash, halved crosswise and deseeded
1 teaspoon coconut oil
1 teaspoon light brown sugar
Few dashes of ground cinnamon
Few dashes of ground nutmeg
1.   On a clean work surface, rub the cut sides of the acorn squash with coconut oil. Scatter with the brown sugar, cinnamon, and nutmeg.
2.   Put the squash halves in the perforated pan, cut-side up.

3. Select Air Fry. Set temperature to 325ºF (163ºC) and set time to 15 minutes. Press Start to begin preheating.
4. Once preheated, place the pan into the oven.
5. When cooking is complete, the squash halves should be just tender when pierced in the center with a paring knife. Remove the pan from the oven. Rest for 5 to 10 minutes and serve warm.

Greek Potatoes with Chives

Prep time: 5 minutes | Cook time: 35 minutes | Serves 4

4 (7-ounce / 198-g) russet potatoes, rinsed
Olive oil spray
½ teaspoon kosher salt, divided
½ cup 2% plain Greek yogurt
¼ cup minced fresh chives
Freshly ground black pepper, to taste
1. Pat the potatoes dry and pierce them all over with a fork. Spritz the potatoes with olive oil spray. Sprinkle with ¼ teaspoon of the salt.
2. Transfer the potatoes to the perforated pan.
3. Select Bake. Set temperature to 400ºF (205ºC) and set time to 35 minutes. Press Start to begin preheating.
4. Once preheated, place the pan into the oven.
5. When cooking is complete, the potatoes should be fork-tender. Remove from the oven and split open the potatoes. Top with the yogurt, chives, the remaining ¼ teaspoon of salt, and finish with the black pepper. Serve immediately.

Garlic Broccoli with Parmesan

Prep time: 5 minutes | Cook time: 4 minutes | Serves 4

1 pound (454 g) broccoli florets
1 medium shallot, minced
2 tablespoons olive oil
2 tablespoons unsalted butter, melted
2 teaspoons minced garlic
¼ cup grated Parmesan cheese
1. Combine the broccoli florets with the shallot, olive oil, butter, garlic, and Parmesan cheese in a medium bowl and toss until the broccoli florets are thoroughly coated.
2. Place the broccoli florets in the perforated pan in a single layer.
3. Select Roast. Set temperature to 360ºF (182ºC) and set time to 4 minutes. Press Start to begin preheating.
4. Once preheated, place the pan into the oven.
5. When cooking is complete, the broccoli florets should be crisp-tender. Remove from the oven and serve warm.

Breaded Asparagus Fries

Prep time: 15 minutes | Cook time: 6 minutes | Serves 4

2 egg whites

¼ cup water
¼ cup plus 2 tablespoons grated Parmesan cheese, divided
¾ cup panko bread crumbs
¼ teaspoon salt
12 ounces (340 g) fresh asparagus spears, woody ends trimmed
Cooking spray
1. In a shallow dish, whisk together the egg whites and water until slightly foamy. In a separate shallow dish, thoroughly combine ¼ cup of Parmesan cheese, bread crumbs, and salt.
2. Dip the asparagus in the egg white, then roll in the cheese mixture to coat well.
3. Place the asparagus in the perforated pan in a single layer, leaving space between each spear. Spritz the asparagus with cooking spray.
4. Select Air Fry. Set temperature to 390ºF (199ºC) and set time to 6 minutes. Press Start to begin preheating.
5. Once preheated, place the pan into the oven.
6. When cooking is complete, the asparagus should be golden brown and crisp. Remove the pan from the oven. Sprinkle with the remaining 2 tablespoons of cheese and serve hot.

Cheddar Broccoli Gratin

Prep time: 5 minutes | Cook time: 14 minutes | Serves 2

$^1/_3$ cup fat-free milk
1 tablespoon all-purpose or gluten-free flour
½ tablespoon olive oil
½ teaspoon ground sage
¼ teaspoon kosher salt
⅛ teaspoon freshly ground black pepper
2 cups roughly chopped broccoli florets
6 tablespoons shredded Cheddar cheese
2 tablespoons panko bread crumbs
1 tablespoon grated Parmesan cheese
Olive oil spray
1. Spritz a baking dish with olive oil spray.
2. Mix the milk, flour, olive oil, sage, salt, and pepper in a medium bowl and whisk to combine. Stir in the broccoli florets, Cheddar cheese, bread crumbs, and Parmesan cheese and toss to coat.
3. Pour the broccoli mixture into the prepared baking dish.
4. Select Bake. Set temperature to 330ºF (166ºC) and set time to 14 minutes. Press Start to begin preheating.
5. Once preheated, place the baking dish into the oven.
6. When cooking is complete, the top should be golden brown and the broccoli should be tender. Remove from the oven and serve immediately.

Roasted Potatoes with Rosemary

Prep time: 5 minutes | Cook time: 20 minutes | Serves 4

1½ pounds (680 g) small red potatoes, cut into 1-inch cubes
2 tablespoons olive oil
2 tablespoons minced fresh rosemary
1 tablespoon minced garlic
1 teaspoon salt, plus additional as needed
½ teaspoon freshly ground black pepper, plus additional as needed
1.   Toss the potato cubes with the olive oil, rosemary, garlic, salt, and pepper in a large bowl until thoroughly coated.
2.   Arrange the potato cubes in the perforated pan in a single layer.
3.   Select Roast. Set temperature to 400ºF (205ºC) and set time to 20 minutes. Press Start to begin preheating.
4.   Once preheated, place the pan into the oven. Stir the potatoes a few times during cooking for even cooking.
5.   When cooking is complete, the potatoes should be tender. Remove from the oven to a plate. Taste and add additional salt and pepper as needed.

Balsamic Asparagus

Prep time: 5 minutes | Cook time: 10 minutes | Serves 4
1 pound (454 g) asparagus, woody ends trimmed
2 tablespoons olive oil
1 tablespoon balsamic vinegar
2 teaspoons minced garlic
Salt and freshly ground black pepper, to taste
1.   In a large shallow bowl, toss the asparagus with the olive oil, balsamic vinegar, garlic, salt, and pepper until thoroughly coated. Put the asparagus in the perforated pan.

2.   Select Roast. Set temperature to 400ºF (205ºC) and set time to 10 minutes. Press Start to begin preheating.
3.   Once preheated, place the pan into the oven. Flip the asparagus with tongs halfway through the cooking time.
4.   When cooking is complete, the asparagus should be crispy. Remove the pan from the oven and serve warm.

Breaded Brussels Sprouts with Paprika

Prep time: 5 minutes | Cook time: 15 minutes | Serves 4
1 pound (454 g) Brussels sprouts, halved
1 cup bread crumbs
2 tablespoons grated Grana Padano cheese
1 tablespoon paprika
2 tablespoons canola oil
1 tablespoon chopped sage
1.   Line the perforated pan with parchment paper. Set aside.
2.   In a small bowl, thoroughly mix the bread crumbs, cheese, and paprika. In a large bowl, place the Brussels sprouts and drizzle the canola oil over the top. Sprinkle with the bread crumb mixture and toss to coat.
3.   Transfer the Brussels sprouts to the prepared pan.
4.   Select Roast. Set temperature to 400ºF (205ºC) and set time to 15 minutes. Press Start to begin preheating.
5.   Once preheated, place the pan into the oven. Stir the Brussels a few times during cooking.
6.   When cooking is complete, the Brussels sprouts should be lightly browned and crisp. Transfer the Brussels sprouts to a plate and sprinkle the sage on top before serving.

CHAPTER 7 MEATS

Beef-Stuffed Bell Peppers

Prep time: 20 minutes | Cook time: 18 minutes | Serves 4
¾ pound (340 g) lean ground beef
4 ounces (113 g) lean ground pork
¼ cup onion, minced
1 (15-ounce / 425-g) can crushed tomatoes
1 teaspoon Worcestershire sauce
1 teaspoon barbecue seasoning
1 teaspoon honey
½ teaspoon dried basil
½ cup cooked brown rice
½ teaspoon garlic powder
½ teaspoon oregano
½ teaspoon salt
2 small bell peppers, cut in half, stems removed, deseeded
Cooking spray
1.	Spritz a baking pan with cooking spray.
2.	Arrange the beef, pork, and onion in the baking pan.
3.	Select Bake. Set temperature to 360ºF (182ºC) and set time to 8 minutes. Press Start to begin preheating.
4.	Once preheated, place the pan into the oven. Break the ground meat into chunks halfway through the cooking.
5.	When cooking is complete, the ground meat should be lightly browned.
6.	Meanwhile, combine the tomatoes, Worcestershire sauce, barbecue seasoning, honey, and basil in a saucepan. Stir to mix well.
7.	Transfer the cooked meat mixture to a large bowl and add the cooked rice, garlic powder, oregano, salt, and ¼ cup of the tomato mixture. Stir to mix well.
8.	Stuff the pepper halves with the mixture, then arrange the pepper halves in the perforated pan.
9.	Select Air Fry. Set time to 10 minutes. Place the pan into the oven.
10.	When cooking is complete, the peppers should be lightly charred.
11.	Serve the stuffed peppers with the remaining tomato sauce on top.

Prosciutto-Wrapped Beef Rolls

Prep time: 15 minutes | Cook time: 10 minutes | Makes 10 rolls
½ pound (227 g) cooked corned beef, chopped
½ cup drained and chopped sauerkraut
1 (8-ounce / 227-g) package cream cheese, softened
½ cup shredded Swiss cheese
20 slices prosciutto
Cooking spray
Thousand Island Sauce:
¼ cup chopped dill pickles
¼ cup tomato sauce
¾ cup mayonnaise
Fresh thyme leaves, for garnish
2 tablespoons sugar
⅛ teaspoon fine sea salt
Ground black pepper, to taste
1.	Spritz the perforated pan with cooking spray.
2.	Combine the beef, sauerkraut, cream cheese, and Swiss cheese in a large bowl. Stir to mix well.
3.	Unroll a slice of prosciutto on a clean work surface, then top with another slice of prosciutto crosswise. Scoop up 4 tablespoons of the beef mixture in the center.
4.	Fold the top slice sides over the filling as the ends of the roll, then roll up the long sides of the bottom prosciutto and make it into a roll shape. Overlap the sides by about 1 inch. Repeat with remaining filling and prosciutto.
5.	Arrange the rolls in the prepared pan, seam side down, and spritz with cooking spray.
6.	Select Air Fry. Set temperature to 400ºF (205ºC) and set time to 10 minutes. Press Start to begin preheating.
7.	Once preheated, place the pan into the oven. Flip the rolls halfway through.
8.	When cooking is complete, the rolls should be golden and crispy.
9.	Meanwhile, combine the ingredients for the sauce in a small bowl. Stir to mix well.
10.	Serve the rolls with the dipping sauce.

Teriyaki-Marinated Rump Steak

Prep time: 5 minutes | Cook time: 13 minutes | Serves 4
½ pound (227 g) rump steak
$^1/_3$ cup teriyaki marinade
1½ teaspoons sesame oil
½ head broccoli, cut into florets
2 red capsicums, sliced
Fine sea salt and ground black pepper, to taste
Cooking spray
1.	Toss the rump steak in a large bowl with teriyaki marinade. Wrap the bowl in plastic and refrigerate to marinate for at least an hour.
2.	Spritz the perforated pan with cooking spray.
3.	Discard the marinade and transfer the steak in the pan. Spritz with cooking spray.
4.	Select Air Fry. Set temperature to 400ºF (205ºC) and set time to 13 minutes. Press Start to begin preheating.
5.	Once preheated, place the pan into the oven. Flip the steak halfway through.
6.	When cooking is complete, the steak should be well browned.
7.	Meanwhile, heat the sesame oil in a nonstick skillet over medium heat. Add the broccoli and capsicum. Sprinkle with salt and ground black

pepper. Sauté for 5 minutes or until the broccoli is tender.

8. Transfer the air fried rump steak on a plate and top with the sautéed broccoli and capsicum. Serve hot.

Beef Meatballs with Salsa

Prep time: 10 minutes | Cook time: 10 minutes | Serves 4

1 pound (454 g) ground beef (85% lean)
½ cup salsa
¼ cup diced green or red bell peppers
1 large egg, beaten
¼ cup chopped onions
½ teaspoon chili powder
1 clove garlic, minced
½ teaspoon ground cumin
1 teaspoon fine sea salt
Lime wedges, for serving
Cooking spray

1. Spritz the perforated pan with cooking spray.
2. Combine all the ingredients in a large bowl. Stir to mix well.
3. Divide and shape the mixture into 1-inch balls. Arrange the balls in the pan and spritz with cooking spray.
4. Select Air Fry. Set temperature to 350ºF (180ºC) and set time to 10 minutes. Press Start to begin preheating.
5. Once preheated, place the pan into the oven. Flip the balls with tongs halfway through.
6. When cooking is complete, the balls should be well browned.
7. Transfer the balls on a plate and squeeze the lime wedges over before serving.

Rosemary Ground Beef with Zucchini

Prep time: 5 minutes | Cook time: 12 minutes | Serves 4

1½ pounds (680 g) ground beef
1 pound (454 g) chopped zucchini
2 tablespoons extra-virgin olive oil
1 teaspoon dried oregano
1 teaspoon dried basil
1 teaspoon dried rosemary
2 tablespoons fresh chives, chopped

1. In a large bowl, combine all the ingredients, except for the chives, until well blended.
2. Place the beef and zucchini mixture in the baking pan.
3. Select Bake. Set temperature to 400ºF (205ºC) and set time to 12 minutes. Press Start to begin preheating.
4. Once preheated, place the pan into the oven.
5. When cooking is complete, the beef should be browned and the zucchini should be tender.

6. Divide the beef and zucchini mixture among four serving dishes. Top with fresh chives and serve hot.

Fried Calf's Liver Sticks

Prep time: 15 minutes | Cook time: 5 minutes | Serves 4

1 pound (454 g) sliced calf's liver, cut into ½-inch wide strips
2 eggs
2 tablespoons milk
½ cup whole wheat flour
2 cups panko bread crumbs
Salt and ground black pepper, to taste
Cooking spray

1. Spritz the perforated pan with cooking spray.
2. Rub the calf's liver strips with salt and ground black pepper on a clean work surface.
3. Whisk the eggs with milk in a large bowl. Pour the flour in a shallow dish. Pour the panko on a separate shallow dish.
4. Dunk the liver strips in the flour, then in the egg mixture. Shake the excess off and roll the strips over the panko to coat well.
5. Arrange the liver strips in the pan and spritz with cooking spray.
6. Select Air Fry. Set temperature to 390ºF (199ºC) and set time to 5 minutes. Press Start to begin preheating.
7. Once preheated, place the pan into the oven. Flip the strips halfway through.
8. When cooking is complete, the strips should be browned.
9. Serve immediately.

Sirloin Steaks with Cucumber Salad

Prep time: 15 minutes | Cook time: 15 minutes | Serves 4

1 (1½-pound / 680-g) boneless top sirloin steak, trimmed and halved crosswise
1½ teaspoons chili powder
1½ teaspoons ground cumin
¾ teaspoon ground coriander
⅛ teaspoon cayenne pepper
⅛ teaspoon ground cinnamon
1¼ teaspoons plus ⅛ teaspoon salt, divided
½ teaspoon plus ⅛ teaspoon ground black pepper, divided
1 teaspoon plus 1½ tablespoons extra-virgin olive oil, divided
3 tablespoons mayonnaise
1½ tablespoons white wine vinegar
1 tablespoon minced fresh dill
1 small garlic clove, minced
8 ounces (227 g) sugar snap peas, strings removed and cut in half on bias
½ English cucumber, halved lengthwise and sliced thin

2 radishes, trimmed, halved and sliced thin
2 cups baby arugula
1.	In a bowl, mix chili powder, cumin, coriander, cayenne pepper, cinnamon, 1¼ teaspoons salt and ½ teaspoon pepper until well combined.
2.	Add the steaks to another bowl and pat dry with paper towels. Brush with 1 teaspoon oil and transfer to the bowl of spice mixture. Roll over to coat thoroughly.
3.	Arrange the coated steaks in the perforated pan, spaced evenly apart.
4.	Select Air Fry. Set temperature to 400ºF (205ºC) and set time to 15 minutes. Press Start to begin preheating.
5.	Once preheated, place the pan into the oven. Flip the steak halfway through to ensure even cooking.
6.	When cooking is complete, an instant-read thermometer inserted in the thickest part of the meat should register at least 145ºF (63ºC).
7.	Transfer the steaks to a clean work surface and wrap with aluminum foil. Let stand while preparing salad.
8.	Make the salad: In a large bowl, stir together 1½ tablespoons olive oil, mayonnaise, vinegar, dill, garlic, ⅛ teaspoon salt, and ⅛ teaspoon pepper. Add snap peas, cucumber, radishes and arugula. Toss to blend well.
9.	Slice the steaks and serve with the salad.

Beef and Pork Sausage Meatloaf

Prep time: 10 minutes | Cook time: 25 minutes | Serves 4
¾ pound (340 g) ground chuck
4 ounces (113 g) ground pork sausage
2 eggs, beaten
1 cup Parmesan cheese, grated
1 cup chopped shallot
3 tablespoons plain milk
1 tablespoon oyster sauce
1 tablespoon fresh parsley
1 teaspoon garlic paste
1 teaspoon chopped porcini mushrooms
½ teaspoon cumin powder
Seasoned salt and crushed red pepper flakes, to taste
1.	In a large bowl, combine all the ingredients until well blended.
2.	Place the meat mixture in the baking pan. Use a spatula to press the mixture to fill the pan.
3.	Select Bake. Set temperature to 360ºF (182ºC) and set time to 25 minutes. Press Start to begin preheating.
4.	Once preheated, place the pan into the oven.
5.	When cooking is complete, the meatloaf should be well browned.
6.	Let the meatloaf rest for 5 minutes. Transfer to a serving dish and slice. Serve warm.

Beef Pizza with Bell Pepper

Prep time: 20 minutes | Cook time: 10 minutes | Serves 4
4 (6-inch) flour tortillas
For the Meat Topping:
4 ounces (113 g) ground lamb or 85% lean ground beef
¼ cup finely chopped green bell pepper
¼ cup chopped fresh parsley
1 small plum tomato, deseeded and chopped
2 tablespoons chopped yellow onion
1 garlic clove, minced
2 teaspoons tomato paste
¼ teaspoon sweet paprika
¼ teaspoon ground cumin
⅛ to ¼ teaspoon red pepper flakes
⅛ teaspoon ground allspice
⅛ teaspoon kosher salt
⅛ teaspoon black pepper
For Serving:
¼ cup chopped fresh mint
1 teaspoon extra-virgin olive oil
1 lemon, cut into wedges
1.	Combine all the ingredients for the meat topping in a medium bowl until well mixed.
2.	Lay the tortillas on a clean work surface. Spoon the meat mixture on the tortillas and spread all over.
3.	Place the tortillas in the perforated pan.
4.	Select Air Fry. Set temperature to 400ºF (205ºC) and set time to 10 minutes. Press Start to begin preheating.
5.	Once preheated, place the pan into the oven.
6.	When cooking is complete, the edge of the tortilla should be golden and the meat should be lightly browned.
7.	Transfer them to a serving dish. Top with chopped fresh mint and drizzle with olive oil. Squeeze the lemon wedges on top and serve.

Curried Beef Meatballs

Prep time: 5 minutes | Cook time: 15 minutes | Serves 4
1 pound (454 g) ground beef
1 tablespoon sesame oil
2 teaspoons chopped lemongrass
1 teaspoon red Thai curry paste
1 teaspoon Thai seasoning blend
Juice and zest of ½ lime
Cooking spray
1.	Spritz the perforated pan with cooking spray.
2.	In a medium bowl, combine all the ingredients until well blended.
3.	Shape the meat mixture into 24 meatballs and arrange them in the pan.
4.	Select Air Fry. Set temperature to 380ºF (193ºC) and set time to 15 minutes. Press Start to begin preheating.
5.	Once preheated, place the pan into the oven. Flip the meatballs halfway through.

6. When cooking is complete, the meatballs should be browned.
7. Transfer the meatballs to plates. Let cool for 5 minutes before serving.

Rosemary Veal Loin with Fennel Seeds

Prep time: 1 hour 10 minutes | Cook time: 12 minutes | Makes 3 veal chops

1½ teaspoons crushed fennel seeds
1 tablespoon minced fresh rosemary leaves
1 tablespoon minced garlic
1½ teaspoons lemon zest
1½ teaspoons salt
½ teaspoon red pepper flakes
2 tablespoons olive oil
3 (10-ounce / 284-g) bone-in veal loin, about ½ inch thick

1. Combine all the ingredients, except for the veal loin, in a large bowl. Stir to mix well.
2. Dunk the loin in the mixture and press to submerge. Wrap the bowl in plastic and refrigerate for at least an hour to marinate.
3. Arrange the veal loin in the perforated pan.
4. Select Air Fry. Set temperature to 400ºF (205ºC) and set time to 12 minutes. Press Start to begin preheating.
5. Once preheated, place the pan into the oven. Flip the veal halfway through.
6. When cooking is complete, the internal temperature of the veal should reach at least 145ºF (63ºC) for medium rare.
7. Serve immediately.

Fried Venison Backstrap

Prep time: 10 minutes | Cook time: 10 minutes | Serves 4

2 eggs
¼ cup milk
1 cup whole wheat flour
½ teaspoon salt
¼ teaspoon ground black pepper
1 pound (454 g) venison backstrap, sliced
Cooking spray

1. Spritz the perforated pan with cooking spray.
2. Whisk the eggs with milk in a large bowl. Combine the flour with salt and ground black pepper in a shallow dish.
3. Dredge the venison in the flour first, then into the egg mixture. Shake the excess off and roll the venison back over the flour to coat well.
4. Arrange the venison in the pan and spritz with cooking spray.
5. Select Air Fry. Set temperature to 360ºF (182ºC) and set time to 10 minutes. Press Start to begin preheating.
6. Once preheated, place the pan into the oven. Flip the venison halfway through.

7. When cooking is complete, the internal temperature of the venison should reach at least 145ºF (63ºC) for medium rare.
8. Serve immediately.

Dijon Lamb Rack with Pistachio

Prep time: 10 minutes | Cook time: 20 minutes | Serves 2

½ cup finely chopped pistachios
1 teaspoon chopped fresh rosemary
3 tablespoons panko bread crumbs
2 teaspoons chopped fresh oregano
1 tablespoon olive oil
Salt and freshly ground black pepper, to taste
1 lamb rack, bones fat trimmed and frenched
1 tablespoon Dijon mustard

1. Put the pistachios, rosemary, bread crumbs, oregano, olive oil, salt, and black pepper in a food processor. Pulse to combine until smooth.
2. Rub the lamb rack with salt and black pepper on a clean work surface, then place it in the perforated pan.
3. Select Air Fry. Set temperature to 380ºF (193ºC) and set time to 12 minutes. Press Start to begin preheating.
4. Once preheated, place the pan into the oven. Flip the lamb halfway through.
5. When cooking is complete, the lamb should be lightly browned.
6. Transfer the lamb on a plate and brush with Dijon mustard on the fat side, then sprinkle with the pistachios mixture over the lamb rack to coat well.
7. Put the lamb rack back to the oven and air fry for 8 more minutes or until the internal temperature of the rack reaches at least 145ºF (63ºC).
8. Remove the lamb rack from the oven with tongs and allow to cool for 5 minutes before slicing to serve.

Beef Tenderloin with Feta Cheese

Prep time: 10 minutes | Cook time: 10 minutes | Serves 4

1½ pounds (680 g) beef tenderloin, pounded to ¼ inch thick
3 teaspoons sea salt
1 teaspoon ground black pepper
2 ounces (57 g) creamy goat cheese
½ cup crumbled feta cheese
¼ cup finely chopped onions
2 cloves garlic, minced
Cooking spray

1. Spritz the perforated pan with cooking spray.
2. Unfold the beef tenderloin on a clean work surface. Rub the salt and pepper all over the beef tenderloin to season.

3.	Make the filling for the stuffed beef tenderloins: Combine the goat cheese, feta, onions, and garlic in a medium bowl. Stir until well blended.
4.	Spoon the mixture in the center of the tenderloin. Roll the tenderloin up tightly like rolling a burrito and use some kitchen twine to tie the tenderloin.
5.	Arrange the tenderloin in the perforated pan.
6.	Select Air Fry. Set temperature to 400ºF (205ºC) and set time to 10 minutes. Press Start to begin preheating.
7.	Once preheated, place the pan into the oven. Flip the tenderloin halfway through.
8.	When cooking is complete, the instant-read thermometer inserted in the center of the tenderloin should register 135ºF (57ºC) for medium-rare.
9.	Transfer to a platter and serve immediately.

Garlic Lamb Chops with Asparagus

Prep time: 10 minutes | Cook time: 15 minutes | Serves 4
4 asparagus spears, trimmed
2 tablespoons olive oil, divided
1 pound (454 g) lamb chops
1 garlic clove, minced
2 teaspoons chopped fresh thyme, for serving
Salt and ground black pepper, to taste
1.	Spritz the perforated pan with cooking spray.
2.	On a large plate, brush the asparagus with 1 tablespoon olive oil, then sprinkle with salt. Set aside.
3.	On a separate plate, brush the lamb chops with remaining olive oil and sprinkle with salt and ground black pepper.
4.	Arrange the lamb chops in the pan.
5.	Select Air Fry. Set temperature to 400ºF (205ºC) and set time to 15 minutes. Press Start to begin preheating.
6.	Once preheated, place the pan into the oven. Flip the lamb chops and add the asparagus and garlic halfway through.
7.	When cooking is complete, the lamb should be well browned and the asparagus should be tender.
8.	Serve them on a plate with thyme on top.

Lamb Kofta with Mint

Prep time: 25 minutes | Cook time: 10 minutes | Serves 4
1 pound (454 g) ground lamb
1 tablespoon ras el hanout (North African spice)
½ teaspoon ground coriander
1 teaspoon onion powder
1 teaspoon garlic powder
1 teaspoon cumin
2 tablespoons mint, chopped
Salt and ground black pepper, to taste
Special Equipment:
4 bamboo skewers

1.	Combine the ground lamb, ras el hanout, coriander, onion powder, garlic powder, cumin, mint, salt, and ground black pepper in a large bowl. Stir to mix well.
2.	Transfer the mixture into sausage molds and sit the bamboo skewers in the mixture. Refrigerate for 15 minutes.
3.	Spritz the perforated pan with cooking spray. Place the lamb skewers in the pan and spritz with cooking spray.
4.	Select Air Fry. Set temperature to 380ºF (193ºC) and set time to 10 minutes. Press Start to begin preheating.
5.	Once preheated, place the pan into the oven. Flip the lamb skewers halfway through.
6.	When cooking is complete, the lamb should be well browned.
7.	Serve immediately.

Horseradish Lamb Loin Chops

Prep time: 10 minutes | Cook time: 13 minutes | Serves 4
For the Lamb:
4 lamb loin chops
2 tablespoons vegetable oil
1 clove garlic, minced
½ teaspoon kosher salt
½ teaspoon black pepper
For the Horseradish Cream Sauce:
1 to 1½ tablespoons prepared horseradish
1 tablespoon Dijon mustard
½ cup mayonnaise
2 teaspoons sugar
Cooking spray
1.	Spritz the perforated pan with cooking spray.
2.	Place the lamb chops on a plate. Rub with the oil and sprinkle with the garlic, salt and black pepper. Let sit to marinate for 30 minutes at room temperature.
3.	Make the horseradish cream sauce: Mix the horseradish, mustard, mayonnaise, and sugar in a bowl until well combined. Set half of the sauce aside until ready to serve.
4.	Arrange the marinated chops in the perforated pan.
5.	Select Air Fry. Set temperature to 325ºF (163ºC) and set time to 10 minutes. Press Start to begin preheating.
6.	Once preheated, place the pan into the oven. Flip the lamb chops halfway through.
7.	When cooking is complete, the lamb should be lightly browned.
8.	Transfer the chops from the oven to the bowl of the horseradish sauce. Roll to coat well. Put the coated chops back to the pan. Return the pan to the oven.
9.	Select Air Fry. Set temperature to 400ºF (205ºC) and set time to 3 minutes.

10.	When cooking is complete, the internal temperature should reach 145ºF (63ºC) on a meat thermometer (for medium-rare). Flip the lamb halfway through.
11.	Serve hot with the horseradish cream sauce.

Bacon-Wrapped Sausage with Tomato Relish

Prep time: 1 hour 15 minutes | Cook time: 32 minutes | Serves 4
8 pork sausages
8 bacon strips
Relish:
8 large tomatoes, chopped
1 small onion, peeled
1 clove garlic, peeled
1 tablespoon white wine vinegar
3 tablespoons chopped parsley
1 teaspoon smoked paprika
2 tablespoons sugar
Salt and ground black pepper, to taste
1.	Purée the tomatoes, onion, and garlic in a food processor until well mixed and smooth.
2.	Pour the purée in a saucepan and drizzle with white wine vinegar. Sprinkle with salt and ground black pepper. Simmer over medium heat for 10 minutes.
3.	Add the parsley, paprika, and sugar to the saucepan and cook for 10 more minutes or until it has a thick consistency. Keep stirring during the cooking. Refrigerate for an hour to chill.
4.	Wrap the sausage with bacon strips and secure with toothpicks, then place them in the perforated pan.
5.	Select Air Fry. Set temperature to 350ºF (180ºC) and set time to 12 minutes. Press Start to begin preheating.
6.	Once preheated, place the pan into the oven. Flip the bacon-wrapped sausage halfway through.
7.	When cooking is complete, the bacon should be crispy and browned.
8.	Transfer the bacon-wrapped sausage on a plate and baste with the relish or just serve with the relish alongside.

Wasabi Spam

Prep time: 5 minutes | Cook time: 12 minutes | Serves 3
$^2/_3$ cup all-purpose flour
2 large eggs
1½ tablespoons wasabi paste
2 cups panko bread crumbs
6½-inch-thick spam slices
Cooking spray
1.	Spritz the perforated pan with cooking spray.
2.	Pour the flour in a shallow plate. Whisk the eggs with wasabi in a large bowl. Pour the panko in a separate shallow plate.

3.	Dredge the spam slices in the flour first, then dunk in the egg mixture, and then roll the spam over the panko to coat well. Shake the excess off.
4.	Arrange the spam slices in the pan and spritz with cooking spray.
5.	Select Air Fry. Set temperature to 400ºF (205ºC) and set time to 12 minutes. Press Start to begin preheating.
6.	Once preheated, place the pan into the oven. Flip the spam slices halfway through.
7.	When cooking is complete, the spam slices should be golden and crispy.
8.	Serve immediately.

Rosemary Pork with Apple Glaze

Prep time: 15 minutes | Cook time: 19 minutes | Serves 4
1 sliced apple
1 small onion, sliced
2 tablespoons apple cider vinegar, divided
½ teaspoon thyme
½ teaspoon rosemary
¼ teaspoon brown sugar
3 tablespoons olive oil, divided
¼ teaspoon smoked paprika
4 pork chops
Salt and ground black pepper, to taste
1.	Combine the apple slices, onion, 1 tablespoon of vinegar, thyme, rosemary, brown sugar, and 2 tablespoons of olive oil in a baking pan. Stir to mix well.
2.	Select Bake. Set temperature to 350ºF (180ºC) and set time to 4 minutes. Press Start to begin preheating.
3.	Once preheated, place the pan into the oven. Stir the mixture halfway through.
4.	Meanwhile, combine the remaining vinegar and olive oil, and paprika in a large bowl. Sprinkle with salt and ground black pepper. Stir to mix well. Dredge the pork in the mixture and toss to coat well. Place the pork in the perforated pan.
5.	When cooking is complete, remove the baking pan from the oven and place in the perforated pan.
6.	Select Air Fry and set time to 10 minutes. Place the pan into the oven. Flip the pork chops halfway through.
7.	When cooking is complete, the pork should be lightly browned.
8.	Remove the pork from the oven and baste with baked apple mixture on both sides. Put the pork back to the oven and air fry for an additional 5 minutes. Flip halfway through.
9.	Serve immediately.

Curried Lamb Chops with Potatoes

Prep time: 10 minutes | Cook time: 20 minutes | Serves 4

8 (½-inch thick) lamb loin chops (about 2 pounds / 907 g)
2 teaspoons kosher salt or 1 teaspoon fine salt, divided
¾ cup plain whole milk yogurt
2 garlic cloves, minced or smashed
1 tablespoon freshly grated ginger (1- or 2-inch piece) or 1 teaspoon ground ginger
1 teaspoon curry powder
1 teaspoon smoked paprika
½ teaspoon cayenne pepper
12 ounces (340 g) small red potatoes, quartered
Cooking spray
1. Sprinkle the lamb chops on both sides with 1 teaspoon of kosher salt and set aside.
2. Meanwhile, make the marinade by stirring together the yogurt, garlic, ginger, curry powder, paprika, cayenne pepper, and remaining 1 teaspoon of kosher salt in a large bowl.
3. Transfer 2 tablespoons of the marinade to a resealable plastic bag, leaving those 2 tablespoons in the bowl. Place the lamb chops in the bag. Squeeze out as much air as possible and squish the bag around so that the chops are well coated with the marinade. Set aside.
4. Add the potatoes to the bowl and toss until well coated. Spritz the sheet pan with cooking spray. Arrange the potatoes in the pan.
5. Select Roast. Set temperature to 375ºF (190ºC) and set time to 10 minutes. Press Start to begin preheating.
6. Once the unit has preheated, place the pan into the oven.
7. Once cooking is complete, remove the pan from the oven.
8. Remove the chops from the marinade, draining off all but a thin coat. Return them to the baking pan.
9. Select Broil. Set temperature to High and set time to 10 minutes. Press Start to begin preheating.
10. Once the unit has preheated, place the pan into the oven. After 5 minutes, remove the pan from the oven and turn over the chops and potatoes. Slide the pan into the oven and continue cooking until the lamb read 145ºF (63ºC) on a meat thermometer. If you want it more well done, continue cooking for another few minutes.
11. Remove the pan from the oven and serve.

Dijon Pork Tenderloin

Prep time: 5 minutes | Cook time: 10 minutes | Serves 6
2 large egg whites
1½ tablespoons Dijon mustard
2 cups crushed pretzel crumbs
1½ pounds (680 g) pork tenderloin, cut into ¼-pound (113-g) sections
Cooking spray
1. Spritz the perforated pan with cooking spray.
2. Whisk the egg whites with Dijon mustard in a bowl until bubbly. Pour the pretzel crumbs in a separate bowl.
3. Dredge the pork tenderloin in the egg white mixture and press to coat. Shake the excess off and roll the tenderloin over the pretzel crumbs.
4. Arrange the well-coated pork tenderloin in the pan and spritz with cooking spray.
5. Select Air Fry. Set temperature to 350ºF (180ºC) and set time to 10 minutes. Press Start to begin preheating.
6. Once preheated, place the pan into the oven.
7. After 5 minutes, remove the pan from the oven. Flip the pork. Return the pan to the oven and continue cooking.
8. When cooking is complete, the pork should be golden brown and crispy.
9. Serve immediately.

Prosciutto Tart with Asparagus

Prep time: 10 minutes | Cook time: 25 minutes | Serves 4
All-purpose flour, for dusting
1 sheet (½ package) frozen puff pastry, thawed
½ cup grated Parmesan cheese
1 pound (454 g) (or more) asparagus, trimmed
8 ounces (227 g) thinly sliced prosciutto, sliced into ribbons about ½-inch wide
2 teaspoons aged balsamic vinegar
1. On a lightly floured cutting board, unwrap and unfold the puff pastry and roll it lightly with a rolling pin so as to press the folds together. Place it on the sheet pan.
2. Roll about ½ inch of the pastry edges up to form a ridge around the perimeter. Crimp the corners together to create a solid rim around the pastry. Using a fork, pierce the bottom of the pastry all over. Scatter the cheese over the bottom of the pastry.
3. Arrange the asparagus spears on top of the cheese in a single layer with 4 or 5 spears pointing one way, the next few pointing the opposite direction. You may need to trim them so they fit within the border of the pastry shell. Lay the prosciutto on top more or less evenly.
4. Select Bake. Set temperature to 375ºF (190ºC) and set time to 25 minutes. Press Start to begin preheating.
5. Once the unit has preheated, place the pan into the oven.
6. After about 15 minutes, check the tart, rotating the pan if the crust is not browning evenly and continue cooking until the pastry is golden brown and the edges of the prosciutto pieces are browned.
7. Remove the pan from the oven. Allow to cool for 5 minutes before slicing.

8. Drizzle with the balsamic vinegar just before serving.

Paprika Lamb Chops with Sage

Prep time: 5 minutes | Cook time: 25 minutes | Serves 4
1 cup all-purpose flour
2 teaspoons dried sage leaves
2 teaspoons garlic powder
1 tablespoon mild paprika
1 tablespoon salt
4 (6-ounce / 170-g) bone-in lamb shoulder chops, fat trimmed
Cooking spray
1. Spritz the perforated pan with cooking spray.
2. Combine the flour, sage leaves, garlic powder, paprika, and salt in a large bowl. Stir to mix well. Dunk in the lamb chops and toss to coat well.
3. Arrange the lamb chops in the pan and spritz with cooking spray.
4. Select Air Fry. Set temperature to 375ºF (190ºC) and set time to 25 minutes. Press Start to begin preheating.
5. Once preheated, place the pan into the oven. Flip the chops halfway through.
6. When cooking is complete, the chops should be golden brown and reaches your desired doneness.
7. Serve immediately.

Ginger Pork Shoulder in Shaoxing Wine

Prep time: 10 minutes | Cook time: 15 minutes | Serves 4
¼ cup honey
1 teaspoon Chinese five-spice powder
1 tablespoon Shaoxing wine (rice cooking wine)
1 tablespoon hoisin sauce
2 teaspoons minced garlic
2 teaspoons minced fresh ginger
2 tablespoons soy sauce
1 tablespoon sugar
1 pound (454 g) fatty pork shoulder, cut into long, 1-inch-thick pieces
Cooking spray
1. Combine all the ingredients, except for the pork should, in a microwave-safe bowl. Stir to mix well. Microwave until the honey has dissolved. Stir periodically.
2. Pierce the pork pieces generously with a fork, then put the pork in a large bowl. Pour in half of the honey mixture. Set the remaining sauce aside until ready to serve.
3. Press the pork pieces into the mixture to coat and wrap the bowl in plastic and refrigerate to marinate for at least 8 hours.
4. Spritz the perforated pan with cooking spray.

5. Discard the marinade and transfer the pork pieces in the perforated pan.
6. Select Air Fry. Set temperature to 400ºF (205ºC) and set time to 15 minutes. Press Start to begin preheating.
7. Once preheated, place the pan into the oven. Flip the pork halfway through.
8. When cooking is complete, the pork should be well browned.
9. Meanwhile, microwave the remaining marinade on high for a minute or until it has a thick consistency. Stir periodically.
10. Remove the pork from the oven and allow to cool for 10 minutes before serving with the thickened marinade.

Citrus Pork Ribs with Oregano

Prep time: 10 minutes | Cook time: 25 minutes | Serves 6
2½ pounds (1.1 kg) boneless country-style pork ribs, cut into 2-inch pieces
3 tablespoons olive brine
1 tablespoon minced fresh oregano leaves
$^1/_3$ cup orange juice
1 teaspoon ground cumin
1 tablespoon minced garlic
1 teaspoon salt
1 teaspoon ground black pepper
Cooking spray
1. Combine all the ingredients in a large bowl. Toss to coat the pork ribs well. Wrap the bowl in plastic and refrigerate for at least an hour to marinate.
2. Spritz the perforated pan with cooking spray.
3. Arrange the marinated pork ribs in the pan and spritz with cooking spray.
4. Select Air Fry. Set temperature to 400ºF (205ºC) and set time to 25 minutes. Press Start to begin preheating.
5. Once preheated, place the pan into the oven. Flip the ribs halfway through.
6. When cooking is complete, the ribs should be well browned.
7. Serve immediately.

Vinegary Pork Schnitzel

Prep time: 5 minutes | Cook time: 14 minutes | Serves 2
½ cup pork rinds
½ tablespoon fresh parsley
½ teaspoon fennel seed
½ teaspoon mustard
$^1/_3$ tablespoon cider vinegar
1 teaspoon garlic salt
$^1/_3$ teaspoon ground black pepper
2 eggs
2 pork schnitzel, halved
Cooking spray

1.   Spritz the perforated pan with cooking spray.
2.   Put the pork rinds, parsley, fennel seeds, and mustard in a food processor. Pour in the vinegar and sprinkle with salt and ground black pepper. Pulse until well combined and smooth.
3.   Pour the pork rind mixture in a large bowl. Whisk the eggs in a separate bowl.
4.   Dunk the pork schnitzel in the whisked eggs, then dunk in the pork rind mixture to coat well. Shake the excess off.
5.   Arrange the schnitzel in the pan and spritz with cooking spray.
6.   Select Air Fry. Set temperature to 350ºF (180ºC) and set time to 14 minutes. Press Start to begin preheating.
7.   Once preheated, place the pan into the oven.
8.   After 7 minutes, remove the pan from the oven. Flip the schnitzel. Return the pan to the oven and continue cooking.
9.   When cooking is complete, the schnitzel should be golden and crispy.
10.   Serve immediately.

Nut-Crusted Pork Rack

Prep time: 5 minutes | Cook time: 35 minutes | Serves 2

1 clove garlic, minced
2 tablespoons olive oil
1 pound (454 g) rack of pork
1 cup chopped macadamia nuts
1 tablespoon bread crumbs
1 tablespoon rosemary, chopped
1 egg
Salt and ground black pepper, to taste
1.   Combine the garlic and olive oil in a small bowl. Stir to mix well.
2.   On a clean work surface, rub the pork rack with the garlic oil and sprinkle with salt and black pepper on both sides.
3.   Combine the macadamia nuts, bread crumbs, and rosemary in a shallow dish. Whisk the egg in a large bowl.
4.   Dredge the pork in the egg, then roll the pork over the macadamia nut mixture to coat well. Shake the excess off.
5.   Arrange the pork in the perforated pan.
6.   Select Air Fry. Set temperature to 350ºF (180ºC) and set time to 30 minutes. Press Start to begin preheating.
7.   Once preheated, place the pan into the oven.
8.   After 30 minutes, remove the pan from the oven. Flip the pork rack. Return the pan to the oven and increase temperature to 390ºF (199ºC) and set time to 5 minutes. Keep cooking.
9.   When cooking is complete, the pork should be browned.
10.   Serve immediately.

Teriyaki-Glazed Pork Ribs

Prep time: 5 minutes | Cook time: 30 minutes | Serves 4

¼ cup soy sauce
¼ cup honey
1 teaspoon garlic powder
1 teaspoon ground dried ginger
4 (8-ounce / 227-g) boneless country-style pork ribs
Cooking spray
1.   Spritz the perforated pan with cooking spray.
2.   Make the teriyaki sauce: combine the soy sauce, honey, garlic powder, and ginger in a bowl. Stir to mix well.
3.   Brush the ribs with half of the teriyaki sauce, then arrange the ribs in the pan. Spritz with cooking spray.
4.   Select Air Fry. Set temperature to 350ºF (180ºC) and set time to 30 minutes. Press Start to begin preheating.
5.   Once preheated, place the pan into the oven.
6.   After 15 minutes, remove the pan from the oven. Flip the ribs and brush with remaining teriyaki sauce. Return the pan to the oven and continue cooking.
7.   When cooking is complete, the internal temperature of the ribs should reach at least 145ºF (63ºC).
8.   Serve immediately.

Bacon-Wrapped Pork Hot Dogs

Prep time: 5 minutes | Cook time: 10 minutes | Serves 5

10 thin slices of bacon
5 pork hot dogs, halved
1 teaspoon cayenne pepper
Sauce:
¼ cup mayonnaise
4 tablespoons low-carb ketchup
1 teaspoon rice vinegar
1 teaspoon chili powder
1.   Arrange the slices of bacon on a clean work surface. One by one, place the halved hot dog on one end of each slice, season with cayenne pepper and wrap the hot dog with the bacon slices and secure with toothpicks as needed.
2.   Place wrapped hot dogs in the perforated pan.
3.   Select Air Fry. Set temperature to 390ºF (199ºC) and set time to 10 minutes. Press Start to begin preheating.
4.   Once preheated, place the pan into the oven. Flip the bacon-wrapped hot dogs halfway through.
5.   When cooking is complete, the bacon should be crispy and browned.
6.   Make the sauce: Stir all the ingredients for the sauce in a small bowl. Wrap the bowl in plastic and set in the refrigerator until ready to serve.
7.   Transfer the hot dogs to a platter and serve hot with the sauce.

Garlic Pork Belly with Bay Leaves

Prep time: 10 minutes | Cook time: 30 minutes | Serves 4

1 pound (454 g) pork belly, cut into three thick chunks
6 garlic cloves
2 bay leaves
2 tablespoons soy sauce
1 teaspoon kosher salt
1 teaspoon ground black pepper
3 cups water
Cooking spray

1.   Put all the ingredients in a pressure cooker, then put the lid on and cook on high for 15 minutes.
2.   Natural release the pressure and release any remaining pressure, transfer the tender pork belly on a clean work surface. Allow to cool under room temperature until you can handle.
3.   Generously Spritz the perforated pan with cooking spray.
4.   Cut each chunk into two slices, then put the pork slices in the pan.
5.   Select Air Fry. Set temperature to 400ºF (205ºC) and set time to 15 minutes. Press Start to begin preheating.
6.   Once preheated, place the pan into the oven.
7.   After 7 minutes, remove the pan from the oven. Flip the pork. Return the pan to the oven and continue cooking.
8.   When cooking is complete, the pork fat should be crispy.
9.   Serve immediately.

Lemon Pork Loin Chop with Marjoram

Prep time: 15 minutes | Cook time: 15 minutes | Serves 4

4 thin boneless pork loin chops
2 tablespoons lemon juice
½ cup flour
¼ teaspoon marjoram
1 teaspoon salt
1 cup panko bread crumbs
2 eggs
Lemon wedges, for serving
Cooking spray

1.   On a clean work surface, drizzle the pork chops with lemon juice on both sides.
2.   Combine the flour with marjoram and salt on a shallow plate. Pour the bread crumbs on a separate shallow dish. Beat the eggs in a large bowl.
3.   Dredge the pork chops in the flour, then dunk in the beaten eggs to coat well. Shake the excess off and roll over the bread crumbs. Arrange the pork chops in the perforated pan and spritz with cooking spray.
4.   Select Air Fry. Set temperature to 400ºF (205ºC) and set time to 15 minutes. Press Start to begin preheating.
5.   Once preheated, place the pan into the oven.

6.   After 7 minutes, remove the pan from the oven. Flip the pork. Return the pan to the oven and continue cooking.
7.   When cooking is complete, the pork should be crispy and golden.
8.   Squeeze the lemon wedges over the fried chops and serve immediately.

Pork and Veggie Kebabs

Prep time: 25 minutes | Cook time: 15 minutes | Serves 4

1 pound (454 g) pork tenderloin, cubed
1 teaspoon smoked paprika
Salt and ground black pepper, to taste
1 green bell pepper, cut into chunks
1 zucchini, cut into chunks
1 red onion, sliced
1 tablespoon oregano
Cooking spray
Special Equipment:
Small bamboo skewers, soaked in water for 20 minutes to keep them from burning while cooking

1.   Spritz the perforated pan with cooking spray.
2.   Add the pork to a bowl and season with the smoked paprika, salt and black pepper. Thread the seasoned pork cubes and vegetables alternately onto the soaked skewers. Arrange the skewers in the pan.
3.   Select Air Fry. Set temperature to 350ºF (180ºC) and set time to 15 minutes. Press Start to begin preheating.
4.   Once preheated, place the pan into the oven.
5.   After 7 minutes, remove the pan from the oven. Flip the pork skewers. Return the pan to the oven and continue cooking.
6.   When cooking is complete, the pork should be browned and vegetables are tender.
7.   Transfer the skewers to the serving dishes and sprinkle with oregano. Serve hot.

Pork and Pineapple Kebabs

Prep time: 10 minutes | Cook time: 12 minutes | Serves 4

¼ teaspoon kosher salt or ⅛ teaspoon fine salt
1 medium pork tenderloin (about 1 pound / 454 g) cut into 1½-inch chunks
1 green bell pepper, seeded and cut into 1-inch pieces
1 red bell pepper, seeded and cut into 1-inch pieces
2 cups fresh pineapple chunks
¾ cup Teriyaki Sauce or store-bought variety, divided
Special Equipment:
12 (9- to 12-inch) wooden skewers, soaked in water for about 30 minutes

1.   Sprinkle the pork cubes with the salt.
2.   Thread the pork, bell peppers, and pineapple onto a skewer. Repeat until all skewers are complete. Brush the skewers generously with about

half of the Teriyaki Sauce. Place them on the sheet pan.

3. Select Roast. Set temperature to 375ºF (190ºC) and set time to 10 minutes. Press Start to begin preheating.

4. Once the unit has preheated, place the pan into the oven.

5. After about 5 minutes, remove the pan from the oven. Turn over the skewers and brush with the remaining half of Teriyaki Sauce. Transfer the pan back to the oven and continue cooking until the vegetables are tender and browned in places and the pork is browned and cooked through.

6. Remove the pan from the oven and serve.

Pork, Squash and Pepper Kebabs

Prep time: 20 minutes | Cook time: 8 minutes | Serves 4

For the Pork:
1 pound (454 g) pork steak, cut in cubes
1 tablespoon white wine vinegar
3 tablespoons steak sauce
¼ cup soy sauce
1 teaspoon powdered chili
1 teaspoon red chili flakes
2 teaspoons smoked paprika
1 teaspoon garlic salt

For the Vegetable:
1 green squash, deseeded and cut in cubes
1 yellow squash, deseeded and cut in cubes
1 red pepper, cut in cubes
1 green pepper, cut in cubes
Salt and ground black pepper, to taste
Cooking spray

Special Equipment:
4 bamboo skewers, soaked in water for at least 30 minutes

1. Combine the ingredients for the pork in a large bowl. Press the pork to dunk in the marinade. Wrap the bowl in plastic and refrigerate for at least an hour.

2. Spritz the perforated pan with cooking spray.

3. Remove the pork from the marinade and run the skewers through the pork and vegetables alternately. Sprinkle with salt and pepper to taste.

4. Arrange the skewers in the pan and spritz with cooking spray.

5. Select Air Fry. Set temperature to 380ºF (193ºC) and set time to 8 minutes. Press Start to begin preheating.

6. Once preheated, place the pan into the oven.

7. After 4 minutes, remove the pan from the oven. Flip the skewers. Return the pan to the oven and continue cooking.

8. When cooking is complete, the pork should be browned and the vegetables should be lightly charred and tender.

9. Serve immediately.

BBQ Kielbasa Sausage

Prep time: 15 minutes | Cook time: 10 minutes | Serves 2 to 4

¾ pound (340 g) kielbasa sausage, cut into ½-inch slices
1 (8-ounce / 227-g) can pineapple chunks in juice, drained
1 cup bell pepper chunks
1 tablespoon barbecue seasoning
1 tablespoon soy sauce
Cooking spray

1. Spritz the perforated pan with cooking spray.

2. Combine all the ingredients in a large bowl. Toss to mix well.

3. Pour the sausage mixture in the perforated pan.

4. Select Air Fry. Set temperature to 390ºF (199ºC) and set time to 10 minutes. Press Start to begin preheating.

5. Once preheated, place the pan into the oven.

6. After 5 minutes, remove the pan from the oven. Stir the sausage mixture. Return the pan to the oven and continue cooking.

7. When cooking is complete, the sausage should be lightly browned and the bell pepper and pineapple should be soft.

8. Serve immediately.

Pork Butt withCoriander-Parsley Sauce

Prep time: 1 hour 15 minutes | Cook time: 30 minutes | Serves 4

1 teaspoon golden flaxseeds meal
1 egg white, well whisked
1 tablespoon soy sauce
1 teaspoon lemon juice, preferably freshly squeezed
1 tablespoon olive oil
1 pound (454 g) pork butt, cut into pieces 2-inches long
Salt and ground black pepper, to taste

Garlicky Coriander-Parsley Sauce:
3 garlic cloves, minced
$^{1}/_{3}$ cup fresh coriander leaves
$^{1}/_{3}$ cup fresh parsley leaves
1 teaspoon lemon juice
½ tablespoon salt
$^{1}/_{3}$ cup extra-virgin olive oil

1. Combine the flaxseeds meal, egg white, soy sauce, lemon juice, salt, black pepper, and olive oil in a large bowl. Dunk the pork strips in and press to submerge.

2. Wrap the bowl in plastic and refrigerate to marinate for at least an hour.

3. Arrange the marinated pork strips in the perforated pan.

4. Select Air Fry. Set temperature to 380ºF (193ºC) and set time to 30 minutes. Press Start to begin preheating.

5. Once preheated, place the pan into the oven.

6. After 15 minutes, remove the pan from the oven. Flip the pork. Return the pan to the oven and continue cooking.
7. When cooking is complete, the pork should be well browned.
8. Meanwhile, combine the ingredients for the sauce in a small bowl. Stir to mix well. Arrange the bowl in the refrigerator to chill until ready to serve.
9. Serve the air fried pork strips with the chilled sauce.

Colby Pork Sausage with Cauliflower

Prep time: 5 minutes | Cook time: 27 minutes | Serves 6
1 pound (454 g) cauliflower, chopped
6 pork sausages, chopped
½ onion, sliced
3 eggs, beaten
$^1/_3$ cup Colby cheese
1 teaspoon cumin powder
½ teaspoon tarragon
½ teaspoon sea salt
½ teaspoon ground black pepper
Cooking spray
1. Spritz the baking pan with cooking spray.
2. In a saucepan over medium heat, boil the cauliflower until tender. Place the boiled cauliflower in a food processor and pulse until puréed. Transfer to a large bowl and combine with remaining ingredients until well blended.
3. Pour the cauliflower and sausage mixture into the pan.
4. Select Bake. Set temperature to 365ºF (185ºC) and set time to 27 minutes. Press Start to begin preheating.
5. Once preheated, place the pan into the oven.
6. When cooking is complete, the sausage should be lightly browned.
7. Divide the mixture among six serving dishes and serve warm.

Pork Chops with Sour Cream and Dill Sauce

Prep time: 5 minutes | Cook time: 4 minutes | Serves 4 to 6
½ cup flour
1½ teaspoons salt
Freshly ground black pepper, to taste
2 eggs
½ cup milk
1½ cups toasted bread crumbs
1 teaspoon paprika
6 boneless, center cut pork chops (about 1½ pounds / 680 g) fat trimmed, pound to ½-inch thick
2 tablespoons olive oil
3 tablespoons melted butter
Lemon wedges, for serving
Sour Cream and Dill Sauce:
1 cup chicken stock
1½ tablespoons cornstarch
$^1/_3$ cup sour cream
1½ tablespoons chopped fresh dill
Salt and ground black pepper, to taste
1. Combine the flour with salt and black pepper in a large bowl. Stir to mix well. Whisk the egg with milk in a second bowl. Stir the bread crumbs and paprika in a third bowl.
2. Dredge the pork chops in the flour bowl, then in the egg milk, and then into the bread crumbs bowl. Press to coat well. Shake the excess off.
3. Arrange the pork chop in the perforated pan, then brush with olive oil and butter on all sides.
4. Select Air Fry. Set temperature to 400ºF (205ºC) and set time to 4 minutes. Press Start to begin preheating.
5. Once preheated, place the pan into the oven.
6. After 2 minutes, remove the pan from the oven. Flip the pork. Return the pan to the oven and continue cooking.
7. When cooking is complete, the pork chop should be golden brown and crispy.
8. Meanwhile, combine the chicken stock and cornstarch in a small saucepan and bring to a boil over medium-high heat. Simmer for 2 more minutes.
9. Turn off the heat, then mix in the sour cream, fresh dill, salt, and black pepper.
10. Remove the schnitzels from the oven to a plate and baste with sour cream and dill sauce. Squeeze the lemon wedges over and slice to serve.

Pork Sausage Ratatouille

Prep time: 10 minutes | Cook time: 25 minutes | Serves 4
4 pork sausages
Ratatouille:
2 zucchinis, sliced
1 eggplant, sliced
15 ounces (425 g) tomatoes, sliced
1 red bell pepper, sliced
1 medium red onion, sliced
1 cup canned butter beans, drained
1 tablespoon balsamic vinegar
2 garlic cloves, minced
1 red chili, chopped
2 tablespoons fresh thyme, chopped
2 tablespoons olive oil
1. Place the sausages in the perforated pan.
2. Select Air Fry. Set temperature to 390ºF (199ºC) and set time to 10 minutes. Press Start to begin preheating.
3. Once preheated, place the pan into the oven.
4. After 7 minutes, remove the pan from the oven. Flip the sausages. Return the pan to the oven and continue cooking.
5. When cooking is complete, the sausages should be lightly browned.
6. Meanwhile, make the ratatouille: arrange the vegetable slices on the prepared pan

alternatively, then add the remaining ingredients on top.
7.	Transfer the air fried sausage to a plate, then place the pan into the oven.
8.	Select Bake. Set time to 15 minutes and bake until the vegetables are tender. Give the vegetables a stir halfway through the baking.
9.	Serve the ratatouille with the sausage on top.

Pork Meatballs with Scallions

Prep time: 5 minutes | Cook time: 15 minutes | Serves 4
1 pound (454 g) ground pork
2 cloves garlic, finely minced
1 cup scallions, finely chopped
1½ tablespoons Worcestershire sauce
½ teaspoon freshly grated ginger root
1 teaspoon turmeric powder
1 tablespoon oyster sauce
1 small sliced red chili, for garnish
Cooking spray
1.	Spritz the perforated pan with cooking spray.
2.	Combine all the ingredients, except for the red chili in a large bowl. Toss to mix well.
3.	Shape the mixture into equally sized balls, then arrange them in the perforated pan and spritz with cooking spray.
4.	Select Air Fry. Set temperature to 350ºF (180ºC) and set time to 15 minutes. Press Start to begin preheating.
5.	Once preheated, place the pan into the oven.
6.	After 7 minutes, remove the pan from the oven. Flip the balls. Return the pan to the oven and continue cooking.
7.	When cooking is complete, the balls should be lightly browned.
8.	Serve the pork meatballs with red chili on top.

Chuck and Sausage Meatballs

Prep time: 15 minutes | Cook time: 24 minutes | Serves 4
1 large egg
¼ cup whole milk
24 saltines, crushed but not pulverized
1 pound (454 g) ground chuck
1 pound (454 g) Italian sausage, casings removed
4 tablespoons grated Parmesan cheese, divided
1 teaspoon kosher salt
4 sub rolls, split
1 cup Marinara sauce
¾ cup shredded Mozzarella cheese
1.	In a large bowl, whisk the egg into the milk, then stir in the crackers. Let sit for 5 minutes to hydrate.
2.	With your hands, break the ground chuck and sausage into the milk mixture, alternating beef and sausage. When you've added half of the meat, sprinkle 2 tablespoons of the grated Parmesan and the salt over it, then continue breaking up the meat until it's all in the bowl. Gently mix everything together. Try not to overwork the meat, but get it all combined.
3.	Form the mixture into balls about the size of a golf ball. You should get about 24 meatballs. Flatten the balls slightly to prevent them from rolling, then place them on a baking pan, about 2 inches apart.
4.	Select Roast. Set temperature to 400ºF (205ºC) and set time to 20 minutes. Press Start to begin preheating.
5.	Once preheated, place the pan into the oven.
6.	After 10 minutes, remove the pan from the oven and turn over the meatballs. Return the pan to the oven and continue cooking.
7.	When cooking is complete, remove the pan from the oven. Place the meatballs on a rack. Wipe off the baking pan.
8.	Open the rolls, cut-side up, on the baking pan. Place 3 to 4 meatballs on the base of each roll, and top each sandwich with ¼ cup of marinara sauce. Divide the Mozzarella among the top halves of the buns and sprinkle the remaining Parmesan cheese over the Mozzarella.
9.	Select Broil. Set temperature to High and set time to 4 minutes. .
10.	Place the pan into the oven. Check the sandwiches after 2 minutes; the Mozzarella cheese should be melted and bubbling slightly.
11.	When cooking is complete, remove the pan from the oven. Close the sandwiches and serve.

Garlic Pork Leg Roast with Candy Onions

Prep time: 10 minutes | Cook time: 52 minutes | Serves 4
2 teaspoons sesame oil
1 teaspoon dried sage, crushed
1 teaspoon cayenne pepper
1 rosemary sprig, chopped
1 thyme sprig, chopped
Sea salt and ground black pepper, to taste
2 pounds (907 g) pork leg roast, scored
½ pound (227 g) candy onions, sliced
4 cloves garlic, finely chopped
2 chili peppers, minced
1.	In a mixing bowl, combine the sesame oil, sage, cayenne pepper, rosemary, thyme, salt and black pepper until well mixed. In another bowl, place the pork leg and brush with the seasoning mixture.
2.	Place the seasoned pork leg in a baking pan. Select Air Fry. Set temperature to 400ºF (205ºC) and set time to 40 minutes. Press Start to begin preheating.
3.	Once preheated, place the pan into the oven.
4.	After 20 minutes, remove the pan from the oven. Flip the pork leg. Return the pan to the oven and continue cooking.

5.	After another 20 minutes, add the candy onions, garlic, and chili peppers to the pan and air fry for another 12 minutes.
6.	When cooking is complete, the pork leg should be browned.
7.	Transfer the pork leg to a plate. Let cool for 5 minutes and slice. Spread the juices left in the pan over the pork and serve warm with the candy onions.

Breaded Pork Loin Chops

Prep time: 5 minutes | Cook time: 10 minutes | Serves 4
$^2/_3$ cup all-purpose flour
2 large egg whites
1 cup panko bread crumbs
4 (4-ounce / 113-g) center-cut boneless pork loin chops (about ½ inch thick)
Cooking spray
1.	Pour the flour in a bowl. Whisk the egg whites in a separate bowl. Spread the bread crumbs on a large plate.
2.	Dredge the pork loin chops in the flour first, press to coat well, then shake the excess off and dunk the chops in the eggs whites, and then roll the chops over the bread crumbs. Shake the excess off.
3.	Arrange the pork chops in the perforated pan and spritz with cooking spray.
4.	Select Air Fry. Set temperature to 375ºF (190ºC) and set time to 10 minutes. Press Start to begin preheating.
5.	Once preheated, place the pan into the oven.
6.	After 5 minutes, remove the pan from the oven. Flip the pork chops. Return the pan to the oven and continue cooking.
7.	When cooking is complete, the pork chops should be crunchy and lightly browned.
8.	Serve immediately.

Thyme Pork Chops with Carrots

Prep time: 10 minutes | Cook time: 15 minutes | Serves 4
2 carrots, cut into sticks
1 cup mushrooms, sliced
2 garlic cloves, minced
2 tablespoons olive oil
1 pound (454 g) boneless pork chops
1 teaspoon dried oregano
1 teaspoon dried thyme
1 teaspoon cayenne pepper
Salt and ground black pepper, to taste
Cooking spray
1.	In a mixing bowl, toss together the carrots, mushrooms, garlic, olive oil and salt until well combined.
2.	Add the pork chops to a different bowl and season with oregano, thyme, cayenne pepper, salt and black pepper.
3.	Lower the vegetable mixture in the greased pan. Place the seasoned pork chops on top.

4.	Select Air Fry. Set temperature to 360ºF (182ºC) and set time to 15 minutes. Press Start to begin preheating.
5.	Once preheated, place the pan into the oven.
6.	After 7 minutes, remove the pan from the oven. Flip the pork and stir the vegetables. Return the pan to the oven and continue cooking.
7.	When cooking is complete, the pork chops should be browned and the vegetables should be tender.
8.	Transfer the pork chops to the serving dishes and let cool for 5 minutes. Serve warm with vegetable on the side.

Balsamic Italian Sausages and Red Grapes

Prep time: 10 minutes | Cook time: 20 minutes | Serves 6
2 pounds (905 g) seedless red grapes
3 shallots, sliced
2 teaspoons fresh thyme
2 tablespoons olive oil
½ teaspoon kosher salt
Freshly ground black pepper, to taste
6 links (about 1½ pounds / 680 g) hot Italian sausage
3 tablespoons balsamic vinegar
1.	Place the grapes in a large bowl. Add the shallots, thyme, olive oil, salt, and pepper. Gently toss. Place the grapes in a baking pan. Arrange the sausage links evenly in the pan.
2.	Select Roast. Set temperature to 375ºF (190ºC) and set time to 20 minutes. Press Start to begin preheating.
3.	Once preheated, place the pan into the oven.
4.	After 10 minutes, remove the pan. Turn over the sausages and sprinkle the vinegar over the sausages and grapes. Gently toss the grapes and move them to one side of the pan. Return the pan to the oven and continue cooking.
5.	When cooking is complete, the grapes should be very soft and the sausages browned. Serve immediately.

Beef Meatloaves with Spinach

Prep time: 15 minutes | Cook time: 45 minutes | Serves 2
1 large egg, beaten
1 cup frozen spinach
$^1/_3$ cup almond meal
¼ cup chopped onion
¼ cup plain Greek milk
¼ teaspoon salt
¼ teaspoon dried sage
2 teaspoons olive oil, divided
Freshly ground black pepper, to taste
½ pound (227 g) extra-lean ground beef
¼ cup tomato paste
1 tablespoon granulated stevia
¼ teaspoon Worcestershire sauce

Cooking spray

1. Coat a shallow baking pan with cooking spray.

2. In a large bowl, combine the beaten egg, spinach, almond meal, onion, milk, salt, sage, 1 teaspoon of olive oil, and pepper.

3. Crumble the beef over the spinach mixture. Mix well to combine. Divide the meat mixture in half. Shape each half into a loaf. Place the loaves in the prepared pan.

4. In a small bowl, whisk together the tomato paste, stevia, Worcestershire sauce, and remaining 1 teaspoon of olive oil. Spoon half of the sauce over each meatloaf.

5. Select Bake. set temperature to 350ºF (180ºC) and set time to 40 minutes. Press Start to begin preheating.

6. Once preheated, place the pan into the oven.

7. When cooking is complete, an instant-read thermometer inserted in the center of the meatloaves should read at least 165ºF (74ºC).

8. Serve immediately.

Breaded Calf's Liver Strips

Prep time: 15 minutes | Cook time: 4 to 5 minutes | Serves 4

1 pound (454 g) sliced calf's liver, cut into about ½-inch-wide strips
Salt and ground black pepper, to taste
2 eggs
2 tablespoons milk
½ cup whole wheat flour
1½ cups panko bread crumbs
½ cup plain bread crumbs
½ teaspoon salt
¼ teaspoon ground black pepper
Cooking spray

1. Sprinkle the liver strips with salt and pepper.

2. Beat together the egg and milk in a bowl. Place wheat flour in a shallow dish. In a second shallow dish, mix panko, plain bread crumbs, ½ teaspoon salt, and ¼ teaspoon pepper.

3. Dip liver strips in flour, egg wash, and then bread crumbs, pressing in coating slightly to make crumbs stick.

4. Spritz the perforated pan with cooking spray. Place strips in a single layer in the perforated pan.

5. Select Air Fry. Set temperature to 400ºF (205ºC) and set time to 4 minutes. Press Start to begin preheating.

6. Once preheated, place the pan into the oven.

7. After 2 minutes, remove the pan from the oven. Flip the strips with tongs. Return the pan to the oven and continue cooking.

8. When cooking is complete, the liver strips should be crispy and golden.

9. Serve immediately.

Pork Chops and Apple Bake

Prep time: 10 minutes | Cook time: 45 minutes | Serves 4

2 apples, peeled, cored, and sliced
1 teaspoon ground cinnamon, divided
4 boneless pork chops (½-inch thick)
Salt and freshly ground black pepper, to taste
3 tablespoons brown sugar
¾ cup water
1 tablespoon olive oil

1. Layer apples in bottom of a baking pan. Sprinkle with ½ teaspoon of cinnamon.

2. Trim fat from pork chops. Lay on top of the apple slices. Sprinkle with salt and pepper.

3. In a small bowl, combine the brown sugar, water, and remaining cinnamon. Pour the mixture over the chops. Drizzle chops with 1 tablespoon of olive oil.

4. Select Bake. Set temperature to 375ºF (190ºC) and set time to 45 minutes. Press Start to begin preheating.

5. Once preheated, place the pan into the oven.

6. When cooking is complete, an instant-read thermometer inserted in the pork should register 165ºF (74ºC).

7. Allow to rest for 3 minutes before serving.

Pork Tenderloin with Rice

Prep time: 10 minutes | Cook time: 12 minutes | Serves 4

3 scallions, diced (about ½ cup)
½ red bell pepper, diced (about ½ cup)
2 teaspoons sesame oil
½ pound (227 g) pork tenderloin, diced
½ cup frozen peas, thawed
½ cup roasted mushrooms
½ cup soy sauce
2 cups cooked rice
1 egg, beaten

1. Place the scallions and red pepper on a baking pan. Drizzle with the sesame oil and toss the vegetables to coat them in the oil.

2. Select Roast. Set temperature to 375ºF (190ºC) and set time to 12 minutes. Press Start to begin preheating.

3. Once preheated, place the pan into the oven.

4. While the vegetables are cooking, place the pork in a large bowl. Add the peas, mushrooms, soy sauce, and rice and toss to coat the ingredients with the sauce.

5. After about 4 minutes, remove the pan from the oven. Place the pork mixture on the pan and stir the scallions and peppers into the pork and rice. Return the pan to the oven and continue cooking.

6. After another 6 minutes, remove the pan from the oven. Move the rice mixture to the sides to create an empty circle in the middle of the pan. Pour the egg in the circle. Return the pan to the oven and continue cooking.

7.	When cooking is complete, remove the pan from the oven and stir the egg to scramble it. Stir the egg into the fried rice mixture. Serve immediately.

Pork and Lettuce Wraps with Almonds

Prep time: 10 minutes | Cook time: 12 minutes | Serves 4
1 (1-pound / 454-g) medium pork tenderloin, silver skin and external fat trimmed
$^2/_3$ cup soy sauce, divided
1 teaspoon cornstarch
1 medium jalapeño, deseeded and minced
1 can diced water chestnuts
½ large red bell pepper, deseeded and chopped
2 scallions, chopped, white and green parts separated
1 head butter lettuce
½ cup roasted, chopped almonds
¼ cup coarsely chopped cilantro
1.	Cut the tenderloin into ¼-inch slices and place them on a baking pan. Baste with about 3 tablespoons of soy sauce. Stir the cornstarch into the remaining sauce and set aside.
2.	Select Roast. Set temperature to 375ºF (190ºC) and set time to 12 minutes. Press Start to begin preheating.
3.	Once preheated, place the pan into the oven.
4.	After 5 minutes, remove the pan from the oven. Place the pork slices on a cutting board. Place the jalapeño, water chestnuts, red pepper, and the white parts of the scallions on the baking pan and pour the remaining sauce over. Stir to coat the vegetables with the sauce. Return the pan to the oven and continue cooking.
5.	While the vegetables cook, chop the pork into small pieces. Separate the lettuce leaves, discarding any tough outer leaves and setting aside the small inner leaves for another use. You'll want 12 to 18 leaves, depending on size and your appetites.
6.	After 5 minutes, remove the pan from the oven. Add the pork to the vegetables, stirring to combine. Return the pan to the oven and continue cooking for the remaining 2 minutes until the pork is warmed back up and the sauce has reduced slightly.
7.	When cooking is complete, remove the pan from the oven. Place the pork and vegetables in a medium serving bowl and stir in half the green parts of the scallions. To serve, spoon some pork and vegetables into each of the lettuce leaves. Top with the remaining scallion greens and garnish with the nuts and cilantro.

Pork Chop Roast with Worcestershire

Prep time: 5 minutes | Cook time: 20 minutes | Serves 2
2 (10-ounce / 284-g) bone-in, center cut pork chops, 1-inch thick
2 teaspoons Worcestershire sauce
Salt and ground black pepper, to taste
Cooking spray
1.	Rub the Worcestershire sauce on both sides of pork chops.
2.	Season with salt and pepper to taste.
3.	Spritz the perforated pan with cooking spray and place the chops in the perforated pan side by side.
4.	Select Roast. Set temperature to 350ºF (180ºC) and set time to 20 minutes. Press Start to begin preheating.
5.	Once preheated, place the pan into the oven.
6.	After 10 minutes, remove the pan from the oven. Flip the pork chops with tongs. Return the pan to the oven and continue cooking.
7.	When cooking is complete, the pork should be well browned on both sides.
8.	Let rest for 5 minutes before serving.

Worcestershire Ribeye Steaks with Garlic

Prep time: 15 minutes | Cook time: 10 to 12 minutes | Serves 2 to 4
2 (8-ounce / 227-g) boneless ribeye steaks
4 teaspoons Worcestershire sauce
½ teaspoon garlic powder
Salt and ground black pepper, to taste
4 teaspoons olive oil
1.	Brush the steaks with Worcestershire sauce on both sides. Sprinkle with garlic powder and coarsely ground black pepper. Drizzle the steaks with olive oil. Allow steaks to marinate for 30 minutes.
2.	Transfer the steaks in the perforated pan.
3.	Select Roast. Set temperature to 400ºF (205ºC) and set time to 4 minutes. Press Start to begin preheating.
4.	Once preheated, place the pan into the oven.
5.	After 2 minutes, remove the pan from the oven. Flip the steaks. Return the pan to the oven and continue cooking.
6.	When cooking is complete, the steaks should be well browned.
7.	Remove the steaks from the perforated pan and let sit for 5 minutes. Salt and serve.

Orange Beef and Broccoli with Sriracha

Prep time: 10 minutes | Cook time: 15 minutes | Serves 4
12 ounces (340 g) broccoli, cut into florets (about 4 cups)
1 pound (454 g) flat iron steak, cut into thin strips
½ teaspoon kosher salt
¾ cup soy sauce
1 teaspoon Sriracha sauce
3 tablespoons freshly squeezed orange juice
1 teaspoon cornstarch
1 medium onion, thinly sliced
1.	Line a baking pan with aluminum foil. Place the broccoli on top and sprinkle with 3 tablespoons of water. Seal the broccoli in the foil in a single layer.

2. Select Roast. Set temperature to 375ºF (190ºC) and set time to 6 minutes. Press Start to begin preheating.
3. Once preheated, place the pan into the oven.
4. While the broccoli steams, sprinkle the steak with the salt. In a small bowl, whisk together the soy sauce, Sriracha, orange juice, and cornstarch. Place the onion and beef in a large bowl.
5. When cooking is complete, remove the pan from the oven. Open the packet of broccoli and use tongs to transfer the broccoli to the bowl with the beef and onion, discarding the foil and remaining water. Pour the sauce over the beef and vegetables and toss to coat. Place the mixture in the baking pan.
6. Select Roast. Set temperature to 375ºF (190ºC) and set time to 9 minutes.
7. Place the pan into the oven.
8. After about 4 minutes, remove the pan from the oven and gently toss the ingredients. Return the pan to oven and continue cooking.
9. When cooking is complete, the sauce should be thickened, the vegetables tender, and the beef barely pink in the center. Serve warm.

Mexican Sirloin Steak and Pepper Fajitas

Prep time: 10 minutes | Cook time: 15 minutes | Serves 4

8 (6-inch) flour tortillas
1 pound (454 g) top sirloin steak, sliced ¼-inch thick
1 red bell pepper, deseeded and sliced ½-inch thick
1 green bell pepper, deseeded and sliced ½-inch thick
1 jalapeño, deseeded and sliced thin
1 medium onion, sliced ½-inch thick
2 tablespoons vegetable oil
2 tablespoons Mexican seasoning
1 teaspoon kosher salt
2 tablespoons salsa
1 small avocado, sliced
1. Line a baking pan with aluminum foil. Place the tortillas on the foil in two stacks and wrap in the foil.
2. Select Roast. Set temperature to 325ºF (163ºC) and set time to 6 minutes. Press Start to begin preheating.
3. Once preheated, place the pan into the oven. After 3 minutes, remove the pan from the oven and flip the packet of tortillas over. Return the pan to the oven and continue cooking.
4. While the tortillas warm, place the steak, bell peppers, jalapeño, and onion in a large bowl and drizzle the oil over. Sprinkle with the Mexican seasoning and salt, and toss to coat.
5. When cooking is complete, remove the pan from the oven and place the packet of tortillas on top of the oven to keep warm. Place the beef and peppers mixture on the baking pan, spreading out into a single layer as much as possible.
6. Select Roast. Set temperature to 375ºF (190ºC) and set time to 9 minutes.

7. Place the pan into the oven.
8. After about 5 minutes, remove the pan from the oven and stir the ingredients. Return the pan to the oven and continue cooking.
9. When cooking is complete, the vegetables will be soft and browned in places, and the beef will be browned on the outside and barely pink inside. Remove the pan from the oven. Unwrap the tortillas and spoon the fajita mixture into the tortillas. Serve with salsa and avocado slices.

Beef Ravioli with Parmesan

Prep time: 10 minutes | Cook time: 10 minutes | Serves 4

1 (20-ounce / 567-g) package frozen cheese ravioli
1 teaspoon kosher salt
1¼ cups water
6 ounces (170 g) cooked ground beef
2½ cups Marinara sauce
¼ cup grated Parmesan cheese, for garnish
1. Place the ravioli in an even layer on a baking pan. Stir the salt into the water until dissolved and pour it over the ravioli.
2. Select Bake. Set temperature to 450ºF (235ºC) and set time to 10 minutes. Press Start to begin preheating.
3. Once preheated, place the pan into the oven.
4. While the ravioli is cooking, mix the ground beef into the marinara sauce in a medium bowl.
5. After 6 minutes, remove the pan from the oven. Blot off any remaining water, or drain the ravioli and return them to the pan. Pour the meat sauce over the ravioli. Return the pan to the oven and continue cooking.
6. When cooking is complete, remove the pan from the oven. The ravioli should be tender and sauce heated through. Gently stir the ingredients. Serve the ravioli with the Parmesan cheese, if desired.

Pork Cutlets with Aloha Salsa

Prep time: 20 minutes | Cook time: 7 minutes | Serves 4

2 eggs
2 tablespoons milk
¼ cup all-purpose flour
¼ cup panko bread crumbs
4 teaspoons sesame seeds
1 pound (454 g) boneless, thin pork cutlets (½-inch thick)
¼ cup cornstarch
Salt and ground lemon pepper, to taste
Cooking spray
Aloha Salsa:
1 cup fresh pineapple, chopped in small pieces
¼ cup red bell pepper, chopped
½ teaspoon ground cinnamon
1 teaspoon soy sauce
¼ cup red onion, finely chopped
⅛ teaspoon crushed red pepper

⅛ teaspoon ground black pepper
1.	In a medium bowl, stir together all ingredients for salsa. Cover and refrigerate while cooking the pork.
2.	Beat together eggs and milk in a large bowl. In another bowl, mix the flour, panko, and sesame seeds. Pour the cornstarch in a shallow dish.
3.	Sprinkle pork cutlets with lemon pepper and salt. Dip pork cutlets in cornstarch, egg mixture, and then panko coating. Spritz both sides with cooking spray.
4.	Select Air Fry. Set temperature to 400ºF (205ºC) and set time to 7 minutes. Press Start to begin preheating.
5.	Once preheated, place the pan into the oven.
6.	After 3 minutes, remove the pan from the oven. Flip the cutlets with tongs. Return the pan to the oven and continue cooking.
7.	When cooking is complete, the pork should be crispy and golden brown on both sides.
8.	Serve the fried cutlets with the Aloha salsa on the side.

Dijon-Honey Pork Tenderloin

Prep time: 15 minutes | Cook time: 15 minutes | Serves 4
3 tablespoons Dijon mustard
3 tablespoons honey
1 teaspoon dried rosemary
1 tablespoon olive oil
1 pound (454 g) pork tenderloin, rinsed and drained
Salt and freshly ground black pepper, to taste
1.	In a small bowl, combine the Dijon mustard, honey, and rosemary. Stir to combine.
2.	Rub the pork tenderloin with salt and pepper on all sides on a clean work surface.
3.	Heat the olive oil in an oven-safe skillet over high heat. Sear the pork loin on all sides in the skillet for 6 minutes or until golden brown. Flip the pork halfway through.
4.	Remove from the heat and spread honey-mustard mixture evenly to coat the pork loin. Transfer the pork to a sheet pan.
5.	Select Bake. Set temperature to 425ºF (220ºC) and set time to 15 minutes. Press Start to begin preheating.
6.	Once preheated, place the pan into the oven.
7.	When cooking is complete, an instant-read thermometer inserted in the pork should register at least 145ºF (63ºC).
8.	Remove from the oven and allow to rest for 3 minutes. Slice the pork into ½-inch slices and serve.

Pork Loin Chops with Butternut Squash

Prep time: 15 minutes | Cook time: 13 minutes | Serves 4
4 boneless pork loin chops, ¾- to 1-inch thick
1 teaspoon kosher salt, divided
2 tablespoons Dijon mustard

2 tablespoons brown sugar
1 pound (454 g) butternut squash, cut into 1-inch cubes
1 large apple, peeled and cut into 12 to 16 wedges
1 medium onion, thinly sliced
½ teaspoon dried thyme
¼ teaspoon freshly ground black pepper
1 tablespoon unsalted butter, melted
½ cup chicken stock
1.	Sprinkle the pork chops on both sides with ½ teaspoon of kosher salt. In a small bowl, whisk together the mustard and brown sugar. Baste about half of the mixture on one side of the pork chops. Place the chops, basted-side up, on a baking pan.
2.	Place the squash in a large bowl. Add the apple, onion, thyme, remaining kosher salt, pepper, and butter and toss to coat. Arrange the squash-fruit mixture around the chops on the pan. Pour the chicken stock over the mixture, avoiding the chops.
3.	Select Roast. Set temperature to 350ºF (180ºC) and set time to 13 minutes. Press Start to begin preheating.
4.	Once preheated, place the pan into the oven.
5.	After about 7 minutes, remove the pan from the oven. Gently toss the squash mixture and turn over the chops. Baste the chops with the remaining mustard mixture. Return the pan to the oven and continue cooking.
6.	When cooking is complete, the pork chops should register at least 145ºF (63ºC) in the center on a meat thermometer, and the squash and apples should be tender. If necessary, continue cooking for up to 3 minutes more.
7.	Remove the pan from the oven. Spoon the squash and apples onto four plates, and place a pork chop on top. Serve immediately.

Mozzarella Sausage Calzones

Prep time: 10 minutes | Cook time: 24 minutes | Serves 4
2 links Italian sausages (about ½ pound / 227 g)
1 pound (454 g) pizza dough, thawed
3 tablespoons olive oil, divided
¼ cup Marinara sauce
½ cup roasted mushrooms
1 cup shredded Mozzarella cheese
1.	Place the sausages in a baking pan.
2.	Select Roast. Set temperature to 375ºF (190ºC) and set time to 12 minutes. Press Start to begin preheating.
3.	Once preheated, place the pan into the oven.
4.	After 6 minutes, remove the pan from the oven and turn over the sausages. Return the pan to the oven and continue cooking.
5.	While the sausages cook, divide the pizza dough into 4 equal pieces. One at a time, place a piece of dough onto a square of parchment paper 9 inches in diameter. Brush the dough on both sides with ¾ teaspoon of olive oil, then top the dough with another piece of parchment. Press the dough into a 7-

inch circle. Remove the top piece of parchment and set aside. Repeat with the remaining pieces of dough.
6.   When cooking is complete, remove the pan from the oven. Place the sausages on a cutting board. Let them cool for several minutes, then slice into ¼-inch rounds and cut each round into 4 pieces.
7.   One at a time, spread a tablespoon of marinara sauce over half of a dough circle, leaving a ½-inch border at the edges. Cover with a quarter of the sausage pieces and add a quarter of the mushrooms. Sprinkle with ¼ cup of cheese. Pull the other side of the dough over the filling and pinch the edges together to seal. Transfer from the parchment to the baking pan. Repeat with the other rounds of dough, sauce, sausage, mushrooms, and cheese.

8.   Brush the tops of the calzones with 1 tablespoon of olive oil.
9.   Select Roast. Set temperature to 450ºF (235ºC) and set time to 12 minutes.
10.   Place the pan into the oven.
11.   After 6 minutes, remove the pan from the oven. The calzones should be golden brown. Turn over the calzones and brush the tops with the remaining olive oil. Return the pan to the oven and continue cooking.
12.   When cooking is complete, the crust should be a deep golden brown on both sides. Remove the pan from the oven. The center should be molten; let cool for several minutes before serving.

CHAPTER 8 FISH AND SEAFOOD

Tuna Casserole with Basil

Prep time: 10 minutes | Cook time: 16 minutes | Serves 4

½ tablespoon sesame oil
$^{1}/_{3}$ cup yellow onions, chopped
½ bell pepper, seeded and chopped
2 cups canned tuna, chopped
Cooking spray
5 eggs, beaten
½ chili pepper, deveined and finely minced
1½ tablespoons sour cream
$^{1}/_{3}$ teaspoon dried basil
$^{1}/_{3}$ teaspoon dried oregano
Fine sea salt and ground black pepper, to taste

1. Heat the sesame oil in a nonstick skillet over medium heat until it shimmers.
2. Add the onions and bell pepper and sauté for 4 minutes, stirring occasionally, or until tender.
3. Add the canned tuna and keep stirring until the tuna is heated through.
4. Meanwhile, coat a baking dish lightly with cooking spray.
5. Transfer the tuna mixture to the baking dish, along with the beaten eggs, chili pepper, sour cream, basil, and oregano. Stir to combine well. Season with sea salt and black pepper.
6. Select Bake. Set temperature to 325ºF (163ºC) and set time to 12 minutes. Press Start to begin preheating.
7. Once preheated, place the baking dish into the oven.
8. When cooking is complete, the eggs should be completely set and the top lightly browned. Remove from the oven and serve on a plate.

Salmon Spring Rolls with Parsley

Prep time: 20 minutes | Cook time: 18 minutes | Serves 4

½ pound (227 g) salmon fillet
1 teaspoon toasted sesame oil
1 onion, sliced
1 carrot, shredded
1 yellow bell pepper, thinly sliced
$^{1}/_{3}$ cup chopped fresh flat-leaf parsley
¼ cup chopped fresh basil
8 rice paper wrappers

1. Arrange the salmon in the perforated pan. Drizzle the sesame oil all over the salmon and scatter the onion on top.
2. Select Air Fry. Set temperature to 370ºF (188ºC) and set time to 10 minutes. Press Start to begin preheating.
3. Once preheated, place the pan into the oven.
4. Meanwhile, fill a small shallow bowl with warm water. One by one, dip the rice paper wrappers into the water for a few seconds or just until moistened, then put them on a work surface.
5. When cooking is complete, the fish should flake apart with a fork. Remove from the oven to a plate.
6. Make the spring rolls: Place ⅛ of the salmon and onion mixture, carrot, bell pepper, parsley, and basil into the center of the rice wrapper and fold the sides over the filling. Roll up the wrapper carefully and tightly like you would a burrito. Repeat with the remaining wrappers and filling.
7. Transfer the rolls to the perforated pan.
8. Select Bake. Set temperature to 380ºF (193ºC) and set time to 8 minutes. Place the pan into the oven.
9. When cooking is complete, the rolls should be crispy and lightly browned. Remove from the oven and cut each roll in half and serve warm.

Cajun Tilapia Tacos

Prep time: 10 minutes | Cook time: 10 to 15 minutes | Serves 6

1 tablespoon avocado oil
1 tablespoon Cajun seasoning
4 (5 to 6 ounce / 142 to 170 g) tilapia fillets
1 (14-ounce / 397-g) package coleslaw mix
12 corn tortillas
2 limes, cut into wedges

1. Line a baking pan with parchment paper.
2. In a shallow bowl, stir together the avocado oil and Cajun seasoning to make a marinade. Place the tilapia fillets into the bowl, turning to coat evenly.
3. Put the fillets in the baking pan in a single layer.
4. Select Air Fry. Set temperature to 375ºF (190ºC) and set time to 10 minutes. Press Start to begin preheating.
5. Once preheated, slide the pan into the oven.
6. When cooked, the fish should be flaky. If necessary, continue cooking for 5 minutes more. Remove the fish from the oven to a plate.
7. Assemble the tacos: Spoon some of the coleslaw mix into each tortilla and top each with $^{1}/_{3}$ of a tilapia fillet. Squeeze some lime juice over the top of each taco and serve immediately.

Hoisin Tuna with Lemongrass

Prep time: 15 minutes | Cook time: 5 minutes | Serves 4

½ cup hoisin sauce
2 tablespoons rice wine vinegar
2 teaspoons sesame oil
2 teaspoons dried lemongrass
1 teaspoon garlic powder
¼ teaspoon red pepper flakes
½ small onion, quartered and thinly sliced
8 ounces (227 g) fresh tuna, cut into 1-inch cubes
Cooking spray

3 cups cooked jasmine rice
1.	In a small bowl, whisk together the hoisin sauce, vinegar, sesame oil, lemongrass, garlic powder, and red pepper flakes.
2.	Add the sliced onion and tuna cubes and gently toss until the fish is evenly coated.
3.	Arrange the coated tuna cubes in the perforated pan in a single layer.
4.	Select Air Fry. Set temperature to 390ºF (199ºC) and set time to 5 minutes. Press Start to begin preheating.
5.	Once preheated, place the pan into the oven. Flip the fish halfway through the cooking time.
6.	When cooking is complete, the fish should begin to flake. Continue cooking for 1 minute, if necessary. Remove from the oven and serve over hot jasmine rice.

Tilapia Meunière with Parsley

Prep time: 10 minutes | Cook time: 20 minutes | Serves 4
10 ounces (283 g) Yukon Gold potatoes, sliced ¼-inch thick
5 tablespoons unsalted butter, melted, divided
1 teaspoon kosher salt, divided
4 (8-ounce / 227-g) tilapia fillets
½ pound (227 g) green beans, trimmed
Juice of 1 lemon
2 tablespoons chopped fresh parsley, for garnish
1.	In a large bowl, drizzle the potatoes with 2 tablespoons of melted butter and ¼ teaspoon of kosher salt. Transfer the potatoes to the sheet pan.
2.	Select Roast. Set temperature to 375ºF (190ºC) and set time to 20 minutes. Press Start to begin preheating.
3.	Once the oven has preheated, place the pan into the oven.
4.	Meanwhile, season both sides of the fillets with ½ teaspoon of kosher salt. Put the green beans in the medium bowl and sprinkle with the remaining ¼ teaspoon of kosher salt and 1 tablespoon of butter, tossing to coat.
5.	After 10 minutes, remove the pan and push the potatoes to one side. Put the fillets in the middle of the pan and add the green beans on the other side. Drizzle the remaining 2 tablespoons of butter over the fillets. Return the pan to the oven and continue cooking, or until the fish flakes easily with a fork and the green beans are crisp-tender.
6.	When cooked, remove the pan from the oven. Drizzle the lemon juice over the fillets and sprinkle the parsley on top for garnish. Serve hot.

Tuna and Fruit Kebabs with Honey Glaze

Prep time: 15 minutes | Cook time: 10 minutes | Serves 4
Kebabs:
1 pound (454 g) tuna steaks, cut into 1-inch cubes
½ cup canned pineapple chunks, drained, juice reserved
½ cup large red grapes
Marinade:
1 tablespoon honey
1 teaspoon olive oil
2 teaspoons grated fresh ginger
Pinch cayenne pepper
Special Equipment:
4 metal skewers
1.	Make the kebabs: Thread, alternating tuna cubes, pineapple chunks, and red grapes, onto the metal skewers.
2.	Make the marinade: Whisk together the honey, olive oil, ginger, and cayenne pepper in a small bowl. Brush generously the marinade over the kebabs and allow to sit for 10 minutes.
3.	When ready, transfer the kebabs to the perforated pan.
4.	Select Air Fry. Set temperature to 370ºF (188ºC) and set time to 10 minutes. Press Start to begin preheating.
5.	Once preheated, place the pan into the oven.
6.	After 5 minutes, remove from the oven and flip the kebabs and brush with the remaining marinade. Return the pan to the oven and continue cooking for an additional 5 minutes.
7.	When cooking is complete, the kebabs should reach an internal temperature of 145ºF (63ºC) on a meat thermometer. Remove from the oven and discard any remaining marinade. Serve hot.

Breaded Fish Fillets with Mustard

Prep time: 20 minutes | Cook time: 7 minutes | Serves 4
1 pound (454 g) fish fillets
1 tablespoon coarse brown mustard
1 teaspoon Worcestershire sauce
½ teaspoon hot sauce
Salt, to taste
Cooking spray
Crumb Coating:
¾ cup panko bread crumbs
¼ cup stone-ground cornmeal
¼ teaspoon salt
1.	On your cutting board, cut the fish fillets crosswise into slices, about 1 inch wide.
2.	In a small bowl, stir together the mustard, Worcestershire sauce, and hot sauce to make a paste and rub this paste on all sides of the fillets. Season with salt to taste.
3.	In a shallow bowl, thoroughly combine all the ingredients for the crumb coating and spread them on a sheet of wax paper.
4.	Roll the fish fillets in the crumb mixture until thickly coated. Spritz all sides of the fish with cooking spray, then arrange them in the perforated pan in a single layer.

5.	Select Air Fry. Set temperature to 400ºF (205ºC) and set time to 7 minutes. Press Start to begin preheating.
6.	Once preheated, place the perforated pan into the oven.
7.	When cooking is complete, the fish should flake apart with a fork. Remove from the oven and serve warm.

Cayenne Cod Fillets

Prep time: 15 minutes | Cook time: 12 minutes | Serves 4
4 cod fillets
¼ teaspoon fine sea salt
1 teaspoon cayenne pepper
¼ teaspoon ground black pepper, or more to taste
½ cup fresh Italian parsley, coarsely chopped
½ cup non-dairy milk
4 garlic cloves, minced
1 Italian pepper, chopped
1 teaspoon dried basil
½ teaspoon dried oregano
Cooking spray
1.	Lightly spritz a baking dish with cooking spray.
2.	Season the fillets with salt, cayenne pepper, and black pepper.
3.	Pulse the remaining ingredients in a food processor, then transfer the mixture to a shallow bowl. Coat the fillets with the mixture.
4.	Select Air Fry. Set temperature to 375ºF (190ºC) and set time to 12 minutes. Press Start to begin preheating.
5.	Once preheated, place the baking dish into the oven.
6.	When cooking is complete, the fish will be flaky. Remove from the oven and serve on a plate.

Breaded Fish Sticks

Prep time: 10 minutes | Cook time: 6 minutes | Serves 8
8 ounces (227 g) fish fillets (pollock or cod) cut into ½ × 3 inches strips
Salt, to taste (optional)
½ cup plain bread crumbs
Cooking spray
1.	Season the fish strips with salt to taste, if desired.
2.	Place the bread crumbs on a plate, then roll the fish in the bread crumbs until well coated. Spray all sides of the fish with cooking spray. Transfer to the perforated pan in a single layer.
3.	Select Air Fry. Set temperature to 400ºF (205ºC) and set time to 6 minutes. Press Start to begin preheating.
4.	Once preheated, place the pan into the oven.
5.	When cooked, the fish sticks should be golden brown and crispy. Remove from the oven to a plate and serve hot.

Tuna and Veggie Salad

Prep time: 10 minutes | Cook time: 15 minutes | Serves 4
10 ounces (283 g) small red potatoes, quartered
8 tablespoons extra-virgin olive oil, divided
1 teaspoon kosher salt, divided
½ pound (227 g) green beans, trimmed
1 pint cherry tomatoes
1 teaspoon Dijon mustard
3 tablespoons red wine vinegar
Freshly ground black pepper, to taste
1 (9-ounce / 255-g) bag spring greens, washed and dried if needed
2 (5-ounce / 142-g) cans oil-packed tuna, drained
2 hard-cooked eggs, peeled and quartered
$^1/_3$ cup kalamata olives, pitted
1.	In a large bowl, drizzle the potatoes with 1 tablespoon of olive oil and season with ¼ teaspoon of kosher salt. Transfer to a sheet pan.
2.	Select Roast. Set temperature to 375ºF (190ºC) and set time to 15 minutes. Press Start to begin preheating.
3.	Once the oven has preheated, place the pan into the oven.
4.	Meanwhile, in a mixing bowl, toss the green beans and cherry tomatoes with 1 tablespoon of olive oil and ¼ teaspoon of kosher salt until evenly coated.
5.	After 10 minutes, remove the pan and fold in the green beans and cherry tomatoes. Return the pan to the oven and continue cooking.
6.	Meanwhile, make the vinaigrette by whisking together the remaining 6 tablespoons of olive oil, mustard, vinegar, the remaining ½ teaspoon of kosher salt, and black pepper in a small bowl. Set aside.
7.	When done, remove the pan from the oven. Allow the vegetables to cool for 5 minutes.
8.	Spread out the spring greens on a plate and spoon the tuna into the center of the greens. Arrange the potatoes, green beans, cheery tomatoes, and eggs around the tuna. Serve drizzled with the vinaigrette and scattered with the olives.

Salmon with Roasted Asparagus

Prep time: 5 minutes | Cook time: 12 minutes | Serves 2
2 teaspoons olive oil, plus additional for drizzling
2 (5-ounce / 142-g) salmon fillets, with skin
Salt and freshly ground black pepper, to taste
1 bunch asparagus, trimmed
1 teaspoon dried tarragon
1 teaspoon dried chives
Fresh lemon wedges, for serving
1.	Rub the olive oil all over the salmon fillets. Sprinkle with salt and pepper to taste.
2.	Put the asparagus on a foil-lined baking sheet and place the salmon fillets on top, skin-side down.

3.	Select Roast. Set temperature to 425ºF (220ºC) and set time to 12 minutes. Press Start to begin preheating.
4.	Once preheated, place the pan into the oven.
5.	When cooked, the fillets should register 145ºF (63ºC) on an instant-read thermometer. Remove from the oven and cut the salmon fillets in half crosswise, then use a metal spatula to lift flesh from skin and transfer to a serving plate. Discard the skin and drizzle the salmon fillets with additional olive oil. Scatter with the herbs.
6.	Serve the salmon fillets with roasted asparagus spears and lemon wedges on the side.

Salmon with Cherry Tomatoes

Prep time: 10 minutes | Cook time: 15 minutes | Serves 4
4 (6-ounce / 170-g) salmon fillets, patted dry
1 teaspoon kosher salt, divided
2 pints cherry or grape tomatoes, halved if large, divided
3 tablespoons extra-virgin olive oil, divided
2 garlic cloves, minced
1 small red bell pepper, seeded and chopped
2 tablespoons chopped fresh basil, divided
1.	Season both sides of the salmon with ½ teaspoon of kosher salt.
2.	Put about half of the tomatoes in a large bowl, along with the remaining ½ teaspoon of kosher salt, 2 tablespoons of olive oil, garlic, bell pepper, and 1 tablespoon of basil. Toss to coat and then transfer to the sheet pan.
3.	Arrange the salmon fillets on the sheet pan, skin-side down. Brush them with the remaining 1 tablespoon of olive oil.
4.	Select Roast. Set temperature to 375ºF (190ºC) and set time to 15 minutes. Press Start to begin preheating.
5.	Once preheated, place the pan into the oven.
6.	After 7 minutes, remove the pan and fold in the remaining tomatoes. Return the pan to the oven and continue cooking.
7.	When cooked, remove the pan from the oven. Serve sprinkled with the remaining 1 tablespoon of basil.

Teriyaki Salmon and Bok Choy

Prep time: 15 minutes | Cook time: 15 minutes | Serves 4
¾ cup Teriyaki sauce, divided
4 (6-ounce / 170-g) skinless salmon fillets
4 heads baby bok choy, root ends trimmed off and cut in half lengthwise through the root
1 teaspoon sesame oil
1 tablespoon vegetable oil
1 tablespoon toasted sesame seeds
1.	Set aside ¼ cup of Teriyaki sauce and pour the remaining sauce into a resealable plastic bag. Put the salmon into the bag and seal, squeezing as much

air out as possible. Allow the salmon to marinate for at least 10 minutes.
2.	Arrange the bok choy halves on the sheet pan. Drizzle the oils over the vegetables, tossing to coat. Drizzle about 1 tablespoon of the reserved Teriyaki sauce over the bok choy, then push them to the sides of the sheet pan.
3.	Put the salmon fillets in the middle of the sheet pan.
4.	Select Roast. Set temperature to 375ºF (190ºC) and set time to 15 minutes. Press Start to begin preheating.
5.	Once the oven has preheated, place the pan into the oven.
6.	When done, remove the pan and brush the salmon with the remaining Teriyaki sauce. Serve garnished with the sesame seeds.

Honey-Lemon Snapper with Grapes

Prep time: 15 minutes | Cook time: 12 minutes | Serves 4
4 (4-ounce / 113-g) red snapper fillets
2 teaspoons olive oil
3 plums, halved and pitted
3 nectarines, halved and pitted
1 cup red grapes
1 tablespoon freshly squeezed lemon juice
1 tablespoon honey
½ teaspoon dried thyme
1.	Arrange the red snapper fillets in the perforated pan and drizzle the olive oil over the top.
2.	Select Air Fry. Set temperature to 390ºF (199ºC) and set time to 12 minutes. Press Start to begin preheating.
3.	Once preheated, place the pan into the oven.
4.	After 4 minutes, remove the pan from the oven. Top the fillets with the plums and nectarines. Scatter the red grapes all over the fillets. Drizzle with the lemon juice and honey and sprinkle the thyme on top. Return the pan to the oven and continue cooking for 8 minutes, or until the fish is flaky.
5.	When cooking is complete, remove from the oven and serve warm.

Ginger Swordfish Steaks with Jalapeño

Prep time: 10 minutes | Cook time: 8 minutes | Serves 4
4 (4-ounce / 113-g) swordfish steaks
½ teaspoon toasted sesame oil
1 jalapeño pepper, finely minced
2 garlic cloves, grated
2 tablespoons freshly squeezed lemon juice
1 tablespoon grated fresh ginger
½ teaspoon Chinese five-spice powder
⅛ teaspoon freshly ground black pepper
1.	On a clean work surface, place the swordfish steaks and brush both sides of the fish with the sesame oil.

2. Combine the jalapeño, garlic, lemon juice, ginger, five-spice powder, and black pepper in a small bowl and stir to mix well. Rub the mixture all over the fish until completely coated. Allow to sit for 10 minutes.
3. When ready, arrange the swordfish steaks in the perforated pan.
4. Select Air Fry. Set temperature to 380ºF (193ºC) and set time to 8 minutes. Press Start to begin preheating.
5. Once preheated, place the pan into the oven. Flip the steaks halfway through.
6. When cooking is complete, remove from the oven and cool for 5 minutes before serving.

Baked Salmon in Wine

Prep time: 5 minutes | Cook time: 10 minutes | Serves 4

4 tablespoons butter, melted
2 cloves garlic, minced
Sea salt and ground black pepper, to taste
¼ cup dry white wine
1 tablespoon lime juice
1 teaspoon smoked paprika
½ teaspoon onion powder
4 salmon steaks
Cooking spray
1. Place all the ingredients except the salmon and oil in a shallow dish and stir to mix well.
2. Add the salmon steaks, turning to coat well on both sides. Transfer the salmon to the refrigerator to marinate for 30 minutes.
3. When ready, put the salmon steaks in the perforated pan, discarding any excess marinade. Spray the salmon steaks with cooking spray.
4. Select Air Fry. Set temperature to 360ºF (182ºC) and set time to 10 minutes. Press Start to begin preheating.
5. Once preheated, place the pan into the oven. Flip the salmon steaks halfway through.
6. When cooking is complete, remove from the oven and divide the salmon steaks among four plates. Serve warm.

Fried Cod Fillets in Beer

Prep time: 5 minutes | Cook time: 15 minutes | Serves 4

2 eggs
1 cup malty beer
1 cup all-purpose flour
½ cup cornstarch
1 teaspoon garlic powder
Salt and pepper, to taste
4 (4-ounce / 113-g) cod fillets
Cooking spray
1. In a shallow bowl, beat together the eggs with the beer. In another shallow bowl, thoroughly combine the flour and cornstarch. Sprinkle with the garlic powder, salt, and pepper.

2. Dredge each cod fillet in the flour mixture, then in the egg mixture. Dip each piece of fish in the flour mixture a second time.
3. Spritz the perforated pan with cooking spray. Arrange the cod fillets in the pan in a single layer.
4. Select Air Fry. Set temperature to 400ºF (205ºC) and set time to 15 minutes. Press Start to begin preheating.
5. Once preheated, place the pan into the oven. Flip the fillets halfway through the cooking time.
6. When cooking is complete, the cod should reach an internal temperature of 145ºF (63ºC) on a meat thermometer and the outside should be crispy. Let the fish cool for 5 minutes and serve.

Cayenne Cod Fillets with Garlic

Prep time: 10 minutes | Cook time: 12 minutes | Serves 4

1 teaspoon olive oil
4 cod fillets
¼ teaspoon fine sea salt
¼ teaspoon ground black pepper, or more to taste
1 teaspoon cayenne pepper
½ cup fresh Italian parsley, coarsely chopped
½ cup nondairy milk
1 Italian pepper, chopped
4 garlic cloves, minced
1 teaspoon dried basil
½ teaspoon dried oregano
1. Lightly coat the sides and bottom of a baking dish with the olive oil. Set aside.
2. In a large bowl, sprinkle the fillets with salt, black pepper, and cayenne pepper.
3. In a food processor, pulse the remaining ingredients until smoothly puréed.
4. Add the purée to the bowl of fillets and toss to coat, then transfer to the prepared baking dish.
5. Select Bake. Set temperature to 380ºF (193ºC) and set time to 12 minutes. Press Start to begin preheating.
6. Once preheated, place the baking dish into the oven.
7. When cooking is complete, the fish should flake when pressed lightly with a fork. Remove from the oven and serve warm.

Lemon Red Snapper with Thyme

Prep time: 13 minutes | Cook time: 10 minutes | Serves 4

1 teaspoon olive oil
1½ teaspoons black pepper
¼ teaspoon garlic powder
¼ teaspoon thyme
⅛ teaspoon cayenne pepper
4 (4-ounce / 113-g) red snapper fillets, skin on
4 thin slices lemon
Nonstick cooking spray

1.	Spritz the perforated pan with nonstick cooking spray.
2.	In a small bowl, stir together the olive oil, black pepper, garlic powder, thyme, and cayenne pepper. Rub the mixture all over the fillets until completely coated.
3.	Lay the fillets, skin-side down, in the perforated pan and top each fillet with a slice of lemon.
4.	Select Bake. Set temperature to 390ºF (199ºC) and set time to 10 minutes. Press Start to begin preheating.
5.	Once preheated, place the pan into the oven. Flip the fillets halfway through.
6.	When cooking is complete, the fish should be cooked through. Let the fish cool for 5 minutes and serve.

Snapper Fillets with Capers

Prep time: 9 minutes | Cook time: 18 minutes | Serves 4

2 tablespoons extra-virgin olive oil
2 large garlic cloves, minced
½ onion, finely chopped
1 (14.5-ounce / 411-g) can diced tomatoes, drained
¼ cup sliced green olives
3 tablespoons capers, divided
2 tablespoons chopped fresh parsley, divided
½ teaspoon dried oregano
4 (6-ounce / 170-g) snapper fillets
½ teaspoon kosher salt
1.	Grease the sheet pan generously with olive oil, then place the pan into the oven.
2.	Select Roast. Set temperature to 375ºF (190ºC) and set time to 18 minutes. Press Start to begin preheating.
3.	When the oven has preheated, remove the pan and add the garlic and onion to the olive oil in the pan, stirring to coat. Return the pan to the oven and continue cooking.
4.	After 2 minutes, remove the pan from the oven. Stir in the tomatoes, olives, 1½ tablespoons of capers, 1 tablespoon of parsley, and oregano. Return the pan to the oven and continue cooking for 6 minutes until heated through.
5.	Meanwhile, rub the fillets with the salt on both sides.
6.	After another 6 minutes, remove the pan. Put the fillets in the center of the sheet pan and spoon some of the sauce over them. Return the pan to the oven and continue cooking, or until the fish is flaky.
7.	When cooked, remove the pan from the oven. Scatter the remaining 1½ tablespoons of capers and 1 tablespoon of parsley on top of the fillets, then serve.

Salmon and Pepper Bowl

Prep time: 115 minutes | Cook time: 12 minutes | Serves 4

12 ounces (340 g) salmon fillets, cut into 1½-inch cubes
1 red onion, chopped
1 jalapeño pepper, minced
1 red bell pepper, chopped
¼ cup low-sodium salsa
2 teaspoons peanut oil or safflower oil
2 tablespoons low-sodium tomato juice
1 teaspoon chili powder
1.	Mix together the salmon cubes, red onion, jalapeño, red bell pepper, salsa, peanut oil, tomato juice, chili powder in a medium metal bowl and stir until well incorporated.
2.	Select Bake. Set temperature to 370ºF (188ºC) and set time to 12 minutes. Press Start to begin preheating.
3.	Once preheated, place the metal bowl into the oven. Stir the ingredients once halfway through the cooking time.
4.	When cooking is complete, the salmon should be cooked through and the veggies should be fork-tender. Serve warm.

Curried Halibut Fillets with Parmesan

Prep time: 5 minutes | Cook time: 10 minutes | Serves 4

2 medium-sized halibut fillets
Dash of tabasco sauce
1 teaspoon curry powder
½ teaspoon ground coriander
½ teaspoon hot paprika
Kosher salt and freshly cracked mixed peppercorns, to taste
2 eggs
1½ tablespoons olive oil
½ cup grated Parmesan cheese
1.	On a clean work surface, drizzle the halibut fillets with the tabasco sauce. Sprinkle with the curry powder, coriander, hot paprika, salt, and cracked mixed peppercorns. Set aside.
2.	In a shallow bowl, beat the eggs until frothy. In another shallow bowl, combine the olive oil and Parmesan cheese.
3.	One at a time, dredge the halibut fillets in the beaten eggs, shaking off any excess, then roll them over the Parmesan cheese until evenly coated.
4.	Arrange the halibut fillets in the perforated pan in a single layer.
5.	Select Roast. Set temperature to 365ºF (185ºC) and set time to 10 minutes. Press Start to begin preheating.
6.	Once preheated, place the pan into the oven.
7.	When cooking is complete, the fish should be golden brown and crisp. Cool for 5 minutes before serving.

Cajun Cod Fillets with Lemon Pepper

Prep time: 5 minutes | Cook time: 12 minutes | Makes 2 cod fillets
1 tablespoon Cajun seasoning
1 teaspoon salt
½ teaspoon lemon pepper
½ teaspoon freshly ground black pepper
2 (8-ounce / 227-g) cod fillets, cut to fit into the perforated pan
Cooking spray
2 tablespoons unsalted butter, melted
1 lemon, cut into 4 wedges
1. Spritz the perforated pan with cooking spray.
2. Thoroughly combine the Cajun seasoning, salt, lemon pepper, and black pepper in a small bowl. Rub this mixture all over the cod fillets until completely coated.
3. Put the fillets in the perforated pan and brush the melted butter over both sides of each fillet.
4. Select Bake. Set temperature to 360ºF (182ºC) and set time to 12 minutes. Press Start to begin preheating.
5. Once preheated, place the pan into the oven. Flip the fillets halfway through the cooking time.
6. When cooking is complete, the fish should flake apart with a fork. Remove the fillets from the oven and serve with fresh lemon wedges.

Honey Halibut Steaks with Parsley

Prep time: 5 minutes | Cook time: 10 minutes | Serves 4
1 pound (454 g) halibut steaks
¼ cup vegetable oil
2½ tablespoons Worcester sauce
2 tablespoons honey
2 tablespoons vermouth
1 tablespoon freshly squeezed lemon juice
1 tablespoon fresh parsley leaves, coarsely chopped
Salt and pepper, to taste
1 teaspoon dried basil
1. Put all the ingredients in a large mixing dish and gently stir until the fish is coated evenly. Transfer the fish to the perforated pan.
2. Select Roast. Set temperature to 390ºF (199ºC) and set time to 10 minutes. Press Start to begin preheating.
3. Once preheated, place the pan into the oven. Flip the fish halfway through cooking time.
4. When cooking is complete, the fish should reach an internal temperature of at least 145ºF (63ºC) on a meat thermometer. Remove from the oven and let the fish cool for 5 minutes before serving.

Catfish Fillets with Pecan Crust

Prep time: 5 minutes | Cook time: 12 minutes | Serves 4
½ cup pecan meal
1 teaspoon fine sea salt
¼ teaspoon ground black pepper
4 (4-ounce / 113-g) catfish fillets
Avocado oil spray
For Garnish (Optional):
Fresh oregano
Pecan halves
1. Spray the perforated pan with avocado oil spray.
2. Combine the pecan meal, sea salt, and black pepper in a large bowl. Dredge each catfish fillet in the meal mixture, turning until well coated. Spritz the fillets with avocado oil spray, then transfer to the perforated pan.
3. Select Air Fry. Set temperature to 375ºF (190ºC) and set time to 12 minutes. Press Start to begin preheating.
4. Once preheated, place the pan into the oven. Flip the fillets halfway through the cooking time.
5. When cooking is complete, the fish should be cooked through and no longer translucent. Remove from the oven and sprinkle the oregano sprigs and pecan halves on top for garnish, if desired. Serve immediately.

Breaded Catfish Nuggets

Prep time: 10 minutes | Cook time: 7 to 8 minutes | Serves 4
2 medium catfish fillets, cut into chunks (approximately 1 × 2 inch)
Salt and pepper, to taste
2 eggs
2 tablespoons skim milk
½ cup cornstarch
1 cup panko bread crumbs
Cooking spray
1. In a medium bowl, season the fish chunks with salt and pepper to taste.
2. In a small bowl, beat together the eggs with milk until well combined.
3. Place the cornstarch and bread crumbs into separate shallow dishes.
4. Dredge the fish chunks one at a time in the cornstarch, coating well on both sides, then dip in the egg mixture, shaking off any excess, finally press well into the bread crumbs. Spritz the fish chunks with cooking spray.
5. Arrange the fish chunks in the perforated pan in a single layer.
6. Select Air Fry. Set temperature to 390ºF (199ºC) and set time to 8 minutes. Press Start to begin preheating.
7. Once preheated, place the pan into the oven. Flip the fish chunks halfway through the cooking time.
8. When cooking is complete, they should be no longer translucent in the center and golden brown. Remove the fish chunks from the oven to a plate. Serve warm.

Paprika Tilapia with Garlic Aioli

Prep time: 5 minutes | Cook time: 15 minutes | Serves 4
Tilapia:
4 tilapia fillets
1 tablespoon extra-virgin olive oil
1 teaspoon garlic powder
1 teaspoon paprika
1 teaspoon dried basil
A pinch of lemon-pepper seasoning
Garlic Aioli:
2 garlic cloves, minced
1 tablespoon mayonnaise
Juice of ½ lemon
1 teaspoon extra-virgin olive oil
Salt and pepper, to taste
1.	On a clean work surface, brush both sides of each fillet with the olive oil. Sprinkle with the garlic powder, paprika, basil, and lemon-pepper seasoning. Place the fillets in the perforated pan.
2.	Select Bake. Set temperature to 400ºF (205ºC) and set time to 15 minutes. Press Start to begin preheating.
3.	Once preheated, place the pan into the oven. Flip the fillets halfway through.
4.	Meanwhile, make the garlic aioli: Whisk together the garlic, mayo, lemon juice, olive oil, salt, and pepper in a small bowl until smooth.
5.	When cooking is complete, the fish should flake apart with a fork and no longer translucent in the center. Remove the fish from the oven and serve with the garlic aioli on the side.

Shrimp Salad with Caesar Dressing

Prep time: 10 minutes | Cook time: 15 minutes | Serves 4
½ baguette, cut into 1-inch cubes (about 2½ cups)
4 tablespoons extra-virgin olive oil, divided
¼ teaspoon granulated garlic
¼ teaspoon kosher salt
¾ cup Caesar dressing, divided
2 romaine lettuce hearts, cut in half lengthwise and ends trimmed
1 pound (454 g) medium shrimp, peeled and deveined
2 ounces (57 g) Parmesan cheese, coarsely grated
1.	Make the croutons: Put the bread cubes in a medium bowl and drizzle 3 tablespoons of olive oil over top. Season with granulated garlic and salt and toss to coat. Transfer to the perforated pan in a single layer.
2.	Select Air Fry. Set temperature to 400ºF (205ºC) and set time to 4 minutes. Press Start to begin preheating.
3.	Once the oven has preheated, place the pan into the oven. Toss the croutons halfway through the cooking time.
4.	When done, remove the perforated pan from the oven and set aside.
5.	Brush 2 tablespoons of Caesar dressing on the cut side of the lettuce. Set aside.

6.	Toss the shrimp with the ¼ cup of Caesar dressing in a large bowl until well coated. Set aside.
7.	Coat the sheet pan with the remaining 1 tablespoon of olive oil. Arrange the romaine halves on the coated pan, cut side down. Brush the tops with the remaining 2 tablespoons of Caesar dressing.
8.	Select Roast. Set temperature to 375ºF (190ºC) and set time to 10 minutes. Place the pan into the oven.
9.	After 5 minutes, remove the pan from the oven and flip the romaine halves. Spoon the shrimp around the lettuce. Return the pan to the oven and continue cooking.
10.	When done, remove the sheet pan from the oven. If they are not quite cooked through, roast for another 1 minute.
11.	On each of four plates, put a romaine half. Divide the shrimp among the plates and top with croutons and grated Parmesan cheese. Serve immediately.

Lemon Tilapia Fillets with Garlic

Prep time: 10 minutes | Cook time: 12 minutes | Serves 4
1 tablespoon olive oil
1 tablespoon lemon juice
1 teaspoon minced garlic
½ teaspoon chili powder
4 tilapia fillets
1.	Line a baking pan with parchment paper.
2.	In a shallow bowl, stir together the olive oil, lemon juice, garlic, and chili powder to make a marinade. Put the tilapia fillets in the bowl, turning to coat evenly.
3.	Place the fillets in the baking pan in a single layer.
4.	Select Air Fry. Set temperature to 375ºF (190ºC) and set time to 12 minutes. Press Start to begin preheating.
5.	Once preheated, slide the pan into the oven.
6.	When cooked, the fish will flake apart with a fork. Remove from the oven to a plate and serve hot.

Old Bay Shrimp with Potatoes

Prep time: 10 minutes | Cook time: 15 minutes | Serves 4
1 pound (454 g) small red potatoes, halved
2 ears corn, shucked and cut into rounds, 1 to 1½ inches thick
2 tablespoons Old Bay or similar seasoning
½ cup unsalted butter, melted
1 (12- to 13-ounce / 340- to 369-g) package kielbasa or other smoked sausages
3 garlic cloves, minced
1 pound (454 g) medium shrimp, peeled and deveined
1.	Place the potatoes and corn in a large bowl.
2.	Stir together the butter and Old Bay seasoning in a small bowl. Drizzle half the butter

mixture over the potatoes and corn, tossing to coat. Spread out the vegetables on a sheet pan.

3. Select Roast. Set temperature to 350ºF (180ºC) and set time to 15 minutes. Press Start to begin preheating.

4. Once the oven has preheated, place the pan into the oven.

5. Meanwhile, cut the sausages into 2-inch lengths, then cut each piece in half lengthwise. Put the sausages and shrimp in a medium bowl and set aside.

6. Add the garlic to the bowl of remaining butter mixture and stir well.

7. After 10 minutes, remove the sheet pan and pour the vegetables into the large bowl. Drizzle with the garlic butter and toss until well coated. Arrange the vegetables, sausages, and shrimp on the sheet pan.

8. Return to the oven and continue cooking. After 5 minutes, check the shrimp for doneness. The shrimp should be pink and opaque. If they are not quite cooked through, roast for an additional 1 minute.

9. When done, remove from the oven and serve on a plate.

Breaded Fish Sticks

Prep time: 10 minutes | Cook time: 8 minutes | Makes 8 fish sticks
8 ounces (227 g) fish fillets (pollock or cod) cut into ½×3-inch strips
Salt, to taste (optional)
½ cup plain bread crumbs
Cooking spray

1. Season the fish strips with salt to taste, if desired.

2. Place the bread crumbs on a plate. Roll the fish strips in the bread crumbs to coat. Spritz the fish strips with cooking spray.

3. Arrange the fish strips in the perforated pan in a single layer.

4. Select Air Fry. Set temperature to 390ºF (199ºC) and set time to 8 minutes. Press Start to begin preheating.

5. Once preheated, place the pan into the oven.

6. When cooking is complete, they should be golden brown. Remove from the oven and cool for 5 minutes before serving.

Dijon Hake Fillets with Garlic Sauce

Prep time: 5 minutes | Cook time: 10 minutes | Serves 3
Fish:
6 tablespoons mayonnaise
1 tablespoon fresh lime juice
1 teaspoon Dijon mustard
1 cup grated Parmesan cheese
Salt, to taste
¼ teaspoon ground black pepper, or more to taste

3 hake fillets, patted dry
Nonstick cooking spray
Garlic Sauce:
¼ cup plain Greek yogurt
2 tablespoons olive oil
2 cloves garlic, minced
½ teaspoon minced tarragon leaves

1. Mix the mayo, lime juice, and mustard in a shallow bowl and whisk to combine. In another shallow bowl, stir together the grated Parmesan cheese, salt, and pepper.

2. Dredge each fillet in the mayo mixture, then roll them in the cheese mixture until they are evenly coated on both sides.

3. Spray the perforated pan with nonstick cooking spray. Place the fillets in the pan.

4. Select Air Fry. Set temperature to 395ºF (202ºC) and set time to 10 minutes. Press Start to begin preheating.

5. Once preheated, place the pan into the oven. Flip the fillets halfway through the cooking time.

6. Meanwhile, in a small bowl, whisk all the ingredients for the sauce until well incorporated.

7. When cooking is complete, the fish should flake apart with a fork. Remove the fillets from the oven and serve warm alongside the sauce.

Cayenne Prawns with Cumin

Prep time: 10 minutes | Cook time: 8 minutes | Serves 2
8 prawns, cleaned
Salt and black pepper, to taste
½ teaspoon ground cayenne pepper
½ teaspoon garlic powder
½ teaspoon ground cumin
½ teaspoon red chili flakes
Cooking spray

1. Spritz the perforated pan with cooking spray.

2. Toss the remaining ingredients in a large bowl until the prawns are well coated.

3. Spread the coated prawns evenly in the perforated pan and spray them with cooking spray.

4. Select Air Fry. Set temperature to 340ºF (171ºC) and set time to 8 minutes. Press Start to begin preheating.

5. Once preheated, place the pan into the oven. Flip the prawns halfway through the cooking time.

6. When cooking is complete, the prawns should be pink. Remove the prawns from the oven to a plate.

Parmesan Fish Fillets with Tarragon

Prep time: 8 minutes | Cook time: 17 minutes | Serves 4
$1/3$ cup grated Parmesan cheese
½ teaspoon fennel seed
½ teaspoon tarragon
$1/3$ teaspoon mixed peppercorns

2 eggs, beaten
4 (4-ounce / 113-g) fish fillets, halved
2 tablespoons dry white wine
1 teaspoon seasoned salt
1. Place the grated Parmesan cheese, fennel seed, tarragon, and mixed peppercorns in a food processor and pulse for about 20 seconds until well combined. Transfer the cheese mixture to a shallow dish.
2. Place the beaten eggs in another shallow dish.
3. Drizzle the dry white wine over the top of fish fillets. Dredge each fillet in the beaten eggs on both sides, shaking off any excess, then roll them in the cheese mixture until fully coated. Season with the salt.
4. Arrange the fillets in the perforated pan.
5. Select Air Fry. Set temperature to 345ºF (174ºC) and set time to 17 minutes. Press Start to begin preheating.
6. Once preheated, place the pan into the oven. Flip the fillets once halfway through the cooking time.
7. When cooking is complete, the fish should be cooked through no longer translucent. Remove from the oven and cool for 5 minutes before serving.

Cajun Catfish Cakes with Parmesan

Prep time: 5 minutes | Cook time: 15 minutes | Serves 4
2 catfish fillets
3 ounces (85 g) butter
1 cup shredded Parmesan cheese
1 cup shredded Swiss cheese
½ cup buttermilk
1 teaspoon baking powder
1 teaspoon baking soda
1 teaspoon Cajun seasoning
1. Bring a pot of salted water to a boil. Add the catfish fillets to the boiling water and let them boil for 5 minutes until they become opaque.
2. Remove the fillets from the pot to a mixing bowl and flake them into small pieces with a fork.
3. Add the remaining ingredients to the bowl of fish and stir until well incorporated.
4. Divide the fish mixture into 12 equal portions and shape each portion into a patty. Place the patties in the perforated pan.
5. Select Air Fry. Set temperature to 380ºF (193ºC) and set time to 15 minutes. Press Start to begin preheating.
6. Once preheated, place the pan into the oven. Flip the patties halfway through the cooking time.
7. When cooking is complete, the patties should be golden brown and cooked through. Remove from the oven. Let the patties sit for 5 minutes and serve.

Coconut Curried Fish with Chilies

Prep time: 10 minutes | Cook time: 22 minutes | Serves 4
2 tablespoons sunflower oil, divided
1 pound (454 g) fish, chopped
1 ripe tomato, pureéd
2 red chilies, chopped
1 shallot, minced
1 garlic clove, minced
1 cup coconut milk
1 tablespoon coriander powder
1 teaspoon red curry paste
½ teaspoon fenugreek seeds
Salt and white pepper, to taste
1. Coat the perforated pan with 1 tablespoon of sunflower oil. Place the fish in the perforated pan.
2. Select Air Fry. Set temperature to 380ºF (193ºC) and set time to 10 minutes. Press Start to begin preheating.
3. Once preheated, place the pan into the oven. Flip the fish halfway through the cooking time.
4. When cooking is complete, transfer the cooked fish to a baking pan greased with the remaining 1 tablespoon of sunflower oil. Stir in the remaining ingredients.
5. Select Air Fry. Set temperature to 350ºF (180ºC) and set time to 12 minutes. Place the pan into the oven.
6. When cooking is complete, they should be heated through. Cool for 5 to 8 minutes before serving.

Shrimp and Veggie Spring Rolls

Prep time: 10 minutes | Cook time: 20 minutes | Serves 4
1 tablespoon olive oil
2 teaspoons minced garlic
1 cup matchstick cut carrots
2 cups finely sliced cabbage
2 (4-ounce / 113-g) cans tiny shrimp, drained
4 teaspoons soy sauce
Salt and freshly ground black pepper, to taste
16 square spring roll wrappers
Cooking spray
1. Spray the perforated pan with cooking spray. Set aside.
2. Heat the olive oil in a medium skillet over medium heat until it shimmers.
3. Add the garlic to the skillet and cook for 30 seconds. Stir in the cabbage and carrots and sauté for about 5 minutes, stirring occasionally, or until the vegetables are lightly tender.
4. Fold in the shrimp and soy sauce and sprinkle with salt and pepper, then stir to combine. Sauté for another 2 minutes, or until the moisture is evaporated. Remove from the heat and set aside to cool.
5. Put a spring roll wrapper on a work surface and spoon 1 tablespoon of the shrimp mixture onto the lower end of the wrapper.

6.	Roll the wrapper away from you halfway, and then fold in the right and left sides, like an envelope. Continue to roll to the very end, using a little water to seal the edge. Repeat with the remaining wrappers and filling.
7.	Place the spring rolls in the perforated pan in a single layer, leaving space between each spring roll. Mist them lightly with cooking spray.
8.	Select Air Fry. Set temperature to 375ºF (190ºC) and set time to 10 minutes. Press Start to begin preheating.
9.	Once preheated, place the pan into the oven. Flip the rolls halfway through the cooking time.
10.	When cooking is complete, the spring rolls will be heated through and start to brown. If necessary, continue cooking for 5 minutes more. Remove from the oven and cool for a few minutes before serving.

Orange Shrimp with Cayenne

Prep time: 40 minutes | Cook time: 12 minutes | Serves 4
$^1/_3$ cup orange juice
3 teaspoons minced garlic
1 teaspoon Old Bay seasoning
¼ to ½ teaspoon cayenne pepper
1 pound (454 g) medium shrimp, thawed, deveined, peeled, with tails off, and patted dry
Cooking spray
1.	Stir together the orange juice, garlic, Old Bay seasoning, and cayenne pepper in a medium bowl. Add the shrimp to the bowl and toss to coat well.
2.	Cover the bowl with plastic wrap and marinate in the refrigerator for 30 minutes.
3.	Spritz the perforated pan with cooking spray. Place the shrimp in the pan and spray with cooking spray.
4.	Select Air Fry. Set temperature to 400ºF (205ºC) and set time to 12 minutes. Press Start to begin preheating.
5.	Once preheated, place the pan into the oven. Flip the shrimp halfway through the cooking time.
6.	When cooked, the shrimp should be opaque and crisp. Remove from the oven and serve hot.

Flounder Fillets with Lemon Pepper

Prep time: 8 minutes | Cook time: 12 minutes | Serves 2
2 flounder fillets, patted dry
1 egg
½ teaspoon Worcestershire sauce
¼ cup almond flour
¼ cup coconut flour
½ teaspoon coarse sea salt
½ teaspoon lemon pepper
¼ teaspoon chili powder
Cooking spray

1.	In a shallow bowl, beat together the egg with Worcestershire sauce until well incorporated.
2.	In another bowl, thoroughly combine the almond flour, coconut flour, sea salt, lemon pepper, and chili powder.
3.	Dredge the fillets in the egg mixture, shaking off any excess, then roll in the flour mixture to coat well.
4.	Spritz the perforated pan with cooking spray. Place the fillets in the pan.
5.	Select Bake. Set temperature to 390ºF (199ºC) and set time to 12 minutes. Press Start to begin preheating.
6.	Once preheated, place the pan into the oven.
7.	After 7 minutes, remove from the oven and flip the fillets and spray with cooking spray. Return the pan to the oven and continue cooking for 5 minutes, or until the fish is flaky.
8.	When cooking is complete, remove from the oven and serve warm.

Paprika Tiger Shrimp

Prep time: 5 minutes | Cook time: 10 minutes | Serves 4
1 pound (454 g) tiger shrimp
2 tablespoons olive oil
½ tablespoon Old Bay seasoning
¼ tablespoon smoked paprika
¼ teaspoon cayenne pepper
A pinch of sea salt
1.	Toss all the ingredients in a large bowl until the shrimp are evenly coated.
2.	Arrange the shrimp in the perforated pan.
3.	Select Air Fry. Set temperature to 380ºF (193ºC) and set time to 10 minutes. Press Start to begin preheating.
4.	Once preheated, place the pan into the oven.
5.	When cooking is complete, the shrimp should be pink and cooked through. Remove from the oven and serve hot.

Curried Prawns with Coconut

Prep time: 15 minutes | Cook time: 8 minutes | Serves 4
12 prawns, cleaned and deveined
1 teaspoon fresh lemon juice
½ teaspoon cumin powder
Salt and ground black pepper, to taste
1 medium egg
$^1/_3$ cup beer
½ cup flour, divided
1 tablespoon curry powder
1 teaspoon baking powder
½ teaspoon grated fresh ginger
1 cup flaked coconut
1.	In a large bowl, toss the prawns with the lemon juice, cumin powder, salt, and pepper until well coated. Set aside.

2.	In a shallow bowl, whisk together the egg, beer, ¼ cup of flour, curry powder, baking powder, and ginger until combined.
3.	In a separate shallow bowl, put the remaining ¼ cup of flour, and on a plate, place the flaked coconut.
4.	Dip the prawns in the flour, then in the egg mixture, finally roll in the flaked coconut to coat well. Transfer the prawns to a baking sheet.
5.	Select Air Fry. Set temperature to 350ºF (180ºC) and set time to 8 minutes. Press Start to begin preheating.
6.	Once preheated, place the baking sheet into the oven.
7.	After 5 minutes, remove from the oven and flip the prawns. Return to the oven and continue cooking for 3 minutes more.
8.	When cooking is complete, remove from the oven and serve warm.

Parsley Shrimp with Lemon

Prep time: 10 minutes | Cook time: 8 minutes | Serves 4
1 pound (454 g) shrimp, deveined
4 tablespoons olive oil
1½ tablespoons lemon juice
1½ tablespoons fresh parsley, roughly chopped
2 cloves garlic, finely minced
1 teaspoon crushed red pepper flakes, or more to taste
Garlic pepper, to taste
Sea salt flakes, to taste
1.	Toss all the ingredients in a large bowl until the shrimp are coated on all sides.
2.	Arrange the shrimp in the perforated pan.
3.	Select Air Fry. Set temperature to 385ºF (196ºC) and set time to 8 minutes. Press Start to begin preheating.
4.	Once preheated, place the pan into the oven.
5.	When cooking is complete, the shrimp should be pink and cooked through. Remove from the oven and serve warm.

Shrimp Kebabs with Cherry Tomatoes

Prep time: 15 minutes | Cook time: 5 minutes | Serves 4
1½ pounds (680 g) jumbo shrimp, cleaned, shelled and deveined
1 pound (454 g) cherry tomatoes
2 tablespoons butter, melted
1 tablespoons Sriracha sauce
Sea salt and ground black pepper, to taste
1 teaspoon dried parsley flakes
½ teaspoon dried basil
½ teaspoon dried oregano
½ teaspoon mustard seeds
½ teaspoon marjoram
Special Equipment:
4 to 6 wooden skewers, soaked in water for 30 minutes
1.	Put all the ingredients in a large bowl and toss to coat well.
2.	Make the kebabs: Thread, alternating jumbo shrimp and cherry tomatoes, onto the wooden skewers. Place the kebabs in the perforated pan.
3.	Select Air Fry. Set temperature to 400ºF (205ºC) and set time to 5 minutes. Press Start to begin preheating.
4.	Once preheated, place the pan into the oven.
5.	When cooking is complete, the shrimp should be pink and the cherry tomatoes should be softened. Remove from the oven. Let the shrimp and cherry tomato kebabs cool for 5 minutes and serve hot.

Shrimp Scampi with Garlic Butter

Prep time: 5 minutes | Cook time: 8 minutes | Serves 4
Sauce:
¼ cup unsalted butter
2 tablespoons fish stock or chicken broth
2 cloves garlic, minced
2 tablespoons chopped fresh basil leaves
1 tablespoon lemon juice
1 tablespoon chopped fresh parsley, plus more for garnish
1 teaspoon red pepper flakes
Shrimp:
1 pound (454 g) large shrimp, peeled and deveined, tails removed
Fresh basil sprigs, for garnish
1.	Put all the ingredients for the sauce in a baking pan and stir to incorporate.
2.	Select Air Fry. Set temperature to 350ºF (180ºC) and set time to 8 minutes. Press Start to begin preheating.
3.	Once preheated, place the baking pan into the oven.
4.	After 3 minutes, remove from the oven and add the shrimp to the baking pan, flipping to coat in the sauce. Return the pan to the oven and continue cooking for 5 minutes until the shrimp are pink and opaque. Stir the shrimp twice during cooking.
5.	When cooking is complete, remove the pan from the oven. Serve garnished with the parsley and basil sprigs.

Lemon Shrimp with Cumin

Prep time: 10 minutes | Cook time: 5 minutes | Serves 4
18 shrimp, shelled and deveined
2 garlic cloves, peeled and minced
2 tablespoons extra-virgin olive oil
2 tablespoons freshly squeezed lemon juice
½ cup fresh parsley, coarsely chopped
1 teaspoon onion powder
1 teaspoon lemon-pepper seasoning

½ teaspoon hot paprika
½ teaspoon salt
¼ teaspoon cumin powder
1.   Toss all the ingredients in a mixing bowl until the shrimp are well coated.
2.   Cover and allow to marinate in the refrigerator for 30 minutes.
3.   When ready, transfer the shrimp to the perforated pan.
4.   Select Air Fry. Set temperature to 400ºF (205ºC) and set time to 5 minutes. Press Start to begin preheating.
5.   Once preheated, place the pan into the oven.
6.   When cooking is complete, the shrimp should be pink on the outside and opaque in the center. Remove from the oven and serve warm.

Hoisin Scallops with Sesame Seeds

Prep time: 10 minutes | Cook time: 8 minutes | Serves 4
1 pound (454 g) sea scallops
3 tablespoons hoisin sauce
½ cup toasted sesame seeds
6 ounces (170 g) snow peas, trimmed
3 teaspoons vegetable oil, divided
1 teaspoon soy sauce
1 teaspoon sesame oil
1 cup roasted mushrooms
1.   Brush the scallops with the hoisin sauce. Put the sesame seeds in a shallow dish. Roll the scallops in the sesame seeds until evenly coated.
2.   Combine the snow peas with 1 teaspoon of vegetable oil, the sesame oil, and soy sauce in a medium bowl and toss to coat.
3.   Grease the sheet pan with the remaining 2 teaspoons of vegetable oil. Put the scallops in the middle of the pan and arrange the snow peas around the scallops in a single layer.
4.   Select Roast. Set temperature to 375ºF (190ºC) and set time to 8 minutes. Press Start to begin preheating.
5.   Once the oven has preheated, place the pan into the oven.
6.   After 5 minutes, remove the pan and flip the scallops. Fold in the mushrooms and stir well. Return the pan to the oven and continue cooking.
7.   When done, remove the pan from the oven and cool for 5 minutes. Serve warm.

Curried King Prawns with Cumin

Prep time: 10 minutes | Cook time: 8 minutes | Serves 2
12 king prawns, rinsed
1 tablespoon coconut oil
Salt and ground black pepper, to taste
1 teaspoon onion powder
1 teaspoon garlic paste
1 teaspoon curry powder
½ teaspoon piri piri powder

½ teaspoon cumin powder
1.   Combine all the ingredients in a large bowl and toss until the prawns are completely coated. Place the prawns in the perforated pan.
2.   Select Air Fry. Set temperature to 360ºF (182ºC) and set time to 8 minutes. Press Start to begin preheating.
3.   Once preheated, place the pan into the oven. Flip the prawns halfway through the cooking time.
4.   When cooking is complete, the prawns will turn pink. Remove from the oven and serve hot.

Old Bay Crab Sticks with Mayo Sauce

Prep time: 5 minutes | Cook time: 12 minutes | Serves 4
Crab Sticks:
2 eggs
1 cup flour
$^1/_3$ cup panko bread crumbs
1 tablespoon Old Bay seasoning
1 pound (454 g) crab sticks
Cooking spray
Mayo Sauce:
½ cup mayonnaise
1 lime, juiced
2 garlic cloves, minced
1.   In a bowl, beat the eggs. In a shallow bowl, place the flour. In another shallow bowl, thoroughly combine the panko bread crumbs and Old Bay seasoning.
2.   Dredge the crab sticks in the flour, shaking off any excess, then in the beaten eggs, finally press them in the bread crumb mixture to coat well.
3.   Arrange the crab sticks in the perforated pan and spray with cooking spray.
4.   Select Air Fry. Set temperature to 390ºF (199ºC) and set time to 12 minutes. Press Start to begin preheating.
5.   Once preheated, place the pan into the oven. Flip the crab sticks halfway through the cooking time.
6.   Meanwhile, make the sauce by whisking together the mayo, lime juice, and garlic in a small bowl.
7.   When cooking is complete, remove the pan from the oven. Serve the crab sticks with the mayo sauce on the side.

Balsamic Shrimp with Goat Cheese

Prep time: 15 minutes | Cook time: 8 minutes | Serves 2
1 pound (454 g) shrimp, deveined
1½ tablespoons olive oil
1½ tablespoons balsamic vinegar
1 tablespoon coconut aminos
½ tablespoon fresh parsley, roughly chopped
Sea salt flakes, to taste
1 teaspoon Dijon mustard
½ teaspoon smoked cayenne pepper

½ teaspoon garlic powder
Salt and ground black peppercorns, to taste
1 cup shredded goat cheese
1. Except for the cheese, stir together all the ingredients in a large bowl until the shrimp are evenly coated.
2. Place the shrimp in the perforated pan.
3. Select Roast. Set temperature to 385ºF (196ºC) and set time to 8 minutes. Press Start to begin preheating.
4. Once preheated, place the pan into the oven.
5. When cooking is complete, the shrimp should be pink and cooked through. Remove from the oven and serve with the shredded goat cheese sprinkled on top.

Jumbo Shrimp with Dijon-Mayo Sauce

Prep time: 5 minutes | Cook time: 7 minutes | Serves 4
Shrimp:
12 jumbo shrimp
½ teaspoon garlic salt
¼ teaspoon freshly cracked mixed peppercorns
Sauce:
4 tablespoons mayonnaise
1 teaspoon grated lemon rind
1 teaspoon Dijon mustard
1 teaspoon chipotle powder
½ teaspoon cumin powder
1. In a medium bowl, season the shrimp with garlic salt and cracked mixed peppercorns.
2. Place the shrimp in the perforated pan.
3. Select Air Fry. Set temperature to 395ºF (202ºC) and set time to 7 minutes. Press Start to begin preheating.
4. Once preheated, place the pan into the oven.
5. After 5 minutes, remove from the oven and flip the shrimp. Return the pan to the oven and continue cooking for 2 minutes more, or until they are pink and no longer opaque.
6. Meanwhile, stir together all the ingredients for the sauce in a small bowl until well mixed.
7. When cooking is complete, remove the shrimp from the oven and serve alongside the sauce.

Crab and Fish Cakes

Prep time: 20 minutes | Cook time: 12 minutes | Serves 4
8 ounces (227 g) imitation crab meat
4 ounces (113 g) leftover cooked fish (such as cod, pollock, or haddock)
2 tablespoons minced celery
2 tablespoons minced green onion
2 tablespoons light mayonnaise
1 tablespoon plus 2 teaspoons Worcestershire sauce
¾ cup crushed saltine cracker crumbs
2 teaspoons dried parsley flakes
1 teaspoon prepared yellow mustard
½ teaspoon garlic powder

½ teaspoon dried dill weed, crushed
½ teaspoon Old Bay seasoning
½ cup panko bread crumbs
Cooking spray
1. Pulse the crab meat and fish in a food processor until finely chopped.
2. Transfer the meat mixture to a large bowl, along with the celery, green onion, mayo, Worcestershire sauce, cracker crumbs, parsley flakes, mustard, garlic powder, dill weed, and Old Bay seasoning. Stir to mix well.
3. Scoop out the meat mixture and form into 8 equal-sized patties with your hands.
4. Place the panko bread crumbs on a plate. Roll the patties in the bread crumbs until they are evenly coated on both sides. Put the patties in the perforated pan and spritz them with cooking spray.
5. Select Bake. Set temperature to 390ºF (199ºC) and set time to 12 minutes. Press Start to begin preheating.
6. Once preheated, place the pan into the oven. Flip the patties halfway through the cooking time.
7. When cooking is complete, they should be golden brown and cooked through. Remove the pan from the oven. Divide the patties among four plates and serve.

Shrimp and Artichoke Paella

Prep time: 5 minutes | Cook time: 16 minutes | Serves 4
1 (10-ounce / 284-g) package frozen cooked rice, thawed
1 (6-ounce / 170-g) jar artichoke hearts, drained and chopped
¼ cup vegetable broth
½ teaspoon dried thyme
½ teaspoon turmeric
1 cup frozen cooked small shrimp
½ cup frozen baby peas
1 tomato, diced
1. Mix together the cooked rice, chopped artichoke hearts, vegetable broth, thyme, and turmeric in a baking pan and stir to combine.
2. Select Bake. Set temperature to 340ºF (171ºC) and set time to 16 minutes. Press Start to begin preheating.
3. Once preheated, place the pan into the oven.
4. After 9 minutes, remove from the oven and add the shrimp, baby peas, and diced tomato to the baking pan. Mix well. Return the pan to the oven and continue cooking for 7 minutes more, or until the shrimp are done and the paella is bubbling.
5. When cooking is complete, remove the pan from the oven. Cool for 5 minutes before serving.

Shrimp and Veggie Patties

Prep time: 15 minutes | Cook time: 12 minutes | Serves 4

½ pound (227 g) raw shrimp, shelled, deveined, and chopped finely
2 cups cooked sushi rice
¼ cup chopped red bell pepper
¼ cup chopped celery
¼ cup chopped green onion
2 teaspoons Worcestershire sauce
½ teaspoon salt
½ teaspoon garlic powder
½ teaspoon Old Bay seasoning
½ cup plain bread crumbs
Cooking spray
1.	Put all the ingredients except the bread crumbs and oil in a large bowl and stir to incorporate.
2.	Scoop out the shrimp mixture and shape into 8 equal-sized patties with your hands, no more than ½-inch thick. Roll the patties in the bread crumbs on a plate and spray both sides with cooking spray. Place the patties in the perforated pan.
3.	Select Air Fry. Set temperature to 390ºF (199ºC) and set time to 12 minutes. Press Start to begin preheating.
4.	Once preheated, place the pan into the oven. Flip the patties halfway through the cooking time.
5.	When cooking is complete, the outside should be crispy brown. Remove the pan from the oven. Divide the patties among four plates and serve warm.

Lemon Crab Cakes with Mayo

Prep time: 5 minutes | Cook time: 10 minutes | Serves 4
8 ounces (227 g) jumbo lump crab meat
1 egg, beaten
Juice of ½ lemon
$^1/_3$ cup bread crumbs
¼ cup diced green bell pepper
¼ cup diced red bell pepper
¼ cup mayonnaise
1 tablespoon Old Bay seasoning
1 teaspoon flour
Cooking spray
1.	Make the crab cakes: Place all the ingredients except the flour and oil in a large bowl and stir until well incorporated.
2.	Divide the crab mixture into four equal portions and shape each portion into a patty with your hands. Top each patty with a sprinkle of ¼ teaspoon of flour.
3.	Arrange the crab cakes in the perforated pan and spritz them with cooking spray.
4.	Select Air Fry. Set temperature to 375ºF (190ºC) and set time to 10 minutes. Press Start to begin preheating.
5.	Once preheated, place the pan into the oven. Flip the crab cakes halfway through.
6.	When cooking is complete, the cakes should be cooked through. Remove the pan from the oven. Divide the crab cakes among four plates and serve.

Balsamic Ginger Scallops

Prep time: 10 minutes | Cook time: 12 minutes | Serves 2
$^1/_3$ cup shallots, chopped
1½ tablespoons olive oil
1½ tablespoons coconut aminos
1 tablespoon Mediterranean seasoning mix
½ tablespoon balsamic vinegar
½ teaspoon ginger, grated
1 clove garlic, chopped
1 pound (454 g) scallops, cleaned
Cooking spray
Belgian endive, for garnish
1.	Place all the ingredients except the scallops and Belgian endive in a small skillet over medium heat and stir to combine. Let this mixture simmer for about 2 minutes.
2.	Remove the mixture from the skillet to a large bowl and set aside to cool.
3.	Add the scallops, coating them all over, then transfer to the refrigerator to marinate for at least 2 hours.
4.	When ready, place the scallops in the perforated pan in a single layer and spray with cooking spray.
5.	Select Air Fry. Set temperature to 345ºF (174ºC) and set time to 10 minutes. Press Start to begin preheating.
6.	Once preheated, place the pan into the oven. Flip the scallops halfway through the cooking time.
7.	When cooking is complete, the scallops should be tender and opaque. Remove from the oven and serve garnished with the Belgian endive.

Fried Bacon-Wrapped Scallops

Prep time: 5 minutes | Cook time: 10 minutes | Serves 4
8 slices bacon, cut in half
16 sea scallops, patted dry
Cooking spray
Salt and freshly ground black pepper, to taste
16 toothpicks, soaked in water for at least 30 minutes
1.	On a clean work surface, wrap half of a slice of bacon around each scallop and secure with a toothpick.
2.	Lay the bacon-wrapped scallops in the perforated pan in a single layer.
3.	Spritz the scallops with cooking spray and sprinkle the salt and pepper to season.
4.	Select Air Fry. Set temperature to 370ºF (188ºC) and set time to 10 minutes. Press Start to begin preheating.
5.	Once preheated, place the pan into the oven. Flip the scallops halfway through the cooking time.
6.	When cooking is complete, the bacon should be cooked through and the scallops should be firm. Remove the scallops from the oven to a plate Serve warm.

Fried Breaded Scallops

Prep time: 5 minutes | Cook time: 7 minutes | Serves 4

1 egg
3 tablespoons flour
1 cup bread crumbs
1 pound (454 g) fresh scallops
2 tablespoons olive oil
Salt and black pepper, to taste

1.	In a bowl, lightly beat the egg. Place the flour and bread crumbs into separate shallow dishes.
2.	Dredge the scallops in the flour and shake off any excess. Dip the flour-coated scallops in the beaten egg and roll in the bread crumbs.
3.	Brush the scallops generously with olive oil and season with salt and pepper, to taste. Transfer the scallops to the perforated pan.
4.	Select Air Fry. Set temperature to 360ºF (182ºC) and set time to 7 minutes. Press Start to begin preheating.
5.	Once preheated, place the pan into the oven. Flip the scallops halfway through the cooking time.
6.	When cooking is complete, the scallops should reach an internal temperature of just 145ºF (63ºC) on a meat thermometer. Remove the pan from the oven. Let the scallops cool for 5 minutes and serve.

Fried Scallops with Thyme

Prep time: 5 minutes | Cook time: 4 minutes | Serves 2

12 medium sea scallops, rinsed and patted dry
1 teaspoon fine sea salt
¾ teaspoon ground black pepper, plus more for garnish
Fresh thyme leaves, for garnish (optional)
Avocado oil spray

1.	Coat the perforated pan with avocado oil spray.
2.	Place the scallops in a medium bowl and spritz with avocado oil spray. Sprinkle the salt and pepper to season.
3.	Transfer the seasoned scallops to the perforated pan, spacing them apart.
4.	Select Air Fry. Set temperature to 390ºF (199ºC) and set time to 4 minutes. Press Start to begin preheating.
5.	Once preheated, place the pan into the oven. Flip the scallops halfway through the cooking time.
6.	When cooking is complete, the scallops should reach an internal temperature of just 145ºF (63ºC) on a meat thermometer. Remove the pan from the oven. Sprinkle the pepper and thyme leaves on top for garnish, if desired. Serve immediately.

Garlic Calamari Rings

Prep time: 5 minutes | Cook time: 12 minutes | Serves 4

2 large eggs
2 garlic cloves, minced
½ cup cornstarch
1 cup bread crumbs
1 pound (454 g) calamari rings
Cooking spray
1 lemon, sliced

1.	In a small bowl, whisk the eggs with minced garlic. Place the cornstarch and bread crumbs into separate shallow dishes.
2.	Dredge the calamari rings in the cornstarch, then dip in the egg mixture, shaking off any excess, finally roll them in the bread crumbs to coat well. Let the calamari rings sit for 10 minutes in the refrigerator.
3.	Spritz the perforated pan with cooking spray. Transfer the calamari rings to the pan.
4.	Select Air Fry. Set temperature to 390ºF (199ºC) and set time to 12 minutes. Press Start to begin preheating.
5.	Once preheated, place the pan into the oven. Stir the calamari rings once halfway through the cooking time.
6.	When cooking is complete, remove the pan from the oven. Serve the calamari rings with the lemon slices sprinkled on top.

Basil Scallops with Broccoli

Prep time: 15 minutes | Cook time: 9 minutes | Serves 4

1 cup frozen peas
1 cup green beans
1 cup frozen chopped broccoli
2 teaspoons olive oil
½ teaspoon dried oregano
½ teaspoon dried basil
12 ounces (340 g) sea scallops, rinsed and patted dry

1.	Put the peas, green beans, and broccoli in a large bowl. Drizzle with the olive oil and toss to coat well. Transfer the vegetables to the perforated pan.
2.	Select Air Fry. Set temperature to 400ºF (205ºC) and set time to 5 minutes. Press Start to begin preheating.
3.	Once preheated, place the pan into the oven.
4.	When cooking is complete, the vegetables should be fork-tender. Transfer the vegetables to a serving bowl. Scatter with the oregano and basil and set aside.
5.	Place the scallops in the perforated pan.
6.	Select Air Fry. Set temperature to 400ºF (205ºC) and set time to 4 minutes. Place the pan into the oven.
7.	When cooking is complete, the scallops should be firm and just opaque in the center. Remove from the oven to the bowl of vegetables and toss well. Serve warm.

Crab Ratatouille with Thyme

Prep time: 5 minutes | Cook time: 12 minutes | Serves 4

Prep time: 15 minutes | Cook time: 13 minutes | Serves 4

1½ cups peeled and cubed eggplant
2 large tomatoes, chopped
1 red bell pepper, chopped
1 onion, chopped
1 tablespoon olive oil
½ teaspoon dried basil
½ teaspoon dried thyme
Pinch salt
Freshly ground black pepper, to taste
1½ cups cooked crab meat
1. In a metal bowl, stir together the eggplant, tomatoes, bell pepper, onion, olive oil, basil and thyme. Season with salt and pepper.
2. Select Roast. Set temperature to 400ºF (205ºC) and set time to 13 minutes. Press Start to begin preheating.
3. Once preheated, place the metal bowl into the oven.
4. After 9 minutes, remove the bowl from the oven. Add the crab meat and stir well and continue roasting for another 4 minutes, or until the vegetables are softened and the ratatouille is bubbling.
5. When cooking is complete, remove from the oven and serve warm.

CHAPTER 9 POULTRY

Chicken Drumsticks with BBQ-Honey Sauce

Prep time: 5 minutes | Cook time: 18 minutes | Serves 5

1 tablespoon olive oil
10 chicken drumsticks
Chicken seasoning or rub, to taste
Salt and ground black pepper, to taste
1 cup barbecue sauce
¼ cup honey

1. Grease the perforated pan with olive oil.
2. Rub the chicken drumsticks with chicken seasoning or rub, salt and ground black pepper on a clean work surface.
3. Arrange the chicken drumsticks in the perforated pan.
4. Select Air Fry. Set temperature to 390ºF (199ºC) and set time to 18 minutes. Press Start to begin preheating.
5. Once preheated, place the pan into the oven. Flip the drumsticks halfway through.
6. When cooking is complete, the drumsticks should be lightly browned.
7. Meanwhile, combine the barbecue sauce and honey in a small bowl. Stir to mix well.
8. Remove the drumsticks from the oven and baste with the sauce mixture to serve.

Chicken and Ham Rochambeau

Prep time: 25 minutes | Cook time: 30 minutes | Serves 4

1 tablespoon melted butter
¼ cup all-purpose flour
4 chicken tenders, cut in half crosswise
4 slices ham, ¼-inch thick, large enough to cover an English muffin
2 English muffins, split in halves
Salt and ground black pepper, to taste
Cooking spray
Mushroom Sauce:
2 tablespoons butter
½ cup chopped mushrooms
½ cup chopped green onions
2 tablespoons flour
1 cup chicken broth
1½ teaspoons Worcestershire sauce
¼ teaspoon garlic powder

1. Put the butter in a baking pan. Combine the flour, salt, and ground black pepper in a shallow dish. Roll the chicken tenders over to coat well.
2. Arrange the chicken in the baking pan and flip to coat with the melted butter.
3. Select Broil. Set temperature to 390ºF (199ºC) and set time to 10 minutes. Press Start to begin preheating.
4. Once preheated, place the pan into the oven. Flip the tenders halfway through.
5. When cooking is complete, the juices of chicken tenders should run clear.
6. Meanwhile, make the mushroom sauce: melt 2 tablespoons of butter in a saucepan over medium-high heat.
7. Add the mushrooms and onions to the saucepan and sauté for 3 minutes or until the onions are translucent.
8. Gently mix in the flour, broth, Worcestershire sauce, and garlic powder until smooth.
9. Reduce the heat to low and simmer for 5 minutes or until it has a thick consistency. Set the sauce aside until ready to serve.
10. When broiling is complete, remove the baking pan from the oven and set the ham slices into the perforated pan.
11. Select Air Fry. Set time to 5 minutes. Flip the ham slices halfway through.
12. When cooking is complete, the ham slices should be heated through.
13. Remove the ham slices from the oven and set in the English muffin halves and warm for 1 minute.
14. Arrange each ham slice on top of each muffin half, then place each chicken tender over the ham slice.
15. Transfer to the oven and set time to 2 minutes on Air Fry.
16. Serve with the sauce on top.

Breaded Chicken Fingers

Prep time: 20 minutes | Cook time: 10 minutes | Makes 12 chicken fingers

½ cup all-purpose flour
2 cups panko bread crumbs
2 tablespoons canola oil
1 large egg
3 boneless and skinless chicken breasts, each cut into 4 strips
Kosher salt and freshly ground black pepper, to taste
Cooking spray

1. Spritz the perforated pan with cooking spray.
2. Pour the flour in a large bowl. Combine the panko and canola oil on a shallow dish. Whisk the egg in a separate bowl.
3. Rub the chicken strips with salt and ground black pepper on a clean work surface, then dip the chicken in the bowl of flour. Shake the excess off and dunk the chicken strips in the bowl of whisked egg, then roll the strips over the panko to coat well.
4. Arrange the strips in the perforated pan.
5. Select Air Fry. Set temperature to 360ºF (182ºC) and set time to 10 minutes. Press Start to begin preheating.
6. Once preheated, place the pan into the oven. Flip the strips halfway through.

7.	When cooking is complete, the strips should be crunchy and lightly browned.
8.	Serve immediately.

Breaded Chicken Tenders with Thyme

Prep time: 15 minutes | Cook time: 5 minutes | Serves 4
½ cup all-purpose flour
1 teaspoon marjoram
½ teaspoon thyme
1 teaspoon dried parsley flakes
½ teaspoon salt
1 egg
1 teaspoon lemon juice
1 teaspoon water
1 cup bread crumbs
4 chicken tenders, pounded thin, cut in half lengthwise
Cooking spray
1.	Spritz the perforated pan with cooking spray.
2.	Combine the flour, marjoram, thyme, parsley, and salt in a shallow dish. Stir to mix well.
3.	Whisk the egg with lemon juice and water in a large bowl. Pour the bread crumbs in a separate shallow dish.
4.	Roll the chicken halves in the flour mixture first, then in the egg mixture, and then roll over the bread crumbs to coat well. Shake the excess off.
5.	Arrange the chicken halves in the perforated pan and spritz with cooking spray on both sides.
6.	Select Air Fry. Set temperature to 390ºF (199ºC) and set time to 5 minutes. Press Start to begin preheating.
7.	Once preheated, place the pan into the oven. Flip the halves halfway through.
8.	When cooking is complete, the chicken halves should be golden brown and crispy.
9.	Serve immediately.

Barbecue Chicken with Coleslaw

Prep time: 15 minutes | Cook time: 10 minutes | Makes 4 tostadas
Coleslaw:
¼ cup sour cream
¼ small green cabbage, finely chopped
½ tablespoon white vinegar
½ teaspoon garlic powder
½ teaspoon salt
¼ teaspoon ground black pepper
Tostadas:
2 cups pulled rotisserie chicken
½ cup barbecue sauce
4 corn tortillas
½ cup shredded Mozzarella cheese
Cooking spray
Make the Coleslaw:
1.	Combine the ingredients for the coleslaw in a large bowl. Toss to mix well.
2.	Refrigerate until ready to serve.
Make the Tostadas:
1.	Spritz the perforated pan with cooking spray.
2.	Toss the chicken with barbecue sauce in a separate large bowl to combine well. Set aside.
3.	Place one tortilla in the perforated pan and spritz with cooking spray.
4.	Select Air Fry. Set temperature to 370ºF (188ºC) and set time to 10 minutes. Press Start to begin preheating.
5.	Once preheated, place the pan into the oven. Flip the tortilla and spread the barbecue chicken and cheese over halfway through.
6.	When cooking is complete, the tortilla should be browned and the cheese should be melted.
7.	Serve the tostadas with coleslaw on top.

Mustard Chicken Thighs in Waffles

Prep time: 1 hour 20 minutes | Cook time: 20 minutes | Serves 4
For the Chicken:
4 chicken thighs, skin on
1 cup low-fat buttermilk
½ cup all-purpose flour
½ teaspoon garlic powder
½ teaspoon mustard powder
1 teaspoon kosher salt
½ teaspoon freshly ground black pepper
¼ cup honey, for serving
Cooking spray
For the Waffles:
½ cup all-purpose flour
½ cup whole wheat pastry flour
1 large egg, beaten
1 cup low-fat buttermilk
1 teaspoon baking powder
2 tablespoons canola oil
½ teaspoon kosher salt
1 tablespoon granulated sugar
1.	Combine the chicken thighs with buttermilk in a large bowl. Wrap the bowl in plastic and refrigerate to marinate for at least an hour.
2.	Spritz the perforated pan with cooking spray.
3.	Combine the flour, mustard powder, garlic powder, salt, and black pepper in a shallow dish. Stir to mix well.
4.	Remove the thighs from the buttermilk and pat dry with paper towels. Sit the bowl of buttermilk aside.
5.	Dip the thighs in the flour mixture first, then into the buttermilk, and then into the flour mixture. Shake the excess off.
6.	Arrange the thighs in the perforated pan and spritz with cooking spray.

7. Select Air Fry. Set temperature to 360ºF (182ºC) and set time to 20 minutes. Press Start to begin preheating.
8. Once preheated, place the pan into the oven. Flip the thighs halfway through.
9. When cooking is complete, an instant-read thermometer inserted in the thickest part of the chicken thighs should register at least 165ºF (74ºC).
10. Meanwhile, make the waffles: combine the ingredients for the waffles in a large bowl. Stir to mix well, then arrange the mixture in a waffle iron and cook until a golden and fragrant waffle forms.
11. Remove the waffles from the waffle iron and slice into 4 pieces. Remove the chicken thighs from the oven and allow to cool for 5 minutes.
12. Arrange each chicken thigh on each waffle piece and drizzle with 1 tablespoon of honey. Serve warm.

Gochujang Chicken Wings

Prep time: 10 minutes | Cook time: 25 minutes | Serves 4
Wings:
2 pounds (907 g) chicken wings
1 teaspoon salt
1 teaspoon ground black pepper
Sauce:
2 tablespoons gochujang
1 tablespoon mayonnaise
1 tablespoon minced ginger
1 tablespoon minced garlic
1 teaspoon agave nectar
2 packets Splenda
1 tablespoon sesame oil
For Garnish:
2 teaspoons sesame seeds
¼ cup chopped green onions
1. Line a baking pan with aluminum foil, then arrange the rack on the pan.
2. On a clean work surface, rub the chicken wings with salt and ground black pepper, then arrange the seasoned wings on the rack.
3. Select Air Fry. Set temperature to 400ºF (205ºC) and set time to 20 minutes. Press Start to begin preheating.
4. Once preheated, place the pan into the oven. Flip the wings halfway through.
5. When cooking is complete, the wings should be well browned.
6. Meanwhile, combine the ingredients for the sauce in a small bowl. Stir to mix well. Reserve half of the sauce in a separate bowl until ready to serve.
7. Remove the air fried chicken wings from the oven and toss with remaining half of the sauce to coat well.
8. Place the wings back to the oven. Select Air Fry. Set time to 5 minutes.
9. When cooking is complete, the internal temperature of the wings should reach at least 165ºF (74ºC).

10. Remove the wings from the oven and place on a large plate. Sprinkle with sesame seeds and green onions. Serve with reserved sauce.

Chili Chicken Skin with Dill

Prep time: 5 minutes | Cook time: 6 minutes | Serves 4
1 pound (454 g) chicken skin, cut into slices
1 teaspoon melted butter
½ teaspoon crushed chili flakes
1 teaspoon dried dill
Salt and ground black pepper, to taste
1. Combine all the ingredients in a large bowl. Toss to coat the chicken skin well.
2. Transfer the skin in the perforated pan.
3. Select Air Fry. Set temperature to 360ºF (182ºC) and set time to 6 minutes. Press Start to begin preheating.
4. Once preheated, place the pan into the oven. Stir the skin halfway through.
5. When cooking is complete, the skin should be crispy.
6. Serve immediately.

Chicken Drumsticks with Cajun Seasoning

Prep time: 5 minutes | Cook time: 18 minutes | Serves 5
1 tablespoon olive oil
10 chicken drumsticks
1½ tablespoons Cajun seasoning
Salt and ground black pepper, to taste
1. Grease the perforated pan with olive oil.
2. On a clean work surface, rub the chicken drumsticks with Cajun seasoning, salt, and ground black pepper.
3. Arrange the seasoned chicken drumsticks in the perforated pan.
4. Select Air Fry. Set temperature to 390ºF (199ºC) and set time to 18 minutes. Press Start to begin preheating.
5. Once preheated, place the pan into the oven. Flip the drumsticks halfway through.
6. When cooking is complete, the drumsticks should be lightly browned.
7. Remove the chicken drumsticks from the oven. Serve immediately.

Breaded Chicken Livers

Prep time: 10 minutes | Cook time: 10 minutes | Serves 4
2 eggs
2 tablespoons water
¾ cup flour
2 cups panko bread crumbs
1 teaspoon salt
½ teaspoon ground black pepper
20 ounces (567 g) chicken livers
Cooking spray

1.   Spritz the perforated pan with cooking spray.
2.   Whisk the eggs with water in a large bowl. Pour the flour in a separate bowl. Pour the panko on a shallow dish and sprinkle with salt and pepper.
3.   Dredge the chicken livers in the flour. Shake the excess off, then dunk the livers in the whisked eggs, and then roll the livers over the panko to coat well.
4.   Arrange the livers in the perforated pan and spritz with cooking spray.
5.   Select Air Fry. Set temperature to 390ºF (199ºC) and set time to 10 minutes. Press Start to begin preheating.
6.   Once preheated, place the pan into the oven. Flip the livers halfway through.
7.   When cooking is complete, the livers should be golden and crispy.
8.   Serve immediately.

Ginger Chicken Bites in Sherry

Prep time: 15 minutes | Cook time: 15 minutes | Serves 4

½ cup pineapple juice
2 tablespoons apple cider vinegar
½ tablespoon minced ginger
½ cup ketchup
2 garlic cloves, minced
½ cup brown sugar
2 tablespoons sherry
½ cup soy sauce
4 chicken breasts, cubed
Cooking spray
1.   Combine the pineapple juice, cider vinegar, ginger, ketchup, garlic, and sugar in a saucepan. Stir to mix well. Heat over low heat for 5 minutes or until thickened. Fold in the sherry and soy sauce.
2.   Dunk the chicken cubes in the mixture. Press to submerge. Wrap the bowl in plastic and refrigerate to marinate for at least an hour.
3.   Spritz the perforated pan with cooking spray.
4.   Remove the chicken cubes from the marinade. Shake the excess off and put in the perforated pan. Spritz with cooking spray.
5.   Select Air Fry. Set temperature to 360ºF (182ºC) and set time to 15 minutes. Press Start to begin preheating.
6.   Once preheated, place the pan into the oven. Flip the chicken cubes at least three times during the air frying.
7.   When cooking is complete, the chicken cubes should be glazed and well browned.
8.   Serve immediately.

Honey-Ginger Chicken Breasts

Prep time: 5 minutes | Cook time: 10 minutes | Serves 4

4 (4-ounce / 113-g) boneless, skinless chicken breasts
Chicken seasoning or rub, to taste
Salt and ground black pepper, to taste
¼ cup honey
2 tablespoons soy sauce
2 teaspoons grated fresh ginger
2 garlic cloves, minced
Cooking spray
1.   Spritz the perforated pan with cooking spray.
2.   Rub the chicken breasts with chicken seasoning, salt, and black pepper on a clean work surface.
3.   Arrange the chicken breasts in the perforated pan and spritz with cooking spray.
4.   Select Air Fry. Set temperature to 400ºF (205ºC) and set time to 10 minutes. Press Start to begin preheating.
5.   Once preheated, place the pan into the oven. Flip the chicken breasts halfway through.
6.   When cooking is complete, the internal temperature of the thickest part of the chicken should reach at least 165ºF (74ºC).
7.   Meanwhile, combine the honey, soy sauce, ginger, and garlic in a saucepan and heat over medium-high heat for 3 minutes or until thickened. Stir constantly.
8.   Remove the chicken from the oven and serve with the honey glaze.

Parmesan Chicken Cutlets

Prep time: 15 minutes | Cook time: 15 minutes | Serves 4

2 tablespoons panko bread crumbs
¼ cup grated Parmesan cheese
⅛ tablespoon paprika
½ tablespoon garlic powder
2 large eggs
4 chicken cutlets
1 tablespoon parsley
Salt and ground black pepper, to taste
Cooking spray
1.   Spritz the perforated pan with cooking spray.
2.   Combine the bread crumbs, Parmesan, paprika, garlic powder, salt, and ground black pepper in a large bowl. Stir to mix well. Beat the eggs in a separate bowl.
3.   Dredge the chicken cutlets in the beaten eggs, then roll over the bread crumbs mixture to coat well. Shake the excess off.
4.   Transfer the chicken cutlets in the perforated pan and spritz with cooking spray.
5.   Select Air Fry. Set temperature to 400ºF (205ºC) and set time to 15 minutes. Press Start to begin preheating.
6.   Once preheated, place the pan into the oven. Flip the cutlets halfway through.

7. When cooking is complete, the cutlets should be crispy and golden brown.
8. Serve with parsley on top.

Rosemary Chicken Breasts with Tomatoes

Prep time: 10 minutes | Cook time: 35 minutes | Serves 8

3 pounds (1.4 kg) chicken breasts, bone-in
1 teaspoon minced fresh basil
1 teaspoon minced fresh rosemary
2 tablespoons minced fresh parsley
1 teaspoon cayenne pepper
½ teaspoon salt
½ teaspoon freshly ground black pepper
4 medium Roma tomatoes, halved
Cooking spray

1. Spritz the perforated pan with cooking spray.
2. Combine all the ingredients, except for the chicken breasts and tomatoes, in a large bowl. Stir to mix well.
3. Dunk the chicken breasts in the mixture and press to coat well.
4. Transfer the chicken breasts to the perforated pan.
5. Select Air Fry. Set temperature to 370ºF (188ºC) and set time to 20 minutes. Press Start to begin preheating.
6. Once preheated, place the pan into the oven. Flip the breasts halfway through the cooking time.
7. When cooking is complete, the internal temperature of the thickest part of the breasts should reach at least 165ºF (74ºC).
8. Remove the cooked chicken breasts from the oven and adjust the temperature to 350ºF (180ºC).
9. Place the tomatoes in the perforated pan and spritz with cooking spray. Sprinkle with a touch of salt.
10. Set time to 10 minutes. Stir the tomatoes halfway through the cooking time.
11. When cooking is complete, the tomatoes should be tender.
12. Serve the tomatoes with chicken breasts on a large serving plate.

Chicken Tacos with Lettuce

Prep time: 10 minutes | Cook time: 6 minutes | Serves 4

1 pound (454 g) ground chicken
2 cloves garlic, minced
¼ cup diced onions
¼ teaspoon sea salt
Cooking spray
Peanut Sauce:
¼ cup creamy peanut butter, at room temperature
2 tablespoons tamari
1½ teaspoons hot sauce
2 tablespoons lime juice
2 tablespoons grated fresh ginger
2 tablespoons chicken broth
2 teaspoons sugar
For Serving:
2 small heads butter lettuce, leaves separated
Lime slices (optional)

1. Spritz a baking pan with cooking spray.
2. Combine the ground chicken, garlic, and onions in the baking pan, then sprinkle with salt. Use a fork to break the ground chicken and combine them well.
3. Select Bake. Set temperature to 350ºF (180ºC) and set time to 5 minutes. Press Start to begin preheating.
4. Once preheated, place the pan into the oven. Stir them halfway through the cooking time.
5. When cooking is complete, the chicken should be lightly browned.
6. Meanwhile, combine the ingredients for the sauce in a small bowl. Stir to mix well.
7. Pour the sauce in the pan of chicken, then bake for 1 more minute or until heated through.
8. Unfold the lettuce leaves on a large serving plate, then divide the chicken mixture on the lettuce leaves. Drizzle with lime juice and serve immediately.

Buttermilk Chicken Drumsticks

Prep time: 10 minutes | Cook time: 14 minutes | Serves 4

8 (4- to 5-ounce / 113- to 142-g) skinless bone-in chicken drumsticks
½ cup plain full-fat or low-fat yogurt
¼ cup buttermilk
2 teaspoons minced garlic
2 teaspoons minced fresh ginger
2 teaspoons ground cinnamon
2 teaspoons ground coriander
2 teaspoons mild paprika
1 teaspoon salt
1 teaspoon Tabasco hot red pepper sauce

1. In a large bowl, stir together all the ingredients except for chicken drumsticks until well combined. Add the chicken drumsticks to the bowl and toss until well coated. Cover in plastic and set in the refrigerator to marinate for 1 hour, tossing once.
2. Arrange the marinated drumsticks in the perforated pan, leaving enough space between them.
3. Select Air Fry. Set temperature to 375ºF (190ºC) and set time to 14 minutes. Press Start to begin preheating.
4. Once preheated, place the pan into the oven. Flip the drumsticks once halfway through to ensure even cooking.
5. When cooking is complete, the internal temperature of the chicken drumsticks should reach 160ºF (71ºC) on a meat thermometer.
6. Transfer the drumsticks to plates. Rest for 5 minutes before serving.

Lime Chicken Breasts with Cilantro

Prep time: 35 minutes | Cook time: 10 minutes | Serves 4

4 (4-ounce / 113-g) boneless, skinless chicken breasts
½ cup chopped fresh cilantro
Juice of 1 lime
Chicken seasoning or rub, to taste
Salt and ground black pepper, to taste
Cooking spray
1.   Put the chicken breasts in the large bowl, then add the cilantro, lime juice, chicken seasoning, salt, and black pepper. Toss to coat well.
2.   Wrap the bowl in plastic and refrigerate to marinate for at least 30 minutes.
3.   Spritz the perforated pan with cooking spray.
4.   Remove the marinated chicken breasts from the bowl and place in the perforated pan. Spritz with cooking spray.
5.   Select Air Fry. Set temperature to 400ºF (205ºC) and set time to 10 minutes. Press Start to begin preheating.
6.   Once preheated, place the pan into the oven. Flip the breasts halfway through.
7.   When cooking is complete, the internal temperature of the chicken should reach at least 165ºF (74ºC).
8.   Serve immediately.

Ground Chicken with Tomatoes

Prep time: 5 minutes | Cook time: 17 minutes | Serves 2

2 red bell peppers, chopped
1 pound (454 g) ground chicken
2 medium tomatoes, diced
½ cup chicken broth
Salt and ground black pepper, to taste
Cooking spray
1.   Spritz a baking pan with cooking spray.
2.   Set the bell pepper in the baking pan.
3.   Select Broil. Set temperature to 365ºF (185ºC) and set time to 5 minutes. Press Start to begin preheating.
4.   Once preheated, place the pan into the oven. Stir the bell pepper halfway through.
5.   When broiling is complete, the bell pepper should be tender.
6.   Add the ground chicken and diced tomatoes in the baking pan and stir to mix well.
7.   Set time to 12 minutes. Stir the mixture and mix in the chicken broth, salt and ground black pepper halfway through.
8.   When cooking is complete, the chicken should be well browned.
9.   Serve immediately.

Chicken with Veggie Couscous Salad

Prep time: 25 minutes | Cook time: 20 minutes | Serves 4

3 tablespoons plus 2 teaspoons pomegranate molasses
½ teaspoon ground cinnamon
1 teaspoon minced fresh thyme
Salt and ground black pepper, to taste
2 (12-ounce / 340-g) bone-in split chicken breasts, trimmed
¼ cup chicken broth
¼ cup water
½ cup couscous
1 tablespoon minced fresh parsley
2 ounces (57 g) cherry tomatoes, quartered
1 scallion, white part minced, green part sliced thin on bias
1 tablespoon extra-virgin olive oil
1 ounce (28 g) feta cheese, crumbled
Cooking spray
1.   Spritz the perforated pan with cooking spray.
2.   Combine 3 tablespoons of pomegranate molasses, cinnamon, thyme, and ⅛ teaspoon of salt in a small bowl. Stir to mix well. Set aside.
3.   Place the chicken breasts in the perforated pan, skin side down, and spritz with cooking spray. Sprinkle with salt and ground black pepper.
4.   Select Air Fry. Set temperature to 350ºF (180ºC) and set time to 20 minutes. Press Start to begin preheating.
5.   Once preheated, place the pan into the oven. Flip the chicken and brush with pomegranate molasses mixture halfway through.
6.   Meanwhile, pour the broth and water in a pot and bring to a boil over medium-high heat. Add the couscous and sprinkle with salt. Cover and simmer for 7 minutes or until the liquid is almost absorbed.
7.   Combine the remaining ingredients, except for the cheese, with cooked couscous in a large bowl. Toss to mix well. Scatter with the feta cheese.
8.   When cooking is complete, remove the chicken from the oven and allow to cool for 10 minutes. Serve with vegetable and couscous salad.

Breaded Chicken Nuggets

Prep time: 10 minutes | Cook time: 8 minutes | Serves 4

1 pound (454 g) boneless, skinless chicken breasts, cut into 1-inch pieces
2 tablespoons panko bread crumbs
6 tablespoons bread crumbs
Chicken seasoning or rub, to taste
Salt and ground black pepper, to taste
2 eggs
Cooking spray
1.   Spritz the perforated pan with cooking spray.
2.   Combine the bread crumbs, chicken seasoning, salt, and black pepper in a large bowl. Stir to mix well. Whisk the eggs in a separate bowl.

3.	Dunk the chicken pieces in the egg mixture, then in the bread crumb mixture. Shake the excess off.
4.	Arrange the well-coated chicken pieces in the perforated pan. Spritz with cooking spray.
5.	Select Air Fry. Set temperature to 400ºF (205ºC) and set time to 8 minutes. Press Start to begin preheating.
6.	Once preheated, place the pan into the oven. Flip the chicken halfway through.
7.	When cooking is complete, the chicken should be crispy and golden brown.
8.	Serve immediately.

Chicken Thighs with Mirin

Prep time: 10 minutes | Cook time: 15 minutes | Serves 4
½ cup mirin
¼ cup dry white wine
½ cup soy sauce
1 tablespoon light brown sugar
1½ pounds (680 g) boneless, skinless chicken thighs, cut into 1½-inch pieces, fat trimmed
4 medium scallions, trimmed, cut into 1½-inch pieces
Cooking spray
Special Equipment:
4 (4-inch) bamboo skewers, soaked in water for at least 30 minutes
1.	Combine the mirin, dry white wine, soy sauce, and brown sugar in a saucepan. Bring to a boil over medium heat. Keep stirring.
2.	Boil for another 2 minutes or until it has a thick consistency. Turn off the heat.
3.	Spritz the perforated pan with cooking spray.
4.	Run the bamboo skewers through the chicken pieces and scallions alternatively.
5.	Arrange the skewers in the perforated pan, then brush with mirin mixture on both sides. Spritz with cooking spray.
6.	Select Air Fry. Set temperature to 400ºF (205ºC) and set time to 10 minutes. Press Start to begin preheating.
7.	Once preheated, place the pan into the oven. Flip the skewers halfway through.
8.	When cooking is complete, the chicken and scallions should be glossy.
9.	Serve immediately.

Garlicky Whole Chicken Bake

Prep time: 10 minutes | Cook time: 1 hour | Serves 2 to 4
½ cup melted butter
3 tablespoons garlic, minced
Salt, to taste
1 teaspoon ground black pepper
1 (1-pound / 454-g) whole chicken
1.	Combine the butter with garlic, salt, and ground black pepper in a small bowl.

2.	Brush the butter mixture over the whole chicken, then place the chicken in the perforated pan, skin side down.
3.	Select Bake. Set temperature to 350ºF (180ºC) and set time to 60 minutes. Press Start to begin preheating.
4.	Once preheated, place the pan into the oven. Flip the chicken halfway through.
5.	When cooking is complete, an instant-read thermometer inserted in the thickest part of the chicken should register at least 165ºF (74ºC).
6.	Remove the chicken from the oven and allow to cool for 15 minutes before serving.

Garlic Chicken Wings

Prep time: 10 minutes | Cook time: 15 minutes | Serves 4
1 tablespoon olive oil
8 whole chicken wings
Chicken seasoning or rub, to taste
1 teaspoon garlic powder
Freshly ground black pepper, to taste
1.	Grease the perforated pan with olive oil.
2.	On a clean work surface, rub the chicken wings with chicken seasoning and rub, garlic powder, and ground black pepper.
3.	Arrange the well-coated chicken wings in the perforated pan.
4.	Select Air Fry. Set temperature to 400ºF (205ºC) and set time to 15 minutes. Press Start to begin preheating.
5.	Once preheated, place the pan into the oven. Flip the chicken wings halfway through.
6.	When cooking is complete, the internal temperature of the chicken wings should reach at least 165ºF (74ºC).
7.	Remove the chicken wings from the oven. Serve immediately.

Chicken and Pepper Baguette with Mayo

Prep time: 10 minutes | Cook time: 20 minutes | Serves 2
1¼ pounds (567 g) assorted small chicken parts, breasts cut into halves
¼ teaspoon salt
¼ teaspoon ground black pepper
2 teaspoons olive oil
½ pound (227 g) mini sweet peppers
¼ cup light mayonnaise
¼ teaspoon smoked paprika
½ clove garlic, crushed
Baguette, for serving
Cooking spray
1.	Spritz the perforated pan with cooking spray.
2.	Toss the chicken with salt, ground black pepper, and olive oil in a large bowl.
3.	Arrange the sweet peppers and chicken in the perforated pan.

4.	Select Air Fry. Set temperature to 375ºF (190ºC) and set time to 20 minutes. Press Start to begin preheating.
5.	Once preheated, place the pan into the oven. Flip the chicken and transfer the peppers on a plate halfway through.
6.	When cooking is complete, the chicken should be well browned.
7.	Meanwhile, combine the mayo, paprika, and garlic in a small bowl. Stir to mix well.
8.	Assemble the baguette with chicken and sweet pepper, then spread with mayo mixture and serve.

Satay Chicken Skewers

Prep time: 5 minutes | Cook time: 10 minutes | Serves 4
4 (6-ounce / 170-g) boneless, skinless chicken breasts, sliced into strips
1 teaspoon sea salt
1 teaspoon paprika
Cooking spray
Satay Sauce:
¼ cup creamy almond butter
½ teaspoon hot sauce
1½ tablespoons coconut vinegar
2 tablespoons chicken broth
1 teaspoon peeled and minced fresh ginger
1 clove garlic, minced
1 teaspoon sugar
For Serving:
¼ cup chopped cilantro leaves
Red pepper flakes, to taste
Thinly sliced red, orange, or / and yellow bell peppers
Special Equipment:
16 wooden or bamboo skewers, soaked in water for 15 minutes
1.	Spritz the perforated pan with cooking spray.
2.	Run the bamboo skewers through the chicken strips, then arrange the chicken skewers in the perforated pan and sprinkle with salt and paprika.
3.	Select Air Fry. Set temperature to 400ºF (205ºC) and set time to 10 minutes. Press Start to begin preheating.
4.	Once preheated, place the pan into the oven. Flip the chicken skewers halfway during the cooking.
5.	When cooking is complete, the chicken should be lightly browned.
6.	Meanwhile, combine the ingredients for the sauce in a small bowl. Stir to mix well.
7.	Transfer the cooked chicken skewers on a large plate, then top with cilantro, sliced bell peppers, red pepper flakes. Serve with the sauce or just baste the sauce over before serving.

Sweet-and-Sour Chicken Breasts

Prep time: 15 minutes | Cook time: 15 minutes | Serves 4
1 cup cornstarch
Chicken seasoning or rub, to taste
Salt and ground black pepper, to taste
2 eggs
2 (4-ounce/ 113-g) boneless, skinless chicken breasts, cut into 1-inch pieces
1½ cups sweet-and-sour sauce
Cooking spray
1.	Spritz the perforated pan with cooking spray.
2.	Combine the cornstarch, chicken seasoning, salt, and pepper in a large bowl. Stir to mix well. Whisk the eggs in a separate bowl.
3.	Dredge the chicken pieces in the bowl of cornstarch mixture first, then in the bowl of whisked eggs, and then in the cornstarch mixture again.
4.	Arrange the well-coated chicken pieces in the perforated pan. Spritz with cooking spray.
5.	Select Air Fry. Set temperature to 360ºF (182ºC) and set time to 15 minutes. Press Start to begin preheating.
6.	Once preheated, place the pan into the oven. Flip the chicken halfway through.
7.	When cooking is complete, the chicken should be golden brown and crispy.
8.	Transfer the chicken pieces on a large serving plate, then baste with sweet-and-sour sauce before serving.

Teriyaki Chicken Thighs

Prep time: 30 minutes | Cook time: 34 minutes | Serves 4
¼ cup chicken broth
½ teaspoon grated fresh ginger
⅛ teaspoon red pepper flakes
1½ tablespoons soy sauce
4 (5-ounce / 142-g) bone-in chicken thighs, trimmed
1 tablespoon mirin
½ teaspoon cornstarch
1 tablespoon sugar
6 ounces (170 g) snow peas, strings removed
⅛ teaspoon lemon zest
1 garlic clove, minced
¼ teaspoon salt
Ground black pepper, to taste
½ teaspoon lemon juice
1.	Combine the broth, ginger, pepper flakes, and soy sauce in a large bowl. Stir to mix well.
2.	Pierce 10 to 15 holes into the chicken skin. Put the chicken in the broth mixture and toss to coat well. Let sit for 10 minutes to marinate.
3.	Transfer the marinated chicken on a plate and pat dry with paper towels.
4.	Scoop 2 tablespoons of marinade in a microwave-safe bowl and combine with mirin, cornstarch and sugar. Stir to mix well. Microwave for 1 minute or until frothy and has a thick consistency. Set aside.

5.	Arrange the chicken in the perforated pan, skin side up.
6.	Select Air Fry. Set temperature to 400ºF (205ºC) and set time to 25 minutes. Press Start to begin preheating.
7.	Once preheated, place the pan into the oven. Flip the chicken halfway through.
8.	When cooking is complete, brush the chicken skin with marinade mixture. Air fry the chicken for 5 more minutes or until glazed.
9.	Remove the chicken from the oven. Allow the chicken to cool for 10 minutes.
10.	Meanwhile, combine the snow peas, lemon zest, garlic, salt, and ground black pepper in a small bowl. Toss to coat well.
11.	Transfer the snow peas in the perforated pan.
12.	Select Air Fry. Set temperature to 400ºF (205ºC) and set time to 3 minutes. Place the pan into the oven.
13.	When cooking is complete, the peas should be soft.
14.	Remove the peas from the oven and toss with lemon juice.
15.	Serve the chicken with lemony snow peas.

Five-Spice Turkey Thighs

Prep time: 10 minutes | Cook time: 25 minutes | Serves 6
2 pounds (907 g) turkey thighs
1 teaspoon Chinese five-spice powder
¼ teaspoon Sichuan pepper
1 teaspoon pink Himalayan salt
1 tablespoon Chinese rice vinegar
1 tablespoon mustard
1 tablespoon chili sauce
2 tablespoons soy sauce
Cooking spray
1.	Spritz the perforated pan with cooking spray.
2.	Rub the turkey thighs with five-spice powder, Sichuan pepper, and salt on a clean work surface.
3.	Put the turkey thighs in the perforated pan and spritz with cooking spray.
4.	Select Air Fry. Set temperature to 360ºF (182ºC) and set time to 22 minutes. Press Start to begin preheating.
5.	Once preheated, place the pan into the oven. Flip the thighs at least three times during the cooking.
6.	When cooking is complete, the thighs should be well browned.
7.	Meanwhile, heat the remaining ingredients in a saucepan over medium-high heat. Cook for 3 minutes or until the sauce is thickened and reduces to two thirds.
8.	Transfer the thighs onto a plate and baste with sauce before serving.

Dijon Turkey Breast with Sage

Prep time: 5 minutes | Cook time: 30 minutes | Serves 4
1 teaspoon chopped fresh sage
1 teaspoon chopped fresh tarragon
1 teaspoon chopped fresh thyme leaves
1 teaspoon chopped fresh rosemary leaves
1½ teaspoons sea salt
1 teaspoon ground black pepper
1 (2-pound / 907-g) turkey breast
3 tablespoons Dijon mustard
3 tablespoons butter, melted
Cooking spray
1.	Spritz the perforated pan with cooking spray.
2.	Combine the herbs, salt, and black pepper in a small bowl. Stir to mix well. Set aside.
3.	Combine the Dijon mustard and butter in a separate bowl. Stir to mix well.
4.	Rub the turkey with the herb mixture on a clean work surface, then brush the turkey with Dijon mixture.
5.	Arrange the turkey in the perforated pan.
6.	Select Air Fry. Set temperature to 390ºF (199ºC) and set time to 30 minutes. Press Start to begin preheating.
7.	Once preheated, place the pan into the oven. Flip the turkey breast halfway through.
8.	When cooking is complete, an instant-read thermometer inserted in the thickest part of the turkey breast should reach at least 165ºF (74ºC).
9.	Transfer the cooked turkey breast on a large plate and slice to serve.

Turkey and Mushroom Meatballs

Prep time: 10 minutes | Cook time: 15 minutes | Serves 6
Sauce:
2 tablespoons tamari
2 tablespoons tomato sauce
1 tablespoon lime juice
¼ teaspoon peeled and grated fresh ginger
1 clove garlic, smashed to a paste
½ cup chicken broth
$^1/_3$ cup sugar
2 tablespoons toasted sesame oil
Cooking spray
Meatballs:
2 pounds (907 g) ground turkey
¾ cup finely chopped button mushrooms
2 large eggs, beaten
1½ teaspoons tamari
¼ cup finely chopped green onions, plus more for garnish
2 teaspoons peeled and grated fresh ginger
1 clove garlic, smashed
2 teaspoons toasted sesame oil
2 tablespoons sugar
For Serving:
Lettuce leaves, for serving
Sliced red chiles, for garnish (optional)

Toasted sesame seeds, for garnish (optional)
1. Spritz the perforated pan with cooking spray.
2. Combine the ingredients for the sauce in a small bowl. Stir to mix well. Set aside.
3. Combine the ingredients for the meatballs in a large bowl. Stir to mix well, then shape the mixture in twelve 1½-inch meatballs.
4. Arrange the meatballs in the perforated pan, then baste with the sauce.
5. Select Air Fry. Set temperature to 350ºF (180ºC) and set time to 15 minutes. Press Start to begin preheating.
6. Once preheated, place the pan into the oven. Flip the balls halfway through.
7. When cooking is complete, the meatballs should be golden brown.
8. Unfold the lettuce leaves on a large serving plate, then transfer the cooked meatballs on the leaves. Spread the red chiles and sesame seeds over the balls, then serve.

Maple Turkey Breast with Rosemary

Prep time: 2 hours 20 minutes | Cook time: 30 minutes | Serves 6
½ teaspoon dried rosemary
2 minced garlic cloves
2 teaspoons salt
1 teaspoon ground black pepper
¼ cup olive oil
2½ pounds (1.1 kg) turkey breast
¼ cup pure maple syrup
1 tablespoon stone-ground brown mustard
1 tablespoon melted vegan butter
1. Combine the rosemary, garlic, salt, ground black pepper, and olive oil in a large bowl. Stir to mix well.
2. Dunk the turkey breast in the mixture and wrap the bowl in plastic. Refrigerate for 2 hours to marinate.
3. Remove the bowl from the refrigerator and let sit for half an hour before cooking.
4. Spritz the perforated pan with cooking spray.
5. Remove the turkey from the marinade and place in the perforated pan.
6. Select Air Fry. Set temperature to 400ºF (205ºC) and set time to 20 minutes. Press Start to begin preheating.
7. Once preheated, place the pan into the oven. Flip the breast halfway through.
8. When cooking is complete, the breast should be well browned.
9. Meanwhile, combine the remaining ingredients in a small bowl. Stir to mix well.
10. Pour half of the butter mixture over the turkey breast in the oven and air fry for 10 more minutes. Flip the breast and pour the remaining half of butter mixture over halfway through.

11. Transfer the turkey on a plate and slice to serve.

Whole Duck with Cherry Sauce

Prep time: 20 minutes | Cook time: 32 minutes | Serves 12
1 whole duck (about 5 pounds / 2.3 kg in total) split in half, back and rib bones removed, fat trimmed
1 teaspoon olive oil
Salt and freshly ground black pepper, to taste
Cherry Sauce:
1 tablespoon butter
1 shallot, minced
½ cup sherry
1 cup chicken stock
1 teaspoon white wine vinegar
¾ cup cherry preserves
1 teaspoon fresh thyme leaves
Salt and freshly ground black pepper, to taste
1. On a clean work surface, rub the duck with olive oil, then sprinkle with salt and ground black pepper to season.
2. Place the duck in the perforated pan, breast side up.
3. Select Air Fry. Set temperature to 400ºF (205ºC) and set time to 25 minutes. Press Start to begin preheating.
4. Once preheated, place the pan into the oven. Flip the ducks halfway through the cooking time.
5. Meanwhile, make the cherry sauce: Heat the butter in a skillet over medium-high heat or until melted.
6. Add the shallot and sauté for 5 minutes or until lightly browned.
7. Add the sherry and simmer for 6 minutes or until it reduces in half.
8. Add the chicken stick, white wine vinegar, and cherry preserves. Stir to combine well. Simmer for 6 more minutes or until thickened.
9. Fold in the thyme leaves and sprinkle with salt and ground black pepper. Stir to mix well.
10. When the cooking of the duck is complete, glaze the duck with a quarter of the cherry sauce, then air fry for another 4 minutes.
11. Flip the duck and glaze with another quarter of the cherry sauce. Air fry for an additional 3 minutes.
12. Transfer the duck on a large plate and serve with remaining cherry sauce.

Chicken Thighs with Peppers

Prep time: 10 minutes | Cook time: 27 minutes | Serves 4
4 bone-in, skin-on chicken thighs (about 1½ pounds / 680 g)
1½ teaspoon kosher salt, divided
1 link sweet Italian sausage (about 4 ounces / 113 g) whole

8 ounces (227 g) miniature bell peppers, halved and deseeded
1 small onion, thinly sliced
2 garlic cloves, minced
1 tablespoon olive oil
4 hot pickled cherry peppers, deseeded and quartered, along with 2 tablespoons pickling liquid from the jar
¼ cup chicken stock
Cooking spray
1. Salt the chicken thighs on both sides with 1 teaspoon of kosher salt. Spritz a baking pan with cooking spray and place the thighs skin-side down on the pan. Add the sausage.
2. Select Roast. Set temperature to 375ºF (190ºC) and set time to 27 minutes. Press Start to begin preheating.
3. Once preheated, place the pan into the oven.
4. While the chicken and sausage cook, place the bell peppers, onion, and garlic in a large bowl. Sprinkle with the remaining kosher salt and add the olive oil. Toss to coat.
5. After 10 minutes, remove the pan from the oven and flip the chicken thighs and sausage. Add the pepper mixture to the pan. Return the pan to the oven and continue cooking.
6. After another 10 minutes, remove the pan from the oven and add the pickled peppers, pickling liquid, and stock. Stir the pickled peppers into the peppers and onion. Return the pan to the oven and continue cooking.
7. When cooking is complete, the peppers and onion should be soft and the chicken should read 165ºF (74ºC) on a meat thermometer. Remove the pan from the oven. Slice the sausage into thin pieces and stir it into the pepper mixture. Spoon the peppers over four plates. Top with a chicken thigh.

Turkey Breast with Strawberries

Prep time: 15 minutes | Cook time: 37 minutes | Serves 2
2 pounds (907 g) turkey breast
1 tablespoon olive oil
Salt and ground black pepper, to taste
1 cup fresh strawberries
1. Rub the turkey bread with olive oil on a clean work surface, then sprinkle with salt and ground black pepper.
2. Transfer the turkey in the perforated pan and spritz with cooking spray.
3. Select Air Fry. Set temperature to 375ºF (190ºC) and set time to 30 minutes. Press Start to begin preheating.
4. Once preheated, place the pan into the oven. Flip the turkey breast halfway through.
5. Meanwhile, put the strawberries in a food processor and pulse until smooth.
6. When cooking is complete, spread the puréed strawberries over the turkey and cook for 7 more minutes.

7. Serve immediately.

Turkey and Cauliflower Meatloaf

Prep time: 15 minutes | Cook time: 50 minutes | Serves 6
2 pounds (907 g) lean ground turkey
1¹/₃ cups riced cauliflower
2 large eggs, lightly beaten
¼ cup almond flour
²/₃ cup chopped yellow or white onion
1 teaspoon ground dried turmeric
1 teaspoon ground cumin
1 teaspoon ground coriander
1 tablespoon minced garlic
1 teaspoon salt
1 teaspoon ground black pepper
Cooking spray
1. Spritz a loaf pan with cooking spray.
2. Combine all the ingredients in a large bowl. Stir to mix well. Pour half of the mixture in the prepared loaf pan and press with a spatula to coat the bottom evenly. Spritz the mixture with cooking spray.
3. Select Bake. Set temperature to 350ºF (180ºC) and set time to 25 minutes. Press Start to begin preheating.
4. Once preheated, place the pan into the oven.
5. When cooking is complete, the meat should be well browned and the internal temperature should reach at least 165ºF (74ºC).
6. Remove the loaf pan from the oven and serve immediately.

Garlic Duck Leg Quarters

Prep time: 5 minutes | Cook time: 45 minutes | Serves 4
4 (½-pound / 227-g) skin-on duck leg quarters
2 medium garlic cloves, minced
½ teaspoon salt
½ teaspoon ground black pepper
1. Spritz the perforated pan with cooking spray.
2. On a clean work surface, rub the duck leg quarters with garlic, salt, and black pepper.
3. Arrange the leg quarters in the perforated pan and spritz with cooking spray.
4. Select Air Fry. Set temperature to 300ºF (150ºC) and set time to 30 minutes. Press Start to begin preheating.
5. Once preheated, place the pan into the oven.
6. After 30 minutes, remove the pan from the oven. Flip the leg quarters. Increase temperature to 375ºF (190ºC) and set time to 15 minutes. Return the pan to the oven and continue cooking.
7. When cooking is complete, the leg quarters should be well browned and crispy.
8. Remove the duck leg quarters from the oven and allow to cool for 10 minutes before serving.

Balsamic Duck Breasts with Orange Marmalade

Prep time: 5 minutes | Cook time: 13 minutes | Serves 4

4 (6-ounce / 170-g) skin-on duck breasts
1 teaspoon salt
¼ cup orange marmalade
1 tablespoon white balsamic vinegar
¾ teaspoon ground black pepper
1. Cut 10 slits into the skin of the duck breasts, then sprinkle with salt on both sides.
2. Place the breasts in the perforated pan, skin side up.
3. Select Air Fry. Set temperature to 400ºF (205ºC) and set time to 10 minutes. Press Start to begin preheating.
4. Once preheated, place the pan into the oven.
5. Meanwhile, combine the remaining ingredients in a small bowl. Stir to mix well.
6. When cooking is complete, brush the duck skin with the marmalade mixture. Flip the breast and air fry for 3 more minutes or until the skin is crispy and the breast is well browned.
7. Serve immediately.

Game Hens with Cucumber Salad

Prep time: 25 minutes | Cook time: 25 minutes | Serves 6

2 (1¼-pound / 567-g) Cornish game hens, giblets discarded
1 tablespoon fish sauce
6 tablespoons chopped fresh cilantro
2 teaspoons lime zest
1 teaspoon ground coriander
2 garlic cloves, minced
2 tablespoons packed light brown sugar
2 teaspoons vegetable oil
Salt and ground black pepper, to taste
1 English cucumber, halved lengthwise and sliced thin
1 Thai chile, stemmed, deseeded, and minced
2 tablespoons chopped dry-roasted peanuts
1 small shallot, sliced thinly
1 tablespoon lime juice
Lime wedges, for serving
Cooking spray
1. Arrange a game hen on a clean work surface, remove the backbone with kitchen shears, then pound the hen breast to flat. Cut the breast in half. Repeat with the remaining game hen.
2. Loose the breast and thigh skin with your fingers, then pat the game hens dry and pierce about 10 holes into the fat deposits of the hens. Tuck the wings under the hens.
3. Combine 2 teaspoons of fish sauce, ¼ cup of cilantro, lime zest, coriander, garlic, 4 teaspoons of sugar, 1 teaspoon of vegetable oil, ½ teaspoon of salt, and ⅛ teaspoon of ground black pepper in a small bowl. Stir to mix well.
4. Rub the fish sauce mixture under the breast and thigh skin of the game hens, then let sit for 10 minutes to marinate.
5. Spritz the perforated pan with cooking spray.
6. Arrange the marinated game hens in the pan, skin side down.
7. Select Air Fry. Set temperature to 400ºF (205ºC) and set time to 25 minutes. Press Start to begin preheating.
8. Once preheated, place the pan into the oven. Flip the game hens halfway through the cooking time.
9. When cooking is complete, the hen skin should be golden brown and the internal temperature of the hens should read at least 165ºF (74ºC).
10. Meanwhile, combine all the remaining ingredients, except for the lime wedges, in a large bowl and sprinkle with salt and black pepper. Toss to mix well.
11. Transfer the fried hens on a large plate, then sit the salad aside and squeeze the lime wedges over before serving.

Turkey Scotch Eggs with Rosemary

Prep time: 15 minutes | Cook time: 12 minutes | Serves 4

1 egg
1 cup panko bread crumbs
½ teaspoon rosemary
1 pound (454 g) ground turkey
4 hard-boiled eggs, peeled
Salt and ground black pepper, to taste
Cooking spray
1. Spritz the perforated pan with cooking spray.
2. Whisk the egg with salt in a bowl. Combine the bread crumbs with rosemary in a shallow dish.
3. Stir the ground turkey with salt and ground black pepper in a separate large bowl, then divide the ground turkey into four portions.
4. Wrap each hard-boiled egg with a portion of ground turkey. Dredge in the whisked egg, then roll over the bread crumb mixture.
5. Place the wrapped eggs in the perforated pan and spritz with cooking spray.
6. Select Air Fry. Set temperature to 400ºF (205ºC) and set time to 12 minutes. Press Start to begin preheating.
7. Once preheated, place the pan into the oven. Flip the eggs halfway through.
8. When cooking is complete, the scotch eggs should be golden brown and crunchy.
9. Serve immediately.

Dijon Turkey with Carrots

Prep time: 10 minutes | Cook time: 25 minutes | Serves 4

2 (12-ounce / 340-g) turkey tenderloins

1 teaspoon kosher salt, divided
6 slices bacon
3 tablespoons balsamic vinegar
2 tablespoons honey
1 tablespoon Dijon mustard
½ teaspoon dried thyme
6 large carrots, peeled and cut into ¼-inch rounds
1 tablespoon olive oil
1.	Sprinkle the turkey with ¾ teaspoon of the salt. Wrap each tenderloin with 3 strips of bacon, securing the bacon with toothpicks. Place the turkey in a baking pan.
2.	In a small bowl, mix the balsamic vinegar, honey, mustard, and thyme.
3.	Place the carrots in a medium bowl and drizzle with the oil. Add 1 tablespoon of the balsamic mixture and ¼ teaspoon of kosher salt and toss to coat. Place these on the pan around the turkey tenderloins. Baste the tenderloins with about one-half of the remaining balsamic mixture.
4.	Select Roast. Set temperature to 375ºF (190ºC) and set time to 25 minutes. Press Start to begin preheating.
5.	Once preheated, place the pan into the oven.
6.	After 13 minutes, remove the pan from the oven. Gently stir the carrots. Flip the tenderloins and baste with the remaining balsamic mixture. Return the pan to the oven and continue cooking.
7.	When cooking is complete, the carrots should tender and the center of the tenderloins should register 165ºF (74ºC) on a meat thermometer. Remove the pan from the oven. Slice the turkey and serve with the carrots.

Chicken and Cheese Sandwiches

Prep time: 12 minutes | Cook time: 13 minutes | Serves 4
2 (8-ounce / 227-g) boneless, skinless chicken breasts
1 teaspoon kosher salt, divided
1 cup all-purpose flour
1 teaspoon Italian seasoning
2 large eggs
2 tablespoons plain yogurt
2 cups panko bread crumbs
$1^1/_3$ cups grated Parmesan cheese, divided
2 tablespoons olive oil
4 ciabatta rolls, split in half
½ cup marinara sauce
½ cup shredded Mozzarella cheese
1.	Lay the chicken breasts on a cutting board and cut each one in half parallel to the board so you have 4 fairly even, flat fillets. Place a piece of plastic wrap over the chicken pieces and use a rolling pin to gently pound them to an even thickness, about ½-inch thick. Season the chicken on both sides with ½ teaspoon of kosher salt.
2.	Place the flour on a plate and add the remaining kosher salt and the Italian seasoning. Mix with a fork to distribute evenly. In a wide bowl, whisk together the eggs with the yogurt. In a small bowl combine the panko, 1 cup of Parmesan cheese, and olive oil. Place this in a shallow bowl.
3.	Lightly dredge both sides of the chicken pieces in the seasoned flour, and then dip them in the egg wash to coat completely, letting the excess drip off. Finally, dredge the chicken in the bread crumbs. Carefully place the breaded chicken pieces in the perforated pan.
4.	Select Air Fry. Set temperature to 375ºF (190ºC) and set time to 10 minutes. Press Start to begin preheating.
5.	Once preheated, place the perforated pan into the oven.
6.	After 5 minutes, remove the perforated pan from the oven. Carefully turn the chicken over. Return the perforated pan to the oven and continue cooking. When cooking is complete, remove the perforated pan from the oven.
7.	Unfold the rolls on the perforated pan and spread each half with 1 tablespoon of marinara sauce. Place a chicken breast piece on the bottoms of the buns and sprinkle the remaining Parmesan cheese over the chicken pieces. Divide the Mozzarella among the top halves of the buns.
8.	Select Broil. Set temperature to High, and set time to 3 minutes.
9.	Place the pan into the oven. Check the sandwiches halfway through. When cooking is complete, the Mozzarella cheese should be melted and bubbly.
10.	Remove the perforated pan from the oven. Close the sandwiches and serve.

Balsamic Chicken Breast with Oregano

Prep time: 35 minutes | Cook time: 40 minutes | Serves 2
¼ cup balsamic vinegar
2 teaspoons dried oregano
2 garlic cloves, minced
1 tablespoon olive oil
⅛ teaspoon salt
½ teaspoon freshly ground black pepper
2 (4-ounce / 113-g) boneless, skinless, chicken-breast halves
Cooking spray
1.	In a small bowl, add the vinegar, oregano, garlic, olive oil, salt, and pepper. Mix to combine.
2.	Put the chicken in a resealable plastic bag. Pour the vinegar mixture in the bag with the chicken, seal the bag, and shake to coat the chicken. Refrigerate for 30 minutes to marinate.
3.	Spritz a baking pan with cooking spray. Put the chicken in the prepared baking pan and pour the marinade over the chicken.
4.	Select Bake. Set temperature to 400ºF (205ºC) and set time to 40 minutes. Press Start to begin preheating.
5.	Once preheated, place the pan into the oven.

6.   After 20 minutes, remove the pan from the oven. Flip the chicken. Return the pan to the oven and continue cooking.
7.   When cooking is complete, the internal temperature of the chicken should registers at least 165ºF (74ºC).
8.   Let sit for 5 minutes, then serve.

Chicken Kebabs with Corn Salad

Prep time: 17 minutes | Cook time: 10 minutes | Serves 4

1 pound (454 g) boneless, skinless chicken breast, cut into 1½-inch chunks
1 green bell pepper, deseeded and cut into 1-inch pieces
1 red bell pepper, deseeded and cut into 1-inch pieces
1 large onion, cut into large chunks
2 tablespoons fajita seasoning
3 tablespoons vegetable oil, divided
2 teaspoons kosher salt, divided
2 cups corn, drained
¼ teaspoon granulated garlic
1 teaspoon freshly squeezed lime juice
1 tablespoon mayonnaise
3 tablespoons grated Parmesan cheese
Special Equipment:
12 wooden skewers, soaked in water for at least 30 minutes
1.   Place the chicken, bell peppers, and onion in a large bowl. Add the fajita seasoning, 2 tablespoons of vegetable oil, and 1½ teaspoons of kosher salt. Toss to coat evenly.
2.   Alternate the chicken and vegetables on the skewers, making about 12 skewers.
3.   Place the corn in a medium bowl and add the remaining vegetable oil. Add the remaining kosher salt and the garlic, and toss to coat. Place the corn in an even layer on a baking pan and place the skewers on top.
4.   Select Roast. Set temperature to 375ºF (190ºC) and set time to 10 minutes. Press Start to begin preheating.
5.   Once preheated, place the pan into the oven.
6.   After about 5 minutes, remove the pan from the oven and turn the skewers. Return the pan to the oven and continue cooking.
7.   When cooking is complete, remove the pan from the oven. Place the skewers on a platter. Put the corn back to the bowl and combine with the lime juice, mayonnaise, and Parmesan cheese. Stir to mix well. Serve the skewers with the corn.

Cheddar Turkey Burgers with Mayo

Prep time: 10 minutes | Cook time: 25 minutes | Serves 4

2 medium yellow onions
1 tablespoon olive oil
1½ teaspoons kosher salt, divided
1¼ pound (567 g) ground turkey
$^1/_3$ cup mayonnaise
1 tablespoon Dijon mustard
2 teaspoons Worcestershire sauce
4 slices sharp Cheddar cheese (about 4 ounces / 113 g in total)
4 hamburger buns, sliced
1.   Trim the onions and cut them in half through the root. Cut one of the halves in half. Grate one quarter. Place the grated onion in a large bowl. Thinly slice the remaining onions and place in a medium bowl with the oil and ½ teaspoon of kosher salt. Toss to coat. Place the onions in a single layer on a baking pan.
2.   Select Roast. Set temperature to 350ºF (180ºC) and set time to 10 minutes. Press Start to begin preheating.
3.   Once preheated, place the pan into the oven.
4.   While the onions are cooking, add the turkey to the grated onion. Add the remaining kosher salt, mayonnaise, mustard, and Worcestershire sauce. Mix just until combined, being careful not to overwork the turkey. Divide the mixture into 4 patties, each about ¾-inch thick.
5.   When cooking is complete, remove the pan from the oven. Move the onions to one side of the pan and place the burgers on the pan. Poke your finger into the center of each burger to make a deep indentation.
6.   Select Broil. Set temperature to High, and set time to 12 minutes.
7.   Place the pan into the oven. After 6 minutes, remove the pan. Turn the burgers and stir the onions. Return the pan to the oven and continue cooking. After about 4 minutes, remove the pan and place the cheese slices on the burgers. Return the pan to the oven and continue cooking for about 1 minute, or until the cheese is melted and the center of the burgers has reached at least 165ºF (74ºC) on a meat thermometer.
8.   When cooking is complete, remove the pan from the oven. Loosely cover the burgers with foil.
9.   Lay out the buns, cut-side up, on the oven rack. Select Broil. Set temperature to High, and set time to 3 minutes. Place the pan into the oven. Check the buns after 2 minutes; they should be lightly browned.
10.   Remove the buns from the oven. Assemble the burgers and serve.

Curried Chicken and Brussels Sprouts

Prep time: 10 minutes | Cook time: 20 minutes | Serves 4

1 pound (454 g) boneless, skinless chicken thighs
1 teaspoon kosher salt, divided
¼ cup unsalted butter, melted
1 tablespoon curry powder
2 medium sweet potatoes, peeled and cut in 1-inch cubes
12 ounces (340 g) Brussels sprouts, halved

1. Sprinkle the chicken thighs with ½ teaspoon of kosher salt. Place them in the single layer on a baking pan.
2. In a small bowl, stir together the butter and curry powder.
3. Place the sweet potatoes and Brussels sprouts in a large bowl. Drizzle half the curry butter over the vegetables and add the remaining kosher salt. Toss to coat. Transfer the vegetables to the baking pan and place in a single layer around the chicken. Brush half of the remaining curry butter over the chicken.
4. Select Roast. Set temperature to 400ºF (205ºC) and set time to 20 minutes. Press Start to begin preheating.
5. Once preheated, place the pan into the oven.
6. After 10 minutes, remove the pan from the oven and turn over the chicken thighs. Baste them with the remaining curry butter. Return the pan to the oven and continue cooking.
7. Cooking is complete when the sweet potatoes are tender and the chicken is cooked through and reads 165ºF (74ºC) on a meat thermometer.

Chicken Thighs with Cherry Tomatoes

Prep time: 10 minutes | Cook time: 18 minutes | Serves 4

1½ pounds (680 g) boneless, skinless chicken thighs
1¼ teaspoon kosher salt, divided
2 tablespoons plus 1 teaspoon olive oil, divided
$^2/_3$ cup plus 2 tablespoons plain Greek yogurt, divided
2 tablespoons freshly squeezed lemon juice (about 1 medium lemon)
4 garlic cloves, minced, divided
1 tablespoon Shawarma Seasoning
4 pita breads, cut in half
2 cups cherry tomatoes
½ small cucumber, peeled, deseeded, and chopped
1 tablespoon chopped fresh parsley

1. Sprinkle the chicken thighs on both sides with 1 teaspoon of kosher salt. Place in a resealable plastic bag and set aside while you make the marinade.
2. In a small bowl, mix 2 tablespoons of olive oil, 2 tablespoons of yogurt, the lemon juice, 3 garlic cloves, and Shawarma Seasoning until thoroughly combined. Pour the marinade over the chicken. Seal the bag, squeezing out as much air as possible. And massage the chicken to coat it with the sauce. Set aside.
3. Wrap 2 pita breads each in two pieces of aluminum foil and place on a baking pan.
4. Select Bake. Set temperature to 300ºF (150ºC) and set time to 6 minutes. Press Start to begin preheating.
5. Once the oven has preheated, place the pan into the oven. After 3 minutes, remove the pan from the oven and turn over the foil packets. Return the

pan to the oven and continue cooking. When cooking is complete, remove the pan from the oven and place the foil-wrapped pitas on the top of the oven to keep warm.
6. Remove the chicken from the marinade, letting the excess drip off into the bag. Place them on the baking pan. Arrange the tomatoes around the sides of the chicken. Discard the marinade.
7. Select Broil. Set temperature to High, and set time to 12 minutes.
8. Place the pan into the oven.
9. After 6 minutes, remove the pan from the oven and turn over the chicken. Return the pan to the oven and continue cooking.
10. Wrap the cucumber in a paper towel to remove as much moisture as possible. Place them in a small bowl. Add the remaining yogurt, kosher salt, olive oil, garlic clove, and parsley. Whisk until combined.
11. When cooking is complete, the chicken should be browned, crisp along its edges, and sizzling. Remove the pan from the oven and place the chicken on a cutting board. Cut each thigh into several pieces. Unwrap the pitas. Spread a tablespoon of sauce into a pita half. Add some chicken and add 2 roasted tomatoes. Serve.

Mozzarella Chicken Breasts with Basil

Prep time: 30 minutes | Cook time: 1 hour | Serves 2

1 large egg
¼ cup almond meal
2 (6-ounce / 170-g) boneless, skinless chicken breast halves
1 (8-ounce / 227-g) jar marinara sauce, divided
4 tablespoons shredded Mozzarella cheese, divided
4 tablespoons grated Parmesan cheese, divided
4 tablespoons chopped fresh basil, divided
Salt and freshly ground black pepper, to taste
Cooking spray

1. Spritz the perforated pan with cooking spray.
2. In a shallow bowl, beat the egg.
3. In a separate shallow bowl, place the almond meal.
4. Dip 1 chicken breast half into the egg, then into the almond meal to coat. Place the coated chicken in the perforated pan. Repeat with the remaining 1 chicken breast half.
5. Select Bake. Set temperature to 350ºF (180ºC) and set time to 40 minutes. Press Start to begin preheating.
6. Once preheated, place the pan into the oven.
7. After 20 minutes, remove the pan from the oven and flip the chicken. Return the pan to oven and continue cooking.
8. When cooking is complete, the chicken should no longer pink and the juices run clear.
9. In a baking pan, pour half of marinara sauce.

10.	Place the cooked chicken in the sauce. Cover with the remaining marinara.
11.	Sprinkle 2 tablespoons of Mozzarella cheese and 2 tablespoons of soy Parmesan cheese on each chicken breast. Top each with 2 tablespoons of basil.
12.	Place the baking pan back in the oven and set the baking time to 20 minutes. Flip the chicken halfway through the cooking time.
13.	When cooking is complete, an instant-read thermometer inserted into the center of the chicken should read at least 165ºF (74ºC).
14.	Remove the pan from oven and divide between 2 plates. Season with salt and pepper and serve.

Chicken Thighs with Cabbage Slaw

Prep time: 10 minutes | Cook time: 27 minutes | Serves 4

4 bone-in, skin-on chicken thighs
1½ teaspoon kosher salt, divided
1 tablespoon smoked paprika
½ teaspoon granulated garlic
½ teaspoon dried oregano
¼ teaspoon freshly ground black pepper
3 cups shredded cabbage
½ small red onion, thinly sliced
4 large radishes, julienned
3 tablespoons red wine vinegar
2 tablespoons olive oil
Cooking spray

1.	Salt the chicken thighs on both sides with 1 teaspoon of kosher salt. In a small bowl, combine the paprika, garlic, oregano, and black pepper. Sprinkle half this mixture over the skin sides of the thighs. Spritz a baking pan with cooking spray and place the thighs skin-side down on the pan. Sprinkle the remaining spice mixture over the other sides of the chicken pieces.
2.	Select Roast. Set temperature to 375ºF (190ºC) and set time to 27 minutes. Press Start to begin preheating.
3.	Once preheated, place the pan into the oven.
4.	After 10 minutes, remove the pan from the oven and turn over the chicken thighs. Return the pan to the oven and continue cooking.
5.	While the chicken cooks, place the cabbage, onion, and radishes in a large bowl. Sprinkle with the remaining kosher salt, vinegar, and olive oil. Toss to coat.
6.	After another 9 to 10 minutes, remove the pan from the oven and place the chicken thighs on a cutting board. Place the cabbage mixture in the pan and toss with the chicken fat and spices.
7.	Spread the cabbage in an even layer on the pan and place the chicken on it, skin-side up. place the pan into the oven and continue cooking. Roast for another 7 to 8 minutes.
8.	When cooking is complete, the cabbage is just becoming tender. Remove the pan from the oven. Taste and adjust the seasoning if necessary. Serve.

Buttery Chicken with Corn

Prep time: 10 minutes | Cook time: 25 minutes | Serves 4

4 bone-in, skin-on chicken thighs
2 teaspoons kosher salt, divided
1 cup Bisquick baking mix
½ cup butter, melted, divided
1 pound (454 g) small red potatoes, quartered
3 ears corn, shucked and cut into rounds 1- to 1½-inches thick
$^1/_3$ cup heavy whipping cream
½ teaspoon freshly ground black pepper

1.	Sprinkle the chicken on all sides with 1 teaspoon of kosher salt. Place the baking mix in a shallow dish. Brush the thighs on all sides with ¼ cup of butter, then dredge them in the baking mix, coating them all on sides. Place the chicken in the center of a baking pan.
2.	Place the potatoes in a large bowl with 2 tablespoons of butter and toss to coat. Place them on one side of the chicken on the pan.
3.	Place the corn in a medium bowl and drizzle with the remaining butter. Sprinkle with ¼ teaspoon of kosher salt and toss to coat. Place on the pan on the other side of the chicken.
4.	Select Roast. Set temperature to 375ºF (190ºC) and set time to 25 minutes. Press Start to begin preheating.
5.	Once preheated, place the pan into the oven.
6.	After 20 minutes, remove the pan from the oven and transfer the potatoes back to the bowl. Return the pan to oven and continue cooking.
7.	As the chicken continues cooking, add the cream, black pepper, and remaining kosher salt to the potatoes. Lightly mash the potatoes with a potato masher.
8.	When cooking is complete, the corn should be tender and the chicken cooked through, reading 165ºF (74ºC) on a meat thermometer. Remove the pan from the oven and serve the chicken with the smashed potatoes and corn on the side.

Vinegary Chicken with Pineapple

Prep time: 10 minutes | Cook time: 10 minutes | Serves 6

1½ pounds (680 g) boneless, skinless chicken breasts, cut into 1-inch chunks
¾ cup soy sauce
2 tablespoons ketchup
2 tablespoons brown sugar
2 tablespoons rice vinegar
1 red bell pepper, cut into 1-inch chunks
1 green bell pepper, cut into 1-inch chunks
6 scallions, cut into 1-inch pieces
1 cup (¾-inch chunks) fresh pineapple, rinsed and drained
Cooking spray

1.	Place the chicken in a large bowl. Add the soy sauce, ketchup, brown sugar, vinegar, red and green peppers, and scallions. Toss to coat.
2.	Spritz a baking pan with cooking spray and place the chicken and vegetables on the pan.
3.	Select Roast. Set temperature to 375ºF (190ºC) and set time to 10 minutes. Press Start to begin preheating.
4.	Once preheated, place the pan into the oven.
5.	After 6 minutes, remove the pan from the oven. Add the pineapple chunks to the pan and stir. Return the pan to the oven and continue cooking.
6.	When cooking is complete, remove the pan from the oven. Serve with steamed rice, if desired.

Chicken Gnocchi with Spinach

Prep time: 10 minutes | Cook time: 13 minutes | Serves 4

1 (1-pound / 454-g) package shelf-stable gnocchi
1¼ cups chicken stock
½ teaspoon kosher salt
1 pound (454 g) chicken breast, cut into 1-inch chunks
1 cup heavy whipping cream
2 tablespoons sun-dried tomato purée
1 garlic clove, minced
1 cup frozen spinach, thawed and drained
1 cup grated Parmesan cheese
1.	Place the gnocchi in an even layer on a baking pan. Pour the chicken stock over the gnocchi.
2.	Select Bake. Set temperature to 450ºF (235ºC) and set time to 7 minutes. Press Start to begin preheating.
3.	Once preheated, place the pan into the oven.
4.	While the gnocchi are cooking, sprinkle the salt over the chicken pieces. In a small bowl, mix the cream, tomato purée, and garlic.
5.	When cooking is complete, blot off any remaining stock, or drain the gnocchi and return it to the pan. Top the gnocchi with the spinach and chicken. Pour the cream mixture over the ingredients in the pan.
6.	Select Roast. Set temperature to 400ºF (205ºC) and set time to 6 minutes. Place the pan into the oven.
7.	After 4 minutes, remove the pan from the oven and gently stir the ingredients. Return the pan to the oven and continue cooking.
8.	When cooking is complete, the gnocchi should be tender and the chicken should be cooked through. Remove the pan from the oven. Stir in the Parmesan cheese until it's melted and serve.

Peach Chicken with Dark Cherry

Prep time: 8 minutes | Cook time: 15 minutes | Serves 4

$^1/_3$ cup peach preserves
1 teaspoon ground rosemary
½ teaspoon black pepper
½ teaspoon salt
½ teaspoon marjoram
1 teaspoon light olive oil
1 pound (454 g) boneless chicken breasts, cut in 1½-inch chunks
1 (10-ounce / 284-g) package frozen dark cherries, thawed and drained
Cooking spray
1.	In a medium bowl, mix peach preserves, rosemary, pepper, salt, marjoram, and olive oil.
2.	Stir in chicken chunks and toss to coat well with the preserve mixture.
3.	Spritz the perforated pan with cooking spray and lay chicken chunks in the perforated pan.
4.	Select Bake. set temperature to 400ºF (205ºC) and set time to 15 minutes. Press Start to begin preheating.
5.	Once preheated, place the pan into the oven.
6.	After 7 minutes, remove the pan from the oven. Flip the chicken chunks. Return the pan to the oven and continue cooking.
7.	When cooking is complete, the chicken should no longer pink and the juices should run clear.
8.	Scatter the cherries over and cook for an additional minute to heat cherries.
9.	Serve immediately.

Turkey Meatloaves with Onion

Prep time: 6 minutes | Cook time: 24 minutes | Serves 4

¼ cup grated carrot
2 garlic cloves, minced
2 tablespoons ground almonds
$^1/_3$ cup minced onion
2 teaspoons olive oil
1 teaspoon dried marjoram
1 egg white
¾ pound (340 g) ground turkey breast
1.	In a medium bowl, stir together the carrot, garlic, almonds, onion, olive oil, marjoram, and egg white.
2.	Add the ground turkey. Mix until combined.
3.	Double 16 foil muffin cup liners to make 8 cups. Divide the turkey mixture evenly among the liners.
4.	Select Bake. Set temperature to 400ºF (205ºC) and set time to 24 minutes. Press Start to begin preheating.
5.	Once preheated, place the muffin cups into the oven.
6.	When cooking is complete, the meatloaves should reach an internal temperature of 165ºF (74ºC) on a meat thermometer.
7.	Serve immediately.

Paprika Hens with Creole Seasoning

Prep time: 10 minutes | Cook time: 40 minutes | Serves 4

½ tablespoon Creole seasoning

½ tablespoon garlic powder
½ tablespoon onion powder
½ tablespoon freshly ground black pepper
½ tablespoon paprika
2 tablespoons olive oil
2 Cornish hens
Cooking spray
1.   Spritz the perforated pan with cooking spray.
2.   In a small bowl, mix the Creole seasoning, garlic powder, onion powder, pepper, and paprika.
3.   Pat the Cornish hens dry and brush each hen all over with the olive oil. Rub each hen with the seasoning mixture. Place the Cornish hens in the perforated pan.
4.   Select Air Fry. Set temperature to 375ºF (190ºC) and set time to 30 minutes. Press Start to begin preheating.
5.   Once preheated, place the pan into the oven.
6.   After 15 minutes, remove the pan from the oven. Flip the hens over and baste it with any drippings collected in the bottom drawer of the oven. Return the pan to the oven and continue cooking.
7.   When cooking is complete, a thermometer inserted into the thickest part of the hens should reach at least 165ºF (74ºC).
8.   Let the hens rest for 10 minutes before carving.

Paprika Hens in Wine

Prep time: 2 hours 15 minutes | Cook time: 30 minutes | Serves 8
4 (1¼-pound / 567-g) Cornish hens, giblets removed, split lengthwise
2 cups white wine, divided
2 garlic cloves, minced
1 small onion, minced
½ teaspoon celery seeds
½ teaspoon poultry seasoning
½ teaspoon paprika
½ teaspoon dried oregano
¼ teaspoon freshly ground black pepper
1.   Place the hens, cavity side up, on a rack in a baking pan. Pour 1½ cups of the wine over the hens; set aside.
2.   In a shallow bowl, combine the garlic, onion, celery seeds, poultry seasoning, paprika, oregano, and pepper. Sprinkle half of the combined seasonings over the cavity of each split half. Cover and refrigerate. Allow the hens to marinate for 2 hours.
3.   Transfer the hens in the perforated pan.
4.   Select Bake. Set temperature to 350ºF (180ºC) and set time to 90 minutes. Press Start to begin preheating.
5.   Once preheated, place the pan into the oven.
6.   Remove the panpan from the oven halfway through the baking, turn breast side up, and remove the skin. Pour the remaining ½ cup of wine over the top, and sprinkle with the remaining seasonings.

7.   When cooking is complete, the inner temperature of the hens should be at least 165ºF (74ºC). Transfer the hens to a serving platter and serve hot.

Chili Chicken Fries

Prep time: 20 minutes | Cook time: 6 minutes | Serves 4 to 6
1 pound (454 g) chicken tenders, cut into about ½-inch-wide strips
Salt, to taste
¼ cup all-purpose flour
2 eggs
¾ cup panko bread crumbs
¾ cup crushed organic nacho cheese tortilla chips
Cooking spray
Seasonings:
½ teaspoon garlic powder
1 tablespoon chili powder
½ teaspoon onion powder
1 teaspoon ground cumin
1.   Stir together all seasonings in a small bowl and set aside.
2.   Sprinkle the chicken with salt. Place strips in a large bowl and sprinkle with 1 tablespoon of the seasoning mix. Stir well to distribute seasonings.
3.   Add flour to chicken and stir well to coat all sides.
4.   Beat eggs in a separate bowl.
5.   In a shallow dish, combine the panko, crushed chips, and the remaining 2 teaspoons of seasoning mix.
6.   Dip chicken strips in eggs, then roll in crumbs. Mist with oil or cooking spray. Arrange the chicken strips in a single layer in the perforated pan.
7.   Select Air Fry. Set temperature to 400ºF (205ºC) and set time to 6 minutes. Press Start to begin preheating.
8.   Once preheated, place the pan into the oven.
9.   After 4 minutes, remove the pan from the oven. Flip the strips with tongs. Return the pan to the oven and continue cooking.
10.   When cooking is complete, the chicken should be crispy and its juices should be run clear.
11.   Allow to cool under room temperature before serving.

Paprika Whole Chicken Roast

Prep time: 15 minutes | Cook time: 1 hour | Serves 6
1 teaspoon Italian seasoning
½ teaspoon garlic powder
½ teaspoon paprika
1 teaspoon salt
½ teaspoon freshly ground black pepper
½ teaspoon onion powder
2 tablespoons olive oil
1 (3-pound / 1.4-kg) whole chicken, giblets removed, pat dry

Cooking spray
1.		Spritz the perforated pan with cooking spray.
2.		In a small bowl, mix the Italian seasoning, garlic powder, paprika, salt, pepper, and onion powder.
3.		Brush the chicken with the olive oil and rub it with the seasoning mixture.
4.		Tie the chicken legs with butcher's twine. Place the chicken in the perforated pan, breast side down.
5.		Select Air Fry. Set temperature to 350ºF (180ºC) and set time to an hour. Press Start to begin preheating.
6.		Once preheated, place the pan into the oven.
7.		After 30 minutes, remove the pan from the oven. Flip the chicken over and baste it with any drippings collected in the bottom drawer of the oven. Return the pan to the oven and continue cooking.
8.		When cooking is complete, a thermometer inserted into the thickest part of the thigh should reach at least 165ºF (74ºC).
9.		Let the chicken rest for 10 minutes before carving and serving.

Lemon Chicken with Oregano

Prep time: 5 minutes | Cook time: 35 minutes | Serves 6
3 (8-ounce / 227-g) boneless, skinless chicken breasts, halved, rinsed
1 cup dried bread crumbs
¼ cup olive oil
¼ cup chicken broth
Zest of 1 lemon
3 medium garlic cloves, minced
½ cup fresh lemon juice
½ cup water
¼ cup minced fresh oregano
1 medium lemon, cut into wedges
¼ cup minced fresh parsley, divided
Cooking spray
1.		Pour the bread crumbs in a shadow dish, then roll the chicken breasts in the bread crumbs to coat.
2.		Spritz a skillet with cooking spray, and brown the coated chicken breasts over medium heat about 3 minutes on each side. Transfer the browned chicken to a baking pan.
3.		In a small bowl, combine the remaining ingredients, except the lemon and parsley. Pour the sauce over the chicken.
4.		Select Bake. Set temperature to 325ºF (163ºC) and set time to 30 minutes. Press Start to begin preheating.
5.		Once preheated, place the pan into the oven.
6.		After 15 minutes, remove the pan from the oven. Flip the breasts. Return the pan to the oven and continue cooking.
7.		When cooking is complete, the chicken should no longer pink.

8.		Transfer to a serving platter, and spoon the sauce over the chicken. Garnish with the lemon and parsley.

Chicken Drumsticks with Green Beans

Prep time: 5 minutes | Cook time: 25 minutes | Serves 4
8 skin-on chicken drumsticks
1 teaspoon kosher salt, divided
1 pound (454 g) green beans, trimmed
2 garlic cloves, minced
2 tablespoons vegetable oil
$^1/_3$ cup Thai sweet chili sauce
1.		Salt the drumsticks on all sides with ½ teaspoon of kosher salt. Let sit for a few minutes, then blot dry with a paper towel. Place on a baking pan.
2.		Select Roast. Set temperature to 375ºF (190ºC) and set time to 25 minutes. Press Start to begin preheating.
3.		Once preheated, place the pan into the oven.
4.		While the chicken cooks, place the green beans in a large bowl. Add the remaining kosher salt, the garlic, and oil. Toss to coat.
5.		After 15 minutes, remove the pan from the oven. Brush the drumsticks with the sweet chili sauce. Place the green beans in the pan. Return the pan to the oven and continue cooking.
6.		When cooking is complete, the green beans should be sizzling and browned in spots and the chicken cooked through, reading 165ºF (74ºC) on a meat thermometer. Serve the chicken with the green beans on the side.

Turkey-Stuffed Peppers with Cheddar

Prep time: 20 minutes | Cook time: 15 minutes | Serves 4
½ pound (227 g) lean ground turkey
4 medium bell peppers
1 (15-ounce / 425-g) can black beans, drained and rinsed
1 cup shredded Cheddar cheese
1 cup cooked long-grain brown rice
1 cup mild salsa
1¼ teaspoons chili powder
1 teaspoon salt
½ teaspoon ground cumin
½ teaspoon freshly ground black pepper
Chopped fresh cilantro, for garnish
Cooking spray
1.		In a large skillet over medium-high heat, cook the turkey, breaking it up with a spoon, until browned, about 5 minutes. Drain off any excess fat.
2.		Cut about ½ inch off the tops of the peppers and then cut in half lengthwise. Remove and discard the seeds and set the peppers aside.
3.		In a large bowl, combine the browned turkey, black beans, Cheddar cheese, rice, salsa, chili

powder, salt, cumin, and black pepper. Spoon the mixture into the bell peppers.
4.   Lightly spray the perforated pan with cooking spray. Arrange the bell peppers in the pan.
5.   Select Air Fry. Set temperature to 350ºF (180ºC) and set time to 15 minutes. Press Start to begin preheating.
6.   Once preheated, place the pan into the oven.
7.   When cooking is complete, the stuffed peppers should be lightly charred and wilted.
8.   Allow to cool for a few minutes and garnish with cilantro before serving.

Lemon Caramelized Pear Tart

Prep time: 15 minutes | Cook time: 25 minutes | Serves 8

Juice of 1 lemon
4 cups water
3 medium or 2 large ripe or almost ripe pears (preferably Bosc or Anjou) peeled, stemmed, and halved lengthwise
1 sheet (½ package) frozen puff pastry, thawed
All-purpose flour, for dusting
4 tablespoons caramel sauce such as Smucker's Salted Caramel, divided

1. Combine the lemon juice and water in a large bowl.
2. Remove the seeds from the pears with a melon baller and cut out the blossom end. Remove any tough fibers between the stem end and the center. As you work, place the pear halves in the acidulated water.
3. On a lightly floured cutting board, unwrap and unfold the puff pastry, roll it very lightly with a rolling pin so as to press the folds together. Place it on the sheet pan.
4. Roll about ½ inch of the pastry edges up to form a ridge around the perimeter. Crimp the corners together so as to create a solid rim around the pastry to hold in the liquid as the tart cooks.
5. Brush 2 tablespoons of caramel sauce over the bottom of the pastry.
6. Remove the pear halves from the water and blot off any remaining water with paper towels.
7. Place one of the halves on the board cut-side down and cut ¼-inch-thick slices radially. Repeat with the remaining halves. Arrange the pear slices over the pastry. Drizzle the remaining 2 tablespoons of caramel sauce over the top.
8. Select Bake. Set temperature to 350ºF (180ºC) and set time to 25 minutes. Press Start to begin preheating.
9. Once the unit has preheated, place the pan into the oven.
10. After 15 minutes, check the tart, rotating the pan if the crust is not browning evenly. Continue cooking for another 10 minutes, or until the pastry is golden brown, the pears are soft, and the caramel is bubbling.
11. When done, remove the pan from the oven and allow to cool for about 10 minutes.
12. Served warm.

Honey Walnut and Pistachios Baklava

Prep time: 10 minutes | Cook time: 16 minutes | Serves 10

1 cup walnut pieces
1 cup shelled raw pistachios
½ cup unsalted butter, melted
¼ cup plus 2 tablespoons honey, divided
3 tablespoons granulated sugar
1 teaspoon ground cinnamon
2 (1.9-ounce / 54-g) packages frozen miniature phyllo tart shells

1. Place the walnuts and pistachios in the perforated pan in an even layer.
2. Select Air Fry. Set temperature to 350ºF (180ºC) and set time to 4 minutes. Press Start to begin preheating.
3. Once the unit has preheated, place the pan into the oven.
4. After 2 minutes, remove the pan and stir the nuts. Transfer the pan back to the oven and cook for another 1 to 2 minutes until the nuts are golden brown and fragrant.
5. Meanwhile, stir together the butter, ¼ cup of honey, sugar, and cinnamon in a medium bowl.
6. When done, remove the pan from the oven and place the nuts on a cutting board and allow to cool for 5minutes. Finely chop the nuts. Add the chopped nuts and all the "nut dust" to the butter mixture and stir well.
7. Arrange the phyllo cups on the pan. Evenly fill the phyllo cups with the nut mixture, mounding it up. As you work, stir the nuts in the bowl frequently so that the syrup is evenly distributed throughout the filling.
8. Select Bake. Set temperature to 350ºF (180ºC) and set time to 12 minutes.
9. Place the pan into the oven. After about 8 minutes, check the cups. Continue cooking until the cups are golden brown and the syrup is bubbling.
10. When cooking is complete, remove the baklava from the oven, drizzle each cup with about ⅛ teaspoon of the remaining honey over the top.
11. Allow to cool for 5 minutes before serving.

Monk Fruit and Hazelnut Cake

Prep time: 5 minutes | Cook time: 20 minutes | Serves 6

1 stick butter, at room temperature
5 tablespoons liquid monk fruit
2 eggs plus 1 egg yolk, beaten
$^1/_3$ cup hazelnuts, roughly chopped
3 tablespoons sugar-free orange marmalade
6 ounces (170 g) unbleached almond flour
1 teaspoon baking soda
½ teaspoon baking powder
½ teaspoon ground cinnamon
½ teaspoon ground allspice
½ ground anise seed
Cooking spray

1. Lightly spritz a baking pan with cooking spray.
2. In a mixing bowl, whisk the butter and liquid monk fruit until the mixture is pale and smooth. Mix in the beaten eggs, hazelnuts, and marmalade and whisk again until well incorporated.

3.   Add the almond flour, baking soda, baking powder, cinnamon, allspice, anise seed and stir to mix well.
4.   Scrape the batter into the prepared baking pan.
5.   Select Bake. Set temperature to 310ºF (154ºC) and set time to 20 minutes. Press Start to begin preheating.
6.   Once the oven has preheated, place the pan into the oven.
7.   When cooking is complete, the top of the cake should spring back when gently pressed with your fingers.
8.   Transfer to a wire rack and let the cake cool to room temperature. Serve immediately.

Blueberry and Peach Tart

Prep time: 10 minutes | Cook time: 30 minutes | Serves 6 to 8
4 peaches, pitted and sliced
1 cup fresh blueberries
2 tablespoons cornstarch
3 tablespoons sugar
1 tablespoon freshly squeezed lemon juice
Cooking spray
1 sheet frozen puff pastry, thawed
1 tablespoon nonfat or low-fat milk
Confectioners' sugar, for dusting
1.   Add the peaches, blueberries, cornstarch, sugar, and lemon juice to a large bowl and toss to coat.
2.   Spritz a round baking pan with cooking spray.
3.   Unfold the pastry and put on the prepared baking pan.
4.   Lay the peach slices on the pan, slightly overlapping them. Scatter the blueberries over the peach.
5.   Drape the pastry over the outside of the fruit and press pleats firmly together. Brush the milk over the pastry.
6.   Select Bake. Set temperature to 400ºF (205ºC) and set time to 30 minutes. Press Start to begin preheating.
7.   Once the unit has preheated, place the pan into the oven.
8.   Bake until the crust is golden brown and the fruit is bubbling.
9.   When cooking is complete, remove the pan from the oven and allow to cool for 10 minutes.
10.   Serve the tart with the confectioners' sugar sprinkled on top.

Butter Shortbread with Lemon

Prep time: 10 minutes | Cook time: 36 to 40 minutes | Makes 4 dozen cookies
1 tablespoon grated lemon zest
1 cup granulated sugar

1 pound (454 g) unsalted butter, at room temperature
¼ teaspoon fine salt
4 cups all-purpose flour
$^1/_3$ cup cornstarch
Cooking spray
1.   Add the lemon zest and sugar to a stand mixer fitted with the paddle attachment and beat on medium speed for 1 to 2 minute. Let stand for about 5 minutes. Fold in the butter and salt and blend until fluffy.
2.   Mix together the flour and cornstarch in a large bowl. Add to the butter mixture and mix to combine.
3.   Spritz the sheet pan with cooking spray and spread a piece of parchment paper onto the pan. Scrape the dough into the pan until even and smooth.
4.   Select Bake. Set temperature to 325ºF (163ºC) and set time to 36 minutes. Press Start to begin preheating.
5.   Once the unit has preheated, place the pan into the oven.
6.   After 20 minutes, check the shortbread, rotating the pan if it is not browning evenly. Continue cooking for another 16 minutes until lightly browned.
7.   When done, remove the pan from the oven. Slice and allow to cool for 5 minutes before serving.

Chocolate Coconut Cake

Prep time: 5 minutes | Cook time: 15 minutes | Serves 10
1¼ cups unsweetened bakers' chocolate
1 stick butter
1 teaspoon liquid stevia
$^1/_3$ cup shredded coconut
2 tablespoons coconut milk
2 eggs, beaten
Cooking spray
1.   Lightly spritz a baking pan with cooking spray.
2.   Place the chocolate, butter, and stevia in a microwave-safe bowl. Microwave for about 30 seconds until melted. Let the chocolate mixture cool to room temperature.
3.   Add the remaining ingredients to the chocolate mixture and stir until well incorporated. Pour the batter into the prepared baking pan.
4.   Select Bake. Set temperature to 330ºF (166ºC) and set time to 15 minutes. Press Start to begin preheating.
5.   Once the oven has preheated, place the pan into the oven.
6.   When cooking is complete, a toothpick inserted in the center should come out clean.
7.   Remove from the oven and allow to cool for about 10 minutes before serving.

Coffee Chocolate Cake with Cinnamon

Prep time: 5 minutes | Cook time: 30 minutes | Serves 8
Dry Ingredients:
1½ cups almond flour
½ cup coconut meal
$^2/_3$ cup Swerve
1 teaspoon baking powder
¼ teaspoon salt
Wet Ingredients:
1 egg
1 stick butter, melted
½ cup hot strongly brewed coffee
Topping:
½ cup confectioner's Swerve
¼ cup coconut flour
3 tablespoons coconut oil
1 teaspoon ground cinnamon
½ teaspoon ground cardamom
1. In a medium bowl, combine the almond flour, coconut meal, Swerve, baking powder, and salt.
2. In a large bowl, whisk the egg, melted butter, and coffee until smooth.
3. Add the dry mixture to the wet and stir until well incorporated. Transfer the batter to a greased baking pan.
4. Stir together all the ingredients for the topping in a small bowl. Spread the topping over the batter and smooth the top with a spatula.
5. Select Bake. Set temperature to 330ºF (166ºC) and set time to 30 minutes. Press Start to begin preheating.
6. Once the oven has preheated, place the pan into the oven.
7. When cooking is complete, the cake should spring back when gently pressed with your fingers.
8. Rest for 10 minutes before serving.

Vanilla Cookies with Chocolate Chips

Prep time: 10 minutes | Cook time: 22 minutes | Makes 30 cookies
$^1/_3$ cup (80g) organic brown sugar
$^1/_3$ cup (80g) organic cane sugar
4 ounces (112g) cashew-based vegan butter
½ cup coconut cream
1 teaspoon vanilla extract
2 tablespoons ground flaxseed
1 teaspoon baking powder
1 teaspoon baking soda
Pinch of salt
2¼ cups (220g) almond flour
½ cup (90g) dairy-free dark chocolate chips
1. Line a baking sheet with parchment paper.
2. Mix together the brown sugar, cane sugar, and butter in a medium bowl or the bowl of a stand mixer. Cream together with a mixer.
3. Fold in the coconut cream, vanilla, flaxseed, baking powder, baking soda, and salt. Stir well.
4. Add the almond flour, a little at a time, mixing after each addition until fully incorporated. Stir in the chocolate chips with a spatula.

5. Scoop the dough onto the prepared baking sheet.
6. Select Bake. Set temperature to 325°F (163°C) and set time to 22 minutes Press Start to begin preheating.
7. Once the unit has preheated, place the baking sheet into the oven.
8. Bake until the cookies are golden brown.
9. When cooking is complete, transfer the baking sheet onto a wire rack to cool completely before serving.

Chocolate Vanilla Cheesecake

Prep time: 5 minutes | Cook time: 18 minutes | Serves 6
Crust:
½ cup butter, melted
½ cup coconut flour
2 tablespoons stevia
Cooking spray
Topping:
4 ounces (113 g) unsweetened baker's chocolate
1 cup mascarpone cheese, at room temperature
1 teaspoon vanilla extract
2 drops peppermint extract
1. Lightly coat a baking pan with cooking spray.
2. In a mixing bowl, whisk together the butter, flour, and stevia until well combined. Transfer the mixture to the prepared baking pan.
3. Select Bake. Set temperature to 350ºF (180ºC) and set time to 18 minutes. Press Start to begin preheating.
4. Once the oven has preheated, place the pan into the oven.
5. When done, a toothpick inserted in the center should come out clean.
6. Remove the crust from the oven to a wire rack to cool.
7. Once cooled completely, place it in the freezer for 20 minutes.
8. When ready, combine all the ingredients for the topping in a small bowl and stir to incorporate.
9. Spread this topping over the crust and let it sit for another 15 minutes in the freezer.
10. Serve chilled.

Strawberry Crumble with Rhubarb

Prep time: 10 minutes | Cook time: 12 to 17 minutes | Serves 6
1½ cups sliced fresh strawberries
$^1/_3$ cup sugar
¾ cup sliced rhubarb
$^2/_3$ cup quick-cooking oatmeal
¼ cup packed brown sugar
½ cup whole-wheat pastry flour
½ teaspoon ground cinnamon
3 tablespoons unsalted butter, melted

1.	Place the strawberries, sugar, and rhubarb in a baking pan and toss to coat.
2.	Combine the oatmeal, brown sugar, pastry flour, and cinnamon in a medium bowl.
3.	Add the melted butter to the oatmeal mixture and stir until crumbly. Sprinkle this generously on top of the strawberries and rhubarb.
4.	Select Bake. Set temperature to 370ºF (188ºC) and set time to 12 minutes. Press Start to begin preheating.
5.	Once the unit has preheated, place the pan into the oven.
6.	Bake until the fruit is bubbly and the topping is golden brown. Continue cooking for an additional 2 to 5 minutes if needed.
7.	When cooking is complete, remove from the oven and serve warm.

Raspberry Muffins

Prep time: 5 minutes | Cook time: 15 minutes | Serves 6
2 cups almond flour
¾ cup Swerve
1¼ teaspoons baking powder
$^1/_3$ teaspoon ground allspice
$^1/_3$ teaspoon ground anise star
½ teaspoon grated lemon zest
¼ teaspoon salt
2 eggs
1 cup sour cream
½ cup coconut oil
½ cup raspberries
1.	Line a muffin pan with 6 paper liners.
2.	In a mixing bowl, mix the almond flour, Swerve, baking powder, allspice, anise, lemon zest, and salt.
3.	In another mixing bowl, beat the eggs, sour cream, and coconut oil until well mixed. Add the egg mixture to the flour mixture and stir to combine. Mix in the raspberries.
4.	Scrape the batter into the prepared muffin cups, filling each about three-quarters full.
5.	Select Bake. Set temperature to 345ºF (174ºC) and set time to 15 minutes. Press Start to begin preheating.
6.	Once the oven has preheated, place the muffin pan into the oven.
7.	When cooking is complete, the tops should be golden and a toothpick inserted in the middle should come out clean.
8.	Allow the muffins to cool for 10 minutes in the muffin pan before removing and serving.

Peach and Apple Crisp with Oatmeal

Prep time: 10 minutes | Cook time: 10 to 12 minutes | Serves 4
2 peaches, peeled, pitted, and chopped
1 apple, peeled and chopped
2 tablespoons honey
3 tablespoons packed brown sugar
2 tablespoons unsalted butter, at room temperature
½ cup quick-cooking oatmeal
$^1/_3$ cup whole-wheat pastry flour
½ teaspoon ground cinnamon
1.	Place the peaches, apple, and honey in a baking pan and toss until thoroughly combined.
2.	Mix together the brown sugar, butter, oatmeal, pastry flour, and cinnamon in a medium bowl and stir until crumbly. Sprinkle this mixture generously on top of the peaches and apples.
3.	Select Bake. Set temperature to 380ºF (193ºC) and set time to 10 minutes. Press Start to begin preheating.
4.	Once the unit has preheated, place the pan into the oven.
5.	Bake until the fruit is bubbling and the topping is golden brown.
6.	Once cooking is complete, remove the pan from the oven and allow to cool for 5 minutes before serving.

Vanilla Walnuts Tart with Cloves

Prep time: 5 minutes | Cook time: 13 minutes | Serves 6
1 cup coconut milk
½ cup walnuts, ground
½ cup Swerve
½ cup almond flour
½ stick butter, at room temperature
2 eggs
1 teaspoon vanilla essence
¼ teaspoon ground cardamom
¼ teaspoon ground cloves
Cooking spray
1.	Coat a baking pan with cooking spray.
2.	Combine all the ingredients except the oil in a large bowl and stir until well blended. Spoon the batter mixture into the baking pan.
3.	Select Bake. Set temperature to 360ºF (182ºC) and set time to 13 minutes. Press Start to begin preheating.
4.	Once the oven has preheated, place the pan into the oven.
5.	When cooking is complete, a toothpick inserted into the center of the tart should come out clean.
6.	Remove from the oven and place on a wire rack to cool. Serve immediately.

Mixed Berry Bake with Almond Topping

Prep time: 5 minutes | Cook time: 17 minutes | Serves 3
½ cup mixed berries
Cooking spray
Topping:
1 egg, beaten
3 tablespoons almonds, slivered
3 tablespoons chopped pecans

2 tablespoons chopped walnuts
3 tablespoons granulated Swerve
2 tablespoons cold salted butter, cut into pieces
½ teaspoon ground cinnamon
1.	Lightly spray a baking dish with cooking spray.
2.	Make the topping: In a medium bowl, stir together the beaten egg, nuts, Swerve, butter, and cinnamon until well blended.
3.	Put the mixed berries in the bottom of the baking dish and spread the topping over the top.
4.	Select Bake. Set temperature to 340ºF (171ºC) and set time to 17 minutes. Press Start to begin preheating.
5.	Once the oven has preheated, place the baking dish into the oven.
6.	When cooking is complete, the fruit should be bubbly and topping should be golden brown.
7.	Allow to cool for 5 to 10 minutes before serving.

Vanilla Coconut Cookies with Pecans

Prep time: 10 minutes | Cook time: 25 minutes | Serves 10
1½ cups coconut flour
1½ cups extra-fine almond flour
½ teaspoon baking powder
$^1/_3$ teaspoon baking soda
3 eggs plus an egg yolk, beaten
¾ cup coconut oil, at room temperature
1 cup unsalted pecan nuts, roughly chopped
¾ cup monk fruit
¼ teaspoon freshly grated nutmeg
$^1/_3$ teaspoon ground cloves
½ teaspoon pure vanilla extract
½ teaspoon pure coconut extract
⅛ teaspoon fine sea salt
1.	Line the perforated pan with parchment paper.
2.	Mix the coconut flour, almond flour, baking powder, and baking soda in a large mixing bowl.
3.	In another mixing bowl, stir together the eggs and coconut oil. Add the wet mixture to the dry mixture.
4.	Mix in the remaining ingredients and stir until a soft dough forms.
5.	Drop about 2 tablespoons of dough on the parchment paper for each cookie and flatten each biscuit until it's 1 inch thick.
6.	Select Bake. Set temperature to 370ºF (188ºC) and set time to 25 minutes. Press Start to begin preheating.
7.	Once the oven has preheated, place the pan into the oven.
8.	When cooking is complete, the cookies should be golden and firm to the touch.
9.	Remove from the oven to a plate. Let the cookies cool to room temperature and serve.

Cinnamon Apple Fritters

Prep time: 30 minutes | Cook time: 7 minutes | Serves 6
1 cup chopped, peeled Granny Smith apple
½ cup granulated sugar
1 teaspoon ground cinnamon
1 cup all-purpose flour
1 teaspoon baking powder
1 teaspoon salt
2 tablespoons milk
2 tablespoons butter, melted
1 large egg, beaten
Cooking spray
¼ cup confectioners' sugar (optional)
1.	Mix together the apple, granulated sugar, and cinnamon in a small bowl. Allow to sit for 30 minutes.
2.	Combine the flour, baking powder, and salt in a medium bowl. Add the milk, butter, and egg and stir to incorporate.
3.	Pour the apple mixture into the bowl of flour mixture and stir with a spatula until a dough forms.
4.	Make the fritters: On a clean work surface, divide the dough into 12 equal portions and shape into 1-inch balls. Flatten them into patties with your hands.
5.	Line the perforated pan with parchment paper and spray it with cooking spray.
6.	Transfer the apple fritters onto the parchment paper, evenly spaced but not too close together. Spray the fritters with cooking spray.
7.	Select Bake. Set temperature to 350ºF (180ºC) and set time to 7 minutes. Press Start to begin preheating.
8.	Once the oven has preheated, place the pan into the oven. Flip the fritters halfway through the cooking time.
9.	When cooking is complete, the fritters should be lightly browned.
10.	Remove from the oven to a plate and serve with the confectioners' sugar sprinkled on top, if desired.

Chocolate Blueberry Cupcakes

Prep time: 5 minutes | Cook time: 15 minutes | Serves 6
¾ cup granulated erythritol
1¼ cups almond flour
1 teaspoon unsweetened baking powder
3 teaspoons cocoa powder
½ teaspoon baking soda
½ teaspoon ground cinnamon
¼ teaspoon grated nutmeg
⅛ teaspoon salt
½ cup milk
1 stick butter, at room temperature
3 eggs, whisked
1 teaspoon pure rum extract
½ cup blueberries
Cooking spray

1.   Spray a 6-cup muffin tin with cooking spray.
2.   In a mixing bowl, combine the erythritol, almond flour, baking powder, cocoa powder, baking soda, cinnamon, nutmeg, and salt and stir until well blended.
3.   In another mixing bowl, mix together the milk, butter, egg, and rum extract until thoroughly combined. Slowly and carefully pour this mixture into the bowl of dry mixture. Stir in the blueberries.
8.   Spoon the batter into the greased muffin cups, filling each about three-quarters full.
4.   Select Bake. Set temperature to 345ºF (174ºC) and set time to 15 minutes. Press Start to begin preheating.
5.   Once the oven has preheated, place the muffin tin into the oven.
6.   When done, the center should be springy and a toothpick inserted in the middle should come out clean.
7.   Remove from the oven and place on a wire rack to cool. Serve immediately.

Vanilla Chocolate Chip Cookies

Prep time: 10 minutes | Cook time: 20 minutes | Makes 4 dozen (1-by-1½-inch) cookies
1 cup unsalted butter, at room temperature
1 cup dark brown sugar
½ cup granulated sugar
2 large eggs
1 tablespoon vanilla extract
Pinch salt
2 cups old-fashioned rolled oats
1½ cups all-purpose flour
1 teaspoon baking powder
1 teaspoon baking soda
2 cups chocolate chips
1.   Stir together the butter, brown sugar, and granulated sugar in a large mixing bowl until smooth and light in color.
2.   Crack the eggs into the bowl, one at a time, mixing after each addition. Stir in the vanilla and salt.
3.   Mix together the oats, flour, baking powder, and baking soda in a separate bowl. Add the mixture to the butter mixture and stir until mixed. Stir in the chocolate chips.
4.   Spread the dough onto the sheet pan in an even layer.
5.   Select Bake. Set temperature to 350ºF (180ºC) and set time to 20 minutes. Press Start to begin preheating.
6.   Once the unit has preheated, place the pan into the oven.
7.   After 15 minutes, check the cookie, rotating the pan if the crust is not browning evenly. Continue cooking for a total of 18 to 20 minutes or until golden brown.
8.   When cooking is complete, remove the pan from the oven and allow to cool completely before slicing and serving.

Vanilla Chocolate Cake

Prep time: 5 minutes | Cook time: 15 minutes | Serves 6
½ cup unsweetened chocolate, chopped
½ stick butter, at room temperature
1 tablespoon liquid stevia
1½ cups coconut flour
2 eggs, whisked
½ teaspoon vanilla extract
A pinch of fine sea salt
Cooking spray
1.   Place the chocolate, butter, and stevia in a microwave-safe bowl. Microwave for about 30 seconds until melted.
2.   Let the chocolate mixture cool for 5 to 10 minutes.
3.   Add the remaining ingredients to the bowl of chocolate mixture and whisk to incorporate.
4.   Lightly spray a baking pan with cooking spray.
5.   Scrape the chocolate mixture into the prepared baking pan.
6.   Select Bake. Set temperature to 330ºF (166ºC) and set time to 15 minutes. Press Start to begin preheating.
7.   Once the oven has preheated, place the pan into the oven.
8.   When cooking is complete, the top should spring back lightly when gently pressed with your fingers.
9.   Let the cake cool for 5 minutes and serve.

Coconut Orange Cake

Prep time: 5 minutes | Cook time: 17 minutes | Serves 6
1 stick butter, melted
¾ cup granulated Swerve
2 eggs, beaten
¾ cup coconut flour
¼ teaspoon salt
$1/3$ teaspoon grated nutmeg
$1/3$ cup coconut milk
1¼ cups almond flour
½ teaspoon baking powder
2 tablespoons unsweetened orange jam
Cooking spray
1.   Coat a baking pan with cooking spray. Set aside.
2.   In a large mixing bowl, whisk together the melted butter and granulated Swerve until fluffy.
3.   Mix in the beaten eggs and whisk again until smooth. Stir in the coconut flour, salt, and nutmeg and gradually pour in the coconut milk. Add the remaining ingredients and stir until well incorporated.
4.   Scrape the batter into the baking pan.
5.   Select Bake. Set temperature to 355ºF (179ºC) and set time to 17 minutes. Press Start to begin preheating.

6.	Once the oven has preheated, place the pan into the oven.
7.	When cooking is complete, the top of the cake should spring back when gently pressed with your fingers.
8.	Remove from the oven to a wire rack to cool. Serve chilled.

Peach and Blueberry Galette

Prep time: 10 minutes | Cook time: 20 minutes | Serves 6
1 pint blueberries, rinsed and picked through (about 2 cups)
2 large peaches or nectarines, peeled and cut into ½-inch slices (about 2 cups)
$^1/_3$ cup plus 2 tablespoons granulated sugar, divided
2 tablespoons unbleached all-purpose flour
½ teaspoon grated lemon zest (optional)
¼ teaspoon ground allspice or cinnamon
Pinch kosher or fine salt
1 (9-inch) refrigerated piecrust (or use homemade)
2 teaspoons unsalted butter, cut into pea-size pieces
1 large egg, beaten
1.	Mix together the blueberries, peaches, $^1/_3$ cup of sugar, flour, lemon zest (if desired) allspice, and salt in a medium bowl.
2.	Unroll the crust on the sheet pan, patching any tears if needed. Place the fruit in the center of the crust, leaving about 1½ inches of space around the edges. Scatter the butter pieces over the fruit. Fold the outside edge of the crust over the outer circle of the fruit, making pleats as needed.
3.	Brush the egg over the crust. Sprinkle the crust and fruit with the remaining 2 tablespoons of sugar.
4.	Select Bake. Set temperature to 350ºF (180ºC) and set time to 20 minutes. Press Start to begin preheating.
5.	Once the unit has preheated, place the pan into the oven.
6.	After about 15 minutes, check the galette, rotating the pan if the crust is not browning evenly. Continue cooking until the crust is deep golden brown and the fruit is bubbling.
7.	When cooking is complete, remove the pan from the oven and allow to cool for 10 minutes before slicing and serving.

Honey Apple-Peach Crumble

Prep time: 10 minutes | Cook time: 11 minutes | Serves 4
1 apple, peeled and chopped
2 peaches, peeled, pitted, and chopped
2 tablespoons honey
½ cup quick-cooking oatmeal
$^1/_3$ cup whole-wheat pastry flour
2 tablespoons unsalted butter, at room temperature
3 tablespoons packed brown sugar
½ teaspoon ground cinnamon

1.	Mix together the apple, peaches, and honey in a baking pan until well incorporated.
2.	In a bowl, combine the oatmeal, pastry flour, butter, brown sugar, and cinnamon and stir to mix well. Spread this mixture evenly over the fruit.
3.	Select Bake. Set temperature to 380ºF (193ºC) and set time to 11 minutes. Press Start to begin preheating.
4.	Once the oven has preheated, place the pan into the oven.
5.	When cooking is complete, the fruit should be bubbling around the edges and the topping should be golden brown.
6.	Remove from the oven and serve warm.

Cinnamon Apple with Apricots

Prep time: 5 minutes | Cook time: 15 to 18 minutes | Serves 4
4 large apples, peeled and sliced into 8 wedges
2 tablespoons olive oil
½ cup dried apricots, chopped
1 to 2 tablespoons sugar
½ teaspoon ground cinnamon
1.	Toss the apple wedges with the olive oil in a mixing bowl until well coated.
2.	Place the apple wedges in the perforated pan.
3.	Select Air Fry. Set temperature to 350ºF (180ºC) and set time to 15 minutes. Press Start to begin preheating.
4.	Once the oven has preheated, place the pan into the oven.
5.	After about 12 minutes, remove from the oven. Sprinkle with the dried apricots and air fry for another 3 minutes.
6.	Meanwhile, thoroughly combine the sugar and cinnamon in a small bowl.
7.	Remove the apple wedges from the oven to a plate. Serve sprinkled with the sugar mixture.

Honey-Glazed Peach and Plum Kebabs

Prep time: 10 minutes | Cook time: 4 minutes | Serves 4
2 peaches, peeled, pitted, and thickly sliced
3 plums, halved and pitted
3 nectarines, halved and pitted
1 tablespoon honey
½ teaspoon ground cinnamon
¼ teaspoon ground allspice
Pinch cayenne pepper
Special Equipment:
8 metal skewers
1.	Thread, alternating peaches, plums, and nectarines onto the metal skewers that fit into the oven.
2.	Thoroughly combine the honey, cinnamon, allspice, and cayenne in a small bowl. Brush generously the glaze over the fruit skewers.

3. Transfer the fruit skewers to the perforated pan.
4. Select Air Fry. Set temperature to 400ºF (205ºC) and set time to 4 minutes. Press Start to begin preheating.
5. Once the oven has preheated, place the pan into the oven.
6. When cooking is complete, the fruit should be caramelized.
7. Remove the fruit skewers from the oven and let rest for 5 minutes before serving.

Vanilla Pound Cake

Prep time: 5 minutes | Cook time: 30 minutes | Serves 8
1 stick butter, at room temperature
1 cup Swerve
4 eggs
1½ cups coconut flour
½ cup buttermilk
½ teaspoon baking soda
½ teaspoon baking powder
¼ teaspoon salt
1 teaspoon vanilla essence
A pinch of ground star anise
A pinch of freshly grated nutmeg
Cooking spray
1. Spray a baking pan with cooking spray.
2. With an electric mixer or hand mixer, beat the butter and Swerve until creamy. One at a time, mix in the eggs and whisk until fluffy. Add the remaining ingredients and stir to combine.
3. Transfer the batter to the prepared baking pan.
4. Select Bake. Set temperature to 320ºF (160ºC) and set time to 30 minutes. Press Start to begin preheating.
5. Once the oven has preheated, place the pan into the oven. Rotate the pan halfway through the cooking time.
6. When cooking is complete, the center of the cake should be springy.
7. Allow the cake to cool in the pan for 10 minutes before removing and serving.

Pumpkin Pudding with Vanilla Wafers

Prep time: 10 minutes | Cook time: 15 minutes | Serves 4
1 cup canned no-salt-added pumpkin purée (not pumpkin pie filling)
¼ cup packed brown sugar
3 tablespoons all-purpose flour
1 egg, whisked
2 tablespoons milk
1 tablespoon unsalted butter, melted
1 teaspoon pure vanilla extract
4 low-fat vanilla wafers, crumbled
Cooking spray
1. Coat a baking pan with cooking spray. Set aside.
2. Mix the pumpkin purée, brown sugar, flour, whisked egg, milk, melted butter, and vanilla in a medium bowl and whisk to combine. Transfer the mixture to the baking pan.
3. Select Bake. Set temperature to 350ºF (180ºC) and set time to 15 minutes. Press Start to begin preheating.
4. Once the oven has preheated, place the pan into the oven.
5. When cooking is complete, the pudding should be set.
6. Remove the pudding from the oven to a wire rack to cool.
7. Divide the pudding into four bowls and serve with the vanilla wafers sprinkled on top.

Vanilla Ricotta Cake with Lemon

Prep time: 5 minutes | Cook time: 25 minutes | Serves 6
17.5 ounces (496 g) ricotta cheese
5.4 ounces (153 g) sugar
3 eggs, beaten
3 tablespoons flour
1 lemon, juiced and zested
2 teaspoons vanilla extract
1. In a large mixing bowl, stir together all the ingredients until the mixture reaches a creamy consistency.
2. Pour the mixture into a baking pan and place in the oven.
3. Select Bake. Set temperature to 320ºF (160ºC) and set time to 25 minutes. Press Start to begin preheating.
4. Once the oven has preheated, place the pan into the oven.
5. When cooking is complete, a toothpick inserted in the center should come out clean.
6. Allow to cool for 10 minutes on a wire rack before serving.

Apple Bake with Cinnamon

Prep time: 15 minutes | Cook time: 12 minutes | Serves 4
1 cup packed light brown sugar
2 teaspoons ground cinnamon
2 medium Granny Smith apples, peeled and diced
1. Thoroughly combine the brown sugar and cinnamon in a medium bowl.
2. Add the apples to the bowl and stir until well coated. Transfer the apples to a baking pan.
3. Select Bake. Set temperature to 350ºF (180ºC) and set time to 12 minutes. Press Start to begin preheating.
4. Once the oven has preheated, place the pan into the oven.

5. After about 9 minutes, stir the apples and bake for an additional 3 minutes. When cooking is complete, the apples should be softened.
6. Serve warm.

Vanilla Fudge Pie

Prep time: 15 minutes | Cook time: 26 minutes | Serves 8

1½ cups sugar
½ cup self-rising flour
$^1/_3$ cup unsweetened cocoa powder
3 large eggs, beaten
12 tablespoons (1½ sticks) butter, melted
1½ teaspoons vanilla extract
1 (9-inch) unbaked pie crust
¼ cup confectioners' sugar (optional)
1. Thoroughly combine the sugar, flour, and cocoa powder in a medium bowl. Add the beaten eggs and butter and whisk to combine. Stir in the vanilla.
2. Pour the prepared filling into the pie crust and transfer to the perforated pan.
3. Select Bake. Set temperature to 350ºF (180ºC) and set time to 26 minutes. Press Start to begin preheating.
4. Once the oven has preheated, place the pan into the oven.
5. When cooking is complete, the pie should be set.
6. Allow the pie to cool for 5 minutes. Sprinkle with the confectioners' sugar, if desired. Serve warm.

Chocolate Cake with Blackberries

Prep time: 10 minutes | Cook time: 22 minutes | Serves 8

½ cup butter, at room temperature
2 ounces (57 g) Swerve
4 eggs
1 cup almond flour
1 teaspoon baking soda
$^1/_3$ teaspoon baking powder
½ cup cocoa powder
1 teaspoon orange zest
$^1/_3$ cup fresh blackberries
1. With an electric mixer or hand mixer, beat the butter and Swerve until creamy.
2. One at a time, mix in the eggs and beat again until fluffy.
3. Add the almond flour, baking soda, baking powder, cocoa powder, orange zest and mix well. Add the butter mixture to the almond flour mixture and stir until well blended. Fold in the blackberries.
4. Scrape the batter into a baking pan.
5. Select Bake. Set temperature to 335ºF (168ºC) and set time to 22 minutes. Press Start to begin preheating.
6. Once the oven has preheated, place the pan into the oven.

7. When cooking is complete a toothpick inserted into the center of the cake should come out clean.
8. Allow the cake cool on a wire rack to room temperature. Serve immediately.

Blackberry Cobbler

Prep time: 15 minutes | Cook time: 20 to 25 minutes | Serves 6

3 cups fresh or frozen blackberries
1¾ cups sugar, divided
1 teaspoon vanilla extract
8 tablespoons (1 stick) butter, melted
1 cup self-rising flour
Cooking spray
1. Spritz a baking pan with cooking spray.
2. Mix the blackberries, 1 cup of sugar, and vanilla in a medium bowl and stir to combine.
3. Stir together the melted butter, remaining sugar, and flour in a separate medium bowl.
4. Spread the blackberry mixture evenly in the prepared pan and top with the butter mixture.
5. Select Bake. Set temperature to 350ºF (180ºC) and set time to 25 minutes. Press Start to begin preheating.
6. Once the oven has preheated, place the pan into the oven.
7. After about 20 minutes, check if the cobbler has a golden crust and you can't see any batter bubbling while it cooks. If needed, bake for another 5 minutes.
8. Remove from the oven and place on a wire rack to cool to room temperature. Serve immediately.

Chocolate Chip Brownies

Prep time: 10 minutes | Cook time: 20 minutes | Makes 1 dozen brownies

1 egg
¼ cup brown sugar
2 tablespoons white sugar
2 tablespoons safflower oil
1 teaspoon vanilla
$^1/_3$ cup all-purpose flour
¼ cup cocoa powder
¼ cup white chocolate chips
Nonstick cooking spray
1. Spritz a baking pan with nonstick cooking spray.
2. Whisk together the egg, brown sugar, and white sugar in a medium bowl. Mix in the safflower oil and vanilla and stir to combine.
3. Add the flour and cocoa powder and stir just until incorporated. Fold in the white chocolate chips.
4. Scrape the batter into the prepared baking pan.
5. Select Bake. Set temperature to 340ºF (171ºC) and set time to 20 minutes. Press Start to begin preheating.

6. Once the oven has preheated, place the pan into the oven.

7. When done, the brownie should spring back when touched lightly with your fingers.

8. Transfer to a wire rack and let cool for 30 minutes before slicing to serve.

White Chocolate Cookies with Nutmeg

Prep time: 5 minutes | Cook time: 11 minutes | Serves 10

8 ounces (227 g) unsweetened white chocolate
2 eggs, well beaten
¾ cup butter, at room temperature
$1^2/_3$ cups almond flour
½ cup coconut flour
¾ cup granulated Swerve
2 tablespoons coconut oil
$^1/_3$ teaspoon grated nutmeg
$^1/_3$ teaspoon ground allspice
$^1/_3$ teaspoon ground anise star
¼ teaspoon fine sea salt

1. Line a baking sheet with parchment paper.

2. Combine all the ingredients in a mixing bowl and knead for about 3 to 4 minutes, or until a soft dough forms. Transfer to the refrigerator to chill for 20 minutes.

3. Make the cookies: Roll the dough into 1-inch balls and transfer to the parchment-lined baking sheet, spacing 2 inches apart. Flatten each with the back of a spoon.

4. Select Bake. Set temperature to 350ºF (180ºC) and set time to 11 minutes. Press Start to begin preheating.

5. Once the oven has preheated, place the baking sheet into the oven.

6. When cooking is complete, the cookies should be golden and firm to the touch.

7. Transfer to a wire rack and let the cookies cool completely. Serve immediately.

Peanut Butter Bread Pudding

Prep time: 10 minutes | Cook time: 10 minutes | Serves 8

1 egg
1 egg yolk
¾ cup chocolate milk
3 tablespoons brown sugar
3 tablespoons peanut butter
2 tablespoons cocoa powder
1 teaspoon vanilla
5 slices firm white bread, cubed
Nonstick cooking spray

1. Spritz a baking pan with nonstick cooking spray.

2. Whisk together the egg, egg yolk, chocolate milk, brown sugar, peanut butter, cocoa powder, and vanilla until well combined.

3. Fold in the bread cubes and stir to mix well. Allow the bread soak for 10 minutes.

4. When ready, transfer the egg mixture to the prepared baking pan.

5. Select Bake. Set temperature to 330ºF (166ºC) and set time to 10 minutes. Press Start to begin preheating.

6. Once the oven has preheated, place the pan into the oven.

7. When done, the pudding should be just firm to the touch.

8. Serve at room temperature.

Cinnamon Pineapple Rings

Prep time: 5 minutes | Cook time: 7 minutes | Serves 6

1 cup rice milk
$^2/_3$ cup flour
½ cup water
¼ cup unsweetened flaked coconut
4 tablespoons sugar
½ teaspoon baking soda
½ teaspoon baking powder
½ teaspoon vanilla essence
½ teaspoon ground cinnamon
¼ teaspoon ground anise star
Pinch of kosher salt
1 medium pineapple, peeled and sliced

1. In a large bowl, stir together all the ingredients except the pineapple.

2. Dip each pineapple slice into the batter until evenly coated.

3. Arrange the pineapple slices in the perforated pan.

4. Select Air Fry. Set temperature to 380ºF (193ºC) and set time to 7 minutes. Press Start to begin preheating.

5. Once the oven has preheated, place the pan into the oven.

6. When cooking is complete, the pineapple rings should be golden brown.

7. Remove from the oven to a plate and cool for 5 minutes before serving.

Mixed Berry Crisp with Cloves

Prep time: 5 minutes | Cook time: 20 minutes | Serves 6

1 tablespoon butter, melted
12 ounces (340 g) mixed berries
$^1/_3$ cup granulated Swerve
1 teaspoon pure vanilla extract
½ teaspoon ground cinnamon
¼ teaspoon ground cloves
¼ teaspoon grated nutmeg
½ cup coconut chips, for garnish

1. Coat a baking pan with melted butter.

2. Put the remaining ingredients except the coconut chips in the prepared baking pan.

3. Select Bake. Set temperature to 330ºF (166ºC) and set time to 20 minutes. Press Start to begin preheating.

4.	Once the oven has preheated, place the pan into the oven.
5.	When cooking is complete, remove from the oven. Serve garnished with the coconut chips.

Pineapple Sticks with Coconut

Prep time: 10 minutes | Cook time: 10 minutes | Serves 4

½ fresh pineapple, cut into sticks
¼ cup desiccated coconut
1.	Place the desiccated coconut on a plate and roll the pineapple sticks in the coconut until well coated.
2.	Lay the pineapple sticks in the perforated pan.
3.	Select Air Fry. Set temperature to 400ºF (205ºC) and set time to 10 minutes. Press Start to begin preheating.
4.	Once the oven has preheated, place the pan into the oven.
5.	When cooking is complete, the pineapple sticks should be crisp-tender.
6.	Serve warm.

Chocolate S'mores

Prep time: 5 minutes | Cook time: 3 minutes | Makes 12 s'mores

12 whole cinnamon graham crackers, halved
2 (1.55-ounce / 44-g) chocolate bars, cut into 12 pieces
12 marshmallows
1.	Arrange 12 graham cracker squares in the perforated pan in a single layer.
2.	Top each square with a piece of chocolate.
3.	Select Bake. Set temperature to 350ºF (180ºC) and set time to 3 minutes. Press Start to begin preheating.
4.	Once the oven has preheated, place the pan into the oven.
5.	After 2 minutes, remove the pan and place a marshmallow on each piece of melted chocolate. Return the pan to the oven and continue to cook for another 1 minute.
6.	Remove from the oven to a serving plate.
7.	Serve topped with the remaining graham cracker squares

Pecan Pie with Chocolate Chips

Prep time: 20 minutes | Cook time: 25 minutes | Serves 8

1 (9-inch) unbaked pie crust
Filling:
2 large eggs
$^1/_3$ cup butter, melted
1 cup sugar
½ cup all-purpose flour
1 cup milk chocolate chips
1½ cups coarsely chopped pecans
2 tablespoons bourbon
1.	Whisk the eggs and melted butter in a large bowl until creamy.
2.	Add the sugar and flour and stir to incorporate. Mix in the milk chocolate chips, pecans, and bourbon and stir until well combined.
3.	Use a fork to prick holes in the bottom and sides of the pie crust. Pour the prepared filling into the pie crust. Place the pie crust in the perforated pan.
4.	Select Bake. Set temperature to 350ºF (180ºC) and set time to 25 minutes. Press Start to begin preheating.
5.	Once the oven has preheated, place the pan into the oven.
6.	When cooking is complete, a toothpick inserted in the center should come out clean.
7.	Allow the pie cool for 10 minutes in the pan before serving.

Vanilla Baked Peaches and Blueberries

Prep time: 10 minutes | Cook time: 10 minutes | Serves 6

3 peaches, peeled, halved, and pitted
2 tablespoons packed brown sugar
1 cup plain Greek yogurt
¼ teaspoon ground cinnamon
1 teaspoon pure vanilla extract
1 cup fresh blueberries
1.	Arrange the peaches in the perforated pan, cut-side up. Top with a generous sprinkle of brown sugar.
2.	Select Bake. Set temperature to 380ºF (193ºC) and set time to 10 minutes. Press Start to begin preheating.
3.	Once the oven has preheated, place the pan into the oven.
4.	Meanwhile, whisk together the yogurt, cinnamon, and vanilla in a small bowl until smooth.
5.	When cooking is complete, the peaches should be lightly browned and caramelized.
6.	Remove the peaches from the oven to a plate. Serve topped with the yogurt mixture and fresh blueberries.

CHAPTER 11 CASSEROLES, FRITTATA, AND QUICHE

Mushroom and Beef Casserole

Prep time: 10 minutes | Cook time: 25 minutes | Serves 4

1½ pounds (680 g) beef steak
1 ounce (28 g) dry onion soup mix
2 cups sliced mushrooms
1 (14.5-ounce / 411-g) can cream of mushroom soup
½ cup beef broth
¼ cup red wine
3 garlic cloves, minced
1 whole onion, chopped

1. Put the beef steak in a large bowl, then sprinkle with dry onion soup mix. Toss to coat well.
2. Combine the mushrooms with mushroom soup, beef broth, red wine, garlic, and onion in a large bowl. Stir to mix well.
3. Transfer the beef steak in a baking pan, then pour in the mushroom mixture.
4. Select Bake. Set temperature to 360ºF (182ºC) and set time to 25 minutes. Press Start to begin preheating.
5. Once preheated, place the pan into the oven.
6. When cooking is complete, the mushrooms should be soft and the beef should be well browned.
7. Remove the baking pan from the oven and serve immediately.

Cauliflower Casserole with Pecan Butter

Prep time: 15 minutes | Cook time: 50 minutes | Serves 6

1 cup chicken broth
2 cups cauliflower florets
1 cup canned pumpkin purée
¼ cup heavy cream
1 teaspoon vanilla extract
2 large eggs, beaten
$^1/_3$ cup unsalted butter, melted, plus more for greasing the pan
¼ cup sugar
1 teaspoon fine sea salt
Chopped fresh parsley leaves, for garnish
Topping:
½ cup blanched almond flour
1 cup chopped pecans
$^1/_3$ cup unsalted butter, melted
½ cup sugar

1. Pour the chicken broth in a baking pan, then add the cauliflower.
2. Select Bake. Set temperature to 350ºF (180ºC) and set time to 20 minutes. Press Start to begin preheating.
3. Once preheated, place the pan into the oven.
4. When cooking is complete, the cauliflower should be soft.
5. Meanwhile, combine the ingredients for the topping in a large bowl. Stir to mix well.
6. Pat the cauliflower dry with paper towels, then place in a food processor and pulse with pumpkin purée, heavy cream, vanilla extract, eggs, butter, sugar, and salt until smooth.
7. Clean the baking pan and grease with more butter, then pour the purée mixture in the pan. Spread the topping over the mixture.
8. Place the baking pan back to the oven. Select Bake and set time to 30 minutes.
9. When baking is complete, the topping of the casserole should be lightly browned.
10. Remove the casserole from the oven and serve with fresh parsley on top.

Cheddar Chicken Sausage Casserole

Prep time: 10 minutes | Cook time: 20 minutes | Serves 8

10 eggs
1 cup Cheddar cheese, shredded and divided
¾ cup heavy whipping cream
1 (12-ounce / 340-g) package cooked chicken sausage
1 cup broccoli, chopped
2 cloves garlic, minced
½ tablespoon salt
¼ tablespoon ground black pepper
Cooking spray

1. Spritz a baking pan with cooking spray.
2. Whisk the eggs with Cheddar and cream in a large bowl to mix well.
3. Combine the cooked sausage, broccoli, garlic, salt, and ground black pepper in a separate bowl. Stir to mix well.
4. Pour the sausage mixture into the baking pan, then spread the egg mixture over to cover.
5. Select Bake. Set temperature to 400ºF (205ºC) and set time to 20 minutes. Press Start to begin preheating.
6. Once preheated, place the pan into the oven.
7. When cooking is complete, the egg should be set and a toothpick inserted in the center should come out clean.
8. Serve immediately.

Corn Casserole with Bell Pepper

Prep time: 10 minutes | Cook time: 20 minutes | Serves 4

1 cup corn kernels
¼ cup bell pepper, finely chopped
½ cup low-fat milk
1 large egg, beaten
½ cup yellow cornmeal
½ cup all-purpose flour
½ teaspoon baking powder
2 tablespoons melted unsalted butter
1 tablespoon granulated sugar
Pinch of cayenne pepper
¼ teaspoon kosher salt
Cooking spray

1. Spritz a baking pan with cooking spray.

2.		Combine all the ingredients in a large bowl. Stir to mix well. Pour the mixture into the baking pan.
3.		Select Bake. Set temperature to 330ºF (166ºC) and set time to 20 minutes. Press Start to begin preheating.
4.		Once preheated, place the pan into the oven.
5.		When cooking is complete, the casserole should be lightly browned and set.
6.		Remove the baking pan from the oven and serve immediately.

Asparagus Casserole with Grits

Prep time: 5 minutes | Cook time: 30 minutes | Serves 4
10 fresh asparagus spears, cut into 1-inch pieces
2 cups cooked grits, cooled to room temperature
2 teaspoons Worcestershire sauce
1 egg, beaten
½ teaspoon garlic powder
¼ teaspoon salt
2 slices provolone cheese, crushed
Cooking spray
1.		Spritz a baking pan with cooking spray.
2.		Set the asparagus in the perforated pan. Spritz the asparagus with cooking spray.
3.		Select Air Fry. Set temperature to 390ºF (199ºC) and set time to 5 minutes. Press Start to begin preheating.
4.		Once preheated, place the pan into the oven. Flip the asparagus halfway through.
5.		When cooking is complete, the asparagus should be lightly browned and crispy.
6.		Meanwhile, combine the grits, Worcestershire sauce, egg, garlic powder, and salt in a bowl. Stir to mix well.
7.		Pour half of the grits mixture in the prepared baking pan, then spread with fried asparagus.
8.		Spread the cheese over the asparagus and pour the remaining grits over.
9.		Select Bake. Set time to 25 minutes. Place the pan into the oven.
10.		When cooking is complete, the egg should be set.
11.		Serve immediately.

Cheddar Broccoli Casserole

Prep time: 5 minutes | Cook time: 30 minutes | Serves 6
4 cups broccoli florets
¼ cup heavy whipping cream
½ cup sharp Cheddar cheese, shredded
¼ cup ranch dressing
Kosher salt and ground black pepper, to taste
1.		Combine all the ingredients in a large bowl. Toss to coat well broccoli well.
2.		Pour the mixture into a baking pan.
3.		Select Bake. Set temperature to 375ºF (190ºC) and set time to 30 minutes. Press Start to begin preheating.
4.		Once preheated, place the pan into the oven.

5.		When cooking is complete, the broccoli should be tender.
6.		Remove the baking pan from the oven and serve immediately.

Tilapia and Rockfish Casserole

Prep time: 8 minutes | Cook time: 22 minutes | Serves 2
1 tablespoon olive oil
1 small yellow onion, chopped
2 garlic cloves, minced
4 ounces (113 g) tilapia pieces
4 ounces (113 g) rockfish pieces
½ teaspoon dried basil
Salt and ground white pepper, to taste
4 eggs, lightly beaten
1 tablespoon dry sherry
4 tablespoons cheese, shredded
1.		Heat the olive oil in a nonstick skillet over medium-high heat until shimmering.
2.		Add the onion and garlic and sauté for 2 minutes or until fragrant.
3.		Add the tilapia, rockfish, basil, salt, and white pepper to the skillet. Sauté to combine well and transfer them on a baking pan.
4.		Combine the eggs, sherry and cheese in a large bowl. Stir to mix well. Pour the mixture in the baking pan over the fish mixture.
5.		Select Bake. Set temperature to 360ºF (182ºC) and set time to 20 minutes. Press Start to begin preheating.
6.		Once preheated, place the pan into the oven.
7.		When cooking is complete, the eggs should be set and the casserole edges should be lightly browned.
8.		Serve immediately.

Parmesan Green Bean Casserole

Prep time: 4 minutes | Cook time: 6 minutes | Serves 4
1 tablespoon melted butter
1 cup green beans
6 ounces (170 g) Cheddar cheese, shredded
7 ounces (198 g) Parmesan cheese, shredded
¼ cup heavy cream
Sea salt, to taste
1.		Grease a baking pan with the melted butter.
2.		Add the green beans, Cheddar, salt, and black pepper to the prepared baking pan. Stir to mix well, then spread the Parmesan and cream on top.
3.		Select Bake. Set temperature to 400ºF (205ºC) and set time to 6 minutes. Press Start to begin preheating.
4.		Once preheated, place the pan into the oven.
5.		When cooking is complete, the beans should be tender and the cheese should be melted.
6.		Serve immediately.

Cheddar Pastrami Casserole

Prep time: 10 minutes | Cook time: 8 minutes | Serves 2

1 cup pastrami, sliced
1 bell pepper, chopped
¼ cup Greek yogurt
2 spring onions, chopped
½ cup Cheddar cheese, grated
4 eggs
¼ teaspoon ground black pepper
Sea salt, to taste
Cooking spray

1. Spritz a baking pan with cooking spray.
2. Whisk together all the ingredients in a large bowl. Stir to mix well. Pour the mixture into the baking pan.
3. Select Bake. Set temperature to 330ºF (166ºC) and set time to 8 minutes. Press Start to begin preheating.
4. Once preheated, place the pan into the oven.
5. When cooking is complete, the eggs should be set and the casserole edges should be lightly browned.
6. Remove the baking pan from the oven and allow to cool for 10 minutes before serving.

Swiss Chicken and Ham Casserole

Prep time: 15 minutes | Cook time: 15 minutes | Serves 4 to 6

2 cups diced cooked chicken
1 cup diced ham
¼ teaspoon ground nutmeg
½ cup half-and-half
½ teaspoon ground black pepper
6 slices Swiss cheese
Cooking spray

1. Spritz a baking pan with cooking spray.
2. Combine the chicken, ham, nutmeg, half-and-half, and ground black pepper in a large bowl. Stir to mix well.
3. Pour half of the mixture into the baking pan, then top the mixture with 3 slices of Swiss cheese, then pour in the remaining mixture and top with remaining cheese slices.
4. Select Bake. Set temperature to 350ºF (180ºC) and set time to 15 minutes. Press Start to begin preheating.
5. Once preheated, place the pan into the oven.
6. When cooking is complete, the egg should be set and the cheese should be melted.
7. Serve immediately.

Spinach and Mushroom Frittata

Prep time: 7 minutes | Cook time: 8 minutes | Serves 2

1 cup chopped mushrooms
2 cups spinach, chopped
4 eggs, lightly beaten
3 ounces (85 g) feta cheese, crumbled
2 tablespoons heavy cream
A handful of fresh parsley, chopped
Salt and ground black pepper, to taste

Cooking spray

1. Spritz a baking pan with cooking spray.
2. Whisk together all the ingredients in a large bowl. Stir to mix well.
3. Pour the mixture in the prepared baking pan.
4. Select Bake. Set temperature to 350ºF (180ºC) and set time to 8 minutes. Press Start to begin preheating.
5. Once preheated, place the pan into the oven. Stir the mixture halfway through.
6. When cooking is complete, the eggs should be set.
7. Serve immediately.

Cauliflower and Okra Casserole

Prep time: 8 minutes | Cook time: 12 minutes | Serves 4

1 head cauliflower, cut into florets
1 cup okra, chopped
1 yellow bell pepper, chopped
2 eggs, beaten
½ cup chopped onion
1 tablespoon soy sauce
2 tablespoons olive oil
Salt and ground black pepper, to taste

1. Spritz a baking pan with cooking spray.
2. Put the cauliflower in a food processor and pulse to rice the cauliflower.
3. Pour the cauliflower rice in the baking pan and add the remaining ingredients. Stir to mix well.
4. Select Bake. Set temperature to 380ºF (193ºC) and set time to 12 minutes. Press Start to begin preheating.
5. Once preheated, place the pan into the oven.
6. When cooking is complete, the eggs should be set.
7. Remove the baking pan from the oven and serve immediately.

Turkey Casserole with Almond Mayo

Prep time: 5 minutes | Cook time: 32 minutes | Serves 4

1 pound (454 g) turkey breasts
1 tablespoon olive oil
2 boiled eggs, chopped
2 tablespoons chopped pimentos
¼ cup slivered almonds, chopped
¼ cup mayonnaise
½ cup diced celery
2 tablespoons chopped green onion
¼ cup cream of chicken soup
¼ cup bread crumbs
Salt and ground black pepper, to taste

1. Put the turkey breasts in a large bowl. Sprinkle with salt and ground black pepper and drizzle with olive oil. Toss to coat well.
2. Transfer the turkey in the perforated pan.
3. Select Air Fry. Set temperature to 390ºF (199ºC) and set time to 12 minutes. Press Start to begin preheating.

4.	Once preheated, place the pan into the oven. Flip the turkey halfway through.
5.	When cooking is complete, the turkey should be well browned.
6.	Remove the turkey breasts from the oven and cut into cubes, then combine the chicken cubes with eggs, pimentos, almonds, mayo, celery, green onions, and chicken soup in a large bowl. Stir to mix.
7.	Pour the mixture into a baking pan, then spread with bread crumbs.
8.	Select Bake. Set time to 20 minutes. Place the pan into the oven.
9.	When cooking is complete, the eggs should be set.
10.	Remove the baking pan from the oven and serve immediately.

Peppery Sausage Casserole with Cheddar

Prep time: 15 minutes | Cook time: 25 minutes | Serves 6
1 pound (454 g) minced breakfast sausage
1 yellow pepper, diced
1 red pepper, diced
1 green pepper, diced
1 sweet onion, diced
2 cups Cheddar cheese, shredded
6 eggs
Salt and freshly ground black pepper, to taste
Fresh parsley, for garnish
1.	Cook the sausage in a nonstick skillet over medium heat for 10 minutes or until well browned. Stir constantly.
2.	When the cooking is finished, transfer the cooked sausage to a baking pan and add the peppers and onion. Scatter with Cheddar cheese.
3.	Whisk the eggs with salt and ground black pepper in a large bowl, then pour the mixture into the baking pan.
4.	Select Bake. Set temperature to 360ºF (182ºC) and set time to 15 minutes. Press Start to begin preheating.
5.	Once preheated, place the pan into the oven.
6.	When cooking is complete, the egg should be set and the edges of the casserole should be lightly browned.
7.	Remove the baking pan from the oven and top with fresh parsley before serving.

Chickpea and Spinach Casserole

Prep time: 10 minutes | Cook time: 21 to 22 minutes | Serves 4
2 tablespoons olive oil
2 garlic cloves, minced
1 tablespoon ginger, minced
1 onion, chopped
1 chili pepper, minced
Salt and ground black pepper, to taste
1 pound (454 g) spinach
1 can coconut milk
½ cup dried tomatoes, chopped
1 (14-ounce / 397-g) can chickpeas, drained

1.	Heat the olive oil in a saucepan over medium heat. Sauté the garlic and ginger in the olive oil for 1 minute, or until fragrant.
2.	Add the onion, chili pepper, salt and pepper to the saucepan. Sauté for 3 minutes.
3.	Mix in the spinach and sauté for 3 to 4 minutes or until the vegetables become soft. Remove from heat.
4.	Pour the vegetable mixture into a baking pan. Stir in coconut milk, dried tomatoes and chickpeas until well blended.
5.	Select Bake. Set temperature to 370ºF (188ºC) and set time to 15 minutes. Press Start to begin preheating.
6.	Once preheated, place the pan into the oven.
7.	When cooking is complete, transfer the casserole to a serving dish. Let cool for 5 minutes before serving.

Beef and Bean Casserole

Prep time: 15 minutes | Cook time: 31 minutes | Serves 4
1 tablespoon olive oil
½ cup finely chopped bell pepper
½ cup chopped celery
1 onion, chopped
2 garlic cloves, minced
1 pound (454 g) ground beef
1 can diced tomatoes
½ teaspoon parsley
½ tablespoon chili powder
1 teaspoon chopped cilantro
1½ cups vegetable broth
1 (8-ounce / 227-g) can cannellini beans
Salt and ground black pepper, to taste
1.	Heat the olive oil in a nonstick skillet over medium heat until shimmering.
2.	Add the bell pepper, celery, onion, and garlic to the skillet and sauté for 5 minutes or until the onion is translucent.
3.	Add the ground beef and sauté for an additional 6 minutes or until lightly browned.
4.	Mix in the tomatoes, parsley, chili powder, cilantro and vegetable broth, then cook for 10 more minutes. Stir constantly.
5.	Pour them in a baking pan, then mix in the beans and sprinkle with salt and ground black pepper.
6.	Select Bake. Set temperature to 350ºF (180ºC) and set time to 10 minutes. Press Start to begin preheating.
7.	Once preheated, place the pan into the oven.
8.	When cooking is complete, the vegetables should be tender and the beef should be well browned.
9.	Remove the baking pan from the oven and serve immediately.

Cheddar Chicken and Broccoli Divan

Prep time: 5 minutes | Cook time: 24 minutes | Serves 4

4 chicken breasts
Salt and ground black pepper, to taste
1 head broccoli, cut into florets
½ cup cream of mushroom soup
1 cup shredded Cheddar cheese
½ cup croutons
Cooking spray
1. Spritz the perforated pan with cooking spray.
2. Put the chicken breasts in the perforated pan and sprinkle with salt and ground black pepper.
3. Select Air Fry. Set temperature to 390ºF (199ºC) and set time to 14 minutes. Press Start to begin preheating.
4. Once preheated, place the pan into the oven. Flip the breasts halfway through the cooking time.
5. When cooking is complete, the breasts should be well browned and tender.
6. Remove the breasts from the oven and allow to cool for a few minutes on a plate, then cut the breasts into bite-size pieces.
7. Combine the chicken, broccoli, mushroom soup, and Cheddar cheese in a large bowl. Stir to mix well.
8. Spritz a baking pan with cooking spray. Pour the chicken mixture into the pan. Spread the croutons over the mixture.
9. Select Bake. Set time to 10 minutes. Place the pan into the oven.
10. When cooking is complete, the croutons should be lightly browned and the mixture should be set.
11. Remove the baking pan from the oven and serve immediately.

Smoked Trout Frittata with Dill

Prep time: 8 minutes | Cook time: 17 minutes | Serves 4
2 tablespoons olive oil
1 onion, sliced
1 egg, beaten
½ tablespoon horseradish sauce
6 tablespoons crème fraiche
1 cup diced smoked trout
2 tablespoons chopped fresh dill
Cooking spray
1. Spritz a baking pan with cooking spray.
2. Heat the olive oil in a nonstick skillet over medium heat until shimmering.
3. Add the onion and sauté for 3 minutes or until translucent.
4. Combine the egg, horseradish sauce, and crème fraiche in a large bowl. Stir to mix well, then mix in the sautéed onion, smoked trout, and dill.
5. Pour the mixture in the prepared baking pan.
6. Select Bake. Set temperature to 350ºF (180ºC) and set time to 14 minutes. Press Start to begin preheating.
7. Once preheated, place the pan into the oven. Stir the mixture halfway through.

8. When cooking is complete, the egg should be set and the edges should be lightly browned.
9. Serve immediately.

Cheddar and Egg Frittata with Parsley

Prep time: 10 minutes | Cook time: 20 minutes | Serves 4
½ cup shredded Cheddar cheese
½ cup half-and-half
4 large eggs
2 tablespoons chopped scallion greens
2 tablespoons chopped fresh parsley
½ teaspoon kosher salt
½ teaspoon ground black pepper
Cooking spray
1. Spritz a baking pan with cooking spray.
2. Whisk together all the ingredients in a large bowl, then pour the mixture into the prepared baking pan.
3. Select Bake. Set temperature to 300ºF (150ºC) and set time to 20 minutes. Press Start to begin preheating.
4. Once preheated, place the pan into the oven. Stir the mixture halfway through.
5. When cooking is complete, the eggs should be set.
6. Serve immediately.

Cheddar Broccoli and Carrot Quiche

Prep time: 6 minutes | Cook time: 14 minutes | Serves 4
4 eggs
1 teaspoon dried thyme
1 cup whole milk
1 steamed carrots, diced
2 cups steamed broccoli florets
2 medium tomatoes, diced
¼ cup crumbled feta cheese
1 cup grated Cheddar cheese
1 teaspoon chopped parsley
Salt and ground black pepper, to taste
Cooking spray
1. Spritz a baking pan with cooking spray.
2. Whisk together the eggs, thyme, salt, and ground black pepper in a bowl and fold in the milk while mixing.
3. Put the carrots, broccoli, and tomatoes in the prepared baking pan, then spread with feta cheese and ½ cup Cheddar cheese. Pour the egg mixture over, then scatter with remaining Cheddar on top.
4. Select Bake. Set temperature to 350ºF (180ºC) and set time to 14 minutes. Press Start to begin preheating.
5. Once preheated, place the pan into the oven.
6. When cooking is complete, the egg should be set and the quiche should be puffed.
7. Remove the quiche from the oven and top with chopped parsley, then slice to serve.

Mexican Beef and Chile Casserole

Prep time: 10 minutes | Cook time: 15 minutes | Serves 4

1 pound (454 g) 85% lean ground beef
1 tablespoon taco seasoning
1 (7-ounce / 198-g) can diced mild green chiles
½ cup milk
2 large eggs
1 cup shredded Mexican cheese blend
2 tablespoons all-purpose flour
½ teaspoon kosher salt
Cooking spray

1. Spritz a baking pan with cooking spray.
2. Toss the ground beef with taco seasoning in a large bowl to mix well. Pour the seasoned ground beef in the prepared baking pan.
3. Combing the remaining ingredients in a medium bowl. Whisk to mix well, then pour the mixture over the ground beef.
4. Select Bake. Set temperature to 350ºF (180ºC) and set time to 15 minutes. Press Start to begin preheating.
5. Once preheated, place the pan into the oven.
6. When cooking is complete, a toothpick inserted in the center should come out clean.
7. Remove the casserole from the oven and allow to cool for 5 minutes, then slice to serve.

Chicken and Broccoli Casserole

Prep time: 15 minutes | Cook time: 15 minutes | Serves 4

4 boneless and skinless chicken breasts, cut into cubes
2 carrots, sliced
1 yellow bell pepper, cut into strips
1 red bell pepper, cut into strips
15 ounces (425 g) broccoli florets
1 cup snow peas
1 scallion, sliced
Cooking spray
Sauce:
1 teaspoon Sriracha
3 tablespoons soy sauce
2 tablespoons oyster sauce
1 tablespoon rice wine vinegar
1 teaspoon cornstarch
1 tablespoon grated ginger
2 garlic cloves, minced
1 teaspoon sesame oil
1 tablespoon brown sugar

1. Spritz a baking pan with cooking spray.
2. Combine the chicken, carrot, and bell peppers in a large bowl. Stir to mix well.
3. Combine the ingredients for the sauce in a separate bowl. Stir to mix well.
4. Pour the chicken mixture into the baking pan, then pour the sauce over. Stir to coat well.
5. Select Bake. Set temperature to 370ºF (188ºC) and set time to 13 minutes. Press Start to begin preheating.
6. Once preheated, place the pan into the oven. Add the broccoli and snow peas to the pan halfway through.
7. When cooking is complete, the vegetables should be tender.
8. Remove the pan from the oven and sprinkle with sliced scallion before serving.

Ricotta Pork Gratin with Mustard

Prep time: 15 minutes | Cook time: 21 minutes | Serves 4

2 tablespoons olive oil
2 pounds (907 g) pork tenderloin, cut into serving-size pieces
1 teaspoon dried marjoram
¼ teaspoon chili powder
1 teaspoon coarse sea salt
½ teaspoon freshly ground black pepper
1 cup Ricotta cheese
1½ cups chicken broth
1 tablespoon mustard
Cooking spray

1. Spritz a baking pan with cooking spray.
2. Heat the olive oil in a nonstick skillet over medium-high heat until shimmering.
3. Add the pork and sauté for 6 minutes or until lightly browned.
4. Transfer the pork to the prepared baking pan and sprinkle with marjoram, chili powder, salt, and ground black pepper.
5. Combine the remaining ingredients in a large bowl. Stir to mix well. Pour the mixture over the pork in the pan.
6. Select Bake. Set temperature to 350ºF (180ºC) and set time to 15 minutes. Press Start to begin preheating.
7. Once preheated, place the pan into the oven. Stir the mixture halfway through.
8. When cooking is complete, the mixture should be frothy and the cheese should be melted.
9. Serve immediately.

Potato and Chorizo Frittata

Prep time: 8 minutes | Cook time: 12 minutes | Serves 4

2 tablespoons olive oil
1 chorizo, sliced
4 eggs
½ cup corn
1 large potato, boiled and cubed
1 tablespoon chopped parsley
½ cup feta cheese, crumbled
Salt and ground black pepper, to taste

1. Heat the olive oil in a nonstick skillet over medium heat until shimmering.
2. Add the chorizo and cook for 4 minutes or until golden brown.
3. Whisk the eggs in a bowl, then sprinkle with salt and ground black pepper.

4. Mix the remaining ingredients in the egg mixture, then pour the chorizo and its fat into a baking pan. Pour in the egg mixture.
5. Select Bake. Set temperature to 330ºF (166ºC) and set time to 8 minutes. Press Start to begin preheating.
6. Once preheated, place the pan into the oven. Stir the mixture halfway through.
7. When cooking is complete, the eggs should be set.
8. Serve immediately.

Asparagus Frittata with Goat Cheese

Prep time: 5 minutes | Cook time: 25 minutes | Serves 2 to 4

1 cup asparagus spears, cut into 1-inch pieces
1 teaspoon vegetable oil
1 tablespoon milk
6 eggs, beaten
2 ounces (57 g) goat cheese, crumbled
1 tablespoon minced chives, optional
Kosher salt and pepper, to taste
1. Add the asparagus spears to a small bowl and drizzle with the vegetable oil. Toss until well coated and transfer to the perforated pan.
2. Select Air Fry. Set temperature to 400ºF (205ºC) and set time to 5 minutes. Press Start to begin preheating.
3. Once preheated, place the pan into the oven. Flip the asparagus halfway through.
4. When cooking is complete, the asparagus should be tender and slightly wilted.
5. Remove the asparagus from the oven to a baking pan.
6. Stir together the milk and eggs in a medium bowl. Pour the mixture over the asparagus in the pan. Sprinkle with the goat cheese and the chives (if using) over the eggs. Season with salt and pepper.
7. Select Bake. Set temperature to 320ºF (160ºC) and set time to 20 minutes. Place the pan into the oven
8. When cooking is complete, the top should be golden and the eggs should be set.
9. Transfer to a serving dish. Slice and serve.

Kale and Egg Frittata with Feta

Prep time: 5 minutes | Cook time: 11 minutes | Serves 2

1 cup kale, chopped
1 teaspoon olive oil
4 large eggs, beaten
Kosher salt, to taste
2 tablespoons water
3 tablespoons crumbled feta
Cooking spray
1. Spritz a baking pan with cooking spray.
2. Add the kale to the baking pan and drizzle with olive oil.
3. Select Broil. Set temperature to 360ºF (182ºC) and set time to 3 minutes. Press Start to begin preheating.

4. Once preheated, place the pan into the oven. Stir the kale halfway through.
5. When cooking is complete, the kale should be wilted.
6. Meanwhile, combine the eggs with salt and water in a large bowl. Stir to mix well.
7. Make the frittata: When broiling is complete, pour the eggs into the baking pan and spread with feta cheese.
8. Select Bake. Set temperature to 300ºF (150ºC) and set time to 8 minutes. Place the pan into the oven.
9. When cooking is complete, the eggs should be set and the cheese should be melted.
10. Remove the baking pan from the oven and serve the frittata immediately.

Spinach and Shrimp Frittata

Prep time: 6 minutes | Cook time: 14 minutes | Serves 4

4 whole eggs
1 teaspoon dried basil
½ cup shrimp, cooked and chopped
½ cup baby spinach
½ cup rice, cooked
½ cup Monterey Jack cheese, grated
Salt, to taste
Cooking spray
1. Spritz a baking pan with cooking spray.
2. Whisk the eggs with basil and salt in a large bowl until bubbly, then mix in the shrimp, spinach, rice, and cheese.
3. Pour the mixture into the baking pan.
4. Select Bake. Set temperature to 360ºF (182ºC) and set time to 14 minutes. Press Start to begin preheating.
5. Once preheated, place the pan into the oven. Stir the mixture halfway through.
6. When cooking is complete, the eggs should be set and the frittata should be golden brown.
7. Slice to serve.

Zucchini and Spinach Frittata

Prep time: 15 minutes | Cook time: 20 minutes | Serves 2

4 eggs
$^1/_3$ cup milk
2 teaspoons olive oil
1 large zucchini, sliced
2 asparagus, sliced thinly
$^1/_3$ cup sliced mushrooms
1 cup baby spinach
1 small red onion, sliced
$^1/_3$ cup crumbled feta cheese
$^1/_3$ cup grated Cheddar cheese
¼ cup chopped chives
Salt and ground black pepper, to taste
1. Line a baking pan with parchment paper.
2. Whisk together the eggs, milk, salt, and ground black pepper in a large bowl. Set aside.

3.	Heat the olive oil in a nonstick skillet over medium heat until shimmering.
4.	Add the zucchini, asparagus, mushrooms, spinach, and onion to the skillet and sauté for 5 minutes or until tender.
5.	Pour the sautéed vegetables into the prepared baking pan, then spread the egg mixture over and scatter with cheeses.
6.	Select Bake. Set temperature to 380ºF (193ºC) and set time to 15 minutes. Press Start to begin preheating.
7.	Once preheated, place the pan into the oven. Stir the mixture halfway through.
8.	When cooking is complete, the egg should be set and the edges should be lightly browned.
9.	Remove the frittata from the oven and sprinkle with chives before serving.

Cheese and Egg Quiche

Prep time: 20 minutes | Cook time: 1 hour | Serves 8
Crust:
1¼ cups blanched almond flour
1 large egg, beaten
1¼ cups grated Parmesan cheese
¼ teaspoon fine sea salt
Filling:
4 ounces (113 g) cream cheese
1 cup shredded Swiss cheese
$^1/_3$ cup minced leeks
4 large eggs, beaten
½ cup chicken broth
⅛ teaspoon cayenne pepper
¾ teaspoon fine sea salt
1 tablespoon unsalted butter, melted
Chopped green onions, for garnish
Cooking spray
1.	Spritz a pie pan with cooking spray.
2.	Combine the flour, egg, Parmesan, and salt in a large bowl. Stir to mix until a satiny and firm dough forms.
3.	Arrange the dough between two grease parchment papers, then roll the dough into a $^1/_{16}$-inch thick circle.
4.	Make the crust: Transfer the dough into the prepared pie pan and press to coat the bottom.

5.	Select Bake. Set temperature to 325ºF (163ºC) and set time to 12 minutes. Press Start to begin preheating.
6.	Once preheated, place the pan into the oven.
7.	When cooking is complete, the edges of the crust should be lightly browned.
8.	Meanwhile, combine the ingredient for the filling, except for the green onions in a large bowl.
9.	Pour the filling over the cooked crust and cover the edges of the crust with aluminum foil.
10.	Select Bake. Set time to 15 minutes. Place the pan into the oven.
11.	When cooking is complete, reduce the heat to 300ºF (150ºC) and set time to 30 minutes.
12.	When cooking is complete, a toothpick inserted in the center should come out clean.
13.	Remove the pie pan from the oven and allow to cool for 10 minutes before serving.

Tomato and Olive Quiche

Prep time: 10 minutes | Cook time: 30 minutes | Serves 4
4 eggs
¼ cup chopped Kalamata olives
½ cup chopped tomatoes
¼ cup chopped onion
½ cup milk
1 cup crumbled feta cheese
½ tablespoon chopped oregano
½ tablespoon chopped basil
Salt and ground black pepper, to taste
Cooking spray
1.	Spritz a baking pan with cooking spray.
2.	Whisk the eggs with remaining ingredients in a large bowl. Stir to mix well.
3.	Pour the mixture into the prepared baking pan.
4.	Select Bake. Set temperature to 340ºF (171ºC) and set time to 30 minutes. Press Start to begin preheating.
5.	Once preheated, place the pan into the oven.
6.	When cooking is complete, the eggs should be set and a toothpick inserted in the center should come out clean.
7.	Serve immediately.

CHAPTER 12 HOLIDAY SPECIALS

Mozzarella Rice Arancini

Prep time: 5 minutes | Cook time: 30 minutes | Makes 10 arancini

$^2/_3$ cup raw white Arborio rice
2 teaspoons butter
½ teaspoon salt
$1^1/_3$ cups water
2 large eggs, well beaten
1¼ cups seasoned Italian-style dried bread crumbs
10 ¾-inch semi-firm Mozzarella cubes
Cooking spray

1. Pour the rice, butter, salt, and water in a pot. Stir to mix well and bring a boil over medium-high heat. Keep stirring.
2. Reduce the heat to low and cover the pot. Simmer for 20 minutes or until the rice is tender.
3. Turn off the heat and let sit, covered, for 10 minutes, then open the lid and fluffy the rice with a fork. Allow to cool for 10 more minutes.
4. Pour the beaten eggs in a bowl, then pour the bread crumbs in a separate bowl.
5. Scoop 2 tablespoons of the cooked rice up and form it into a ball, then press the Mozzarella into the ball and wrap.
6. Dredge the ball in the eggs first, then shake the excess off the dunk the ball in the bread crumbs. Roll to coat evenly. Repeat to make 10 balls in total with remaining rice.
7. Transfer the balls in the perforated pan and spritz with cooking spray.
8. Select Air Fry. Set temperature to 375ºF (190ºC) and set time to 10 minutes. Press Start to begin preheating.
9. Once preheated, place the pan into the oven.
10. When cooking is complete, the balls should be lightly browned and crispy.
11. Remove the balls from the oven and allow to cool before serving.

Pork Egg Rolls with Vinegar Dipping

Prep time: 40 minutes | Cook time: 33 minutes | Makes 25 egg rolls

Egg Rolls:
1 tablespoon mirin
3 tablespoons soy sauce, divided
1 pound (454 g) ground pork
3 tablespoons vegetable oil, plus more for brushing
5 ounces (142 g) shiitake mushrooms, minced
4 cups shredded Napa cabbage
¼ cup sliced scallions
1 teaspoon grated fresh ginger
1 clove garlic, minced
¼ teaspoon cornstarch
1 (1-pound / 454-g) package frozen egg roll wrappers, thawed

Dipping Sauce:
1 scallion, white and light green parts only, sliced
¼ cup rice vinegar
¼ cup soy sauce
Pinch sesame seeds
Pinch red pepper flakes
1 teaspoon granulated sugar

1. Line the perforated pan with parchment paper. Set aside.
2. Combine the mirin and 1 tablespoon of soy sauce in a large bowl. Stir to mix well.
3. Dunk the ground pork in the mixture and stir to mix well. Wrap the bowl in plastic and marinate in the refrigerator for at least 10 minutes.
4. Heat the vegetable oil in a nonstick skillet over medium-high heat until shimmering. Add the mushrooms, cabbage, and scallions and sauté for 5 minutes or until tender.
5. Add the marinated meat, ginger, garlic, and remaining 2 tablespoons of soy sauce. Sauté for 3 minutes or until the pork is lightly browned. Turn off the heat and allow to cool until ready to use.
6. Put the cornstarch in a small bowl and pour in enough water to dissolve the cornstarch. Put the bowl alongside a clean work surface.
7. Put the egg roll wrappers in the perforated pan.
8. Select Air Fry. Set temperature to 400ºF (205ºC) and set time to 15 minutes. Press Start to begin preheating.
9. Once preheated, place the pan into the oven. Flip the wrappers halfway through the cooking time.
10. When cooked, the wrappers will be golden brown. Remove the egg roll wrappers from the oven and allow to cool for 10 minutes or until you can handle them with your hands.
11. Lay out one egg roll wrapper on the work surface with a corner pointed toward you. Place 2 tablespoons of the pork mixture on the egg roll wrapper and fold corner up over the mixture. Fold left and right corners toward the center and continue to roll. Brush a bit of the dissolved cornstarch on the last corner to help seal the egg wrapper. Repeat with remaining wrappers to make 25 egg rolls in total.
12. Arrange the rolls in the pan and brush the rolls with more vegetable oil.
13. Select Air Fry and set time to 10 minutes. Place the pan into the oven When done, the rolls should be well browned and crispy.
14. Meanwhile, combine the ingredients for the dipping sauce in a small bowl. Stir to mix well.
15. Serve the rolls with the dipping sauce immediately.

Cinnamon Churros

Prep time: 35 minutes | Cook time: 10 minutes | Makes 12 churros

4 tablespoons butter
¼ teaspoon salt
½ cup water
½ cup all-purpose flour
2 large eggs
2 teaspoons ground cinnamon
¼ cup granulated white sugar
Cooking spray

1.	Put the butter, salt, and water in a saucepan. Bring to a boil until the butter is melted on high heat. Keep stirring.
2.	Reduce the heat to medium and fold in the flour to form a dough. Keep cooking and stirring until the dough is dried out and coat the pan with a crust.
3.	Turn off the heat and scrape the dough in a large bowl. Allow to cool for 15 minutes.
4.	Break and whisk the eggs into the dough with a hand mixer until the dough is sanity and firm enough to shape.
5.	Scoop up 1 tablespoon of the dough and roll it into a ½-inch-diameter and 2-inch-long cylinder. Repeat with remaining dough to make 12 cylinders in total.
6.	Combine the cinnamon and sugar in a large bowl and dunk the cylinders into the cinnamon mix to coat.
7.	Arrange the cylinders on a plate and refrigerate for 20 minutes.
8.	Spritz the perforated pan with cooking spray. Place the cylinders in the perforated pan and spritz with cooking spray.
9.	Select Air Fry. Set temperature to 375ºF (190ºC) and set time to 10 minutes. Press Start to begin preheating.
10.	Once preheated, place the pan into the oven. Flip the cylinders halfway through the cooking time.
11.	When cooked, the cylinders should be golden brown and fluffy.
12.	Serve immediately.

Vanilla Banana Cake

Prep time: 25 minutes | Cook time: 20 minutes | Serves 8
1 cup plus 1 tablespoon all-purpose flour
¼ teaspoon baking soda
¾ teaspoon baking powder
¼ teaspoon salt
9½ tablespoons granulated white sugar
5 tablespoons butter, at room temperature
2½ small ripe bananas, peeled
2 large eggs
5 tablespoons buttermilk
1 teaspoon vanilla extract
Cooking spray
1.	Spritz a baking pan with cooking spray.
2.	Combine the flour, baking soda, baking powder, and salt in a large bowl. Stir to mix well.
3.	Beat the sugar and butter in a separate bowl with a hand mixer on medium speed for 3 minutes.
4.	Beat in the bananas, eggs, buttermilk, and vanilla extract into the sugar and butter mix with a hand mixer.
5.	Pour in the flour mixture and whip with hand mixer until sanity and smooth.
6.	Scrape the batter into the pan and level the batter with a spatula.
7.	Select Bake. Set temperature to 325ºF (163ºC) and set time to 20 minutes. Press Start to begin preheating.

8.	Once the oven has preheated, place the pan into the oven.
9.	After 15 minutes, remove the pan from the oven. Check the doneness. Return the pan to the oven and continue cooking.
10.	When done, a toothpick inserted in the center should come out clean.
11.	Invert the cake on a cooling rack and allow to cool for 15 minutes before slicing to serve.

Chocolate Macaroons with Coconut

Prep time: 10 minutes | Cook time: 8 minutes |Makes 24 macaroons
3 large egg whites, at room temperature
¼ teaspoon salt
¾ cup granulated white sugar
4½ tablespoons unsweetened cocoa powder
2¼ cups unsweetened shredded coconut
1.	Line the perforated pan with parchment paper.
2.	Whisk the egg whites with salt in a large bowl with a hand mixer on high speed until stiff peaks form.
3.	Whisk in the sugar with the hand mixer on high speed until the mixture is thick. Mix in the cocoa powder and coconut.
4.	Scoop 2 tablespoons of the mixture and shape the mixture in a ball. Repeat with remaining mixture to make 24 balls in total.
5.	Arrange the balls in a single layer in the perforated pan and leave a little space between each two balls.
6.	Select Air Fry. Set temperature to 375ºF (190ºC) and set time to 8 minutes. Press Start to begin preheating.
7.	Once the oven has preheated, place the pan into the oven.
8.	When cooking is complete, the balls should be golden brown.
9.	Serve immediately.

Chocolate-Glazed Donut Holes

Prep time: 1 hour 50 minutes | Cook time: 4 minutes | Makes 24 donut holes
Dough:
1½ cups bread flour
2 egg yolks
1 teaspoon active dry yeast
½ cup warm milk
½ teaspoon pure vanilla extract
2 tablespoons butter, melted
1 tablespoon sugar
¼ teaspoon salt
Cooking spray
Custard Filling:
1 (3.4-ounce / 96-g) box French vanilla instant pudding mix
¼ cup heavy cream
¾ cup whole milk
Chocolate Glaze:
$^1/_3$ cup heavy cream
1 cup chocolate chips

Special Equipment:
A pastry bag with a long tip
1.		Combine the ingredients for the dough in a food processor, then pulse until a satiny dough ball forms.
2.		Transfer the dough on a lightly floured work surface, then knead for 2 minutes by hand and shape the dough back to a ball.
3.		Spritz a large bowl with cooking spray, then transfer the dough ball into the bowl. Wrap the bowl in plastic and let it rise for 1½ hours or until it doubled in size.
4.		Transfer the risen dough on a floured work surface, then shape it into a 24-inch long log. Cut the log into 24 parts and shape each part into a ball.
5.		Transfer the balls on two baking sheets and let sit to rise for 30 more minutes.
6.		Spritz the balls with cooking spray.
7.		Select Bake. Set temperature to 400ºF (205ºC) and set time to 4 minutes. Press Start to begin preheating.
8.		Once preheated, place the baking sheets into the oven. Flip the balls halfway through the cooking time.
9.		When cooked, the balls should be golden brown.
10.		Meanwhile, combine the ingredients for the filling in a large bowl and whisk for 2 minutes with a hand mixer until well combined.
11.		Pour the heavy cream in a saucepan, then bring to a boil. Put the chocolate chips in a small bowl and pour in the boiled heavy cream immediately. Mix until the chocolate chips are melted and the mixture is smooth.
12.		Transfer the baked donut holes to a large plate, then pierce a hole into each donut hole and lightly hollow them.
13.		Pour the filling in a pastry bag with a long tip and gently squeeze the filling into the donut holes. Then top the donut holes with chocolate glaze.
14.		Allow to sit for 10 minutes, then serve.

Balsamic Cherry Tomatoes

Prep time: 5 minutes | Cook time: 10 minutes | Serves 4 to 6
2 pounds (907 g) cherry tomatoes
2 tablespoons olive oil
2 teaspoons balsamic vinegar
½ teaspoon salt
½ teaspoon ground black pepper
1.		Toss the cherry tomatoes with olive oil in a large bowl to coat well. Pour the tomatoes in a baking pan.
2.		Select Air Fry. Set temperature to 400ºF (205ºC) and set time to 10 minutes. Press Start to begin preheating.
3.		Once preheated, slide the pan into the oven. Stir the tomatoes halfway through the cooking time.
4.		When cooking is complete, the tomatoes will be blistered and lightly wilted.
5.		Transfer the blistered tomatoes to a large bowl and toss with balsamic vinegar, salt, and black pepper before serving.

Vanilla Butter Cake

Prep time: 25 minutes | Cook time: 20 minutes | Serves 8
1 cup all-purpose flour
1¼ teaspoons baking powder
¼ teaspoon salt
½ cup plus 1½ tablespoons granulated white sugar
9½ tablespoons butter, at room temperature
2 large eggs
1 large egg yolk
2½ tablespoons milk
1 teaspoon vanilla extract
Cooking spray
1.		Spritz a baking pan with cooking spray.
2.		Combine the flour, baking powder, and salt in a large bowl. Stir to mix well.
3.		Whip the sugar and butter in a separate bowl with a hand mixer on medium speed for 3 minutes.
4.		Whip the eggs, egg yolk, milk, and vanilla extract into the sugar and butter mix with a hand mixer.
5.		Pour in the flour mixture and whip with hand mixer until sanity and smooth.
6.		Scrape the batter into the baking pan and level the batter with a spatula.
7.		Select Bake. Set temperature to 325ºF (163ºC) and set time to 20 minutes. Press Start to begin preheating.
8.		Once the oven has preheated, place the pan into the oven.
9.		After 15 minutes, remove the pan from the oven. Check the doneness. Return the pan to the oven and continue cooking.
10.		When done, a toothpick inserted in the center should come out clean.
11.		Invert the cake on a cooling rack and allow to cool for 15 minutes before slicing to serve.

Dill Pickles with Buttermilk Dressing

Prep time: 45 minutes | Cook time: 8 minutes | Serves 6 to 8
Buttermilk Dressing:
¼ cup buttermilk
¼ cup chopped scallions
¾ cup mayonnaise
½ cup sour cream
½ teaspoon cayenne pepper
½ teaspoon onion powder
½ teaspoon garlic powder
1 tablespoon chopped chives
2 tablespoons chopped fresh dill
Kosher salt and ground black pepper, to taste
Fried Dill Pickles:
¾ cup all-purpose flour
1 (2-pound / 907-g) jar kosher dill pickles, cut into 4 spears, drained
2½ cups panko bread crumbs
2 eggs, beaten with 2 tablespoons water
Kosher salt and ground black pepper, to taste
Cooking spray

1.	Combine the ingredients for the dressing in a bowl. Stir to mix well.
2.	Wrap the bowl in plastic and refrigerate for 30 minutes or until ready to serve.
3.	Pour the flour in a bowl and sprinkle with salt and ground black pepper. Stir to mix well. Put the bread crumbs in a separate bowl. Pour the beaten eggs in a third bowl.
4.	Dredge the pickle spears in the flour, then into the eggs, and then into the panko to coat well. Shake the excess off.
5.	Arrange the pickle spears in a single layer in the perforated pan and spritz with cooking spray.
6.	Select Air Fry. Set temperature to 400ºF (205ºC) and set time to 8 minutes. Press Start to begin preheating.
7.	Once the oven has preheated, place the pan into the oven. Flip the pickle spears halfway through the cooking time.
8.	When cooking is complete, remove the pan from the oven.
9.	Serve the pickle spears with buttermilk dressing.

Olive and Basil Stromboli with Garlic

Prep time: 25 minutes | Cook time: 25 minutes | Serves 8
4 large cloves garlic, unpeeled
3 tablespoons grated Parmesan cheese
½ cup packed fresh basil leaves
½ cup marinated, pitted green and black olives
¼ teaspoon crushed red pepper
½ pound (227 g) pizza dough, at room temperature
4 ounces (113 g) sliced provolone cheese (about 8 slices)
Cooking spray
1.	Spritz the perforated pan with cooking spray. Put the unpeeled garlic in the perforated pan.
2.	Select Air Fry. Set temperature to 370ºF (188ºC) and set time to 10 minutes. Press Start to begin preheating.
3.	Once preheated, place the pan into the oven.
4.	When cooked, the garlic will be softened completely. Remove from the oven and allow to cool until you can handle.
5.	Peel the garlic and place into a food processor with 2 tablespoons of Parmesan, basil, olives, and crushed red pepper. Pulse to mix well. Set aside.
6.	Arrange the pizza dough on a clean work surface, then roll it out with a rolling pin into a rectangle. Cut the rectangle in half.
7.	Sprinkle half of the garlic mixture over each rectangle half, and leave ½-inch edges uncover. Top them with the provolone cheese.
8.	Brush one long side of each rectangle half with water, then roll them up. Spritz the perforated pan with cooking spray. Transfer the rolls to the perforated pan. Spritz with cooking spray and scatter with remaining Parmesan.
9.	Select Air Fry and set time to 15 minutes. Place the pan into the oven. Flip the rolls halfway through the cooking time. When done, the rolls should be golden brown.
10.	Remove the rolls from the oven and allow to cool for a few minutes before serving.

Pigs in a Blanket with Sesame Seeds

Prep time: 10 minutes | Cook time: 8 minutes | Makes 16 rolls
1 can refrigerated crescent roll dough
1 small package mini smoked sausages, patted dry
2 tablespoons melted butter
2 teaspoons sesame seeds
1 teaspoon onion powder
1.	Place the crescent roll dough on a clean work surface and separate into 8 pieces. Cut each piece in half and you will have 16 triangles.
2.	Make the pigs in the blanket: Arrange each sausage on each dough triangle, then roll the sausages up.
3.	Brush the pigs with melted butter and place of the pigs in the blanket in the perforated pan. Sprinkle with sesame seeds and onion powder.
4.	Select Bake. Set temperature to 330ºF (166ºC) and set time to 8 minutes Press Start to begin preheating.
5.	Once the oven has preheated, place the pan into the oven. Flip the pigs halfway through the cooking time.
6.	When cooking is complete, the pigs should be fluffy and golden brown.
7.	Serve immediately.

Cream-Glazed Cinnamon Rolls

Prep time: 2 hours 15 minutes | Cook time: 5 minutes | Serves 8
1 pound (454 g) frozen bread dough, thawed
2 tablespoons melted butter
1½ tablespoons cinnamon
¾ cup brown sugar
Cooking spray
Cream Glaze:
4 ounces (113 g) softened cream cheese
½ teaspoon vanilla extract
2 tablespoons melted butter
1¼ cups powdered erythritol
1.	Place the bread dough on a clean work surface, then roll the dough out into a rectangle with a rolling pin.
2.	Brush the top of the dough with melted butter and leave 1-inch edges uncovered.
3.	Combine the cinnamon and sugar in a small bowl, then sprinkle the dough with the cinnamon mixture.
4.	Roll the dough over tightly, then cut the dough log into 8 portions. Wrap the portions in plastic, better separately, and let sit to rise for 1 or 2 hours.
5.	Meanwhile, combine the ingredients for the glaze in a separate small bowl. Stir to mix well.
6.	Spritz the perforated pan with cooking spray. Transfer the risen rolls to the perforated pan.

7. Select Air Fry. Set temperature to 350ºF (180ºC) and set time to 5 minutes. Press Start to begin preheating.
8. Once the oven has preheated, place the pan into the oven. Flip the rolls halfway through the cooking time.
9. When cooking is complete, the rolls will be golden brown.
10. Serve the rolls with the glaze.

Buttermilk Chocolate Cake

Prep time: 20 minutes | Cook time: 20 minutes | Serves 8

1 cup all-purpose flour
$^2/_3$ cup granulated white sugar
¼ cup unsweetened cocoa powder
¾ teaspoon baking soda
¼ teaspoon salt
$^2/_3$ cup buttermilk
2 tablespoons plus 2 teaspoons vegetable oil
1 teaspoon vanilla extract
Cooking spray

1. Spritz a baking pan with cooking spray.
2. Combine the flour, cocoa powder, baking soda, sugar, and salt in a large bowl. Stir to mix well.
3. Mix in the buttermilk, vanilla, and vegetable oil. Keep stirring until it forms a grainy and thick dough.
4. Scrape the chocolate batter from the bowl and transfer to the pan, level the batter in an even layer with a spatula.
5. Select Bake. Set temperature to 325ºF (163ºC) and set time to 20 minutes. Press Start to begin preheating.
6. Once preheated, place the pan into the oven.
7. After 15 minutes, remove the pan from the oven. Check the doneness. Return the pan to the oven and continue cooking.
8. When done, a toothpick inserted in the center should come out clean.
9. Invert the cake on a cooling rack and allow to cool for 15 minutes before slicing to serve.

Teriyaki-Marinated Shrimp Skewers

Prep time: 10 minutes | Cook time: 6 minutes | Makes 12 skewered shrimp

1½ tablespoons mirin
1½ teaspoons ginger juice
1½ tablespoons soy sauce
12 large shrimp (about 20 shrimps per pound) peeled and deveined
1 large egg
¾ cup panko bread crumbs
Cooking spray

1. Combine the mirin, ginger juice, and soy sauce in a large bowl. Stir to mix well.
2. Dunk the shrimp in the bowl of mirin mixture, then wrap the bowl in plastic and refrigerate for 1 hour to marinate.
3. Spritz the perforated pan with cooking spray.
4. Run twelve 4-inch skewers through each shrimp.
5. Whisk the egg in the bowl of marinade to combine well. Pour the bread crumbs on a plate.
6. Dredge the shrimp skewers in the egg mixture, then shake the excess off and roll over the bread crumbs to coat well.
7. Arrange the shrimp skewers in the perforated pan and spritz with cooking spray.
8. Select Air Fry. Set temperature to 400ºF (205ºC) and set time to 6 minutes. Press Start to begin preheating.
9. Once preheated, place the pan into the oven. Flip the shrimp skewers halfway through the cooking time.
10. When done, the shrimp will be opaque and firm.
11. Serve immediately.

Garlic Nuggets

Prep time: 15 minutes | Cook time: 4 minutes | Makes 20 nuggets

1 cup all-purpose flour, plus more for dusting
1 teaspoon baking powder
½ teaspoon butter, at room temperature, plus more for brushing
¼ teaspoon salt
¼ cup water
⅛ teaspoon onion powder
¼ teaspoon garlic powder
⅛ teaspoon seasoning salt
Cooking spray

1. Line the perforated pan with parchment paper.
2. Mix the flour, baking powder, butter, and salt in a large bowl. Stir to mix well. Gradually whisk in the water until a sanity dough forms.
3. Put the dough on a lightly floured work surface, then roll it out into a ½-inch thick rectangle with a rolling pin.
4. Cut the dough into about twenty 1- or 2-inch squares, then arrange the squares in a single layer in the perforated pan. Spritz with cooking spray.
5. Combine onion powder, garlic powder, and seasoning salt in a small bowl. Stir to mix well, then sprinkle the squares with the powder mixture.
6. Select Air Fry. Set temperature to 370ºF (188ºC) and set time to 4 minutes. Press Start to begin preheating.
7. Once the oven has preheated, place the pan into the oven. Flip the squares halfway through the cooking time.
8. When cooked, the dough squares should be golden brown.
9. Remove the golden nuggets from the oven and brush with more butter immediately. Serve warm.

Vanilla Cheese Blintzes

Prep time: 5 minutes | Cook time: 10 minutes | Makes 8 blintzes

2 (7½-ounce / 213-g) packages farmer cheese, mashed
¼ cup cream cheese
¼ teaspoon vanilla extract
¼ cup granulated white sugar
8 egg roll wrappers
4 tablespoons butter, melted
1. Combine the farmer cheese, cream cheese, vanilla extract, and sugar in a bowl. Stir to mix well.
2. Unfold the egg roll wrappers on a clean work surface, spread ¼ cup of the filling at the edge of each wrapper and leave a ½-inch edge uncovering.
3. Wet the edges of the wrappers with water and fold the uncovered edge over the filling. Fold the left and right sides in the center, then tuck the edge under the filling and fold to wrap the filling.
4. Brush the wrappers with melted butter, then arrange the wrappers in a single layer in the perforated pan, seam side down. Leave a little space between each two wrappers.
5. Select Air Fry. Set temperature to 375ºF (190ºC) and set time to 10 minutes. Press Start to begin preheating.
6. Once preheated, place the pan into the oven.
7. When cooking is complete, the wrappers will be golden brown.
8. Serve immediately.

Maple Pecan Tart

Prep time: 2 hours 25 minutes | Cook time: 26 minutes | Serves 8
Tart Crust:
¼ cup firmly packed brown sugar
$^1/_3$ cup butter, softened
1 cup all-purpose flour
¼ teaspoon kosher salt
Filling:
¼ cup whole milk
4 tablespoons butter, diced
½ cup packed brown sugar
¼ cup pure maple syrup
1½ cups finely chopped pecans
¼ teaspoon pure vanilla extract
¼ teaspoon sea salt
1. Line a baking pan with aluminum foil, then spritz the pan with cooking spray.
2. Stir the brown sugar and butter in a bowl with a hand mixer until puffed, then add the flour and salt and stir until crumbled.
3. Pour the mixture in the prepared baking pan and tilt the pan to coat the bottom evenly.
4. Select Bake. Set temperature to 350ºF (180ºC) and set time to 13 minutes. Press Start to begin preheating.
5. Once the oven has preheated, place the pan into the oven.
6. When done, the crust will be golden brown.
7. Meanwhile, pour the milk, butter, sugar, and maple syrup in a saucepan. Stir to mix well. Bring to a simmer, then cook for 1 more minute. Stir constantly.
8. Turn off the heat and mix the pecans and vanilla into the filling mixture.

9. Pour the filling mixture over the golden crust and spread with a spatula to coat the crust evenly.
10. Select Bake and set time to 12 minutes. Place the pan into the oven. When cooked, the filling mixture should be set and frothy.
11. Remove the baking pan from the oven and sprinkle with salt. Allow to sit for 10 minutes or until cooled.
12. Transfer the pan to the refrigerator to chill for at least 2 hours, then remove the aluminum foil and slice to serve.

Asiago Balls

Prep time: 37 minutes | Cook time: 12 minutes | Makes 12 balls
2 tablespoons butter, plus more for greasing
½ cup milk
1½ cups tapioca flour
½ teaspoon salt
1 large egg
$^2/_3$ cup finely grated aged Asiago cheese
1. Put the butter in a saucepan and pour in the milk, heat over medium heat until the liquid boils. Keep stirring.
2. Turn off the heat and mix in the tapioca flour and salt to form a soft dough. Transfer the dough in a large bowl, then wrap the bowl in plastic and let sit for 15 minutes.
3. Break the egg in the bowl of dough and whisk with a hand mixer for 2 minutes or until a sanity dough forms. Fold the cheese in the dough. Cover the bowl in plastic again and let sit for 10 more minutes.
4. Grease a baking pan with butter.
5. Scoop 2 tablespoons of the dough into the baking pan. Repeat with the remaining dough to make dough 12 balls. Keep a little distance between each two balls.
6. Select Bake. Set temperature to 375ºF (190ºC) and set time to 12 minutes. Press Start to begin preheating.
7. Once preheated, place the pan into the oven. Flip the balls halfway through the cooking time.
8. When cooking is complete, the balls should be golden brown and fluffy.
9. Remove the balls from the oven and allow to cool for 5 minutes before serving.

Sriracha Shrimp with Mayo

Prep time: 15 minutes | Cook time: 10 minutes | Serves 4
1 tablespoon Sriracha sauce
1 teaspoon Worcestershire sauce
2 tablespoons sweet chili sauce
¾ cup mayonnaise
1 egg, beaten
1 cup panko bread crumbs
1 pound (454 g) raw shrimp, shelled and deveined, rinsed and drained
Lime wedges, for serving
Cooking spray

1.	Spritz the perforated pan with cooking spray.
2.	Combine the Sriracha sauce, Worcestershire sauce, chili sauce, and mayo in a bowl. Stir to mix well. Reserve $^1/_3$ cup of the mixture as the dipping sauce.
3.	Combine the remaining sauce mixture with the beaten egg. Stir to mix well. Put the panko in a separate bowl.
4.	Dredge the shrimp in the sauce mixture first, then into the panko. Roll the shrimp to coat well. Shake the excess off.
5.	Place the shrimp in the perforated pan, then spritz with cooking spray.
6.	Select Air Fry. Set temperature to 360ºF (182ºC) and set time to 10 minutes. Press Start to begin preheating.
7.	Once preheated, place the pan into the oven. Flip the shrimp halfway through the cooking time.
8.	When cooking is complete, the shrimp should be opaque.
9.	Remove the shrimp from the oven and serve with reserve sauce mixture and squeeze the lime wedges over.

Risotto Croquettes with Tomato Sauce

Prep time: 1 hour 40 minutes | Cook time: 54 minutes | Serves 6
Risotto Croquettes:
4 tablespoons unsalted butter
1 small yellow onion, minced
1 cup Arborio rice
3½ cups chicken stock
½ cup dry white wine
3 eggs
Zest of 1 lemon
½ cup grated Parmesan cheese
2 ounces (57 g) fresh Mozzarella cheese
¼ cup peas
2 tablespoons water
½ cup all-purpose flour
1½ cups panko bread crumbs
Kosher salt and ground black pepper, to taste
Cooking spray
Tomato Sauce:
2 tablespoons extra-virgin olive oil
4 cloves garlic, minced
¼ teaspoon red pepper flakes
1 (28-ounce / 794-g) can crushed tomatoes
2 teaspoons granulated sugar
Kosher salt and ground black pepper, to taste

1.	Melt the butter in a pot over medium heat, then add the onion and salt to taste. Sauté for 5 minutes or until the onion in translucent.
2.	Add the rice and stir to coat well. Cook for 3 minutes or until the rice is lightly browned. Pour in the chicken stock and wine.
3.	Bring to a boil. Then cook for 20 minutes or until the rice is tender and liquid is almost absorbed.
4.	Make the risotto: When the rice is cooked, break the egg into the pot. Add the lemon zest and Parmesan cheese. Sprinkle with salt and ground black pepper. Stir to mix well.
5.	Pour the risotto in a baking sheet, then level with a spatula to spread the risotto evenly. Wrap the baking sheet in plastic and refrigerate for1 hour.
6.	Meanwhile, heat the olive oil in a saucepan over medium heat until shimmering.
7.	Add the garlic and sprinkle with red pepper flakes. Sauté for a minute or until fragrant.
8.	Add the crushed tomatoes and sprinkle with sugar. Stir to mix well. Bring to a boil. Reduce the heat to low and simmer for 15 minutes or until lightly thickened. Sprinkle with salt and pepper to taste. Set aside until ready to serve.
9.	Remove the risotto from the refrigerator. Scoop the risotto into twelve 2-inch balls, then flatten the balls with your hands.
10.	Arrange a about ½-inch piece of Mozzarella and 5 peas in the center of each flattened ball, then wrap them back into balls.
11.	Transfer the balls to a baking sheet lined with parchment paper, then refrigerate for 15 minutes or until firm.
12.	Whisk the remaining 2 eggs with 2 tablespoons of water in a bowl. Pour the flour in a second bowl and pour the panko in a third bowl.
13.	Dredge the risotto balls in the bowl of flour first, then into the eggs, and then into the panko. Shake the excess off.
14.	Transfer the balls to the perforated pan and spritz with cooking spray.
15.	Select Bake. Set temperature to 400ºF (205ºC) and set time to 10 minutes. Press Start to begin preheating.
16.	Once the oven has preheated, place the pan into the oven. Flip the balls halfway through the cooking time.
17.	When cooking is complete, the balls should be until golden brown.
18.	Serve the risotto balls with the tomato sauce.

CHAPTER 13 ROTISSERIE RECIPES

Whiskey-Basted Prime Rib Roast

Prep time: 10 minutes | Cook time: 2 hours | Serves 8 to 10

1 4-bone prime rib roast (8 to 10 pounds / 3.6 to 4.5 kg)

Rub:
¼ cup coarse salt
1 small shallot, finely chopped
2 cloves garlic, minced
2 tablespoons olive oil
1 tablespoon coarsely ground black pepper
Zest of 1 large lemon
1 teaspoon paprika
1 teaspoon sugar

Baste:
$^1/_3$ cup whiskey
¼ cup water
Juice of 1 lemon
⅛ teaspoon salt

1. Trim off any straggling pieces of meat or fat from the roast. If the fat cap is too thick, cut it down to between ¼ to ½ inch in thickness depending on how you like your prime rib.
2. Run a long sword skewer through the center of the roast lengthwise to create a pilot hole. Run the rotisserie spit through the hole and secure with the forks. Balance as necessary.
3. To make the rub: Combine the rub ingredients in a small bowl to form an even paste. Use additional olive oil if necessary to get it to a thick but workable consistency. Apply evenly to the roast, focusing on the outer shell of the roast.
4. To make the baste: Combine the baste ingredients in a small bowl and set aside for 15 to 30 minutes to come to room temperature.
5. Select Roast, set temperature to 400ºF (205ºC), Rotate, and set time to 2 hours. Select Start to begin preheating.
6. Once preheated, place the prepared roast with rotisserie spit into the oven. Set a drip tray underneath, and add 1 to 2 cups hot water to the tray. If you intend to make a gravy from the drippings, monitor the drip tray to make sure it does not run dry. Add extra water if needed.
7. During the last hour of cooking time, begin basting. Apply the baste gently so as not to wash away the seasonings on the outside of the roast. Do this 6 to 8 times, until the roast is well coated with the baste. Roast until it is near the desired doneness: 125ºF (52ºC) for rare, 135ºF (57ºC) for medium rare, 145ºF (63ºC) for medium, 155ºF (68ºC) for medium well, or 165ºF (74ºC) for well done. The roast will shrink during cooking, so adjust the forks when appropriate.
8. When cooking is complete, remove the roast using the rotisserie lift. Carefully remove the rotisserie forks and slide the spit out, and then set the roast on a large cutting board. Tent the roast with aluminum foil and let the meat rest for 15 to 20 minutes. Cut away the bones first by passing a knife against the bones and cutting through (save the bones for later). Cut the meat into thin slices.

Paprika Pulled Pork Butt

Prep time: 10 minutes | Cook time: 6 hours | Serves 10

1 pork butt, 5 to 6 pounds (2.3 to 2.7 kg)

Rub:
2 tablespoons paprika
2 tablespoons packed brown sugar
1 tablespoon kosher salt
1 tablespoon mild chili powder
1 teaspoon freshly ground black pepper
1 teaspoon celery salt
½ teaspoon cayenne
½ teaspoon garlic powder

1. Run a long sword skewer through the center of the roast lengthwise to create a pilot hole. Run the rotisserie spit through the hole and secure with the forks. Balance as necessary.
2. To make the rub: Combine the rub ingredients in a small bowl and apply evenly all over the roast. Let sit at room temperature for 15 minutes. By this time the air fryer oven should be ready.
3. Select Roast, set temperature to 350ºF (180ºC), Rotate, and set time to 6 hours. Select Start to begin preheating.
4. Once preheated, place the prepared roast with rotisserie spit into the oven. Set a drip tray underneath. Roast until the internal temperature reaches 185ºF (85ºC). The roast will shrink during cooking, so adjust the forks when appropriate.
5. When cooking is complete, remove the roast using the rotisserie lift. Carefully remove the rotisserie forks and slide the spit out, and then set the pork on a large cutting board. Tent the roast with aluminum foil and let the meat rest for 20 minutes. Remove the foil and let stand for an additional 10 minutes.
6. Using two forks, check to see how easily the meat shreds. Some parts will do this more easily than others. Be sure to use heat-resistant gloves to break the roast apart. Begin shredding each large chunk one at a time. Add pieces to a large bowl and either add the barbecue sauce directly to the shredded meat or serve on the side. Keep the bowl covered as you're working on each section. This will help keep the meat warm. Serve by itself or with your favorite sides or in sandwiches.

Porchetta with Lemony Sage Rub

Prep time: 15 minutes | Cook time: 3½ hours | Serves 6

1 slab pork belly, skin on, 5 to 6 pounds (2.3 to 2.7 kg)

1 boneless pork loin roast, about 3 pounds (1.4 kg)
Rub:
2 tablespoons fennel seeds
1 tablespoon finely chopped fresh sage
Zest of 1 lemon
4 or 5 cloves garlic
2 teaspoons coarse salt
2 teaspoons freshly ground black pepper
1 teaspoon chopped fresh rosemary
1 teaspoon red pepper flakes
1½ teaspoons coarse salt
1 teaspoon freshly ground black pepper

1. Lay the pork belly, skin-side down, on a large cutting board. Place the pork loin on top and roll the pork belly together so that the ends meet. Trim any excess pork belly and loin so that it is a uniform cylinder. Do not tie yet.

2. To make the rub: Using a mortar and pestle or spice grinder, crush the fennel seeds to a medium grind. Combine with the remaining rub ingredients in a small bowl and apply all over the pork loin.

3. Roll the pork loin inside the pork belly and tie with kitchen twine every inch into a secure, round bundle. Season the outside of the pork belly with the coarse salt and pepper. Set onto a baking sheet and place in the refrigerator, uncovered, for 24 hours.

4. Run a long sword skewer through the center of the roast lengthwise to create a pilot hole. Run the rotisserie spit through the hole and secure with the forks. Balance as necessary.

5. Select Roast, set temperature to 400ºF (205ºC), Rotate, and set time to 3½ hours. Select Start to begin preheating.

6. Once preheated, place the prepared porchetta with rotisserie spit into the oven. Set a drip tray underneath. Watch for burning or excessive browning and adjust the heat as necessary. Once the porchetta has reached an internal temperature of 145ºF (63ºC), the roast is done. If the skin is not a deep brown and crispy in texture, increase the temperature to 450ºF (235ºC) and roast for an additional 10 minutes.

7. When cooking is complete, remove the porchetta using the rotisserie lift. Carefully remove the rotisserie forks and slide the spit out, and then set the meat on a large cutting board. Tent the roast with aluminum foil and let the meat rest for 15 minutes. Slice the meat ½ inch thick and serve.

Orange Honey Glazed Ham

Prep time: 10 minutes | Cook time: 45 minutes | Serves 12 to 14
1 ham, bone in and unsliced, 7 to 8 pounds (3.2 to 3.6 kg)
1 cup packed brown sugar
Glaze:
1½ cups orange juice
½ cup honey
2 tablespoons packed brown sugar
¼ teaspoon ground cinnamon
⅛ teaspoon ground nutmeg
⅛ teaspoon ground allspice
⅛ teaspoon ground cloves
⅛ teaspoon white pepper
2 tablespoons unsalted butter

1. To make the glaze: Combine the orange juice, honey, brown sugar, and spices in a saucepan and bring almost to a boil over medium-high heat. Decrease the heat to medium and simmer for 10 minutes, stirring often. The mixture should be a little runnier than real maple syrup. Remove from the heat and add the butter, stirring until melted. Let the mixture cool.

2. Run a long sword skewer through the center of the ham lengthwise to create a pilot hole. There is a bone in the middle of this ham, but generally it is just to one side. The skewer should easily go through, but feel for the bone before you start so you will know how to navigate around it. Run the rotisserie spit through the hole and secure with the forks. Balance the ham on the spit as well as possible.

3. Select Roast, set temperature to 375ºF (190ºC), Rotate, and set time to 45 minutes. Select Start to begin preheating.

4. Once preheated, place the prepared ham with rotisserie spit into the oven. Set a drip tray underneath. The ham should not take too long to heat up. Look for an internal temperature around 130ºF (54ºC). The surface should be hot.

5. Baste the ham with the glaze after 20 minutes on the air fryer oven. Repeat the process every 5 minutes and about 3 more times.

6. During the last 5 to 10 minutes of cooking time, the ham should be hot as well as sticky from the glaze. Increase the temperature to 400ºF (205ºC) and sprinkle the brown sugar evenly on the surface of the ham in small amounts until it is completely coated. Continue to cook until the sugar starts to bubble. Move quickly, as sugar tends to burn.

7. Once the sugar is bubbling rapidly, remove the ham using the rotisserie lift and place on a large cutting board. Remove the rotisserie forks and slide the spit out, loosely cover the ham with aluminum foil, and let it rest for 5 minutes. Carve into thin slices and serve warm.

Ham with Dijon Bourbon Baste

Prep time: 5 minutes | Cook time: 50 minutes | Serves 10 to 12
1 ham, unsliced, 5 to 6 pounds (2.3 to 2.7 kg)
Baste:
$^1/_3$ cup apple butter
¼ cup packed brown sugar
2 tablespoons bourbon
1½ teaspoons Dijon mustard
¼ teaspoon ground ginger
¼ teaspoon white pepper

1. Run a long sword skewer through the center of the ham lengthwise to create a pilot hole.

Run the rotisserie spit through the hole and secure with the forks. Balance as necessary and secure tightly. Place the ham on the preheated air fryer oven and cook for 50 to 60 minutes. If there is room, set a drip tray underneath.

2.   To make the baste: Combine all the baste ingredients in a small saucepan and simmer over medium heat for 2 minutes, stirring often. Remove from the heat and let sit for 5 to 10 minutes before using.

3.   Select Roast, set temperature to 400ºF (205ºC), Rotate, and set time to 45 minutes. Select Start to begin preheating.

4.   Once preheated, place the prepared ham with rotisserie spit into the oven. Set a drip tray underneath. During the last 20 minutes of the cooking time, begin basting the ham with the apple butter-bourbon mixture. Make at least 4 or 5 passes with the baste to coat evenly. Focus the coating on the outside of the ham and not on the cut side. The ham should not take too long to heat up. Look for an internal temperature around 130ºF (54ºC). The surface should be hot.

5.   When cooking is complete, remove the ham using the rotisserie lift. Carefully remove the rotisserie forks and slide the spit out, and then set the ham on a large cutting board. Tent the ham with aluminum foil and let the meat rest for 10 minutes. Carve and serve immediately.

Spareribs with Paprika Rub

Prep time: 15 minutes | Cook time: 3½ hours | Serves 4 to 6

2 racks spareribs

Sauce:

1 tablespoon olive oil

2 cloves garlic, minced

1 cup ketchup

¾ cup water

$^1/_3$ cup packed brown sugar

1 tablespoon paprika

2 teaspoons mild chili powder

¼ teaspoon cayenne

Rub:

$^1/_3$ cup packed brown sugar

2 tablespoons paprika

2 teaspoons salt

2 teaspoons mild chili powder

1 teaspoon onion powder

½ teaspoon garlic powder

¼ teaspoon cayenne

1.   To make the sauce: Heat the oil in a medium-size saucepan over medium heat and sauté the garlic for 15 seconds, until aromatic. Add the remaining sauce ingredients and simmer for 5 minutes, stirring often. Remove from the heat and let cool to room temperature before using.

2.   To make the rub: Combine the rub ingredients in a small bowl and set aside.

3.   Place the ribs on a cutting board and pat dry with paper towels. Cut away any excess fat from the ribs. Remove the membrane from the back of the ribs by using a blunt knife to work the membrane away from the bone in one corner. Grab hold of the membrane with a paper towel for a good grip and gently peel away. With a little practice, this becomes an easy process.

4.   Lay the rib racks meat-side down. Apply a small portion of the rub, just enough to season, to the bone side of the racks. Lay one rack on top of the other, bone side to bone side, to form an even shape. Tie the two racks together with kitchen twine between every other bone. The ribs should be held tightly together. Run the rotisserie spit between the racks and secure with the forks. The fork tines should run through the meat as best as possible. The ribs will move a little as the rotisserie turns. They should not flop around, however. Secure to prevent this. Apply the remaining rub evenly over the outer surface of the ribs. A general rule with rubs is that what sticks is the amount needed.

5.   Select Roast, set temperature to 375ºF (190ºC), Rotate, and set time to 3½ hours. Select Start to begin preheating.

6.   Once preheated, place the prepared ribs with rotisserie spit into the oven. Set a drip tray underneath. Roast until the ribs reach an internal temperature of 185ºF (85ºC). Test the temperature in several locations. Baste the ribs several times with the sauce during the last hour of cooking to build up a sticky surface.

7.   When cooking is complete, remove the ribs using the rotisserie lift. Carefully remove the rotisserie forks and slide the spit out, and then set the ribs on a large cutting board. Tent the ribs with aluminum foil and let the meat rest for 5 to 10 minutes. Cut away the twine and cut the racks into individual ribs. Serve.

Smoked Paprika Lamb Leg

Prep time: 10 minutes | Cook time: 1 hour 20 minutes | Serves 6 to 8

1 boneless leg of lamb (partial bone-in is fine), 4 to 5 pounds (1.8 to 2.3 kg)

Rub:

¼ cup packed brown sugar

1 tablespoon coarse salt

2 teaspoons smoked paprika

1½ to 2 teaspoons spicy chili powder or cayenne

2 teaspoons onion powder

1 teaspoon garlic powder

1 teaspoon freshly ground black pepper

½ teaspoon ground cloves

⅛ teaspoon ground cinnamon

1.   Trim off the excess fat and any loose hanging pieces from the lamb. With kitchen twine, tie the roast into a uniform and solid roast. It will take four to five ties to hold it together properly. Run a long sword skewer through the center of the roast

lengthwise to create a pilot hole. Run the rotisserie spit through the hole and secure with the forks. Balance as necessary.

2.   To make the rub: Combine the rub ingredients in a small bowl and apply evenly to the lamb. Make sure you get as much of the rub on the meat as possible.

3.   Select Roast, set temperature to 375ºF (190ºC), Rotate, and set time to 80 minutes. Select Start to begin preheating.

4.   Once preheated, place the prepared lamb with rotisserie spit into the oven. Set a drip tray underneath. Roast until the lamb reaches an internal temperature of 140ºF (60ºC) for medium or 150ºF (66ºC) for medium well. The lamb will shrink during cooking, so adjust the forks when appropriate.

5.   When cooking is complete, remove the lamb using the rotisserie lift. Carefully remove the rotisserie forks and slide the spit out, and then set the lamb on a large cutting board. Tent the roast with aluminum foil and let the meat rest for 10 to 12 minutes. Cut off the twine and carve. Serve.

BBQ Chicken with Mustard Rub

Prep time: 15 minutes | Cook time: 1 hour 10 minutes | Serves 4 to 6
1 whole chicken, 3 to 4 pounds (1.4 to 1.8 kg)
1 medium-size onion, peeled but whole (for cavity)
Barbecue Sauce:
¾ cup ketchup
$^2/_3$ cup cherry cola
¼ cup apple cider vinegar
2 tablespoons packed brown sugar
1 tablespoon molasses
¼ teaspoon salt
¼ teaspoon freshly ground black pepper
Rub:
2 teaspoons salt
2 teaspoons onion powder
1 teaspoon mustard powder
½ teaspoon freshly ground black pepper
½ teaspoon garlic powder

1.   To make the barbecue sauce: Combine all the ingredients in a medium-size saucepan over medium heat and simmer for 5 to 6 minutes, until the mixture is smooth and well blended. Stir often and watch for burning. Remove from the heat and let the sauce cool at least 10 minutes before using.

2.   To make the rub: Combine all the rub ingredients in a small bowl.

3.   Pat the chicken dry inside and out with paper towels. Apply the rub all over the bird, under the breast skin, and inside the body cavity.

4.   Truss the chicken with kitchen twine. Run the rotisserie spit through the onion and insert it into the chicken cavity. Use a paring knife to cut a pilot hole in the onion to make this easier. Continue to run the spit through the chicken and secure with the rotisserie forks.

5.   Select Roast, set temperature to 400ºF (205ºC), Rotate, and set time to 70 minutes. Select Start to begin preheating.

6.   Once preheated, place the prepared chicken with rotisserie spit into the oven. Set a drip tray underneath. Roast until the meat in the thighs and legs reaches 175ºF (79ºC). The breasts should be 165ºF (74ºC). Baste the chicken with the barbecue sauce during the last half of the cooking time. Do so every 7 to 10 minutes, until the bird is nearly done and well coated with the sauce.

7.   When cooking is complete, remove the chicken using the rotisserie lift. Carefully remove the rotisserie forks and slide the spit out, and then set the chicken on a large cutting board. Tent the chicken with aluminum foil and let it rest for 10 to 15 minutes before cutting off the twine and carving.

Sirloin Roast with Porcini-Wine Baste

Prep time: 20 minutes | Cook time: 2 hours | Serves 8
1 top sirloin roast, 4 to 4½ pounds (1.8 to 2.0 kg)
Wet Rub:
½ cup dried porcini mushrooms
¼ cup olive oil
4 teaspoons salt
1 tablespoon chopped fresh thyme
2 cloves garlic, minced
1 teaspoon onion powder
1 teaspoon chili powder
1 teaspoon coarsely ground black pepper
Baste:
½ cup dried porcini mushrooms
1 or 2 cups boiling water
½ cup red wine (Cabernet Sauvignon recommended)
1 tablespoon wet rub mixture
1 teaspoon Worcestershire sauce

1.   For the wet rub: Chop the mushrooms into small pieces. Place in a clean spice or coffee grinder and grind to a fine powder. Transfer to a bowl and add the remaining rub ingredients. Remove 1 tablespoon (6 g) of the mixture and set aside.

2.   If the sirloin roast is loose or uneven, tie it with kitchen twine to hold it to a consistent and even shape. Run a long sword skewer through the center of the roast lengthwise to create a pilot hole. Run the rotisserie spit through the hole and secure with the forks. Balance as necessary. Apply the wet rub evenly to the meat.

3.   Select Roast, set temperature to 400ºF (205ºC), Rotate, and set time to 2 hours. Select Start to begin preheating.

4.   Once preheated, place the prepared roast with rotisserie spit into the oven. Set a drip tray underneath, and add 1 to 2 cups hot water to the tray. Roast until it reaches the desired doneness: 125ºF (52ºC) for rare, 135ºF (57ºC) for medium rare, 145ºF (63ºC) for medium, 155ºF (68ºC) for medium well, or 165ºF (74ºC) for well done. Adjust the forks when appropriate.

5.	While the roast cooks, make the baste: Add the dried porcini mushrooms to 1 cup boiling water, or 2 cups boiling water if you would like to use the porcini broth for the gravy. Steep the mushrooms for 30 minutes, covered. Strain the broth and reserve the porcinis (for the gravy) and broth separately. Divide the broth into two equal portions, one for the baste and one for the gravy. Combine 1 cup broth with remaining baste ingredients. Let sit for 15 to 30 minutes to come to room temperature before using. Begin basting the roast during the last half of the cooking time and repeat every 10 to 12 minutes until the roast is ready.

6.	When cooking is complete, remove the roast using the rotisserie lift. Carefully remove the rotisserie forks and slide the spit out. Tent the roast with aluminum foil and let the meat rest for 20 minutes. Cut into ¼-inch slices and serve.

Balsamic Chuck Roast

Prep time: 15 minutes | Cook time: 1 hour | Serves 8

1 chuck roast, 4 to 4½ pounds (1.8 to 2.0 kg)
1¼ teaspoons salt
½ teaspoon freshly ground black pepper
Marinade:
1 tablespoon olive oil
1 shallot, finely chopped
2 or 3 cloves garlic, minced
1½ cups tawny port
¼ cup beef broth
1½ tablespoons balsamic vinegar
1 teaspoon Worcestershire sauce
1 teaspoon chopped fresh thyme
¼ teaspoon salt
¼ teaspoon freshly ground black pepper

1.	To make the marinade: Heat the olive oil in a saucepan over medium-low heat and cook the shallot for 3 minutes until translucent. Add the garlic and cook for 30 seconds. Increase the heat to medium-high and add the port. Stir thoroughly and cook for 1 minute. Add the remaining ingredients and simmer the sauce for 5 minutes, stirring occasionally. Remove from the heat and let cool for 10 to 15 minutes. Divide the mixture into two even portions, reserving one half for the baste and one for the marinade. Store in the refrigerator until ready to cook, then bring to room temperature before using.

2.	Trim away excess fat from the outer edges of the chuck roast. Place the roast in a resealable plastic bag. Add half of the port mixture to the bag, making sure that all of the meat is well covered. Seal the bag and place in the refrigerator for 6 to 8 hours.

3.	Remove the roast from the bag, discarding the marinade, and place on a large cutting board or platter. With kitchen twine, tie the roast into a round and uniform shape, pulling tightly. Start in the center and work toward the ends until it is tied into a solid round roast. This will take four or five ties. Run a long sword skewer through the center of the roast lengthwise to create a pilot hole. Run the rotisserie spit through the hole and secure with the forks. Balance as necessary. Season the roast with the salt and pepper.

4.	Select Roast, set temperature to 400ºF (205ºC), Rotate, and set time to 1 hour. Select Start to begin preheating.

5.	Once preheated, place the prepared roast with rotisserie spit into the oven. Set a drip tray underneath. Roast until it reaches the desired doneness: 125ºF (52ºC) for rare, 135ºF (57ºC) for medium rare, 145ºF (63ºC) for medium, 155ºF (68ºC) for medium well, or 165ºF (74ºC) for well done. Baste halfway through the cooking time, and repeat the process at least 3 times until the roast is done.

6.	When cooking is complete, remove the roast using the rotisserie lift. Carefully remove the rotisserie forks and slide the spit out, and then set the roast on a large cutting board. Tent the roast with aluminum foil and let the meat rest for 15 to 20 minutes. Cut off the twine. Slice into ¼-inch slices and serve.

Baby Back Ribs with Paprika Rub

Prep time: 15 minutes | Cook time: 2½ hours | Serves 4 to 6

2 racks baby back ribs
Sauce:
1 tablespoon vegetable oil
1 cup finely chopped sweet onion
2 cloves garlic, minced
1½ cups ketchup
¼ cup red wine vinegar
¼ cup packed brown sugar
2 tablespoons yellow mustard
⅛ teaspoon salt
Rub:
1 tablespoon paprika
2 teaspoons salt
2 teaspoons freshly ground black pepper
½ teaspoon cayenne

1.	To make the sauce: Heat the oil in a medium-size saucepan over medium heat. Add the onions and sauté for 5 minutes. Add the garlic and sauté for 15 seconds. Add the remaining sauce ingredients and simmer for 4 to 5 minutes, stirring often. Remove from the heat and let cool for 15 to 30 minutes before using.

2.	To make the rub: Combine the rub ingredients in a small bowl and set aside.

3.	Place the ribs on a cutting board and pat dry with paper towels. Cut away any excess fat from the ribs. Remove the membrane from the back of the ribs by using a blunt knife to work the membrane away from the bone in one corner. Grab hold of the membrane with a paper towel for a good grip and gently peel away. With a little practice, this becomes an easy process. Apply the rub all over the ribs' surface, focusing more on the meat side than the bone side.

4. Place one rack of ribs bone-side up on a large cutting board. Place the other rack of ribs bone-side down on top. Position to match up the racks of ribs as evenly as possible. With kitchen twine, tie the racks together between ever other bone, end to end. The whole bundle should be secure and tight. Run the rotisserie spit between the racks and secure tightly with the rotisserie forks. There will be a little movement in the middle, which is fine. As the ribs cook it may be necessary to tighten the forks to keep them secure. Make sure the forks pass through the meat of each rack on each end.
5. Select Roast, set temperature to 375ºF (190ºC), Rotate, and set time to 2½ hours. Select Start to begin preheating.
6. Once preheated, place the prepared ribs with rotisserie spit into the oven. Set a drip tray underneath. Roast until the internal temperature reaches 185ºF (85ºC). Test the temperature in several locations. Baste the ribs evenly with barbecue sauce during the last 45 minutes of cooking time.
7. When cooking is complete, remove the ribs using the rotisserie lift. Carefully remove the rotisserie forks and slide the spit out, and then set the ribs on a large cutting board. Tent the ribs with aluminum foil and let the meat rest for 5 to 10 minutes.
8. Cut away the twine and cut the racks into individual ribs. Serve.

Teriyaki Chicken

Prep time: 5 minutes | Cook time: 1 hour 10 minutes | Serves 4
1 (4-pound / 1.8-kg) chicken
1 tablespoon kosher salt
Teriyaki Sauce:
¼ cup soy sauce
¼ cup mirin
¼ cup honey (or sugar)
¼ inch slice of ginger, smashed
1. Season the chicken with the salt, inside and out. Gently work your fingers under the skin on the breast, then rub some of the salt directly onto the breast meat. Fold the wingtips under the wings and truss the chicken. Skewer the chicken on the rotisserie spit, securing it with the rotisserie forks. Let the chicken rest at room temperature.
2. Select Roast, set temperature to 450ºF (235ºC), Rotate, and set time to 1 hour. Select Start to begin preheating.
3. While the air fryer oven is preheating, combine the soy sauce, mirin, honey, and ginger in a saucepan. Bring to a boil over medium-high heat, stirring often, then decrease the heat to low and simmer for 10 minutes, until the liquid is reduced by half.
4. Once preheated, place the prepared chicken with rotisserie spit into the oven. Set a drip tray underneath. Roast until the chicken reaches 160ºF

(70ºC) in the thickest part of the breast. During the last 15 minutes of cooking, brush the chicken with the teriyaki sauce every five minutes.
5. When cooking is complete, remove the chicken using the rotisserie lift. Remove the chicken from the rotisserie spit and transfer to a platter. Be careful - the spit and forks are blazing hot. Remove the trussing twine, then brush the chicken one last time with the teriyaki sauce. Let the chicken rest for 15 minutes, then carve and serve, passing any remaining teriyaki sauce at the table.

Chicken Roast with Mustard Paste

Prep time: 5 minutes | Cook time: 1 hour | Serves 4
1 (4-pound / 1.8-kg) chicken
Mustard Paste:
¼ cup Dijon mustard
1 tablespoon kosher salt
1 tablespoon Herbes de Provence
1 teaspoon freshly ground black pepper
1. Mix the mustard paste ingredients in a small bowl. Rub the chicken with the mustard paste, inside and out. Gently work your fingers under the skin on the breast, then rub some of the paste directly onto the breast meat. Refrigerate for at least two hours, preferably overnight.
2. One hour before cooking, remove the chicken from the refrigerator. Fold the wingtips under the wings and truss the chicken. Skewer the chicken on the rotisserie spit, securing it with the rotisserie forks. Let the chicken rest at room temperature.
3. Select Roast, set temperature to 450ºF (235ºC), Rotate, and set time to 1 hour. Select Start to begin preheating.
4. Once preheated, place the prepared chicken with rotisserie spit into the oven. Set a drip tray underneath. Roast until the chicken reaches 160ºF (70ºC) in the thickest part of the breast.
5. When cooking is complete, remove the chicken using the rotisserie lift. Remove the chicken from the rotisserie spit and remove the twine trussing the chicken. Be careful - the spit and forks are blazing hot. Let the chicken rest for 15 minutes, then carve and serve.

Chicken with Brown Sugar Brine

Prep time: 5 minutes | Cook time: 1 hour | Serves 4
1 (4-pound / 1.8-kg) chicken
Brine:
2 quarts cold water
½ cup table salt (or 1 cup kosher salt)
¼ cup brown sugar
½ head of garlic (6 to 8 cloves), skin on, crushed
3 bay leaves, crumbled
1 tablespoon peppercorns, crushed or coarsely ground

1.   Combine the brine ingredients in large container, and stir until the salt and sugar dissolve. Submerge the chicken in the brine. Store in the refrigerator for at least one hour, preferably four hours, no longer than eight hours.
2.   Remove the chicken from the brine and pat dry with paper towels, picking off any pieces of bay leaves or garlic that stick to the chicken. Fold the wingtips underneath the wings, then truss the chicken. Skewer the chicken on the rotisserie spit, securing it with the rotisserie forks. Let the chicken rest at room temperature.
3.   Select Roast, set temperature to 450ºF (235ºC), Rotate, and set time to 1 hour. Select Start to begin preheating.
4.   Once preheated, place the prepared chicken with rotisserie spit into the oven. Set a drip tray underneath. Roast until the chicken reaches 160ºF (70ºC) in the thickest part of the breast.
5.   When cooking is complete, remove the chicken using the rotisserie lift. Remove the chicken from the rotisserie spit and remove the twine trussing the chicken. Be careful - the spit and forks are blazing hot. Let the chicken rest for 15 minutes, then carve and serve.

Turkey with Thyme-Sage Brine

Prep time: 5 minutes | Cook time: 2½ hours | Serves 12 to 14
1 (12- to 14-pound / 5.4- to 6.3-kg) turkey
Dry Brine:
¼ cup kosher salt
1 tablespoon minced fresh sage
1 tablespoon minced fresh thyme
1 teaspoon fresh ground black pepper
Fist sized chunk of smoking wood (or 1 cup wood chips)
1.   Mix the dry brine ingredients in a small bowl. Sprinkle the turkey with the dry brine, inside and out. Gently work your fingers under the skin on the breast, then rub some of the dry brine directly onto the breast meat. Refrigerate at least overnight, preferably two to three days. If dry brining more than a day in advance, cover the turkey with plastic wrap until the night before cooking, then remove the plastic wrap to let the skin dry out overnight.
2.   Two hours before cooking, remove the turkey from the refrigerator. Fold the wingtips underneath the wings, then truss the turkey. Skewer the turkey on the rotisserie spit, securing it with the rotisserie forks. Let the turkey rest at room temperature. Submerge the smoking wood in water and let it soak until the air fryer oven is ready.
3.   Select Roast, set temperature to 375ºF (190ºC), Rotate, and set time to 2½ hours. Select Start to begin preheating.
4.   Once preheated, place the prepared turkey with rotisserie spit into the oven. Set a drip tray underneath. Roast until the turkey reaches 155ºF (68ºC) in the thickest part of the breast.

5.   When cooking is complete, remove the turkey using the rotisserie lift. Remove the turkey from the rotisserie spit and remove the twine trussing the turkey. Be very careful - the spit and forks are blazing hot. Let the turkey rest for 15 to 30 minutes, then carve and serve.

Pork Loin Roast with Brown Sugar Brine

Prep time: 10 minutes | Cook time: 45 minutes | Serves 4
1 (4-pound / 1.8-kg) bone-in pork loin roast
Brine:
3 quarts water
½ cup table salt (or 1 cup kosher salt)
¼ cup brown sugar
Spice Rub:
4 cloves garlic, minced or pressed through a garlic press
1 teaspoon minced rosemary
1 teaspoon fresh ground black pepper
½ teaspoon hot red pepper flakes
1.   Combine the brine ingredients in a large container and stir until the salt and sugar dissolve. Submerge the pork in the brine. Store in the refrigerator for four to eight hours.
2.   One hour before cooking, remove the pork from the brine and pat dry with paper towels. Mix the rub ingredients in a small bowl, then rub over the pork shoulder, working the rub into any natural seams in the meat. Truss the pork roast, skewer it on the rotisserie spit, and secure it with the rotisserie forks. Let the pork rest at room temperature.
3.   Select Roast, set temperature to 450ºF (235ºC), Rotate, and set time to 45 minutes. Select Start to begin preheating.
4.   Once preheated, place the prepared pork roast with rotisserie spit into the oven. Set a drip tray underneath. Roast until it reaches 135ºF (57ºC) in its thickest part.
5.   When cooking is complete, remove the pork using the rotisserie lift. Remove the pork from the rotisserie spit and remove the twine trussing the roast. Be careful - the spit and forks are blazing hot. Let the pork rest for 15 minutes, then slice and serve.

Dried Fruit Stuffed Pork Loin

Prep time: 10 minutes | Cook time: 50 minutes | Serves 4
2 (2-pound / 907-g) boneless pork loin roasts
Apple Cider Brine:
2 quarts apple cider
1 quart water
½ cup table salt
Dried Fruit Stuffing:
2 cups mixed dried fruit, chopped (apples, apricots, cranberries and raisins)
1 teaspoon fresh ground black pepper
½ teaspoon dried ginger

1.   Combine the brine ingredients in a large container and stir until the salt and sugar dissolve. Roll cut the pork roasts to open them up like a book. Set a roast with the fat cap facing down. Make a cut the length of the roast, one third of the way from the bottom, which goes almost all the way to the other side of the roast but not through. Open the roast up like a book along that cut, then make another cut halfway up the opened part of the roast, almost all the way to the other side, and open up the roast again. Submerge the pork roasts in the brine. Store in the refrigerator for one to four hours.
2.   One hour before cooking, remove the pork from the brine and pat dry with paper towels. Open up the pork with the cut side facing up, and sprinkle evenly with the chopped fruit, ginger, and pepper. Carefully roll the pork back into a cylinder, then truss each roast at the edges to hold the cylinder shape. Truss the roasts together with the fat caps facing out, then skewer on the rotisserie spit, running the spit between the roasts and securing them with the rotisserie forks. Let the pork rest at room temperature.
3.   Select Roast, set temperature to 450ºF (235ºC), Rotate, and set time to 50 minutes. Select Start to begin preheating.
4.   Once preheated, place the prepared pork with rotisserie spit into the oven. Set a drip tray underneath. Roast until it reaches 135ºF (57ºC) in its thickest part.
5.   When cooking is complete, remove the pork using the rotisserie lift. Remove the pork from the rotisserie spit and remove the twine trussing the roast. Be careful - the spit and forks are blazing hot. Let the pork rest for 15 minutes, then slice into ½ inch thick rounds and serve.

Feta Stuffed Lamb Leg

Prep time: 5 minutes | Cook time: 45 minutes | Serves 3
1 (2½-pound / 1.1-kg) boneless leg of lamb roast
2 teaspoons kosher salt
Feta Stuffing:
2 ounces crumbled feta cheese
1 teaspoon minced fresh rosemary
1 teaspoon minced fresh thyme
Zest of ½ lemon
1.   Season the leg of lamb with the salt, then refrigerate for at least two hours, preferably overnight.
2.   One hour before cooking, remove the lamb from the refrigerator. Just before heating the air fryer oven, mix the stuffing ingredients. Open up the lamb like a book, then spread the stuffing over the cut side of the lamb. Fold the roast back into its original shape. Truss the lamb, then skewer it on the rotisserie spit, securing it with the rotisserie forks. (You're going to lose a little of the stuffing when you tie down the trussing twine; that's OK.) Let the lamb rest at room temperature until the air fryer oven is ready.

3.   Select Roast, set temperature to 450ºF (235ºC), Rotate, and set time to 45 minutes. Select Start to begin preheating.
4.   Once preheated, place the prepared lamb with rotisserie spit into the oven. Set a drip tray underneath. Roast until it reaches 130ºF (54ºC) in its thickest part for medium. (Cook to 115ºF (46ºC) for rare, 120ºF (49ºC) for medium-rare.)
5.   When cooking is complete, remove the lamb using the rotisserie lift. Remove the lamb from the rotisserie spit and remove the twine trussing the roast. Be careful - the spit and forks are blazing hot. Let the lamb rest for 15 minutes, then carve and serve.

Mustard Lamb Shoulder

Prep time: 5 minutes | Cook time: 2 hours | Serves 4
1 (4-pound / 1.8-kg) boneless lamb shoulder roast
Mustard Herb Paste:
¼ cup whole grain mustard
1 tablespoon kosher salt
1 tablespoon minced fresh thyme
1 teaspoon minced fresh oregano
1 teaspoon minced fresh rosemary
1 teaspoon fresh ground black pepper
1.   Mix the paste ingredients in a small bowl. Open up the lamb like a book, then rub all over with the paste, working it into any natural seams in the meat. Refrigerate for at least two hours, preferably overnight.
2.   One hour before cooking, remove the lamb from the refrigerator. Fold the lamb into its original shape, truss the lamb, and skewer it on the rotisserie spit, securing it with the rotisserie forks. Let the lamb rest at room temperature until the air fryer oven is ready.
3.   Select Roast, set temperature to 375ºF (190ºC), Rotate, and set time to 2 hours. Select Start to begin preheating.
4.   Once preheated, place the prepared lamb with rotisserie spit into the oven. Set a drip tray underneath. Roast the lamb until it reaches 190ºF (88ºC) in its thickest part.
5.   When cooking is complete, remove the lamb shoulder using the rotisserie lift. Remove the lamb shoulder from the rotisserie spit and remove the twine trussing the roast. Be careful - the spit and forks are blazing hot. Let the lamb rest for 15 minutes, then carve and serve.

Bacon-Wrapped Sirloin Roast

Prep time: 5 minutes | Cook time: 45 minutes | Serves 4
1 (4-pound / 1.8-kg) sirloin roast
1 tablespoon kosher salt
4 slices bacon

1.		Season the sirloin roast with the salt, then refrigerate for at least two hours, preferably overnight.

2.		One hour before cooking, remove the sirloin roast from the refrigerator. Cut the butcher's twine and lay the strings on a platter, spaced where you want to tie the sirloin roast. Put two slices of bacon on top of the string, with a gap between them. Put the sirloin roast on top of the bacon, then lay the last two pieces of bacon on top of the sirloin roast. Tie the twine to truss the sirloin roast and the bacon. Trim off any loose ends of bacon so they don't burn in the air fryer oven. Skewer the sirloin roast on the rotisserie spit, securing it with the rotisserie forks. Let the beef rest at room temperature until the air fryer oven is ready.

3.		Select Roast, set temperature to 450ºF (235ºC), Rotate, and set time to 45 minutes. Select Start to begin preheating.

4.		Once preheated, place the prepared sirloin roast with rotisserie spit into the oven. Set a drip tray underneath. Roast until it reaches 120ºF (49ºC) in its thickest part for medium-rare. (Cook to 115ºF (46ºC) for rare, 130ºF (54ºC) for medium.)

5.		When cooking is complete, remove the sirloin roast using the rotisserie lift. Remove the sirloin roast from the rotisserie spit and remove the twine trussing the roast, leaving as much bacon behind as possible. Be careful - the spit and forks are blazing hot. Let the beef rest for 15 minutes, then carve into thin slices and serve.

APPENDIX : RECIPES INDEX

A

Air Fried Tofu Sticks 50
Apple Bake with Cinnamon 128
Artichoke and Mushroom Frittata 17
Asiago Balls 145
Asparagus Casserole with Grits 133
Asparagus Frittata with Goat Cheese 138
Asparagus Strata with Havarti Cheese 14
Avocado and Egg Burrito 14
Avocado and Tomato Wraps 36
Avocado Chips with Lime 27

B

Baby Back Ribs with Paprika Rub 151
Bacon and Egg Wraps with Salsa 35
Bacon Knots with Maple Sugar 7
Bacon-Wrapped Pork Hot Dogs 73
Bacon-Wrapped Sausage with Tomato Relish 70
Bacon-Wrapped Sirloin Roast 154
Baked Avocado with Eggs and Tomato 16
Baked Cornmeal Pancake 9
Baked Eggs with Kale Pesto 15
Baked Eggs with Spinach and Basil 47
Baked Salmon in Wine 88
Baked White Rice 45
Balsamic Asparagus 64
Balsamic Cherry Tomatoes 142
Balsamic Chicken Breast with Oregano 113
Balsamic Chuck Roast 151
Balsamic Duck Breasts with Orange Marmalade 112
Balsamic Ginger Scallops 98
Balsamic Italian Sausages and Red Grapes 78
Balsamic Prosciutto-Wrapped Pears 24
Balsamic Shrimp with Goat Cheese 96
Balsamic-Glazed Beets 55
Banana Carrot Muffin 17
Banana Chocolate Bread with Walnuts 15
Barbecue Chicken with Coleslaw 102
Basil Scallops with Broccoli 99
BBQ Cheese Chicken Pizza 30
BBQ Chicken with Mustard Rub 150
BBQ Kielbasa Sausage 75
Beef and Bean Casserole 135
Beef and Pork Sausage Meatloaf 67
Beef Burgers with Korean Mayo 40
Beef Burgers with Seeds 42
Beef Hash with Eggs 19
Beef Meatballs with Salsa 66
Beef Meatloaves with Spinach 78
Beef Pizza with Bell Pepper 67
Beef Ravioli with Parmesan 81
Beef Steak and Bell Pepper Rolls 39
Beef Tenderloin with Feta Cheese 68
Beef-Stuffed Bell Peppers 65
Bell Pepper and Carrot Frittata 10
Bell Pepper and Ham Omelet 12
Bell Pepper Rings with Eggs 9

Black Bean and Salsa Tacos 46
Blackberry Cobbler 129
Blueberries Quesadillas 15
Blueberry and Peach Tart 122
Blueberry Cake with Lemon 18
Breaded Artichoke Bites 31
Breaded Asparagus Fries 63
Breaded Brussels Sprouts with Paprika 64
Breaded Calf's Liver Strips 79
Breaded Catfish Nuggets 90
Breaded Chicken Fingers 101
Breaded Chicken Livers 103
Breaded Chicken Nuggets 106
Breaded Chicken Tenders with Thyme 102
Breaded Fish Fillets with Mustard 85
Breaded Fish Sticks 86
Breaded Fish Sticks 92
Breaded Pork Loin Chops 78
Breaded Zucchini Chips with Parmesan 54
Breaded Zucchini Tots 24
Breakfast Sausage Quiche 10
Brie Pear Sandwiches 30
Broccoli and Red Pepper Quiche 11
Brown Rice Porridge with Dates 13
Brown Rice Quiches with Pimiento 14
Brown Sugar Acorn Squash 62
Butter Shortbread with Lemon 122
Buttermilk Biscuits 8
Buttermilk Chicken Drumsticks 105
Buttermilk Chocolate Cake 144
Buttermilk-Marinated Chicken Wings 31
Butternut Squash and Parsnip with Thyme 49
Butternut Squash with Goat Cheese 49
Buttery Chicken with Corn 116
Buttery Mushrooms 44

C

Cabbage and Prawn Wraps 35
Cajun Beef and Bell Pepper Fajitas 37
Cajun Catfish Cakes with Parmesan 93
Cajun Cod Fillets with Lemon Pepper 89
Cajun Tilapia Tacos 84
Carrot and Mushroom Spring Rolls 36
Carrot Chips 28
Carrot, Tofu and Cauliflower Rice 53
Catfish Fillets with Pecan Crust 90
Cauliflower and Okra Casserole 134
Cauliflower Casserole with Pecan Butter 132
Cauliflower with Teriyaki Sauce 55
Cayenne Cod Fillets 86
Cayenne Cod Fillets with Garlic 88
Cayenne Green Beans 51
Cayenne Prawns with Cumin 92
Cheddar and Egg Frittata with Parsley 136
Cheddar Bacon Casserole 12
Cheddar Baked Potatoes with Chives 21
Cheddar Black Bean and Corn Salsa 30
Cheddar Broccoli and Carrot Quiche 136
Cheddar Broccoli Casserole 133

Cheddar Broccoli Gratin 63
Cheddar Chicken and Broccoli Divan 135
Cheddar Chicken Empanadas 43
Cheddar Chicken Sausage Casserole 132
Cheddar Ham Toast 7
Cheddar Hash Brown Casserole 12
Cheddar Mushrooms with Pimientos 22
Cheddar Pastrami Casserole 133
Cheddar Sausage Balls 23
Cheddar Turkey Burgers with Mayo 114
Cheese and Bacon Muffin Sandwiches 10
Cheese and Egg Quiche 139
Cheesy Broccoli with Rosemary 47
Chicken and Broccoli Casserole 137
Chicken and Cabbage Wraps 37
Chicken and Cheese Sandwiches 113
Chicken and Ham Rochambeau 101
Chicken and Pepper Baguette with Mayo 107
Chicken Breakfast Sausages 15
Chicken Drumsticks with BBQ-Honey Sauce 101
Chicken Drumsticks with Cajun Seasoning 103
Chicken Drumsticks with Green Beans 119
Chicken Gnocchi with Spinach 117
Chicken Kebabs with Corn Salad 114
Chicken Roast with Mustard Paste 152
Chicken Tacos with Lettuce 105
Chicken Thighs with Cabbage Slaw 116
Chicken Thighs with Cherry Tomatoes 115
Chicken Thighs with Mirin 107
Chicken Thighs with Peppers 110
Chicken with Brown Sugar Brine 152
Chicken with Veggie Couscous Salad 106
Chicken Wraps with Ricotta Cheese 35
Chickpea and Mushroom Wraps 38
Chickpea and Spinach Casserole 135
Chickpea-Stuffed Bell Peppers 57
Chili Chicken Fries 118
Chili Chicken Skin with Dill 103
Chocolate Blueberry Cupcakes 125
Chocolate Cake with Blackberries 129
Chocolate Chip Brownies 129
Chocolate Coconut Cake 122
Chocolate Macaroons with Coconut 141
Chocolate S'mores 131
Chocolate Vanilla Cheesecake 123
Chocolate-Glazed Donut Holes 141
Chuck and Sausage Meatballs 77
Cinnamon Apple Chips 27
Cinnamon Apple Fritters 125
Cinnamon Apple Turnovers 18
Cinnamon Apple with Apricots 127
Cinnamon Churros 140
Cinnamon Monkey Bread 7
Cinnamon Peach Wedges 30
Cinnamon Pineapple Rings 130
Cinnamon Rolls with Brown Sugar 16
Citrus Carrots with Balsamic Glaze 61
Citrus Pork Ribs with Oregano 72
Coconut Curried Fish with Chilies 93

Coconut Orange Cake 126
Cod Fish Tacos with Mango Salsa 34
Coffee Chocolate Cake with Cinnamon 122
Colby Pork Sausage with Cauliflower 76
Corn Casserole with Bell Pepper 132
Corn Casserole with Swiss Cheese 62
Corn Frittata with Avocado Dressing 10
Crab and Fish Cakes 97
Crab Ratatouille with Thyme 99
Cream Cheese and Crab Wontons 40
Cream-Glazed Cinnamon Rolls 143
Creamy Grits 44
Crispy Cream Cheese Wontons 39
Cumin Fried Chickpeas 28
Cumin Tortilla Chips 27
Curried Beef Meatballs 67
Curried Cauliflower with Cashews 52
Curried Chicken and Brussels Sprouts 114
Curried Halibut Fillets with Parmesan 89
Curried King Prawns with Cumin 96
Curried Lamb Chops with Potatoes 70
Curried Pork Sliders 38
Curried Prawns with Coconut 94
Curried Shrimp and Zucchini Potstickers 34

D

Deviled Eggs with Mayo 25
Dijon Hake Fillets with Garlic Sauce 92
Dijon Lamb Rack with Pistachio 68
Dijon Pork Tenderloin 71
Dijon Turkey Breast with Sage 109
Dijon Turkey with Carrots 112
Dijon-Honey Pork Tenderloin 82
Dill Pickles with Buttermilk Dressing 142
Dried Fruit Stuffed Pork Loin 153

E

Egg and Bacon Bread Cups 9
Eggplant and Bell Peppers with Basil 46
English Muffins with Spinach and Pear 9

F

Feta Stuffed Lamb Leg 154
Five-Spice Turkey Thighs 109
Flounder Fillets with Lemon Pepper 94
French Toast Sticks with Strawberries 18
Fried Bacon-Wrapped Scallops 98
Fried Breaded Scallops 99
Fried Calf's Liver Sticks 66
Fried Cod Fillets in Beer 83
Fried Pickle Spears with Chili 27
Fried Root Veggies with Thyme 52
Fried Scallops with Thyme 99
Fried Venison Backstrap 68

G

Game Hens with Cucumber Salad 112
Garlic Bell Peppers with Marjoram 53
Garlic Broccoli with Parmesan 63
Garlic Butternut Squash Croquettes 61
Garlic Calamari Rings 99
Garlic Carrots with Sesame Seeds 48
Garlic Chicken Wings 107
Garlic Duck Leg Quarters 111

Garlic Eggplant Slices with Parsley 51
Garlic Fried Edamame 29
Garlic Lamb Chops with Asparagus 69
Garlic Nuggets 144
Garlic Pork Belly with Bay Leaves 74
Garlic Pork Leg Roast with Candy Onions 77
Garlic Potatoes with Heavy Cream 60
Garlic Potatoes with Peppers and Onions 14
Garlic Ratatouille 54
Garlic Tofu with Basil 51
Garlic Tomato Sauce 44
Garlic Turnip and Zucchini 55
Garlic Zucchini Crisps 60
Garlic Zucchini Sticks 60
Garlicky Cabbage with Red Pepper 60
Garlicky Whole Chicken Bake 107
Garlic-Lime Shishito Peppers 60
Ginger Apple Wedges 27
Ginger Chicken Bites in Sherry 104
Ginger Pork Shoulder in Shaoxing Wine 72
Ginger Shrimp with Sesame Seeds 24
Ginger Swordfish Steaks with Jalapeño 87
Ginger-Garlic Dipping Sauce 44
Ginger-Pepper Broccoli 50
Gochujang Beef and Onion Tacos 34
Gochujang Chicken Wings 103
Greek Potatoes with Chives 63
Green Chiles and Cheese Nachos 23
Grits with Cheddar Cheese 8
Ground Chicken with Tomatoes 106

H

Halloumi Zucchinis and Eggplant 54
Ham with Dijon Bourbon Baste 148
Hash Brown Cups with Cheddar Cheese 8
Hoisin Scallops with Sesame Seeds 96
Hoisin Tuna with Lemongrass 84
Honey Apple-Peach Crumble 127
Honey Baby Carrots with Dill 51
Honey Cashew Granola with Cranberries 19
Honey Eggplant with Yogurt Sauce 48
Honey Halibut Steaks with Parsley 90
Honey Roasted Grapes with Basil 21
Honey Snack Mix 26
Honey Walnut and Pistachios Baklava 121
Honey-Ginger Chicken Breasts 104
Honey-Glazed Peach and Plum Kebabs 127
Honey-Lemon Snapper with Grapes 87
Horseradish Green Tomatoes 32
Horseradish Lamb Loin Chops 69
Hush Puppies with Jalapeño 26

I

Italian Rice Balls with Olives 33

J

Jalapeño Poppers with Cheddar 22
Jalapeño Turkey Sliders with Chive Mayo 40
Jumbo Shrimp with Dijon-Mayo Sauce 97

K

Kale and Egg Frittata with Feta 138
Kale with Tahini-Lemon Dressing 47

L

Lamb Hamburgers with Feta Cheese 41
Lamb Kofta with Mint 69
Lemon Anchocy Dressing 44
Lemon Caramelized Pear Tart 121
Lemon Chicken with Oregano 119
Lemon Crab Cakes with Mayo 98
Lemon Pork Loin Chop with Marjoram 74
Lemon Red Snapper with Thyme 88
Lemon Ricotta with Capers 25
Lemon Shrimp with Cumin 95
Lemon Tilapia Fillets with Garlic 91
Lemon-Pepper Chicken Wings 22
Lime Chicken Breasts with Cilantro 105
Lime Sweet Potatoes with Allspice 61

M

Maple Banana Bread Pudding 16
Maple French Toast Casserole 19
Maple Garlic Brussels Sprouts 61
Maple Granola 7
Maple Pecan Tart 145
Maple Turkey Breast with Rosemary 110
Mexican Beef and Chile Casserole 137
Mexican Sirloin Steak and Pepper Fajitas 81
Mixed Berry Bake with Almond Topping 124
Mixed Berry Crisp with Cloves 130
Monk Fruit and Hazelnut Cake 121
Mozzarella Chicken Breasts with Basil 115
Mozzarella Chicken Taquitos 38
Mozzarella Rice Arancini 140
Mozzarella Sausage Calzones 82
Mozzarella Tomato-Stuffed Squash 58
Mozzarella Walnut Stuffed Mushrooms 56
Muffuletta Sliders with Olive Mix 33
Mushroom and Beef Casserole 132
Mushroom and Sausage Empanadas 28
Mushroom and Spinach Frittata 12
Mustard Chicken Thighs in Waffles 102
Mustard Lamb Shoulder 154

N

Nut-Crusted Pork Rack 73
Nutmeg Apple Chips 29

O

Old Bay Crab Sticks with Mayo Sauce 96
Old Bay Fried Chicken Wings 28
Old Bay Shrimp with Potatoes 91
Olive and Basil Stromboli with Garlic 143
Onion-Stuffed Mushrooms 55
Orange Beef and Broccoli with Sriracha 80
Orange Honey Glazed Ham 148
Orange Scones with Blueberries 18
Orange Shrimp with Cayenne 94

P

Paprika Hens in Wine 118
Paprika Hens with Creole Seasoning 117
Paprika Lamb Chops with Sage 72
Paprika Nut Mix 29
Paprika Polenta Fries with Chili-Lime Mayo 25
Paprika Potato Chips 26
Paprika Pulled Pork Butt 147
Paprika Tiger Shrimp 94

Paprika Tilapia with Garlic Aioli 90
Paprika Whole Chicken Roast 118
Paprika-Oregano Seasoning 45
Parmesan Bruschetta with Tomato 29
Parmesan Brussels Sprouts 50
Parmesan Cabbage Wedges 48
Parmesan Cauliflower with Turmeric 21
Parmesan Chicken Cutlets 104
Parmesan Corn on the Cob 62
Parmesan Crab Toasts 31
Parmesan Eggplant Hoagies 38
Parmesan Fish Fillets with Tarragon 92
Parmesan Green Bean Casserole 133
Parmesan Snack Mix 26
Parsley Shrimp with Lemon 95
Peach and Apple Crisp with Oatmeal 124
Peach and Blueberry Galette 127
Peach Chicken with Dark Cherry 117
Peanut Butter Bread Pudding 130
Pecan Pie with Chocolate Chips 131
Pepperoni Pizza Bites with Marinara 23
Pepper-Stuffed Portobellos 57
Peppery Sausage Casserole with Cheddar 135
Pigs in a Blanket with Sesame Seeds 143
Pineapple Sticks with Coconut 131
Poblano Garlic Sauce 45
Porchetta with Lemony Sage Rub 147
Pork and Cabbage Gyoza 40
Pork and Lettuce Wraps with Almonds 80
Pork and Pineapple Kebabs 74
Pork and Turkey Sandwiches 31
Pork and Veggie Kebabs 74
Pork Butt withCoriander-Parsley Sauce 75
Pork Chop Roast with Worcestershire 80
Pork Chops and Apple Bake 79
Pork Chops with Sour Cream and Dill Sauce 76
Pork Cutlets with Aloha Salsa 81
Pork Egg Rolls with Vinegar Dipping 140
Pork Loin Chops with Butternut Squash 82
Pork Loin Roast with Brown Sugar Brine 153
Pork Meatballs with Scallions 77
Pork Momos with Carrot 39
Pork Sausage Ratatouille 76
Pork Tenderloin with Rice 79
Pork, Squash and Pepper Kebabs 75
Potato and Asparagus Platter 57
Potato and Chorizo Frittata 137
Potato Samosas with Mint Chutney 42
Potato Taquitos with Mexican Cheese 37
Prosciutto Tart with Asparagus 71
Prosciutto-Wrapped Beef Rolls 65
Pumpkin Pudding with Vanilla Wafers 128

R

Raspberry Muffins 124
Ratatouille with Bread Crumb Topping 49
Red Chili Okra 52
Rice and Olives Stuffed Peppers 58
Ricotta Pork Gratin with Mustard 137
Ricotta Spinach and Basil Pockets 36
Risotto Croquettes with Tomato Sauce 146

Roasted Mushrooms with Garlic 22
Roasted Potatoes with Rosemary 63
Roasted Veggie and Tofu 46
Roasted Veggie Rice with Eggs 50
Roasted Veggie Salad with Lemon 56
Roasted Veggies with Honey-Garlic Glaze 54
Rosemary Chicken Breasts with Tomatoes 105
Rosemary Ground Beef with Zucchini 66
Rosemary Pork with Apple Glaze 70
Rosemary Veal Loin with Fennel Seeds 68

S

Salmon and Pepper Bowl 89
Salmon Spring Rolls with Parsley 84
Salmon with Cherry Tomatoes 87
Salmon with Roasted Asparagus 86
Satay Chicken Skewers 108
Sausage and Onion Rolls with Mustard 21
Sesame Green Beans with Sriracha 62
Sesame Kale Chips 30
Sesame Mushrooms with Thyme 49
Shawarma Seasoning 45
Shrimp and Artichoke Paella 97
Shrimp and Spinach Frittata 11
Shrimp and Veggie Patties 97
Shrimp and Veggie Spring Rolls 93
Shrimp Kebabs with Cherry Tomatoes 95
Shrimp Salad with Caesar Dressing 91
Shrimp Scampi with Garlic Butter 95
Sirloin Roast with Porcini-Wine Baste 150
Sirloin Steaks with Cucumber Salad 66
Smoked Paprika Chicken Burgers 41
Smoked Paprika Lamb Leg 149
Smoked Trout Frittata with Dill 136
Snapper Fillets with Capers 89
Spareribs with Paprika Rub 149
Spinach and Egg Florentine 16
Spinach and Mushroom Frittata 134
Spinach and Shrimp Frittata 138
Spinach Calzones with Mushrooms 32
Spinach-Stuffed Beefsteak Tomatoes 56
Sriracha Shrimp with Mayo 145
Strawberry Crumble with Rhubarb 123
Stuffed Bell Peppers with Cream Cheese 58
Sugar Roasted Walnuts 24
Sweet Potato and Spinach Burritos 35
Sweet-and-Sour Chicken Breasts 108
Swiss Chicken and Ham Casserole 134

T

Tater Tot and Chicken Sausage Casserole 8
Teriyaki Chicken 152
Teriyaki Chicken Thighs 108
Teriyaki Salmon and Bok Choy 87
Teriyaki Sauce 44
Teriyaki-Glazed Pork Ribs 73
Teriyaki-Marinated Rump Steak 65
Teriyaki-Marinated Shrimp Skewers 144
Thai Curried Veggies 46
Thai-Flavored Brussels Sprouts 48
Thyme Pork Chops with Carrots 78
Tilapia and Rockfish Casserole 133

Tilapia Meunière with Parsley 85
Tomato and Olive Quiche 139
Tomato-Stuffed Portobello Mushrooms 56
Tuna and Fruit Kebabs with Honey Glaze 85
Tuna and Veggie Salad 86
Tuna Casserole with Basil 84
Tuna Melts with Mayo 23
Turkey and Cauliflower Meatloaf 111
Turkey and Mushroom Meatballs 109
Turkey and Pepper Hamburger 43
Turkey Breast with Strawberries 111
Turkey Casserole with Almond Mayo 134
Turkey Meatloaves with Onion 117
Turkey Scotch Eggs with Rosemary 112
Turkey with Thyme-Sage Brine 153
Turkey-Stuffed Peppers with Cheddar 119
Turkey-Wrapped Dates and Almonds 32

V

Vanilla Baked Peaches and Blueberries 131
Vanilla Banana Bread Pudding 11
Vanilla Banana Cake 141
Vanilla Blueberry Cobbler 13
Vanilla Butter Cake 142
Vanilla Cheese Blintzes 144
Vanilla Chocolate Cake 126

Vanilla Chocolate Chip Cookies 126
Vanilla Coconut Cookies with Pecans 125
Vanilla Cookies with Chocolate Chips 123
Vanilla French Toast withBourbon 7
Vanilla Fudge Pie 129
Vanilla Pancake with Mixed Berries 13
Vanilla Pancake with Walnuts 13
Vanilla Pound Cake 128
Vanilla Ricotta Cake with Lemon 128
Vanilla Walnuts Tart with Cloves 124
Vegetable Mélange with Garlic 47
Veggie and Oat Meatballs 53
Vinegary Asparagus 47
Vinegary Chicken with Pineapple 116
Vinegary Pork Schnitzel 72

W

Wasabi Spam 70
Whiskey-Basted Prime Rib Roast 147
White Chocolate Cookies with Nutmeg 130
Whole Duck with Cherry Sauce 110
Whole-Wheat Blueberries Muffins 17
Worcestershire Ribeye Steaks with Garlic 80

Z

Zucchini and Spinach Frittata 138
Zucchini Quesadilla with Gouda Cheese 51

Printed by Libri Plureos GmbH in Hamburg,
Germany